A Book of Scattered Leaves

Volume 2

A Book of Scattered Leaves

Poetry of Poverty in Broadside Ballads
of Nineteenth-Century England

STUDY AND ANTHOLOGY

James Hepburn

VOLUME 2

Lewisburg
Bucknell University Press
London: Associated University Presses

© 2001 by James Hepburn.

All rights reserved. Authorization to photocopy items for internal or personal use, or the internal or personal use of specific clients, is granted by the copyright owner, provided that a base fee of $10.00, plus eight cents per page, per copy is paid directly to the Copyright Clearance Center, 222 Rosewood Dr., Danvers, Massachusetts 01923. [0-8387-5472-4/01 $10.00 + 8¢ pp, pc.]

Associated University Presses
440 Forsgate Drive
Cranbury, NJ 08512

Associated University Presses
16 Barter Street
London WC1A 2AH, England

Associated University Presses
P.O. Box 338, Port Credit
Mississauga, Ontario
Canada L5G 4L8

The paper used in this publication meets the requirements of the American National Standard for Permanence of Paper for Printed Library Materials Z39.48-1984.

Library of Congress Cataloging-in-Publication Data

Hepburn, James G.
   A book of scattered leaves : poetry of poverty in broadside ballads of nineteenth-century England : study and anthology / James Hepburn.
      v. <1-> : ill.; 25 cm.
   Includes bibliographical references (v. 1, p. 271–283)
   Contents: v. 1. Study and Anthology, pt. 1 — v. 2, Anthology, pt. 2.
   ISBN 0-8387-5397-3 (alk. paper)
   ISBN 0-8387-5472-4 (v. 2)
    1. Ballads, English—England—History and criticism. 2. English poetry—19th century—History and criticism. 3. Poverty—England—History—19th century—Sources. 4. Poor—England—History—19th century—Sources. 5. English poetry—19th century. 6. Poverty—England—Poetry. 7. Poverty in literature. 8. Poor—England—Poetry. 9. Broadsides—England. 10. Poor in literature. I. Title.

PR976 .H47 2000
821'.04409355—dc21

                                                99-043700

PRINTED IN THE UNITED STATES OF AMERICA

Editorial Note. Five authors represented and discussed in this volume receive slight or no mention in volume 1: James Bruton, E. Green, Miss A. Strickland, and Henry Valentine represented with one ballad each, and Thomas Peckett Prest represented with three ballads. They all seem to have belonged to the middle rank of society: Miss Strickland apparently the niece of a member of parliament, Bruton a successful professional singer and songwriter, Prest an industrious author and editor very likely living near poverty, Valentine a perhaps modestly monied self-publicist, and Green a would-be writer of concert songs.

In volume 1 the first version of "The Workhouse Boy" is now dated to the first half of 1834 or earlier. The "parochial authority" who wrote it is now identified as "Aldridge Esq." He is otherwise unknown except as the author also of "The Vorkhus Gal," which itself is now dated to about January 1835. The second version of "The Workhouse Boy" is now dated to about July 1834, and its author "Mr. Flint" is now identified as R. Flint, about whom nothing further is known. Information derives from *Singer's Penny Magazine and Reciter's Album,* 1834–35, Preface and nos. 3 and 29. The magazine is discussed on pages 511–12 below.

The number of ballads in the collection with authors named for them, discussed on page 27 of volume 1, now stands at 43 of the 123 ballads printed in full (counting the photograph of John Morgan's "Camberwell & Reform!"), the name given either on the broadside used or on a broadside seen (16), discovered (25), or guessed (2). Ballads marked with asterisks in the table below are (to the best of my knowledge) printed for the first time since their appearance on the street or elsewhere in the years before 1871. Ballads marked with daggers have more nearly exact dates of publication given for them than the dates provided in the table of contents for this volume on pages 11–13 of volume 1.

Contents
Volume 2

List of Illustrations   293

Anthology, Part 2: The Poor

1. Beggars and Paupers   299
    INTRODUCTION   299

BALLADS AND COMMENTARIES 303
 The Beggar: c. 1791–92* / 303
 The Beggar Girl: c. 1802* / 305
 The Merry Will & Testament of Master
  Black Billy: 1823* / 308
 The Pauper's Drive: 1841 or before / 311
 The Beggar's Lament: 1849* / 313
 As I Wandered by the Cook Shop: 1855 or before* / 317

2. Children on the Street 319
 INTRODUCTION 319
 BALLADS AND COMMENTARIES 319
  The Match Song: early 1800s* / 320
  Little Jessey, the Poor Flower Girl: 1838*† / 322
  The Child's Inquiry: 1853–55?* / 323
  The Poor Lost Child Restored to His Mother:: 1855?* / 325
  The Policeman's Pet: 1860s* / 328

3. Criminals 332
 INTRODUCTION 332
 BALLADS AND COMMENTARIES 338
  The Last Sorrowful Lamentation of a Boy
   under Twelve Years of Age: 1826* / 338
  The Mill: 1830–35* / 343
  Very Respectable: c. 1831† / 347
  Ax My Eye: 1834–35*† / 349
  The Cove Vot Has Seen Better Days: 1830–37* / 352
  Parson Brown's Sheep: 1835–40* / 354
  Farewell Address to Their Countrymen and Friends: 1842 / 357
  After Serving Seven Years: 1840*† / 361
  The Dreadful Murder of a Wife and Six Children: 1869* / 362

4. People In and Out of Work 374
 INTRODUCTION 374
 BALLADS AND COMMENTARIES 381
  Turn the Carpet: 1796* / 381
  Joan o' Grinfield: c. 1815 / 384
  John Taylor, Cotton Spinner . . . , Being Out
   of Employ: c. 1827?* / 387
  Bill Bounce, the Swell Cove Out of Luck: c. 1831*† / 389
  The Dead Alive: c. 1830* / 392
  The Pitman's Widow's Lament: c. 1835* / 393

The White Slave: c. 1835* / 396
Naked Truth: c. 1838* / 399
The Lucky Factory Boy: 1830s?* / 402
The Factory Child: 1840–41*† / 403
Stitch Goes the Needle: 1840s* / 405
The Hungry Army: c. 1852* / 407
God Speed the Good Ship; or, the English
 Emigrant!: c. 1855 / 408

5. Maidens and Lovers — 411
   INTRODUCTION — 411
   BALLADS AND COMMENTARIES — 415
   Squire and Milkmaid: or, Blackberry Fold:
     early 1800s / 415
   Poverty's No Sin: c. 1815* / 421
   The Fancy Lad: 1817–25 / 422
   The Dogs-Meat Man: c. 1824* / 425
   The Weaver's Daughter: 1820s* / 432
   Advice to Country Maidens on the Poor Law
     Bill: 1834* / 433
   Artichokes & Cauliflowers: 1830s / 436
   Rigs and Flares-Up of the Fair: 1837* / 438
   The Lady and the Welsh Ploughboy:
     c. 1840?* / 440
   The Village Beauty: 1840s–1850s* / 445
   Oh, Ain't I Nuts on Sarah: c. 1860* / 448
   Polly Perkins, of Paddington Green: c. 1865 / 449

6. Husbands and Wives — 452
   INTRODUCTION — 452
   BALLADS AND COMMENTARIES — 458
   Love and Liver: c. 1832* / 458
   Struggle for the Breeches: c. 1832–35* / 460
   The Blessings of a Good Little Wife: c. 1835* / 461
   The Wives Lamentation: 1832–36* / 463
   Mrs. Johnson: 1834*† / 466
   A Week's Matrimony: 1832–36* / 468
   The Drunken Husband: 1836–37 / 471
   The Woman That Wished She'd Never Got
     Married: c. 1840?* / 473
   My Wife's First Baby: c. 1845–48 / 475
   Poor Married Man: c. 1851* / 477

7. Poets	480
INTRODUCTION	480
BALLADS AND COMMENTARIES	482
Wandering Bard: c. 1800?*† / 482	
Billy Nutts, the Poet: c. 1853–55*† / 484	
Anything to Earn a Crust: c. 1850–55* / 494	
8. Scenes of Mirth and Contentment	500
INTRODUCTION	500
BALLADS AND COMMENTARIES	505
Hot Codlings: c. 1806?† / 505	
Beggars Opera—Tom, Jerry, & Logick Among the Cadgers in the Holy Land: 1822* / 506	
The Coalheaver's Feast: c. 1833–36*† / 509	
Monmouth Street: c. 1836*† / 514	
The Way to Live: 1840s / 517	
The Last Farewell to Poor St. Giles's: c. 1848* / 519	
Owdham Streets at Dinner Time: 1850s / 523	
The Brixton Lady and Her Nice Beetle Pies: c. 1856–57* / 525	
Appendix 1. The Broadside Cock	529
Appendix 2. "Justifiable Homicide" of a Policeman: Jurors Versus Coroner, the *Times*, and the Government, May 1833	542
Notes	548
Bibliography	561
Title List of English Broadsides (mainly ballads) on Poverty, 1790–1870, Used, Quoted, Referred to, with Locations	569
First-Line List of Ballads	621
General Index	653

List of Illustrations

Billy Waters	307
Beggars Opera	310
The Tread Mill	345
"Farewell Address to Their Countrymen and Friends"	358
The Dogs-Meat Man and Miss Dorothy	424
"The Village Beauty"	446
"The Last Farewell to Poor St. Giles's"	520
"The Brixton Lady and Her Nice Beetle Pies"	526

A Book of Scattered Leaves

Volume 2

Anthology, Part 2: The Poor

1
Beggars and Paupers

In 1814–15 a House of Commons Select Committee investigated the matter of beggary in London. They knew that in 1803 there were reckoned to be some fifteen thousand beggars in and around the city, and that numbers had increased since then. They knew that the law of the land, emanating from the Poor Law Act of 1601, required every parish to take care of its poor, either by finding work for them or by providing relief. Why should beggars be on the street at all? The committee reported what they had learned:

> Street beggars with very few exceptions are utterly worthless and incorrigible.
> Beggars on their being searched . . . , a great deal of money has been found about them.
> A blind man with a dog got 30s. in one day [a sum that would keep an honest beggar alive for well more than a month].
> A Negro beggar retired to the West Indies with a fortune, it was supposed, of £1500.
> A highly respected manufacturer in Spitalfields stated . . . that there were instances of his people leaving profitable work for the purpose of begging.

The committee saw that certain aspects of beggary were organized:

> Beggars are furnished with children at houses in Whitechapel, Shoreditch; some who look like twins.
> A woman with twins, who never grew older, sat [in the street] for ten years.
> An old woman . . . kept a night-school for instructing children in the street language.

The committee gave special attention to St. Giles's:

> Out of 400 beggars in St. Giles's, 350 are capable of earning their own living.

In conclusion the committee recommended the establishment of a mendicant police board to enquire further into the causes of beggary and to examine beggars brought before it.[1]

Such a board seems not to have been formally set into being; but two years later the Society for the Suppression of Mendicity was founded, with views consonant with those of the Select Committee, and possessed of quasi-legal powers. It was a society of rich men, with the duke of York (second son of George III) as patron, the duke of Northumberland as president, and a number of other dukes, several earls and lords, and a few esquires as vice-presidents. In later years Queen Victoria was patron, and in last years the present Queen Mother, the society surviving into the 1950s.

The basic principle of the society was that "indiscriminate alms-giving is not charity," and the implication of the principle was that requests for alms should be investigated. Neither dukes nor esquires should be duped. Members of the society did not give alms; rather, they risked giving tickets that might be exchanged for meals. The price of each ticket was interrogation, possible investigation, possible prosecution. The society employed constables who had authority to apprehend under the laws of vagrancy.

The task before the society was considerable, and in its first year it examined only one-sixth or one-seventh of the reported number of beggars in and around London. The first annual report gave a total of 3,284 cases examined. Of that number, nearly 50 percent were referred to their original parishes for relief, 3 percent were provided with employment, another 3 percent were clothed and sent to sea, 4 percent disappeared without trace, 7 percent were found to be able to take care of themselves, and 16 percent were ordered to be prosecuted. The remaining number were divided among those sent directly into workhouses or hospitals, those sent to their countries of origin, and so forth. After another twelve years the society reported that in sum it had examined 25,558 cases, and that its constables had apprehended 9,565 seeming beggars and obtained convictions of 4,795. If the figures do not fully support the statements of the Select Committee that nearly all beggars were worthless and that seven-eighths of them in a given sample (St. Giles's) were able to earn their own livings, they nevertheless suggest that a considerable percentage were impostors, undeserving of alms. (See the endnote for further information on the Mendicity Society, on attacks on the society, and on another attempt to suppress beggary.)[2]

Among the beggars described in the ballads reprinted below, only one was a real person instead of a poetic invention, and it would perhaps have been a matter of regret to both Select Committee and Mendicity Society if they could have known that Black Billy Waters was thought by Douglas Jerrold to be highly gifted instead of worthless, that his wooden leg was real instead of fake, and that he died in a workhouse instead of the West Indies. It is the case, though, that the ballad history of invented beggary offers much to support the views of Select Committee and Mendicity Society. "The Beggars Chorus" of the 1600s, attributed to Richard Brome, asks, "Then who would be a king, / When a beggar lives so well?" Brome's beggar tells of the good food, drink, wenches he enjoys—all in between pretenses of being crippled. The ballad survived into the nineteenth century, essentially unaltered under the same title, mutilated in "The Beggar" ("Of all the trades in London, / A beggar is the best"). Other earlier ballads showing well-fed beggars are "The Jolly Beggar" (attributed to James V of Scotland), "The Dorsetshire Garland, or, the Beggars' Wedding," "Sandman's Wedding," and "The Bunter's Wedding" (the whore's wedding).[3] More clearly criminal beggars can be seen in "The Beggar Wench of Hull" and "The Stout Cripple of Cornwall," both of which ballads apparently date from the 1600s. In the first, the beggar wench lures a merchant's son to a tavern, and with the presumed connivance of landlord and landlady, gets him drunk, gives him a sleeping potion, and runs off with his money and clothing. The second describes a beggar-highwayman who is caught and hanged.[4]

Even in tales of Robin Hood, beggars are sometimes not what they ought to be. In "Robin Hood and the Beggar," Robin picks a quarrel with a beggar. The beggar is no starveling, and lays Robin low and departs. Robin sends two men after him for revenge, and the beggar bribes them with an offer of £100, a sum that apparently seems reasonable to them for a beggar to carry. When they agree to the bribe, he throws meal in their faces and lays them low too. In "Bold Robin Hood," Robin disguises himself as a beggar to dupe the Sheriff of Nottingham and save the lives of three poachers. The moral for sheriffs and others in high and low places is not to trust beggars.[5]

There was, though, occasional appearance to the contrary, as in the old ballad "The Maunding Soldier; or, the Fruits of Warre is Beggary." Another old ballad, "The Map of Mock-Beggar Hall," sought to expose deception more profound than that practiced by beggars:

> Some gentlemen and citizens have,
> In divers eminent places
> Erected houses, rich and brave,
> Which stood for the owners graces;
> Let any poore to such a doore
> Come, they expecting plenty,
> They there may ask till their throats are sore,
> *For mock beggar hall stands empty.*[6]

Broadside ballads of the nineteenth century show considerable numbers of both unworthy and worthy beggars. Among the first sort are "The Manchester Cadger! or Ve Vants No Vork to Do" (a mixture of prose and verse, the verse sometimes printed alone as "Life of a Cadger!"), "Let Us Go Cadging Together," "Life of a Vagabond," and "A Rummy Old Cadger am I." All of these ballads describe dodges employed by beggars to excite pity. "The Manchester Cadger!" mentions sham fits abetted by soap in the mouth, suicide attempts as by drowning while numbers of people are standing by, going out in the rain to shiver, and writing begging letters to the duke of Wellington as from veterans of Waterloo and

Bunker Hill. Of particular interest is the baby dodge, which the ballad-writer might have got from the Select Committee. The lines parody the song "All Round My Hat."[7]

> All round the squares, Sal lugs a pair of babbies—
> All round the squares, Sal lugs a pair of twins;
> And when the public passes by she pinches them voraciously,
> Vich makes the babbies for to cry, and sympathy it brings.

The cadger himself observes that the other day a woman came up to Sal and said, "How is it, mum, your children never grows any older?" Sal is momentarily at a loss, then says, "The fact on it is, marm, the kids is hobstinate, and won't grow."

The dishonesty of such cadgers is in gulling the public rather than in criminal activity. More criminal cadging, as in the thievery described in "Tim Snooken, the Cadger," is dealt with in the section below on the criminal poor. Ballads purporting to describe the plight of genuine beggars are on the whole of less interest than those about cadgers. The doleful mode was perhaps more difficult to sustain than the ironic mode. Nevertheless, doleful ballads seem to have sold in much the greater numbers, possibly an indication of the importance of charitable impulse in the buying of ballads. One of the dodges mentioned in "The Manchester Cadger!" is Sal's going out to sing and sell ballads. It seems unlikely that either true or false beggars would choose to offer "The Manchester Cadger!" itself.

Illustrative of the hazard of the doleful mode is "The Blind Man's Lamentation," which is a succession of quatrains of the following kind:

> How heartless is my situation,
>   Good Christians all now pity me;
> And when you hear my lamentation,
>   Bestow on me your charity.

One ballad that in part survives the hazard is "The Lamentation of Sarah Bursnell, Composed by Herself, a Blind Woman," in which apparently real dole lent energy to poetic—though the first line is possibly drawn from an unknown source:

> All you that fear the Lord, who rules the sky,
> Praise his holy name that lives on high,
> Regard the helpless, lame, and blind, that can no comfort find.
> In pity pray be kind, my wants supply.

Prominent among worthy beggars in the ballads are children, soldiers and sailors, and wanderers from other lands. "The Beggar Girl," given below, was perhaps the most popular of all beggar ballads. It seems to have been written for a theatrical entertainment at the turn of the century, it came directly onto the street, and it sold widely for forty years or more. It had counterparts in two ballads entitled "The Beggar Boy" and others entitled "Please, Give Me a Penny, Sir," "Poor Mechanic's Boy," and "The Friendless Boy." The last of these has a footnote saying, "When sung by a lady, the word 'boy' must be sung 'girl'." Ballads such as "The Poor Discharged Soldier" and "The British Tars" concern men who have served the nation and then been left to starve. Two of the most widely popular beggar ballads were "The Poor Old Worn Out Sailor" and "The Poor Irish Stranger." The old sailor comes to a village to beg, and a young woman there discovers he is her father. The poor Irishman has been robbed of his idyllic rural home by a rich man who has built a splendid mock-beggar hall and has taken the produce of the land.

Overall, it would appear that buyers of street ballads were much more disposed to think generously of beggars than were the Select Committee, the Mendicity Society, or certain ballad writers enjoying a cynical vein. One of these last was a man named George Sykes, otherwise unknown, who waved aside the problem of beggary with a ballad entitled "We Are All Beggars" ("We are all beggars, beg, beg, beggars"). The ballad is a litany of beggars, from milkman and baker, who beg customers to buy chalk and water and bone dust of them, to Poor Law Commissioners, Prince Albert, and Robert Peel, who beg for poor rates, pension, and income tax. The ballad exists in three versions, with one giving considerable space to begging from the public purse by the monarchy. The hit at Robert Peel echoes a ballad called "The Begging Box," written at the turn of the century, which attacks the original income tax introduced by the younger Pitt. The ballad is republican, and sees the French wars filling foreign coffers and producing famine in England.

The longest view of beggary is taken in a ballad called "The Gospel Beggar," which seems to date from mid-century. It says that all true Christians are beggars, and they do not even think of knocking on the door of mock-beggar hall.

> I've done well with begging since first I set out,
> I have begged a kingdom without any doubt;
> A crown for my head, and a harp for my hand,
> I am making home to glory at Jesus's command.
>
> Come all faithful beggars, fresh courage now take,
> And beg your way through, and his ways don't forsake;
> Knock at mercy's door, Christ will not deny,
> There's a crown and a kingdom for you by and by.

The Beggar

> Why good people all at what do you pry,
> Is it the stump of my arm or my leg

Or the place where I lost my good looking eye,
    Or is it to see me beg.
Lord love you hard fortune is nothing at all
    And he's but a fool and a dunce
Who expects when he's running full butt 'gainst a wall
    Not to get a good rap on the sconce.
If beg borrow or steal be the choice of mankind
    Sure I chose the best of the three,
Besides as times go what a comfort to find,
    That in this bad world there's some charity.

For a soldier I listed to grow great in fame,
    To be shot at for eight pence a day,
Lord help the poor poultry where'er I came,
    For how could I live on my pay.
I went to the wars to fight the king's foes
    Where bullets came whistling by,
Till they shivered three ribs, broke the bridge of my nose,
    Queer'd my napper and knock'd out my eye.
Well what of all this I'd my legs and my arms,
    And at Chelsea to lie up was free,
Where my pipe I could smoke, talk of battles and storm,
    And bless his good Majesty's charity.

But thinking it shameful to live at my ease,
    Away while the frolic was warm,
In search of good fortune I sail'd the salt seas,
    And so lost my leg and my arm.
With two strings to my bow I thought myself sure,
    But such is the fortune of war,
A lobster at Greenwich they shewed me the door,
    At Chelsea they call'd me a tar;
So falling to nothing between those two stools,
    I the whole world before me had free,
To ask comfort from misers and pity from fools,
    And live on that air, men's charity.

And what now of all this here patter at last,
    How many who hold their head high,
And in fashion's fine whirligig fly round so fast,
    Are but beggars as well as I?

1 / BEGGARS AND PAUPERS

> The courtier he begs for a sinecure,
>   For a smile beg your amorous elves,
> Churchwardens hand the plate round and beg the poor,
>   Just to pamper and fatten themselves.
> Thus we're beggars throughout the whole race of mankind,
>   As by daily experience we see,
> And as time goes what a comfort to find
>   That in this bad world there's some charity.

Lobster—soldier

Words and music of the ballad were written by Charles Dibdin (1745–1814) in about 1791–92. He was the precocious son of a parish clerk in Southampton, and grandson of a substantial merchant there. He was gifted as poet, dramatist, musician, composer, and painter. At age fifteen he was in London, singing in the chorus at Covent Garden. At age nineteen he sang the leading role there in *The Shepherd's Artifice*, for which he had written the words and music. During succeeding years he had very considerable success at Covent Garden and elsewhere. Over many years he wrote several hundred songs. Among well more than a hundred that found their way as broadsides are "Bill Bobstay," "Honesty in Tatters," "The Labourer's Welcome Home," "The Last Shilling," "The Thrasher," and "Tom Tackle." These all touch upon poverty. Dibdin wrote many naval songs, and was called "Poet Laureate of the British Navy." "The Beggar" was written for an entertainment called "Private Theatricals," given at the Royal Polygraphic Rooms in the Strand. Presumably it came onto the street soon thereafter, though the text given here, as printed by Pitts, could not have been issued before about 1797. Pitts's printing has minor differences from the ballad as printed in George Hogarth's *The Songs of Charles Dibdin*, 1842. Punctuation is conventional and much heavier in Hogarth, and the beggar is shot at for sixpence a day instead of eight. The latter difference suggests that the text Hogarth worked from antedated Pitts's printing by some years.[8] I have added punctuation to Pitts's printing.

The Beggar Girl

Over the mountain and over the moor,
    Hungry and barefoot I wander forlorn;
My father is dead, and my mother is poor,
    And she grieves for the day that will never return.

CHORUS

Pity, kind gentlefolks, friends of humanity,
   Cold blows the wind and the night's coming on,
Give me some food for my mother for charity,
   Give me some food as I may go home.

Call me not lazy-back, beggar, or bold enough,
   Fain would I learn for to knit or sew,
I've two little brothers at home, when they're old enough,
   They shall work hard for the gifts you'll bestow.

So think while you're able, so careless and free,
   Safe from the winds, well cloathed and fed,
If fortune should change, how hard it would be
   To beg at a door for a morsel of bread!

Pity, kind gentlefolks, friends of humanity,
   Cold blows the wind, and the night's coming on,
Give me some food for my mother, for charity,
   Give me some food as I may go home.

    The ballad appears to have been one of the most popular broadside ballads of the century. The copy printed from was "published and sold by George Huntley, a disabled soldier," and he had the song from the Theatre Royal, Covent Garden, where, he says, it was "sung with great applause by Mr. Mountain." Words and music were composed by John Westbrook Chandler, who is not otherwise known except as the composer of another song, "Adieu My Native Land Adieu" (1797), which also appeared in broadside form.[9]

    The published sheet music of the present ballad dates from about 1802. It has minor differences: "mountains" and "moors" in the first line, "pity, kind gentlemen" and "then I will be gone" in the chorus, and "while you revel so careless" and "should fortune so change it" in the third stanza.

    The beggar girl is lucky in that she has a mother to return to. Most other beggar-children are orphans, as seen in "The Soldier's Orphan's Prayer," "The Drunkard's Child," and "The Savoyard Boy." Other ballads show such orphans on the point of rescue: "Fisherman's Girl," "The Pauper's Child," and "The Soldier's Boy." The narratives of the latter two ballads are very much the same.

BILLY WATERS.
Billy Waters. By permission of the British Library.

The Merry Will & Testament of Master Black Billy

I Master William Waters, O,
    A *Minstrel of the Holy Land*;
Well known among my betters, O,
    And at the Adelphi, in the Strand,
Convinc'd that death will me soon call,
    This day for my old *Palls* I've sent,
And in the presence of them all,
    Thus make my Will and Testament.

I do declare with my last breath,
    And sign it in plain black and white,
That Tom and Jerry's sudden death,
    Has poor Black Billy kill'd outright.
And when that Billy's dead and gone,
    I hope his friends will not be slack,
About his death to make a song,
    And hang St. Giles's church in black.

Now, I do advise my little son,
    If he should live to be a man,
To do just as his daddy's done,
    And drink good gin whene'er he can.
To the British Museum I bequeath,
    My smart cock'd hat and feathers three,
And hope the same they will receive,
    As poor Black Billy's legacy.

Next, to the Adelphi I bequeath
    My Fiddle, which is worth a groat;
And unto Dusty Bob I leave
    My jacket for to mend his coat.
Unto Bob Logic, that rum swell,
    I do present my timber toe,
In hopes that he will hand it well,
    In flooring of the charlies, O.

I do bequeath unto Black Sall,
    One Penny for to buy a bun;

1 / BEGGARS AND PAUPERS

  Likewise my Shirt so full of holes,
   A flea thereon he could not run.
  My Trousers (tho' not worth a pin)
   By Public Auction shall be Sold,
  All for to buy a drop of gin,
   To warm her heart when it is cold.

  Thus poor Black Billy's made his Will,
   His property was small good-lack,
  For 'til the day death did him kill
   His house he carried on his back.
  The Adelphi now may say alas!
   And to his memory raise a stone;
  Their gold will be exchang'd for brass,
   Since poor Black Billy's dead and gone.

  The ballad, printed on one of James Catnach's large and splendid sheets, sold for twopence instead of the customary halfpence or penny. The copy printed from is described as a tenth edition. I have retained the spellings Pall and Sall as given on the sheet. The overall title of the sheet is "The Death, Last Will, and Funeral of 'Black Billy'; also the Tears of London for the Death of Tom and Jerry." Tom and Jerry, along with their friend Bob Logic (sometimes Logick), are the contentious swells of Pierce Egan's great literary and dramatic success of the early 1820s, *Life in London*. The three men get into a variety of scrapes as they go about town drinking, gaming, and whoring. The book was dramatized several times, most successfully by W. T. Moncrieff. His version, with the title *Tom and Jerry*, had a long run at the Adelphi Theatre, outside of which Billy Waters was accustomed to play his fiddle and dance on his wooden leg. Moncrieff gave proportionately more space to Tom and Jerry's adventures in the slums of St. Giles's (the Holy Land) than did Egan in his book. Anyone attending Moncrieff's "operatic extravaganza" might first see Billy Waters outside, and then see representations inside of him and other denizens of the Holy Land: Dusty Bob, Black Sal, and Little Jemmy. The death of Tom and Jerry refers to the closing of Moncrieff's piece shortly before Billy Waters' death.

  Much of Catnach's sheet is taken up with three cuts. The first cut shows Death the Boxer standing triumphant over Tom and Jerry (in spite of their boxing skills), with surrounding rejoicing figures of the chief enemies of the men, the night-watchmen (Charlies) of the city. The second cut shows the funeral procession for Tom and Jerry passing the Adelphi Theatre. In attendance are Logic (carrying an opened umbrella), Kate and Susan (Tom and Jerry's women) walking together, Black Billy playing his fiddle, Black Sal drinking gin as she walks, Dusty Bob with his bell, and others. The third cut shows the funeral procession for Black Billy. On top of the draped coffin are his cocked hat, fiddle, wooden leg, perhaps shirt and trousers, and other things. The mourners here are not clearly identifiable except for Little Jemmy, a cripple, who is carried. The procession is passing the Beggars Opera, familiar name for the pub the Rose and Crown. The illustration of the interior of the Beggars Opera comes from another Catnach sheet, "Life in London." Black Billy fiddles, Dusty Bob raises his bell and hat, Little Jemmy sits in his high chair, Jerry sits beside him, and Tom talks with Peg the ballad singer. Peg, mentioned in a passage quoted from Egan's book on page 422, is presumably fictional. For another ballad concerning Black Billy and his friends, and for more detail on Moncrieff, see pages 506–9.

CUT VI. *Beggars Opera---Tom, Jerry, & Logick, among the Cadgers in the Holy Land.*

Beggars Opera. By permission of the St. Bride Printing Library.

The verses on Black Billy are followed by an account of him written by Catnach himself and dated 25 March 1823:

Life of Black Billy

On Friday in St. Giles's workhouse the famous Billy Waters. Billy endeavoured up to the period of his illness to obtain for a wife and two children what he termed an honest living by the scraping of catgut, by which he amassed a considerable portion of browns (halfpence) at the west end of the town, where his hat and feathers with his peculiar antics excited much mirth and attention. He was obliged prior to his death to part with his old friend, the fiddle, for a trifling sum at the pawnbrokers. His wooden pin had twice saved him from the treadmill. He lost his leg in his majesty's service for which he received a pension. Every child in London knew him. A short time before he died he was elected King of the Beggars.

In his *True History of Tom and Jerry* (1892), Charles Hindley offers a fanciful account of Waters's origins, attributing it to Moncrieff. An appreciation of Black Billy appears in Douglas Jerrold's essay "The Ballad Singer," in his *Writings:*

> Blackest of blacks! Ethiopian Grimaldi! They who saw thee not, cannot conceive the amount of grace coexistent with a wooden leg—the comedy budding from timber . . . ; his face seemed polished, trickling with good humour. Who ever danced as he danced? Waters was a genius.[10]

In a letter to Hindley of 29 February 1876, John Morgan recalls "Waters, with his wooden leg, dancing and playing his fiddle, and singing":

> Polly will you marry me—Polly don't you cry,
> Polly come to bed with me, and get a little boy.[11]

What sort of funeral Black Billy actually received is unknown. In *John Pitts, Ballad Printer,* Leslie Shepard describes the funeral in 1815 of a famous blind ballad singer named Jack Stuart.

> Crowds of spectators, including the leading beggars and balladmongers of London, followed the procession from Somers Town to St. Pancras churchyard, afterwards celebrating a wake of dancing, drinking, swearing and fighting.[12]

The church of St. Giles-in-the-Fields dates back to 1101. It was rebuilt twice, the second time handsomely in the 1730s, when the district was descending from high respectability into squalor. Ninety years later, at the time of Billy Waters' death, the church stood in lonely splendor amidst some of the worst slums in London. Today it is overlooked by Centre Point.

The Pauper's Drive

> There's a grim one-horse hearse in a jolly round trot;
> To the churchyard a pauper is going, I wot;
> The road it is rough, and the hearse has no springs,
> And hark to the *dirge* that the *sad* driver sings:—
>   "Rattle his bones over the stones;
>   He's *only* a Pauper, whom nobody owns!"

Oh, where are the mourners? alas! there are none;—
He has left not a gap in the world now he's gone;
Not a tear in the eye of child, woman, or man;—
To the grave with his carcase as fast as you can;
    "Rattle his bones over the stones;
    He's *only* a Pauper, whom nobody owns!"

What a jolting and creaking, and splashing and din!
The whip, how it cracks! and the wheels how they spin!
How the dirt, right and left, o'er the hedges is hurl'd!
The Pauper at length makes a noise in the world!
    "Rattle his bones over the stones;
    He's *only* a Pauper, whom nobody owns!"

Poor Pauper defunct! he has made some approach
To gentility, now that he's stretch'd in a coach;
He's taking a drive in his carriage at last;
But it will not be long, if he goes on so fast!
    "Rattle his bones over the stones;
    He's *only* a Pauper, whom nobody owns!"

You bumpkin! who stare at your brother convey'd,
Behold what respect to a cloddy is paid,
And be joyful to think, when by death you're laid low,
You've a chance to the grave like a *gemman* to go.
    "Rattle his bones over the stones;
    He's *only* a Pauper, whom nobody owns!"

But a truce to this strain,—for my soul it is sad,
To think that a heart in humanity clad,
Should make, like the brutes, such a desolate end,
And depart from the light without leaving a friend!
    Bear softly his bones over the stones;
    Though a Pauper, *he's one whom his Maker yet owns!*

    The ballad is by Thomas Noel (1799–1861). He was born in Kirk Mallory, son of a clergyman, and was educated at Merton College, Oxford. Much or most of his life after leaving Oxford in 1824 was spent in seclusion at Boyne Cottage, Boyne Hill, Maidenhead. He published three known collections of poetry: *The Cottage Muse* (1833), and *Village Verse* and *Rymes and Roundelayes*, both 1841. "The Pauper's Drive" appeared in the last of these volumes, along with the one other poem by which he is chiefly remembered, "Rocked in the Cradle of the

Deep." "The Pauper's Drive" was reprinted in the Chartist *Northern Star*, Leeds, 5 February 1842, and moved from there onto broadsides. Broadside versions often bring an early truce to the strain, omitting stanzas 4 and 5. I have followed the 1841 volume.

Boyne Cottage was near the Cookham Union Workhouse, and Noel must often have seen carts carrying the dead over the rough roads from the workhouse to burial places in Cookham and Bray.

(Most of my information derives from two articles on Noel by F. J. B. in the *Maidenhead Advertiser*, 29 October and 19 November 1941. I am grateful to Rhodri Thomas and Gail Stuckey of the Maidenhead Library for their help, and to the County Local Studies Library, Reading, for making available a copy of "The Pauper's Drive" from *Rymes and Roundelayes*.)

The Beggar's Lament

The beggars are ruined oh, dear,—oh, dear,
The beggars are ruined oh, dear,—oh, dear,
The lash of the *Times* has made them feel queer,
The beggars are ruined oh, dear, oh, dear.
Duck Lane and Old Pie Street are all up in arms,
Cow Cross and the Rookery teem with alarms,
Wooden legs and sore noses have lost all their charms,
And pity no more awaits sermons or psalms.
The beggars are ruined, &c.

Once I could wait at a pastry cook's shop,
While lusty young ladies were filling their crop,
Then follow them close with a whine and a hop,
Until their odd coppers they were glad to drop.
I've been ruined by steam, I've been maim'd in the wars,
And I've chanted a ditty with fresh water tars
All bandaged with rags, and deformed with sham scars
And I've oft bribed the bobbies to keep out of jars.

I've chew'd yellow soap, and been troubled with fits,
'Till the ladies dropp'd tears with their fourpenny bits,
Since the days of my boyhood I've liv'd by my wits,
By concocting petitions, distresses and writs!
I've chalked on the pavement "no food for a week!"
"Kind Christians in vain for employment I seek;"

And when with reluctance I've bowed to the beak,
The poor box rewarded my tale told so meek.

Near the Bank and Exchange I could once safely lurk,
In every dark alley, and corner and quirk,
And sooner than stoop to degrading hard work,
I'll go on the highway with pistol and dirk.
The papers may talk of the swindle and sin,
Of easing the rich of a little spare tin,
What tho' we expend it in brandy and gin,
We enrich the excise, all the more we gulf in.

My wife and my daughters are plunged in dejection,
They could act the poor widow in first rate perfection,
And mourn their dear husbands with tears of affection,
While exposing hired babies who had no connexion.
My sons shamm'd consumption, with long tallow faces,
And studied the glass to learn awful grimaces,
In the parks and the squares they picked the best places
And reaped cash galore at the fairs and the races.

The Puppet-show put us in a terrible pickle,
And *Punch* has thought proper our tobies to tickle,
The whole public press to condemn us don't stickle,
But the *Times* to our harvest put in the first sickle.
At night in the play-house no longer we shine,
Chicken and ham we're compelled to resign,
We gladly drink porter in lieu of port wine,
And the cry in real earnest is, "where shall I dine?"

We will wait on the Queen with a monster petition,
And humbly ask Her Most Gracious permission,
To hang foreign beggars of every condition,
Who have bought up the press to defy competition;
Let the beggarly Germans be made go-a-head!
And the beggarly Poles at home seek their bread,
And when from our shore all the mongrels have fled,
Let beggarly Britons get fat in their stead.

Duck Lane and Old Pie Street—streets of the poor in Westminster; today what survives of Duck Lane is Matthew Street

Cow Cross—a similar street, leading today from the Farringdon Road at the Underground Station to St. John Street
The Rookery—the cluster of cheap lodging houses in St. Giles's; two of the most notorious, Rats Castle and Mother Swankey's, disappeared in 1848 to make way for New Oxford Street; see the illustration, page 32
Ruined by steam—supposedly put out of work by steam-driven machinery
Jars—police cells?
Quirk—odd corner?
Tin—money
Tobies—buttocks

The ballad was issued by C. Paul of 18 Great St. Andrew's Street, presumably in January or February of 1849. It is a substantial improvement over a printing in the second volume of *Model Song Book,* issued in London by T. Goode in about 1848. There it appears on page 253 under the name of Henry Valentine. Its first stanza therein is merely a four-line chorus, the first two lines of which are the same as Paul's first two lines, with the next two both saying, "The crusade of the press has inspired them with fear." The image of the alarm felt by beggars in Old Pie Street and the Rookery occurs nowhere in the ballad, and presumably has yet to be invented. In general, Paul's version is more fluent in rhythm, more lively in language. "Let the thunderer grieve at the heinous sin" becomes "The papers may speak of the swindle and sin" and "While exposing hired babies sans daddy's protection" becomes "While exposing hired babies who had no connexion." Paul omits one altogether weak stanza.

Valentine is an obscure figure with a very brief known life in print. Twenty or so ballads have been seen that bear his name, mainly as published in the two volumes of *Model Song Book.* Most of the songs are innocuous. Only one other of his ballads, "Johnny Jiggletoes," is known in broadside form. Valentine is presumably the author also of two little books published in about 1848 under his name. One of them, *Behind the Curtain,* consists of several monologues delivered in the persons of Charles Macready, Madame Vestris, the elder Kean, and others in their dressing rooms. The book is dedicated to Macready and speaks of reforms at the Theatre Royal, Covent Garden suggested by Valentine and carried into effect by Macready. No reference to Valentine appears in a number of books by or about Macready that have been seen. The other little book is *The Comic Dictionary, or, Multum in Parvo of Fun and Fact.* E.g.:

> YORE, ad. of long past time, of old time. John Bull's greatest aggravation is, being taunted with "the days of yore."
>
> > In days of yore, 'tis in history said,
> > One halfpenny would buy a bushel of bread.
> > > Bard of the Seven Dials.

Following the dictionary is a list of some forty celebrated men and women, who include Black Sal and Dusty Bob, Billy Waters, and Walker the Twopenny Postman—the first three of whom can be seen, the last of whom is mentioned, elsewhere in this volume.

Like John Martin, Thomas Hudson, Thomas Peckett Prest, James Bruton, Pierce Egan, W. T. Moncrieff and others, Valentine apparently knew in some measure the diverse literature and life of street, concert, and stage. It seems more likely than not that he was the improver of his concert song for street publication.

The good fight against beggary was conducted in the *Times* for several years in the 1840s. The immediate reference is presumably to a leader there on 24 January 1849, in which the editors took at least as stern a view as the parliamentary Select Committee in 1816 and the Mendicity Society.

> The plague of beggars is beginning to abate. It is possible now for a middle-aged gentleman of portly form and benignant expression to walk abroad without a retinue of mendicants. Even elderly ladies are allowed an occasional respite. Lucifer matches, pocket-books, bouquets, lead pencils, penknives, and key-rings are no longer forced on the reluctant public. Artificial flowers and pin-cushions are left to the law of demand and supply. By the operation of the same laws we have no doubt that little children have fallen in the market, and may be hired for less than 9d. a day by such as are willing to brave the policeman. Beggars' hotels, coffee-houses, and ordinaries cannot now be in so thriving a condition as they were a few months ago. Where the poor creatures go we can hardly divine. One only knows that as one wind brought the locusts, another has swept them away.... Humane people need not conclude that beggars perish when they are driven from the pavement, like insects in a frost. They are only a little inconvenienced by being compelled to do something for their subsistence....
>
> A few weeks ago begging was the best trade in London. Many a sturdy fellow earned more by bullying ladies than the industrious tradesman whose shop-door he blockaded. The public indignation has been roused, and the craft is at a discount....
>
> It is established by a vast mass of evidence that nine hundred and ninety-nine beggars out of a thousand are persons who will not work honestly for their daily bread. An inspired apostle, and withal a very sensible man, tells us that such persons ought not to live. We think so too, and will only mitigate the severity of this maxim so far as to let them live in prison....

On the next day the *Times* reprinted from *Punch* several stanzas entitled "The Jolly London Beggars." The stanzas illustrate the jolly life that deserves to be dealt with so sternly.

Spelling is notably careless in the printing. I have corrected it along with one or two other slips.

(I am grateful to Steve Roud for making available to me his copy of *Model Song Book*. Valentine came to my attention as the author of "The Beggar's Lament" by way of Roud's *Broadside Index,* listed in the bibliography, page 566.

As I Wandered by the Cook Shop

As I wandered by the Cook Shop,
    A wishing for a meal,
I looked up at the old town clock,
    And in my pockets did feel;
There was no sign of any coppers,
    Nor clink of other coins,
But the grumbling of my inside
    Was the only sound I heard.

I stood beneath the window,
    'Twas there I licked the steam,
And as it grew more stronger,
    How very queer I did seem;
But I waited for the pot boy,
    I listened for his word,
But the grumbling of my inside
    Was the only sound I heard.

He came not, oh! he came not,
    For some soup I did long,
Hot smoking joints lay one by one,
    Surrounded by puddings strong;
The chill air rolled around me,
    The blinds above were stained,
But the grumbling of my inside
    Was the only sound I heard.

Fast, fast, sad tears were flowing,
    When a Peeler he stood behind,
He grabbed me by the shoulder,
    I thought he was unkind;
He made me quake and quiver,
    I could not speak one word,
So the grumbling of my inside
    Was the only sound I heard.

Peeler—Sir Robert Peel's new policeman

The ballad is a parody of sentimental verses by Lord Houghton (Richard Monckton Milnes, 1809–85). Houghton's verses, called "The Brook-Side," describe a young woman waiting for her lover, who does not come until "fast silent tears" are flowing. For her "the beating of my own heart / Was all the sound I heard," until at the end "the beating of our own hearts / Was all the sound we heard."[13] These verses appeared in broadside form under the title "The Beating of My Own Heart" at least as early as 1845 in a printing by Hodges at 31 Monmouth Street—just before Monmouth Street was renamed Dudley Street.[14] The verses were set to music at least four times within forty years, the first time apparently being in 1858. In three of the settings the composer took the liberty of changing Houghton's opening line, "I wandered by the brook side" to "As I wandered . . . ," perhaps relying upon the liberty taken by earlier broadside printers in changing the line for parody.[15] Printings of the parody in 1855 or earlier by Bebbington and by Hodges use "as I wandered" in both title and first line.[16]

Every printing I have seen of "As I Wandered by the Cook Shop" has "she came not, oh, she came not" following from "I waited for the pot boy." I have changed it. Some printings, apparently trying to improve the verses, give "sauntered" in the first line instead of "wandered," and "awful," "horrid," or "growling" instead of "only" in the refrain line.

Lord Houghton—poet, biographer of Keats, friend of Swinburne, collector of pornography, and political figure—published a slender volume of verse in 1840 called *Poetry for the People*. In one of its poems, "Rich and Poor," he wrote:

> When God built up the dome of blue,
> And portioned earth's prolific floor,
> The measure of his wisdom drew
> A line between the Rich and Poor.

Houghton imagined that the line would hold until either Judgment Day or the day when love triumphed on earth. Meanwhile he took some satisfaction in things as they were:

> What paupers are the ambitious Rich!
> How wealthy the contented Poor![17]

He himself, as described by his biographer, James Pope Hennessy, was an easy-going rich man.[18]

2
Children on the Street

Of several sorts of ballads about children on the street, those that apparently sold most widely were pathetic ones. Whether sales owed more to popularity or more to charity is unknown. Some of them sold from printer to printer over many years ("The Primrose Girl," "Poor Little Child of a Tar," "The Little Chimney Sweep"), and they survive in large numbers in collections of ballads. A considerable proportion, perhaps 50 percent or more, are the same ballads that were sung in polite parlors and concert rooms, and probably in most cases were written for such places—as, apparently, was "Little Jessey, the Poor Flower Maid" given below. It seems likely that on the street such ballads raised the same sympathy in the same breasts as they had done before, and that they were the particular stock in trade of balladmongers asking for charity. They usually display popular notions of poetic language: "In a little blue garment all ragged and torn," "'Twas a keen frosty morn and the snow heavy falling," "The bitter wind blew keen and cold." These are the first lines of three of many ballads with titles beginning "Poor Little. . . ." The first two were written for stage, concert room, parlor.

Some of the pathetic ballads are little more than depictions of doleful scenes. One of the better ones is "The London Newsboy," a late ballad (1876) written by F. W. Green. It shows the boy at five o'clock in the evening making his "piteous cry" for sales while a "pitiless wind" howls. Then the time shifts to midnight, with the streets empty, the boy gone, and the observer haunted by thought of him. Most of the pathetic ballads carry their brief narratives forward to some sort of conclusion. The popular ballad "The Wandering Boy," by the gifted and ill-fated Henry Kirk White (1785–1806), begins thus:

> When the winter wind whistles along the wild moor,
> And the cottager shuts on the beggar his door...;

and ends thus:

> I'll go to the grave where my parents both lie,
> And death shall befriend the poor Wandering Boy.

Alternative happy endings are sometimes only marginally so. In one of the most lugubrious of such ballads, "Poor Little Joe," the question is asked, "Who wouldn't pity poor little Joe?" The answer is that he has "no one to soothe him…, no one to pity him." He dies, and the alleviating thought for the teller of the tale is that "now in Heaven surely he's resting." Other ballads speak more confidently of Heaven, but pathos remains their general aim. It is with rescue here on earth that pathos yields to joy. In "The Pauper's Child" the poor child weeps at a mansion door, tells his tale of dead parents and workhouse to the lady there, and is seized by her to her bosom to replace "my own dear girl [who] is with the angels." The most remarkable of such reversals occurs with "The Little Chimney Sweep," which in one printing is described as "a favourite ballad founded on fact." The sweep weeps "unnotic'd, unpity'd" until a kind damsel comes along, takes him to a neighbor's home, warms and washes him, and discovers that he is her lost brother.

> In rapture she gaz'd on each black sooty feature,
> And hugg'd to her bosom the foul-smelling creature!
> Who, sav'd by a sister, no longer need creep
> Thro' lanes, courts, and alleys a poor little sweep.

A similar story is told, less dramatically, in "Fisherman's Girl."

For every several dozen ballads of the pathetic sort, there are one or two that are cheerful. The young girl in "The Nosegay Girl" ("Sweet nosegays, buy my sweet nosegays") asks "not alms or pity." But she is on the verge of womanhood, and presently she and "my William sweet" will marry and live happily, and the ballad moves into another sort concerned with true love among the poor. A more straightforward example, given below, is "The Match Song," in which the boy knows that he will get no supper if he fails to sell his matches, but he does not pity himself nor does his verse ask for pity.

The three other ballads in this section are unusual ones. They have been seen in only one or two copies.

The Match Song

> Come buy my deal matches, come buy of me,
> They are the best matches that ever was seen,
> For lighting your candles, and kindling your fires,
> They are the best matches you can desire.
> My mother she lives at the sign of the skimmer,
> If I don't sell my matches I shall have no dinner.

I cries my matches all round Charing-Cross,
There sits King Charles upon a black horse.
I cries my matches all round the King's mews,
God bless you ma'am give me an old pair of shoes.
I cries my matches all round Wapping,
God bless you ma'am give me an old pair of stockings.
I cries my matches round hedges and ditches,
God bless you ma'am give me an old pair of breeches.
I cries my matches all round the hay-cock,
God bless you ma'am give my mother an old smock.
I cries my matches my matches my trade,
For Johnny the footman kiss'd Molly the maid.
I cries my matches and am no thief,
God bless you ma'am give me a piece of roast beef.
I cries my matches all round the gutter,
God bless you ma'am give me a piece of bread and butter.
I cries my matches all round Covent-garden,
Two for a halfpenny and one for a farthing,
I cries my matches all round the green trees,
God bless you ma'am give me a piece of bread and cheese.
If I don't sell them today I must sell tomorrow,
If I don't sell them today it will be my sorrow.

In its cheerful matter-of-factness, "The Match Song" contrasts with two companion ballads called "The Match Boy." In one, match boy Ned describes how a lady saw him one day and took him into her home, where:

> I live as nicely as a prince,
>   And lest I swell with pride,
> Call to mind not long time since,
>   I rare deal matches cry'd.

In the other a moral and poetical observer exhorts the rich to "give a mite to the poor" (rather than take them in):

> Ye wealthy and proud, while in splendour you roll
> Behold a poor orphan, pale, hungry, and wan.

The earliest copy I have seen of the present ballad was published by John Pitts at 14 Great St. Andrew's Street. Pitts was there from about 1797 to 1819.

Little Jessey, the Poor Flower Maid

I am poor little Jessey, I come here to show
To dear charming ladies and gentlemen too,
My basket of flowers so lovely and gay,
So buy my sweet posies, oh, buy them I pray;
I've pinks all so blooming, I've lilies so fair,
I've blue bells so pretty your choice to share,
I've roses and tulips, and violets sweet,
I've gather'd them lovely from nature's retreat.
Oh, my father he died many long years ago
When I was too little the sad loss to know,
And my dearest mother on a sick bed is laid,
Oh, buy them of Jessey, the poor flower maid.

I've wandered from cottage to cottage around,
But few to assist me in truth I have found,
Yet my dear little brothers and sisters at home,
So hungry and sorrowing wait my return.
I heed not the jeer nor the jest of the rude,
I proceed on my way for my purpose is good,
And I know that my mother is breathing a prayer
To Heaven, to take me beneath its good care.
Oh, proud shall I be when I see home again,
To gladden her heart, and to soften her pain,
Assisted by you, all her sad wants to aid,
Pray buy them of Jessey the poor flower maid.

The ballad appears, with negligible differences, in the *London Singer's Magazine* in 1838, with a note describing it as "an original song, written by Mr. John Martin, and sung at the London concerts." On John Martin see pages 484–94. Few copies of it as a broadside ballad survive.

One of the most widely sold ballads of the sort was "The Swiss Toy Girl," sometimes known as "Rose of Lucerne." Rose is in England for the sake of "a brother dear to me," and she offers ribbons, perfume, and crosses for sale to young ladies. The ballad appears in Catnach's 1832 catalogue, and was issued as sheet music perhaps two years earlier. "The Primrose Girl" (whose name is sometimes Kate, sometimes Mary) was first sung in a theatrical entertainment, *The Sultan*, by John Moulds, in about 1790. Kate is a poor and honest orphan, and she hopes that pity allied with virtue will produce a tear and a buyer. "Bessy Bloom the Flower Girl" is very much the same ballad as "Little Jessey."

"Poor Little Child of a Tar" (In a little blue garment all ragged and torn) was written in about 1800 by T. G. Ingall (otherwise unknown) and sung at the Theatre Royal, Drury Lane, by Mrs. Bland. "The Little Chimney Sweep" ('Twas a keen frosty morn and the snow heavy falling) was written eight years later by Mr. Upton (otherwise unknown) and sold as sheet music from Fentum's in the Strand. On the street it more often appeared under the title "Poor Little Sweep," with altered lines, including the first: "On a cold winter's morn as the snow was a falling."

The Child's Inquiry

You oft have told me, mother dear,
    As o'er the green we've trod,
The voice I fancied ever near,
    Was the spirit of our God!
Have not these accents, sweet and mild,
    To all mankind appeal'd?
Or is it only to your child
    That mystery is revealed?

Are all those little ragged boys,
    Who look so pale and cold—
Shut out from Heaven's promis'd joys?
    Can these be bought with gold?
Have they not hearts, my dear mamma,
    The same as you and I?
Or are they born beneath some star,
    Of outcast destiny?

Are they created to be lost—
    To know no fostering care?
Have not their souls the same price cost,
    That saved us from despair?
Have they no parent kind to teach
    The truth we should adore?
Is it a crime, mamma, "to preach
    The Gospel to the poor?"

>They seem to smile, when they are gay—
>   To weep, when they are sad;
>As tho' their feelings own'd the sway
>   That rich folks all have had:
>Then, why does wealth so chary give,
>   To train this ragged band?
>Have they no claim to learn, or live,
>   In this a Christian land?
>
>Nay! do not turn away your head,
>   But tell me is it right,
>That, on a velvet downy bed,
>   Your lap dog rests at night;
>While these poor ragged children stray,
>   For want of your kind aid,
>In vice's dark, unhallow'd way,
>   Their rags—their ruin made?

The printer put a question mark at the end of line 4 in the first stanza. I have replaced it with an exclamation point, following another printing.

The child's precocious view that poverty can lead children into dark unhallowed ways is rarely expressed in broadside ballads. Children on the street or in other scenes of poverty are characteristically innocent and virtuous. In ballads about professional beggars, children are usually neutral instruments of adult deception, as with the hired babies in "The Beggar's Lament" given elsewhere in these pages. One broadside ballad that does depict an evil child is "The Vulgar Little Girl." The girl uses pity or sexual interest to deliver unwary men into the hands of ruffians. The narrator of the ballad tells of returning from a Bible meeting on a dark and rainy night, of coming upon a weeping girl on a doorstep, and of aiming to succor her and her starving family. He is nevertheless aware that people look askance at him in the company of the girl. Presently the girl's accomplices set upon him. They tell him (as afterwards the police confirm) that no one will believe that his intentions towards the girl were honorable. The author standing behind the narrator tells the slightly salacious tale without expression of moral concern either for the girl or for her innocence-protesting victim. He is preoccupied with the superior literary style of his good-humored mockery, as in the passage in which the accomplices seize the narrator:

>Amazement on me quickly sat, oh, what a dreadful state;
>On horror's head, as Shakespeare writes, horrors accumulate.

"The Vulgar Little Girl" is a companion piece to another ballad, "Vulgar Little Boy" (broadside title), written by the clergyman-author R. H. Barham (1788–1845).[1]

The narrator of Barham's ballad is robbed after he takes home a boy who tells a sad tale of mother dead and father gone to sea.

The present ballad was published by John Gilbert, Royal Arcade, Newcastle upon Tyne, whose only known active dates are 1853–55. The tenor of the ballad—its direct appeal to mothers in Christian terms alternately sentimental and ironic—suggests that the author is a woman. Some of the lines have unusual poetic force, notably "Or are they born beneath some star, / Of outcast destiny?"

The Poor Lost Child Restored to His Mother

Founded on Facts

The following affecting narrative shows the remarkable discovery of Henry Yates, a little boy about two years of age, who was stolen away from his mother's door by a daring ruffian, now in custody, and who gives the name of Henry Ramsden; he is connected with a daring gang of miscreants, who in various ways manage to practise their vile schemes upon a too generous and confiding public.

No pen can write or tongue can describe the grief and anguish of the afflicted mother, who for weeks lay upon a bed of sickness, lingering between life and death, and at times would cry out in endearing terms for her lost child, imagining that it was near. In this manner years passed away. She was advised by her medical attendants to try change of scene, which might in some degree compose her troubled mind. She accordingly went to the favourite watering town of Scarbro' to reside for a short time. One morning, taking her accustomed walk on the beach, attended by a female servant, her attention was arrested at hearing the cries of a poor blind child, led by the hand of an old man, soliciting charity. The lady gave him a piece of money, at the same time asking some questions. The poor child instantly stretched out his hand in the direction of the voice that spoke, and exclaimed, Mother! don't you know your poor boy? The lady was transfixed to the spot, and perceived in the pallid features of the little sufferer before her, her long lost and only offspring.

The hoary headed villain seeing this, began to drag the child away, but did not succeed: assistance being at hand, he was secured, and consequently committed to gaol to take his trial at the assizes.

> The mother mourned her infant lost,
> She mourned her lot severe;
> And on her silent pillow shed
> Affliction's bitter tear.

It chanced one hour of evil fate,
　　The child strolled out to play,
A ruffian, passing by the gate,
　　Decoyed the child away.

Paler than death were the mother's cheeks,
　　Her looks were sad and wild;
And loud and fearful were her shrieks,
　　When first she missed her child.

With quivering lips she call'd his name,
　　She call'd him o'er and o'er;
No little voice responsive came,
　　She saw his face no more.

The neighbours all ran far and near,
　　To search the country round;
But yet no tidings could they hear—
　　They thought the child was drowned.

But who can tell the mother's pain?
　　Her heart with anguish bled;
Thick coming fancies racked her brain,
　　Her troubled reason fled.

At morning dawn she'd bid him rise,
　　And kneel him down to prayer;
Then start with anguish and surprise
　　Seeing he was not there.

Then bending o'er his little bed,
　　At each return of even,
She'd pray for blessings on his head,
　　Then cry, We'll meet in heaven.

Thus two tedious years had passed away,
　　When she grew more resigned;
And reason's intellectual sway
　　Revisited her mind.

It was on Scarbro's beach she strayed,
　　Two beggars met her eye;

2 / CHILDREN ON THE STREET

One with locks all silvery grey,
    Implored her charity.

Your charity, O Lady, give,
    Our small boon don't deny,
Pity my age opprest with want,
    Think on this poor blind boy.

Think on our sad disastrous state,
    Outcasts of human kind;
I'm poor, and old, and desolate,
    He's miserable and blind.

The child his sightless eyeballs rolled,
    And bowed his little head;
His face a tale of sorrow told,
    But not a word he said.

Pity the child I do indeed,
    Poor darling doom'd to rove;
Thou of a mother's care hast need,
    Above all a mother's love.

The child he started as she spoke,
    And a gleam of sudden joy,
Like daylight, on his features broke,
    That burned with ecstasy.

The astonished beggar vainly tried
    The child then to restrain;
It's my own mother's voice, he cried,
    O mother, speak again.

You used to see my father's hair,
    His features fondly trace;
And kiss my eyes so bright and clear,
    And stroke my little face.

Quick as the vivid lightning's dart
    Across the desert wild,
Conviction struck the mother's heart,—
    But Oh! the child was blind.

Whether the tale is true or fabricated is unknown. If the latter, and if it was sold as true account, it is what is called a cock. See appendix 1 for a discussion of the type.

Three printings have been seen. The one used here bears no printer's name. The first of the other two was issued by J. O. Bebbington, 26 Goulden Street, Oldham Road, Manchester, possibly in 1855.[2] The second was issued by W. S. Fortey, who took over the Catnach establishment from Catnach's sister Anne Ryle in 1859. The Bebbington and Fortey printings have an additional stanza and other minor differences. Rhyming is slightly irregular in all three printings.

Another similar tale, with a happy ending and a warning to mothers, is "The Lost Child Found," issued by T. Birt in the late 1830s. In it a child is stolen away from a meadow near its home in Stoney Middleton, Derbyshire. The abductor is a woman. Three years later the mother invites a passing sweep and his climbing boy in to sweep the chimney. She recognizes the sooty boy by a mark under his eye.[3] Catnach lists "Lost Child Restored" in his 1832 catalogue, but no copy of it has been seen.

The Policeman's Pet

"That boy?" No, he's not mine exactly,
    Though I look on him now as a son,
And he looks upon me as a father;
    But for me, his young life had been done.

My beat lay along the Embankment,
    Rather pleasant for me, did they say?
Yes, but sometimes I had all my work, sir,
    To keep the young mudlarks away.

They go like young ducks for the water,
    Though they seem rather shy of the soap;
They hop like young frogs on the barges,
    Or like monkeys they swing on a rope.

I remember the evening; at sunset
    I was watching the swift changing sky,
And the beautiful glow on the river,
    And the steamers that swept swiftly by.

When I heard a loud splash and a holloo—
    A boy tumbled in! Then a scream;

I flung off my helmet and tunic,
    And leaped in the fast flowing stream.

I had dived where I saw the air bubbles,
    I had missed him, then came to the brink;
And I saw his white face for a moment,
    Then I swam where I last saw him sink.

I seized on his coat, 'twas too flimsy,
    The rags in a moment gave way,
I made one last effort and caught him,
    And swam where the coal barges lay.

I thought he was dead when we landed,
    He lay there so still and so white;
But he opened his eyes at the doctor's,
    And seemed almost killed with the fright.

When they asked where he lived, he fell crying,
    And told us his parents were dead:
When they said he must go to the workhouse,
    I thought I would take him instead.

So I carried him home on my shoulder—
    My wife was as pleased as could be;
We had only had one "little stranger,"
    Who had lived but three months, so you see.

My Betsy took kindly to Willie,
    For that was the name of the lad;
It's true he was only a street waif,
    Rather rough, but not vulgar or bad.

I made some inquiries about him,
    And found that his story was true;
His father had come up to London,
    And he could get nothing to do.

It was the old story of struggle,
    Of poverty hidden away,
Until they went down in the battle,
    And both parents died in one day.

> A man who made toys for a living,
>   Which his wife sold at night in the street,
> Had done what he could for the orphan,
>   Had given him something to eat.
>
> They had such a little to give him,
>   And they said they could trust in me;
> So I hurried off home and told Betsy,
>   Dear woman! she shouted with glee.
>
> So that's how we came by our darling,
>   He's a brave little chap you can see;
> And he almost worships my Betsy,
>   And he's quite a companion for me.

Mudlarks are described by Henry Mayhew in the second volume of *London Labour and the London Poor:*

> These poor creatures are certainly about the most deplorable in their appearance of any I have met with in the course of my inquiries. They may be seen of all ages, from mere childhood to positive decrepitude, crawling among the barges at the various wharfs along the river; it cannot be said that they are clothed in rags, for they are scarcely half covered by the tattered indescribable things that serve them for clothing; their bodies are grimed with the foul soil of the river, and their torn garments stiffened up like boards with dirt. . . .
>
> The mudlarks collect whatever they happen to find, such as coals, bits of old iron, rope, bones, and copper nails. . . . The coals . . . they sell to the poor people of the neighbourhood at 1d. per pot, holding about 14 lbs. . . . ; they dispose of the iron at 5 lbs. for 1d., the bones at 3 lbs. for 1d. . . . In this manner they earn from 2½d. to 8d. per day. . . .

Mayhew then turns to the scene behind and beyond:

> That the majority of this class are ignorant, and without even the rudiments of education, and that many of them from time to time are committed to prison for petty thefts, cannot be wondered at. . . . As for the females . . . , I have found . . . that very many of the unfortunate creatures who swell the tide of prostitution . . . have originally been mudlarks, and only remained at that occupation till such time as they were capable of adopting the more easy and more lucrative life. . . .

He estimates that daily some forty to fifty boys would go down King James's Stairs in Wapping Wall for mudlarking, and that overall nearly three hundred boys could be seen daily at the foot of these and other stairs along that stretch of the

Thames. He concludes with his own tale of a mudlark saved from a miserable life by a kindly person, and he draws the moral that misery and thence crime are in some part caused by social indifference.[4]

I have seen only one copy of the ballad. It bears no printer's name. The casual reference to steamers and the wholly positive view of the policeman—after years of considerable distrust of Sir Robert Peel's bobbies—suggest a late date, perhaps the 1860s.

3
Criminals

"Poverty's No Sin" says one ballad (on page 421), and "Poverty No Crime" says another. The latter ballad tells the supposedly true tale of John Hanson of Manchester. He and his wife and four children were near to starvation, and he saw nothing to do but to commit robbery. He went onto the highway and demanded money of a gentleman. The gentleman surrendered £5, a sum that Hanson considered too much to take. The gentleman thereupon asked Hanson about his circumstances, offered to help, and promised to come to Hanson's home the next day. He did come, and found the whole family dead. The same tale is told in different form as "The Lancashire Tragedy." Both ballads recall an eighteenth-century ballad entitled "The Nobleman's Generous Kindness to the Poor Man in Distress." The nobleman is identified in the ballad as Sir Walter Blackett of Newcastle upon Tyne, and presumably he was Sir Walter Blackett of that city who died in 1777. The poor man in the case had wife and four children, and they faced starvation. He went to the bread shop where he had had credit before, but the woman of the shop would give no further credit.

> This poor man took a loaf away,
> And unto her these words did say,
> I'll take it home with me indeed;
> My children starve for want of bread.

Presently he was arrested and brought before Sir Walter, to whom he told his situation. Sir Walter sent two men to investigate, and when they reported back that wife and children were indeed near to starvation, Sir Walter gave money to the man, released him, and promised to find work for him, saying,

> 'Tis against the laws of God and man,
> To starve the poor in a Christian land.[1]

Three ballads that tell altogether grim tales in which the desperate poor man sees no other course than destruction of himself and wife or of himself and family are

"Horrid Murder of Four Children," "Copy of Verses on the Lamentable Death of Mr. and Mrs. Jessup," and "The Dreadful Murder of a Wife and Six Children." The last is given below.

All six ballads implicitly concern one question: can a desperate poor person be excused of desperate crime? They offer evidence on another question: how significant is poverty as a cause of crime? "The Nobleman's Generous Kindness" suggests a third: is the law of the land criminal that starves the poor? None of them mentions a fourth and fifth: is the law of the land criminal that makes petty crime—such as minor theft—a hanging offense? and is the law more severe on the criminal poor than on the criminal rich? These questions are rarely faced directly in nineteenth-century broadside balladry. The second is dealt with substantially in two known ballads: "Can You Wonder at Crime," given on page 134, and "Farewell Address to Their Countrymen and Friends," given below. The fifth question, the one most often faced, is dealt with in three ballads in the section on "Contrasts of Rich and Poor."

In the main, nineteenth-century broadsides about actual crimes are preoccupied with sensation. The typical broadside tells of unconscionable violent act and consequent trial and violent punishment. It focuses upon grim and unusual detail. It takes the side of the law, and observes guilt, remorse, obduracy, and punishment with conventional piety. It is unconcerned with excuses, exculpation. Even with crimes involving very young persons, where pity may be urged, the typical broadside speaks of wicked example and natural bent towards wickedness. Most such sensational broadsides are prose rather than verse; and if the two appear together, the verse is usually mere coda to the prose. Versification is generally crude, and phrases and stanzas are sometimes repeated from one ballad to another. Four stanzas towards the end of "Anything to Earn a Crust," given on page 494, are close parody of such verse.

Among crimes punishable by death, theft was prominent. It was the crime most likely to be associated with poverty. It was by all odds the most prevalent of crimes. Thus in the years 1802–8 more than seven thousand men, women, and children were charged at Newgate with criminal offenses committed in the City of London, Westminster, and the county of Middlesex. Of that total, 73 percent were charged with one or another sort of theft: highway and street robbery—190; horse, sheep, and cattle stealing—74; stealing in dwelling houses—1,013; stealing in shops—859; stealing from wagons—106; picking pockets—235; women stealing from men—279; robbery in lodgings—130; burglary (with housebreaking)—233; unidentified and other miscellaneous larcenies—2,695. This information appears on a broadside issued in 1809 by Eyre & Strahan, His Majesty's Printers. The 73 percent excludes embezzling—852; receiving stolen goods—193; and making and uttering false coins and notes—195. Violent crimes against persons—murder, manslaughter, maiming, shooting, and rape: characteristic crimes reported on broadsides—accounted for just under 2 percent.[2]

Assize broadside calendars of the time show sentences imposed—though not necessarily carried out. The 18 August 1814 assize calendar of prisoners in the gaols of Durham, Newcastle, and Morpeth gives the following information:

stealing a horse, two men—death
stealing eight ewe sheep—death
stealing a pig—transportation, seven years
breaking and entering, stealing handkerchiefs, silver, other small items—death
stealing from wagons, two men—transportation, seven years
stealing three silver spoons and other small items—one year
"charged with suspicion of" stealing a gown—one year

An assize calendar of the same towns in August 1829 shows among other sentences:

breaking and entering a house and stealing two pieces of broadcloth and other articles—death
stealing goods—transportation, fourteen years
stealing a gamecock—transportation, fourteen years[3]

Old Bailey records of September–December 1819 reveal the following extraordinary numbers of youths among all men lying under sentence of death in Middlesex:

14 of ages 15–19
14 of ages 20–29
6 of ages 30–39
1 in his 40s
1 of age 62[4]

Behind such bald facts and figures must have been many true tales of poverty, but such tales were rarely told in broadside form. Theft lacked sensation, and so did poverty as cause. "Poverty No Crime" and "The Nobleman's Generous Kindness" are among rare exceptions—assuming that they are true accounts. So is "The Last Sorrowful Lamentation," given below. Unlike the two preceding ballads, it makes no mention of poverty, and one guesses that poverty was the cause. In any event, the ballad suggests more starkly, more sensationally, than any other ballad that in numberless cases theft was a minor crime committed by poor people, and criminal justice a great crime committed against them. For it concerns the theft of six handkerchiefs. The criminal was nine years old. The sentence was death.

Other sorts of crimes that were likely to involve poor people were trade union activity, riot, and rebellion. Although these subjects are outside the scope of this book, something should be said about them. Trade union activity was made illegal by the Combination Acts of 1799–1800, and riot and rebellion were covered by earlier legislation and by the Six Acts passed after Peterloo. Though the Combination Acts did not wholly succeed in their aim, and though they were repealed in 1824, legal oppression of trade union activity continued. The notable later instance of oppression was the 1834 sentencing of Tolpuddle laborers to seven years transportation for administering unlawful oaths. The men said in defense of their attempt to organize a union: "We have injured no man's reputation, character, person, or property. We were meeting together to preserve ourselves, our wives, and our children from utter degradation and starvation."[5]

Riot and rebellion sometimes came from degradation and starvation too. Notable among many such occurrences were riots in the middle 1790s, riots in 1800 (described on pages 83–87). Luddite uprisings in the years from 1811, riots in 1816, Peterloo in 1819 (with the killing of eleven people in anticipation of riot), Captain Swing rebellion in 1830–31, Chartist riot and rebellion in 1839, and riots and other violence in the north of England in 1842 (described on pages 358–60). Some of the riot and rebellion brought severest retribution. Luddite frame-breaking was briefly made a capital offense in 1812—with maximum punishment reduced to transportation for life a year and a half later. "Trials and Executions of the Rick Burners in Different Parts of England" gives accounts of nine men executed in December 1830 and January 1831. According to Eric Hobsbawm and George Rudé in *Captain Swing* (1969), 19 people were executed in connection with the rebellion (from 252 sentences of death), and 505 people were transported.[6]

All this tragedy for the poor finds little direct expression in the pages of this book. The harsh verses of "The Double Dealer" (page 109) are a call to strike. "The Riot" and "Poverty and Contentment," mentioned on pages 58 and 501, are pious warnings against riot. "The Labourer's Horizon at Sunrise," "The New Poor Law and the Farmer's Glory," and "Haughty Lords Have Us Degraded" (pages 140, 163, 206) threaten uprising. Among other items seen, two are worth mentioning. The first is a broadside proclamation issued in Newcastle during a strike of keelmen in November 1822.

> The Civil Authorities regret to find the deluded keelmen still continue to insult His Majesty's boats, by throwing stones when protecting those that are willing to work; and finding forbearance any longer will endanger the lives of those so employed,— this is to caution the peaceable inhabitants, and women and children, to keep within their houses during the time the keels are passing from the Staiths to Shields, as the marines have orders to fire on the first man that shall dare to throw a stone at them.[7]

The *Newcastle Chronicle* reported on the exemplary restraint of the marines and the violence of the strikers. It noted that seamen and steamboats had been brought in by the coal owners to move the coal, that some thirty strikers who had obtained work elsewhere were arrested (because still under bond to the coal owners) and put on the treadmill in Durham Gaol, and that further stone-throwing had brought "discharge of fire arms from the men of war's boats." The *Chronicle* was confident that the coal owners were winning the contest.[8]

The second item is a broadside petition to William IV for mercy in several sentences of death imposed in Newcastle in 1831. The petition acknowledges

> acts of incendiarism, and of riotous violence and depredation; but acts, may it please your Majesty, committed under the influence of popular excitement, arising out of extreme and long-continued suffering, such as it has rarely been the lot of any people to endure, and never before, as in the present case, arising out of erroneous legislation, inefficient and perverted institutions, with the virtual subversion of public rights, and the total annihilation of all public weight and influence in the common house of parliament.[9]

Trade union balladry exists in considerable profusion in the broadside ballad collections seen, and may exist in greater profusion elsewhere. A single strike, the so-called Preston ten-percent strike of 1853, elicited forty-five or more ballads, many of them gathered in the Madden Collection at Cambridge University.[10] Peterloo is remembered chiefly in Samuel Bamford's "Peterloo" (See! see! where Freedom's noblest champion stands) and one or two other broadside ballads seen in the collections.[11] Luddism, Captain Swing, Chartist agitation, and other disturbances are fitfully represented in the collections. See the endnote for listings of broadside and some other material on them.[12]

The connection between riot and poverty is rarely exposed in such material. "Trials and Executions of the Rick Burners" offers no suggestion of poverty as a cause for the crimes. The brief verses on the sheet show familiar piety.

> Ill fated youths how could you thus all laws divine defy,
> The precious food which God had sent, you basely did destroy.

Perhaps the absence of such material reflects actual or perceived constraints on freedom of the press. Perhaps it merely reflects preference for sensation over issues of social justice among people who wanted to read about trials and executions. One may suppose, though, that some people who read "The Last Sorrowful Lamentation" were appalled by the legal crime committed. One may also suppose that the general concern for poverty in broadside balladry had at least slight bearing upon the amelioration of criminal law. Over the first seventy years of the century the number of capital crimes was reduced from two hundred to four (aside from military and naval offenses). Transportation was removed as a form of sentence. Punishment generally became less brutal. By 1870, being poor was less criminal than it had been, and the law was less criminal.

Insofar as gallows and other like literature were predominantly prose, it is probably fair to say that the most popular broadside ballads on crime were descriptions of prison life and sketches of petty criminals. Much of this material touches tangentially if at all upon poverty. Little of it professes to be more than generalized account. A ballad called "County Gaol"—sometimes called "Bellevue

Gaol," "Preston Gaol," "Wakefield Gaol"—was popular in the 1840s and later. It offers a lighthearted description of the routine of prison life. A somewhat more serious view is taken in the ballad "Skilly Night and Morning." One grim ballad professing to be true is "The Birmingham Investigation," which describes deliberate starving of inmates. Of apparently greater popularity were a number of ballads that focused upon the prison instrument the treadmill, illustrated on page 000. The best of them is given below. A related ballad worth mentioning is "The Devil." Originally a longish ballad by Coleridge, it describes several sights pleasing to the devil on his earthly rambles. His last sight is of the prison in Cold Bath Fields.

> As he passed by Cold Bath Fields he saw
> A solitary cell,
> And the Devil was pleased for it gave him a hint,
> For improving the prisons of hell.[13]

Four other ballads about petty criminals are given below. Three of the four employ special language of the criminal underworld. The self-consciousness of the display perhaps undermines their concern for poverty—although much the same thing might be said of the fourth ballad, which is interested in more conventional poetic tricks. All four ballads are typical in their relatively lighthearted and generalized view of the petty criminal and his situation.

The one crime that might seem most inevitably to have concerned poverty, and thus to have provoked ballads so concerned was poaching. Acts of enclosure over the centuries had deprived the poor of ancient rights on common land. Game laws in support of landowners meant penalties up to and including death for poor men who reasserted those rights. Other law allowed landowners to use man traps and spring guns to protect game for their own table and sport. A poor man in search of food risked being maimed by trap or gun, attacked by gamekeeper and associates, and punished severely in court. It seems inexplicable that among fifty or more ballads seen on poaching, most are preoccupied with the melodrama or daring of the activity. None deals substantially with poverty. "Claughton Wood Poachers" gives one line of forty-four to poverty: "I'm afraid more game there will be slain unless the times do mend." Most of the ballad is given to the affray between six "men of courage" and gamekeeper and allies, and to the sentencing of two of the six to seven years transportation and the others to two years imprisonment. "Gallant Poachers" tells of a youth who is shot and killed by a gamekeeper. Poverty is not clearly the impetus for him and his friends:

> I and five more a poaching went,
> To kill some game was our intent,
> Our money gone and all was spent,
> We nothing else would try.

Otherwise the ballad is preoccupied with melodrama, pathos of the youth's death, and (rather vaguely) guilt and ostracism for a murderer.[14] Poaching ballads illustrate the general truth that nineteenth-century broadside ballads about crime are seldom ballads explicitly about poverty.

The Last Sorrowful Lamentation
Of a Boy Under Twelve Years of Age
Now Lying in Newgate, Under Sentence of Death

CHARLES ELLIOTT, a boy under 12 years of age was capitally convicted at the last Old Bailey Sessions for privately stealing six silk handkerchiefs out of the shop of Mrs. Blakeman, in Oxford Street………

Guilty,—Death.

All tender mothers lend an ear
    Unto this tale of woe,
'Twill make the tear of sympathy
    From every eye to flow:
In Newgate's dark and dreary cell,
    In bitter grief does lie,
A little boy of twelve years old,
    Who is condemn'd to die.

When he was sentenc'd at the bar,
    The court was drown'd in tears,
To see a child so young cut off,
    All in his tender years.
His father wept, his mother tore
    Her hair, in agony,—
A heart of stone would melt to hear
    How bitter she did cry.

Be warn'd, my little children dear,
    By this poor boy's downfall,
Keep from dishonest courses clear,
    And God will bless you all.
O think how this poor little boy
    Laments his woeful state,
Lock'd in a cell—he has no joy,
    How dreadful is his fate!

I

Charles Elliott committed his crime on 8 February 1820, while Martha Blakeman, widow, stood in a back room of her shop. She saw him run out of the shop, saw that five or six handkerchiefs were missing, and ran after him, calling "stop, thief." A constable heard her, caught Charles Elliott, and found the handkerchiefs under his hat. Martha Blakeman's testimony and that of the constable were recorded in *Old Bailey Sessions Papers* for 18 February. So was Charles Elliott's defense:

> I heard the cry, and saw a little boy about my size going along; he dropped the handkerchiefs. I told him he had dropped them; he said, "Never mind, keep them," and I put them into my hat.[15]

The value of the handkerchiefs was said to be £1, and Charles Elliott's age was given—in the *Sessions Papers* and in other official documents— not as twelve or under twelve but nine. The judge sentenced Charles Elliott to death. No recommendation to mercy by either prosecutor or jury accompanied sentence, in contrast to the sentencing to death of two other boys, ages eleven and fourteen, likewise for petty theft, in the same session of the court. The indictment form for Charles Elliott was filled in by hand, with brief details of crime and sentence, and final words given in the margin: "to be hanged by the neck till he be dead."[16]

Though unqualified sentence of death for petty crime for a child so young was extraordinary and perhaps unique for the time, the case seems to have aroused no public horror, shame, concern. Among broadsheet newspapers in London, the *Times, Morning Chronicle, Globe,* and *Morning Post* all took frequent notice of Old Bailey proceedings, but they passed Charles Elliott by with barely a word. The *Times* on the morning of 19 February was preoccupied with the murder of the duc de Berri in Paris, and made no mention of the Old Bailey session of the 18th. By the 24th, and for several days thereafter, it was even more preoccupied with the Cato Street conspiracy. It did on the 21st take note of a case of forgery heard on the previous day, and commented in a leader on the prevalence of that crime. The *Morning Chronicle* remarked upon the session of the 18th, and was interested in a case of forgery, and said nothing about Charles Elliott. The *Globe* reported nothing of any session until the 29th, when it considered a case of mail coach robbery. Only the *Morning Post* took heed of Charles Elliott, and it had this, and only this, to say:

> Early depravity,— Charles Elliott, a boy aged but nine years, was capitally indicted for stealing six pocket handkerchiefs privately from the shop of Mrs. Blakeman. — Guilty. —Death.[17]

The one other known public comment on Charles Elliott made certainly at the time of his trial came in a broadside: "The Trials of All the Prisoners at the Old Bailey, Commenced Wednesday, Feb. 17th. 1820." It describes six cases of perhaps twice as many heard on the 17th and 18th. The sheet itself is small, and the typography is modest. There is no aim for sensation. The case of Charles Elliott comes second in the list, and it is distinguished from the others only in the respects that it gets as many words as all the others put together and that it is the only one on which the broadside author offers an opinion. He paraphrases Charles Elliott's testimony as given in the *Sessions Papers*, and characterizes it as a "defence usually adopted by the most hackneyed thieves." Twenty-four lines of verse follow in very small type. They are very much the same as those given here.

A second, and briefer, broadside account of the trial, "A Warning to Youth," appeared several weeks later. It was a filler on a broadside more largely concerned with the execution of the Cato Street conspirators on 1 May: "The Sorrowful and Weeping Lamentation of the Wives and Orphans of the Late Sufferers. . . ." This account of Elliott says nothing about date, testimony, and verdict except that "notwithstanding the boy made a most remarkable and astonishing defence, hardly to be credited, the Jury found him Guilty—Death. At the last assizes." It too offers a "Lamentation of the Boy," adding sixteen lines to twenty-four that are virtually the same as those in "The Trials of All the Prisoners" and "The Last Sorrowful Lamentation."

Charles Elliott was lucky, or could count himself lucky. Though the law in 1820 was barbaric enough to sentence him to death, it was not so barbaric as to do the deed. The judge doubtless assumed the black cap to pronounce sentence of death, but his act was presumably a charade of deeper dye than that imputed to Charles Elliott by the author of "The Trials of All the Prisoners." A further Old Bailey document, "Prisoners on Orders," of 12 April 1820, lists twenty-eight prisoners under sentence of death. Charles Elliott and nineteen others are shown there to have had their sentences respited to transportation for life. Three others, including a youth said to be fifteen, are noted as having been executed. Five remain under sentence of death. Another document of the same sort, of 19 May, indicates that Charles Elliott has been removed to a penitentiary.[18] Only one thing more is known of the boy who stole six handkerchiefs. The *Criminal Register* for 1820 lists him, gives his age again as nine, and under "Remarks" says, "His brother transported."[19]

II

The present ballad with its brief prose account has been excerpted from a broadside printed by Mary Shepherd of Bristol. The full title of the broadside is, "The Last Sorrowful Lamentation of 15 Young Men Now Lying in Newgate Under Sentence of Death, Two of Whom are Brothers and Natives of this City, and One, a Boy under Twelve Years of Age." Charles Elliott's case is described first, then that of eight men convicted of forgery—including John and Joseph Bird of Bristol, then that of six men convicted of housebreaking. A letter follows that

3 / CRIMINALS 341

purports to be from one of the housebreakers to his wife. The broadside concludes with two ballads of twenty-four lines each. The first ballad is that concerned with Charles Elliott. The second is general in its first sixteen lines, and turns to Charles Elliott in the last eight. The first four of these last eight lines are the same as lines 33–36 in "A Warning to Youth."

> You sisters who have tender hearts,
> Was this your brother's case,
> The world to you would be no joy,
> Whilst he was in that place.
>
> Inform your friends both far and near,
> Wherever they are fix'd,
> To pray for this boy who is to die,
> On Monday morning next.

The broadside is thus to some extent a particular sort of cock—a fabricated sensational tale that offers circumstantial detail to suggest it is true. The type is discussed in appendix 1. The fabrication begins with the title phrase "last sorrowful lamentation," which implies the impending execution that both "die on Monday morning next" and the letter from the housebreaker make explicit. The fabrication apparently involves most of the fourteen men as well. Several of the listed names—Thomas Deller, Richard Gipson, William Wills, and George Wise—do not appear in *Old Bailey Sessions Papers* in the years 1819–28, and other listed names appear but are associated with crimes other than forgery and housebreaking, with lighter sentences or acquittals recorded. The two brothers alone have some substance. They were convicted and sentenced to death at the Old Bailey session of 24 February 1820, although their crime was breaking and entering, with theft, instead of forgery as on the broadside, and their names were John and George Bird instead of John and Joseph. None of the small amount of evidence in the *Sessions Papers* links them to Bristol. As reported in the *Criminal Register* and the *Times*, their ages were twenty-one and twenty. The *Times* said they were leaders of "a gang of desperate fellows" in the Fulham and Hammersmith area of London. They were executed at Newgate on 12 April 1820.[20]

One other broadside survives on Charles Elliott. It is a fairly thoroughgoing cock. It bears the title "A Warning to Young Men, the Last Awful Moments of Charles Elliott, a Boy Nine Years Old, Who Was Executed at the Old Bailey on Monday Last, July 10, for Privately Stealing Six Pocket Handkerchiefs in a Shop." It describes briefly the true circumstance of trial and sentencing, then repeats "A Warning to Youth" in saying that Charles Elliott "made a most remarkable and astonishing defence, hardly to be credited," tells of his contrition for a dissipated life brought on by indulgent parents, and describes the execution, with "thousands of people assembled to witness so novel and mournful a scene." There follows in verse "The Boy's Lamentation" in thirty-two lines that are exactly the same (except for "You" in place of "ye") as the first thirty-two lines in "A Warning to Youth."

Among the slight differences in the four lamentations of Charles Elliott, one is of special interest. The last four lines of "The Trials of All the Prisoners" and lines 21–24 of "A Warning to Youth" go thus:

> O think how this poor wretched boy,
> Laments his woeful fate,
> Lock'd in a cell—he has no joy,
> How dreadful is his state.

The sense of the four lines is Charles Elliott's present dreadful situation, emphasized with "state" as the last word instead of "fate." Impending execution is not implied. Were "fate" and "state" reversed, the basic sense would not alter, but the emphasis on present situation would perhaps be less. In the last four lines of "The Last Sorrowful Lamentation," the reversed order of the same two words serves to emphasize the impending doom of execution suggested in the title and made plain by "die on Monday morning next" in the adjoining ballad. In "A Warning to Young Men" the four lines are the antepenultimate quatrain of eight quatrains. The order in them is "fate" / "state"; but insofar as the preceding prose describes the execution, the order is unimportant—though "state" / "fate" would better express the progress to doom.

The verses of "The Trials of All the Prisoners" came first chronologically, and it is all but certain that they preceded similar verses on broadsides about T. King / Thomas Mitchel, mentioned on pages 531–32. Mary Shepherd printed one of the broadsides on King / Mitchel. Whether the author of "The Trials of All the Prisoners" was the original author of the verses is another matter.

The year in which Mary Shepherd printed "The Last Sorrowful Lamentation" is uncertain. The suspicion is that she printed it in about 1826 instead of in 1820. If she did, it becomes an unusual sort of cock, and rather more thoroughgoing than it otherwise seems. The evidence for 1820 is the conjunction of trials of Charles Elliott and the Bird brothers in February of that year. However, Mary Shepherd is not known otherwise to have been in business so early. Bristol street directories list her only for the years 1826–28. They give Henry Shepherd at the same address, 6 Broad Weir, in the years 1823–25. One or the other of them, or a third Shepherd, was in business as early as 1821, for "Shepherd" at the address Temple Gate issued a broadside on the death of Queen Caroline in that year. All of Mary Shepherd's known publications are sensational, and at least a few are cocks. One of the cocks provides the reason for thinking that she printed her broadside on Charles Elliott in about 1826. It is devoted to the Bird brothers, and bears the title "The Last Words, Dying Speech, Confession and Behaviour of John and Joseph Bird, Two Brothers, and Natives of This City, Who Were Executed Yesterday Morning, March 13, 1826, at the Old Bailey for Forgery."[21]

One broadside issued by "H. Shepherd" is a cock with a difference. It offers "A Full and Particular Account of the Sufferings and Melancholy Death of Three Atheists, Who in a Fit of Impiety Roasted the Bible!" The three men, all of Bristol, were "subscribers to the works of Tom Paine and Richard Carlyle." Two of the three have now "died wretched," and the third—surprisingly—is not dead but "dragging out a miserable existence in a madhouse." The author of the broadside hopes that a merciful God will bring him to his senses and thence to repentance.[22]

The printer of "A Warning to Young Men" is a more interesting figure than Mary Shepherd. He is Harry Bonner, likewise of Bristol; and though street directories list him only for the years 1814–18, he certainly had to be printing in 1820 or later to have dealt in any way with Charles Elliott. That he issued "A Warning to Young Men" in 1820 is unknown. The year may indeed have been 1826, for in that year "H. Bonner" issued a broadside entitled "Dreadful and Awful Effects of Acute Distress," which tells of an unemployed shoemaker in Cheltenham who poisoned his starving family "on Saturday last, the 21st of October 1826." If H. Bonner is Harry, one may guess that Harry Bonner and Mary Shepherd were closely associated. Three broadsides similar to "Dreadful and Awful Effects" and bearing Harry Bonner's name are mentioned on page 373. Bonner's interest in sensation seems to have ranged more widely than Mary Shepherd's. He printed several broadsides on Waterloo, on the Spa Field and other riots of 1816 and later, on the activities of the radical orator Henry Hunt, and on the Cato Street conspirators. He issued a broadside lamenting the death of Sir Samuel Romilly, who fought for many years to ameliorate the laws on capital crime and who might have approved of "A Warning to Young Men" if it seemed helpful in dramatizing the horrors of those laws. Bonner came of a family of printers who were active in Bristol over the years 1775 to 1867. In 1833 one of the family, identified only as "Bonner," printed "National Convention and Murder," having to do with the events discussed in appendix 2.[23]

Further comment on the Charles Elliott broadsides and on the Bonners and Shepherds appears in appendix 1.

(I am very much obliged to Harriet Jones of the London Metropolitan Archive, and Nigel Taylor of the Public Record Office, Kew, for advice on criminal records, and to Elizabeth Jeffrey, assistant reference librarian, Bristol Central Library, for information on the Shepherds and Bonners.)

The Mill

The Mill!—the Mill—the Brixton treading-mill,
The whirligig that ne'er stands still;
Without a mark, without a bound,

It moveth both morn and night around.
It plays with the feet, it dazzles the eyes,
And like a caton-wheel round it flies.
I'm on the Mill, I'm on the Mill,
I am where I have had my fill,
Of treading above and treading below,
And a basin of skilley when off I go:
If the mice, or the bugs, or the fleas should bite,
What matter, what matter—the Mill is my delight.

I love, I love—oh, how I love to ride
With a scurvy pal all by my side;
Where every kiddy whistles a tune,
And snorts away in his blue shaloon;
And tells of the joys he once espied,
With his fancy woman by his side.
I never was on the Thames or the shore,
But I loved the treading-mill more and more,
And backward flew to its ribby breast,
Like a chicken which flies to its mother's nest;
And a mother she was and shall be still,
For I was born—was born to work at the Mill.

The night was queer and foggy the morn,
In the noisy hour when I was born;
The cat molrow'd and the dog it howl'd,
And my father dead drunk on the floor he roll'd,
And never was heard such a hubbaboo wild
As welcomed to life the pilfering child:
I've lived since then without a wife,
Though not exactly a single life;
With blunt to spend and a power to range,
And a swellish coat for a Sunday change;
And Death may come whenever he will,
He'll find me treading away at the Brixton Mill.

Caton-wheel—corruption of Catherine Wheel?[24]
Skilley—gruel
Kiddy—fellow criminal
Blunt—money

THE TREAD-MILL.

The Tread Mill. By permission of the British Library.

In a broadside entitled "The Tread Mill," James Catnach provided the cut shown here, the account given below, and a ballad about Tom, Jerry, and Logic on the treadmill. The mill was built in 1817.

> The treadmill at Brixton, that "terror to evildoers," has excited so much attention that a correct view and description of it cannot fail of being acceptable to the public. The treadmill is the invention of Mr. Cubitt, of Ipswich, and is considered a great improvement in prison discipline; so much so that since its beneficial effects have been experienced at Brixton, mills of a similar construction have been erected at Cold-bath-fields, and several places in the country.
>
> The above engraving exhibits a party of prisoners in the act of working the Brixton Tread-Mill, of which it is a correct representation. The view is taken from a corner of one of the ten airing yards of the prison, all of which radiate from the Governor's house in the centre; so that from the window of his room he commands a complete view into all the yards.[25]

The ballad is a parody of the song "The Sea," which aside from "The Fine Old English Gentleman" is probably the most parodied of all verses in nineteenth-century broadside literature. The parodies characteristically follow the structure of the original song, the narrator identifying and characterizing the object of his attention in the first twelve lines, dilating upon his love in the second twelve, and recalling his birth and upbringing in the last twelve. Among such parodies are "The Bishop's See," "The Fight," "The Gin," "The Land," "The Omnibus," "The Road," "The Spree," "The Tea," and "The Ugly Sea."[26]

"The Sea" was written by Barry Cornwall (Bryan Waller Proctor, 1787–1874). Cornwall's professional life was that of a barrister, but he wrote poetry for some fifteen years with considerable popular success, and later wrote biographies of Edmund Kean and Charles Lamb. Whether "The Sea" was first published in a journal is unknown, but its first appearance otherwise was in *English Songs* (1832), Cornwall's last volume of verse. Cornwall remarks in the volume that he has "for some years past abandoned verse-writing," and he adds that the popularity of several of his songs is largely owing to Sigismund Neukom's musical settings of them.[27] The earliest known publication of Neukom's music for "The Sea" is 1832. The British Library gives—on what basis is unknown—a provisional dating of 1825 for "The Gin: An Out-and-Out Parody on 'The Sea'."

"The Sea" itself was apparently more popular in broadside form than all or most of its parodies. W. M. Thackeray, probable author of "Horae Catnachianae," in *Fraser's Magazine* (1839), speaks of its being "roared through the streets of the metropolis."[28] I give it here as published in *English Songs* in six stanzas.

The Sea

The sea! the sea! the open sea!
The blue, the fresh, the ever free!
Without a mark, without a bound,
It runneth the earth's wide regions round;
It plays with the clouds; it mocks the skies;
Or like a cradled creature lies.

I'm on the sea! I'm on the sea!
I am where I would ever be;
With the blue above, and the blue below,
And silence wheresoe'er I go;
If a storm should come and awake the deep,
What matter? I shall ride and sleep.

I love, oh! *how* I love to ride
On the fierce foaming bursting tide,

Where every mad wave drowns the moon,
Or whistles aloft his tempest tune,
And tells how goeth the world below,
And why the Sou'-west's blasts do blow.

I never was on the dull tame shore,
But I lov'd the great sea more and more,
And backwards flew to her billowy breast,
Like a bird that seeks its mother's nest;
And a mother she was and *is* to me;
For I was born on the open sea!

The waves were white, and red the morn,
In the noisy hour when I was born;
And the whale it whistled, the porpoise rolled,
And the dolphins bared their backs of gold,
And never was heard such an outcry wild
As welcomed to life the ocean child!

I've lived since then in calm and strife,
Full fifty summers a sailor's life,
With wealth to spend and a power to range,
But never have sought nor sighed for change;
And Death, whenever he comes to me,
Shall come on the wild unbounded sea!

In Cornwall's *Autobiographical Fragment* (1877), the editor remarks that Cornwall was on the sea only once in his life, and was seasick.[29]

Among other ballads on treadmills are "Brixton Tread Mill," "The Newcastle Treadmill," and "Tom, Jerry, and Logic at the Tread Mill."[30] John Camden Hotten says that criminals called the treadmill the everlasting staircase.[31]

Very Respectable

One day, going out for a walk,
    A thought it popp'd into my noddle, sir,
Of St. James's Park I had heard great talk,
    So to it I resolved for to toddle, sir.
But when I got there, lack a day!
    A figure I saw so dejectable,

His face was fill'd with dismay,
    But yet he looked very respectable.

I beheld him with wonder surprised,
    I felt myself quite in confusion,
I scarcely could credit my eyes,
    For I thought it was all an illusion.
No shoes to his feet he had got,
    His hat appear'd quite rejectable,
His hair it grew out of the top,
    But yet it look'd very respectable.

I approach'd him, intending to speak,
    As he on the bench was reclining,
His name I began for to seek,
    But he answer'd me so undefining:
In business he said he had been,
    But things they did not go delectable,
For the bailiffs on him were so keen,
    But once he was very respectable.

I with him most deeply sympathized,
    And he made me a bow with such grace, sir,
In stooping, his limbs I descried,
    To see him it was a disgrace, sir.
His trousers were slit up so neat,
    That his knees they peep'd thro' so perfectable,
No stockings he had—what a treat!
    But yet he look'd very respectable.

I talk'd with him till it got dark,
    And then I invited him home, sir,
To be seen in the day with this spark,
    I wasn't much inclin'd for to roam, sir;
For his beard was as black as a coal,
    So rough, and so very projectable,
As he stood, oh! he shivered with cold,
    But yet he look'd very respectable.

When we got home I instantly fed
    This man, for I thought it a charity;
I made him have part of my bed,
    And both of us seem'd in hilarity;

But when he undress'd did appear,
    No waistcoat or shirt—'twas delectable,
To have seen him it would make you stare,
    But yet he look'd very respectable.

In the morning, O when I awoke,
    I look'd for my friend, but alack! sir!
I soon found that it was not a joke,
    For off with my clothes he had pack'd, sir;
My watch he had taken—so strange!
    And every thing that was selectable;
His rags he had left me in exchange,
    But yet he was very respectable.

The dejectable but perhaps once respectable man was a frequent figure in the ballads, and he was often to be found in St. James's Park. In "Study Economy" a "gent reduced by railway speculation" remarks:

> When I've no pieces of cigars, and am getting low in coppers.
> I toddle round St. James's Park and pick up all the toppers.

Toppers—cigar and cigarette ends

The man in that ballad does not resort to crime.

"Very Respectable" dates from about 1831. It appears with negligible differences on page 189 of a song collection, *London Melodist,* published in London by Diprose in about that year. Diprose was a notable publisher of song collections. The earliest broadside publication noticed is by Catnach at 2 Monmouth Court. It does not appear in his 1832 catalogue.

Ax My Eye

I deals in costermongery,
    And in my calling make some noise,
And to them wot is hungry,
    I sarves out 'taters and sawoys.
Some may sport a boney pony,
    Or lean knacker for a job,

> But I've a randy, dandy, tear up, flare up
>   Moke, that cost eleven bob.
>
> Stow your gab and guffery,
>   To every fakement I am fly,
> I never takes no fluffery,
>   I am regular—AX MY EYE.
>
> I can sport the mopusses,
>   Amongst the kiddies I'm the kick,
> With them wi' empty gropusses,
>   I sport my ochre like a brick.
> Then I keeps a rousing tousling
>   Moll, full fat and finely shaped,
> Who, when she's togged out flashy dashy,
>   Is like a carrot newly scraped.
>   Stow your gab, &c.
>
> You'll think I'll tell a pack o' lies,
>   But toggety tip top put on,
> My Sunday subligacholees,
>   Have fetched me fifteen hog in pawn.
> Besides I sport a hellish swellish
>   Coat, wot stands the weathers rubs,
> A tile too, and a slashing dashing
>   Stunning pair of pickling tubs.
>
> Of grub I stows a dollop in
>   My tripes at least four times a day,
> And as for lush I gollop in,
>   Like fun, the gatter—that's the way.
> Sometimes at home I sidle idle,
>   All day long and scarcely wag,
> Then at night am working, burking,
>   Hocussing, or kenning swag.
>
> I oft go out and cant and jaw,
>   And turn parson in the open air,
> My rolling eyes and lantern jaws,
>   Do wonders 'mongst the pious there.
> I strikes them dumb with moaning, groaning,
>   And while they stare with upturn'd eyes,

3 / CRIMINALS 351

> My pals go round, and ogle fogles,
> And empts of all their blunt their clies.
> Stow your gab, &c.

Ax my eye—a very alert fellow
Costermonger—seller of fruit, vegetables, fish, etc., from a barrow
Savoy—a kind of cabbage
Moke—donkey
Fakement—trick
Fly—knowing
Mopusses—halfpennies, farthings
Kiddies—petty criminals
Kick—the dandy among the kiddies
Gropusses—coat pockets
Subligacholees—best clothes? (see end of commentary below)
Hog—shilling
Tile—hat
Pickling tubs—Wellington boots
Tripes—paunch
Lush—drink
Gatter—beer
Wag—go out
Burking—criminal activity, here presumably not the strangling and suffocating done by William Burke
Fogles—handkerchiefs
Blunt—money
Clies—pockets

Partridge gives the term "ax my eye" as current 1850–1910, but the printing of this ballad in the copy used here was issued by Catnach from 2 and 3 Monmouth Court between 1836 and 1838. Its appearance in number 18 of the *Singer's Penny Magazine,* where it is described as "a celebrated song," apparently dates it from 1835 or 1834. I have amended "like a carrot" to "Is like a carrot," from a printing by Birt. I have changed "Did wonders" (both printings) to "Do wonders." I have changed punctuation, mainly to remove commas from the ends of run-on lines. The Birt printing gives "rousling, tousling."

The special language of the ballad is that of the criminal underworld. Ballads of this sort—so-called canting ballads—have a long history. Poets from Thomas Dekker to Thomas Moore wrote them, along with many other people without names to remember. They were popular in supper clubs and on the street in the nineteenth century. Further examples are on the next pages. Perhaps most notable among a number of collections of such ballads is J. S. Farmer's *Musa Pedestris*, first published in 1896 and reissued in 1964.[32]

"Subligacholees" may be a playful addition to cant offered by the perhaps middle class author of the ballad. The word could not be found in a number of cant, slang, and conventional dictionaries of the English language. The nearest fit to it seems to be Latin *subligaculum*, waistband or breechcloth.

The Cove Vot Has Seen Better Days

I once could sport the blunt about,
    But people now cocks up their nose;
'Cause on the bounce I hunt about,
    And crawls along in sickery clothes;
My coat is rather seedy, needy,
    My kicksies all in holes I wow,
From which my shirt might angle dangle,
    But then I doesn't vear von now!
Spoken.—Cause! my swells, you don't know vot you may come to!

For though you may cock up your nose,
    Your admiration I must raise;
My *gentlemanly* conduct shows
    I'm a "Cove vot has seen *better days!*"

Of tradesmen I vos vonce the top,
    And brought much hoker to my till,
I kept a slashing cat's meat shop,
    And hung out just by Mutton-hill.
From an old crony I collared a pony,
    Vith vhich they saddled me next day,
The beak so bulky, gallows sulky,
    Sent me off to *Bottomhouse-bay*;
Spoken.—Cause! you see, I only vent on a woyage o' discovery.
    For though, &c.

Ven hunger does my belly fib,
    I like a cur don't sneak about;
I bolts into a wittling crib,
    And has a rummy good blow out!
I gorge and guzzle to the muzzle
    On meat and lots o' gatter too;

>   Then out I vaulks me, if they baulks me,
>   I gives to them my I, O, U.!
> *Spoken.*—Cause! so help me bob, I'll pay you on the honour of
>   a gentleman.
>
>   For, &c.
>
>
>   I begging letters writes so fine,
>   And gets much money by my vit;
>   Street crawlers I gets in a line,
>   By shamming the cholera or a fit.
>   In gemmen's kitchens, there I'm pitching,
>   Many a yarn that seems so true,
>   And vhile the maid is sidling, idling,
>   I nibbles a silver spoon or two.
> *Spoken.*—Cause, you know, my coves, consider vot a
>   temptation that ere is.
>
>   For, &c.
>
>
>   I likes a honest life I'm sure,
>   And vhen that I can raise the shine,
>   Of schofels, I then buy a score,
>   And does vonders in the smashing line.
>   But them there Peelers are no feelers,
>   Vith honesty they never chimes.
>   So me they fixt on, and to Brixton,
>   Sent me five and twenty times.
> *Spoken.*—Cause ———
>
>
>   They say I'm gallows saucy now,
>   To common kids I vill not speak,
>   'Cause from the vorkhouse you must know,
>   I gets my eighteen vin a week.
>   Next veek I'll marry Molly, jolly,
>   'Then low lifed ways I means to drop,
>   I'll send round cards to cracksmen, flashmen,
>   And open a roaring fencing shop.
> *Spoken.*—Cause, shan't I flare-up then, my rum uns?
>
>   For though, &c.

Blunt—money
On the bounce—swindling with impudence?

Sickery (shickery)—shabby
Kicksies—breeches
Hoker (ochre)—money
Mutton-hill—unidentified, presumably an informal name, referred to also in "The Costermonger"
Slashing—brilliant
Collared—i.e., stole
Bottom-house-bay—unidentified, presumably an informal name for a local Botany Bay
Fib—strike
Wittling—victualing
Crib—shop
Gatter—beer
Raise the shine—raise money
Schofels—bad money
Smashing line—dealing in bad money
Peelers—police
Brixton—Brixton prison
Vin—unknown; perhaps a misprint for *tin*—money
Cracksmen—housebreakers, burglars
Fencing—dealing in stolen goods
Flashmen—thieves, criminals

Another ballad, "The Man That Has Seen Better Days" (No doubt you all wonder what object this is), of apparently later date, repeats title and refrain and general subject. Its first line echoes that of "The Charity Boy," page 243.

The reference to Sir Robert Peel's new police in the present ballad dates it some while after 1829. The printing used here is by Taylor at 14 Waterloo Road near the Victoria Theatre, and must have been issued in 1837.

Parson Brown's Sheep

Not long ago, in our town,
A little place of great renown,
There lived a man named Mr. Brown,
    And he was our parson.
Father he was very poor,
Christmas it was very near;
We'd neither mutton, beef, nor beer
    For our Christmas dinner.

Spoken.—They were very hard times for poor folks! Faider had lost his work 'cause he was getting old and couldn't do much; so I went to Parson Brown's, and asked him for some broken wittols; but he wouldn't gi' me any, but sot the dog at me, and sent me beeak broken hearted. When I came beeak, who should there be but Faider wi' one o' Parson Brown's fat wether sheep. There, said the old man, that's the first time I ever robbed in my life; but they won't let me work, and I can't starve. Egad! I was nation pleased to see the old sheep: I ran and kissed mother, father, and the old sheep and all, and ran up and down, singing—

> CHORUS
> Faider stole the parson's sheep,
> And we shall have both pudding and meat,
> And a merry Christmas we shall keep,
>   But I mayn't say nought about it.
>
> I sung up and down the street all day,
> Parson heard what I did say,
> And asked me in a civil way,
>   If I'd sing it o'er again, sir.
> Says he, I'll gi' thee half-a-crown,
> A suit of clothes and money down,
> If to church you'll go along,
>   And sing it to the people.

Spoken.—Egad! then, I said, I will. He gave me a bran new suit of clothes and half-a-crown. I ran home and told mother what parson had given me to go to church to tell who 'twas that stole the parson's sheep.

> My mother thought as I was mad,
> Says she, what ever ails the lad?
> You know they'll surely hang your dad
>   If you say aught about it.
> Says I, then, mother, I'll tell thee
> What I will do as sure as can be;
> I'll tell the folks what I did see
>   The parson doing to Molly.

Spoken.—I said, I'm dang'd if I doant, mother. Well, she said, Do lad, but don't thee say a word about the old sheep: if thee do, they'll hang thee and thy faider too. No, I said, I woan't then. So off I went, all in my bran new clothes. I'm sure I never looked so fine in all my life afore. I was as pleased as a cat with a pepper-box. I goes clink-o-me-clank, clink-o-me-clank, right up to the parson. He began to tell the folk what I had come for. Now, he says, I hope you'll hearken attentively to what this lad be about to sing; for it is a most notorious and outrageous crime as ever was committed, and ought to be severely punished, and every word he says is as true as the gospel I am now preaching. Then he swelled himself up like a turkey-cock, blew his nose, and told me to begin. Then I began singing—

> As I was in the field one day,
> I saw our parson very gay,
> Romping Molly on the hay,
>   And turn her upside down, sir.
> And for fear it shouldn't be known,
> A suit of clothes and half-a-crown,
> Were all given me by Mr. Brown,
>   For I to come and tell you.

Spoken.—He! he! he! I thought parson would have gone ramping mad. He stamped and swore it was the biggest lie that ever was told; but folk wouldn't believe him. They all ran out of church and cried shame of parson. He sent a big book at me, but it hit an old lady on the head: down she went and parson plump on top of her. I ran off, singing—

> CHORUS
> I have done old parson Brown,
> Of a suit of clothes and half-a-crown
> For telling all the folk around,
>   What he had done to Molly.

Sheep-stealing was a capital offense until 1832. The earliest printing I have seen of the ballad dates from around 1840. It was followed by an inferior and apparently less popular "Second Edition of Parson Brown's Sheep," in which Parson Brown sends for the lad and offers to "marry I for nothing and...give Molly three hundred golden sovereigns and a bran new suit of wedding clothes if I would only make an honest woman of her, and . . . he would put I into a great farm and stand godfather to our first boy." The lad likes Molly and agrees, and now he is "blest with a lovely sweet temper'd wife, two smiling babes and in possession of every blessing."

> So was it not a lucky day,
> When I saw Parson Brown so gay,
> A romping Molly on the hay,
>   And turned her upside down sir,

Another ballad that apparently waited even longer after 1832 to make its appearance is "The Englishman, Irishman, and Scotchman; or, Dearly You Must Pay For Your Mutton." The three men are travelling together, and "to keep them from starving" they kill a sheep. They are caught, tried, and sentenced to hang. The judge in his mercy allows them to choose where they will hang. The Englishman chooses an oak tree, the Scotchman the highest hill in Scotland, the Irishman a gooseberry bush. The judge grants the first two requests but is doubtful that a gooseberry bush would be high enough.

> Hold hard, says Paddy, don't be in a flurry,
>   There isn't one high enough, sure everyone knows;
> But as for the hanging, I'm in no hurry,
>   If it pleases your honour, I'll wait till it grows.

A variant of "Parson Brown's Sheep" was printed in Glasgow in 1854. The printer, "The Poet," says that the ballad is a great favorite around Glasgow.

Farewell Address
To Their Countrymen and Friends
Of All Those Unfortunate Men Who Received
Their Several Sentences of Transportation
At the Summer Assizes for the Year 1842
By the Judges of the Northern Circuit

The assizes they are over now, the judge is gone away,
But many aching hearts are left within the town today;
The crime is bad, yet poverty's made many one to be
A transport from his native land, and cross the raging sea.

Oh! 'tis a cruel sentence for a man to leave his wife,
His children, and his dearest friends, all dearer than his life;
To leave the land that gave him birth, to see it p'rhaps no more,
And drag a wretched life in chains, upon a distant shore.

The rich have no temptations, they have all things at command,
And 'tis for pleasure or for health, they leave their native land;
But a starving wife and family, makes a poor man's heart to break,
And makes him do what brings the blush of shame upon his cheek.

Their sentence some deserve to get, and laws were made to be
Preservers of the public peace, and of society;
But great distress and want of work, starvation, and disease,
Make inmates for the prison-house, and transports for the seas.

FAREWELL ADDRESS

To their Countrymen and Friends,

Of all those unfortunate Men who received their several Sentences, of Transportation, at the Summer Assizes for the year 1842, by the Judges on the Northern Circuit.

The assizes they are over now, the Judge is gone away,
But many aching hearts are left within the town to day;
Tho' crime is bad, yet poverty's made many one to be
A transport from his native land, and cross the raging sea.

Oh! 'tis a cruel sentence for a man to leave his wife,
His children, and his dearest friends, all dearer than his life;
To leave the land that gave him birth, to see it p'rhaps no more,
And drag a wretched life in chains, upon a distant shore.

The rich have no temptations, they have all things at command,
And 'tis for pleasure or for health, they leave their native land;
But a starving wife and family, makes a poor man's heart to break,
And makes him do what brings the blush of shame upon his cheek.

Their sentence some deserve to get, and laws were made to be
Preservers of the public peace, and of society;
But great distress and want of work, starvation, and disease,
Make inmates for the prison-house, and transports for the seas.

Oh! think a sentence for one's life, for fifteen years or less,
What tears they cost a family—what anguish and distress;
What heart but mourns the transport's fate, what eye but sheds a tear,
For tho' we hate the crime we hold man's liberty more dear.

Oh would our Rulers make a law for man to earn his bread,
And make sufficient wage to keep his wife and children fed,
The Judge's would have less to do, and half their pay might be
Devoted to this public good, and bless society,

The Prisons would be empty soon, and transport ships would then
Bring o'er the seas a load of corn, and not a load of men;
Act after act our rulers make, but one they will not do,
To do to others as they would—themselves be done unto.

Would they but pass an act for man to work and earn his bread,
Crime would soon dwindle from the land, and transportation fled;
Would providence direct their hearts to make such laws, and then
Instead of outlawed slaves—we might have free and honest men.

T. DODDS, Printer, No. 43, Head of the Side,

No. 26.

"Farewell Address to Their Countrymen and Friends." By permission of the Syndics of Cambridge University Library.

Oh! think a sentence for one's life, for fifteen years or less,
What tears they cost a family—what anguish and distress;
What heart but mourns the transport's fate, what eye but sheds a tear,
For tho' we hate the crime we hold man's liberty more dear.

Oh would our rulers make a law for man to earn his bread,
And make sufficient wage to keep his wife and children fed,
The judges would have less to do, and half their pay might be
Devoted to this public good, and bless society.

The prisons would be empty soon, and transport ships would then
Bring o'er the seas a load of corn, and not a load of men;
Act after act our rulers make, but one they will not do,
To do to others as they would-themselves be done unto.

Would they but pass an act for man to work and earn his bread,
Crime would soon dwindle from the land and transportation fled;
Would providence direct their hearts to make such laws, and then
Instead of outlawed slaves—we might have free and honest men.

The immediate incident or incidents that the ballad refers to are unknown. The ballad was issued by T. Dodds, 43 Head of the Side, Newcastle upon Tyne, who is described by C. J. Hunt as "the most important radical printer in Newcastle."[33] The *Newcastle Chronicle* (16 and 23 July) and assize records in the Public Record Office, Kew, give sparse information on the Newcastle and Northumberland summer assizes held in Newcastle in 1842. Together they report six sentences of transportation, three of twelve years for theft of a purse containing three five-pound notes and seventeen sovereigns, one of fifteen years for burglary of three silver candlesticks and another item, one of fourteen years for stealing from a silversmith, one of ten years for breaking and entering. They give no hint of cause—of poverty, mental unbalance, natural tendency towards wickedness, or anything else. Of the first case it is reported that the three youths involved, ages 16, 19, and 20, subsequently bought three pairs of boots (one pair women's) and a hat with the money.[34] It might be surmised that desperate poverty—starvation—was not the cause of the crime. Other evidence suggests that "Farewell Address" may not refer to local matters. J. Latimer's *Local Records* (1857) says of the year 1842 that "although much alarm was felt, and the lower classes were suffering to an extent rarely known in this country, not a single attack upon property occurred in this district [of Newcastle]."[35]

It seems likely that the ballad refers to incidents over a wider area. Along with being a year of special hardship for the poor, 1842 was the year of the second Chartist petition, presented to Parliament in May with more than three million signatures. Its failure brought widespread rioting in the north of England. Records of Yorkshire summer assizes show many riots in the summer months. Mainly they seem to have been "plug riots"—masses of men coming upon mills to demand higher wages and to force the removal of boiler plugs, so stopping machinery. One deposition concerning a riot in Bradford speaks of "the riotous state of the town."

Another concerning Halifax speaks of a mob of about a thousand people aiming to release men who were being taken to prison. At Leeds a deposition made on 19 August by Rainer Stamfield says:

> I am a magistrate of the borough of Leeds and also for the West Riding of Yorkshire —owing to the disturbed and excited state of the borough of Leeds and the neighbourhood thereof and other parts of the West Riding of Yorkshire I have for several days past in conjunction with my brother justices of the borough of Leeds thought it my duty to increase the civil and military force of the borough of Leeds in order to preserve the public peace —that on Wednesday last a party of the police force and the troops left Leeds attended by the mayor and some of the magistrates with the object of preventing outrages and for the apprehension of offenders —that after those magistrates had returned to Leeds with the civil and military force namely between four and five in the afternoon of the same day (Wednesday) information was communicated to the justices at Leeds that a mob were at Messrs Marshall's Mill attempting to stop it and the mayor requested myself and Mr. Benyon (another magistrate) to take the civil force to protect it and we accordingly proceeded towards Messrs Marshall's Mill attended by a body of police and Mr. Read the chief constable —on our way we learnt that the mob had left Marshall's Mill and had gone to Benyon's Mill. We then proceeded there. When we came in view of Benyon's Mill Mr. Read saw some of the people running and he left us and went after them —on turning the corner which brought us in view of Marsh and Maclea's Mill we saw a riot at their gates, some people were striving to force into the mill and others inside were endeavouring to keep them out —a cry was then made that Read the chief constable was killed, upon which I rode up to the mill gate of Marsh and Maclea and read the Riot Act —I had hardly finished when a volley of stones came in the direction where we were standing —I urged the police forwards and then I galloped back into the corner for the military and returned with them. When we returned with the military we found the whole street filled with a mob of rioters and the police were struggling in various directions and endeavouring to seize their respective prisoners. Previous to turning the corner which brought us in view of the mob I had given orders to His Royal Highness Prince George of Cambridge to disperse the mob and clear the streets and he and his troops accordingly did so.[36]

That one of the magistrates was named Benyon, and one of the mills also, suggests the manifold forces arrayed against the laboring poor. In the 1832 parliamentary report on child labor in mills and factories, the first recorded testimony was that of a young man who had begun work at Benyon's at age 10 in 1813. He said that during the year and a half that he was there, he regularly worked sixteen hours a day, and his sister eighteen hours, 5 A.M. to 9 P.M. and 5 A.M. to 11 P.M. He said that he had no break for meals except forty minutes at noon, and that both boys and girls were sometimes severely strapped for failing in their work.[37]

Most of the lines of "Farewell Address" appear in another ballad entitled "The Transport's Lamentation," which tells the tale of a man from Lancashire who was driven by poverty into robbery. That ballad is decidedly less skillful, and looks to be a piece of plagiarism. For other ballads on transportation, see the endnote.[38]

(I am obliged to Barbara Heathcote, local studies librarian, Central Library, Newcastle, for providing information on economic conditions in Newcastle in 1842.)

After Serving Seven Years

After serving seven years,
    Vot a shame it is to thrust
A fellow on the treading mill,
    'Cos he strove to cadge a crust,
I turn away from morn till night,
    And fancy by the powers,
Too many ups and downs through life,
    I takes my cauliflowers.
            After serving, &c.

Lord, how I'm changed since last I stept,
    On yonder strange machine,
For slipping 'neath von old bloke's arm,
    To pinch another's screen.
Then if by chance I prigg'd a vipe,
    Of any sort of wally—
'Twas safe to walk to Ikey's fence,
    Vot stood in Cranbourn Alley.
            After serving, &c.

I would not now recall those scenes,
    They bring to me no joy,
But summons to this weary back,
    The thrashings of a boy.
I gaze on yonder whipping post,
    Where I've been tied so often—
As a cracksman 'neath the hangman's noose,
    Squints queerly on his coffin.
            After serving, &c.

Cauliflowers—hard knocks?
Screen—bank note
Prig—steal
Wipe—nose handkerchief
Wally—foolish fellow?
Ikey's fence—Jewish dealer in stolen goods
Whipping post—whipping was frequent punishment through the 1820s and later; it was not formally abandoned as legal punishment until 1948
Cracksman—housebreaker, burglar

The ballad was printed by H. Paul, 22 Brick Lane, who was active there from 1840 to 1845 (dates given by William Todd).[39] Paul presumably printed it in 1840 soon after its appearance, with negligible differences, in issue number 35 of *London Singer's Magazine*. That number perhaps appeared in spring 1840. There it is described as "a celebrated parody on 'After Many Roving Years,' written by Mr. E. Green, and sung at the London Concerts." (For a note on *London Singer's Magazine* and its dates see page 513. Green is the known author of a dozen songs published in *London Singer's Magazine* and *Model Song Book* in the 1840s. Most of them are of little interest. "Confessions of a Bachelor" describes several young women the speaker has courted. "I Will Never Deceive Him" professes faithfulness to the speaker's lover. Along with "After Serving Seven Years," Green's best ballad is "The Marsh-Gate Costermonger," which is known only in broadside form. It was printed by Henry Disley in 1860 or later under Green's name. Marsh-Gate Joe takes his woman to the Victoria Theatre, and there in the Gods he comments noisily and ignorantly on famous actors, provokes a fight, and gets locked up.

"After Many Roving Years," which had some popularity as a broadside ballad, brings a man home who has traveled because of ambitions. Its third and final stanza goes thus:

> I would I could recall once more,
>   That blest and peaceful joy,
> And summon to this weary heart,
>   The feelings of a boy;
> I gaze on scenes of fond delight,
>   Without that wonted pleasure,
> As a miser on his bed of death,
>   Looks coldly on his treasure.

The Dreadful Murder of a Wife and Six Children

Early on Monday morning a whole family, consisting of the father, mother, and six children named Duggan were found poisoned at a house in Hosier-lane,

City. The father was a working silversmith. A letter in the father's own hand, directed to the police, led to the discovery, and on going to the house indicated they found in one room on the bed, the dead bodies of the mother and three of the youngest children, one on each side of her, and the other across the foot of the bed. Two daughters were stretched upon another bed in the same room, and that of the eldest boy lay upon an adjoining crib, while the body of the father lay alone in the back room. A bottle labelled "Poison" in conspicuous letters was by his side. The whole of the dead bodies were in their night dress, and lay just as if they had resigned themselves to sleep for the night. The man Duggan appears to have been much respected by his fellow-workmen, and to have been of sober and steady habits. In a letter he wrote to his brother, he accused his late employer of being a hard, selfish, narrow-minded man. Duggan also said that he had looked for work and for lodgings, but could obtain neither, and that they had to face the alternatives of starving in the streets, the workhouse or death. We prefer the latter. He requested his brother to break the news gently to his mother, and bade them all an eternal farewell.

> Draw near all you fathers, and mothers as well,
>   The young, too, as well as the old,
> A tragedy, dreadful, I will to you tell,
>   As shocking as ever was told:—
> Of Walter J. Duggan, a father so dear,
>   His wife, him six children had borne,
> In Hosier-lane, City, they all did live there,
>   But now to their graves they have gone:
> Of life they were all there denied,
> With their father and mother they died.
>
> Six children have perished you hear,
>   A father and mother besides,
> For them, poverty he so greatly did fear,
>   So from poison eight souls they have died.
>
> Oh, poverty, poverty, hard is thy sting!
>   How many thy load have to bear,
> Your burden on poor Duggan's back you did fling,
>   It drove him to death and despair;
> His troubles were great, he affliction had borne,
>   Grim want it stared hard in his face,
> Let's hope to a far better land he has gone,
>   Where there's neither crime, shame, or disgrace.

Oh, hear his last words to his brother he penn'd:—
 To my mother the news gently break,
For when you receive this, I'm no more among men,
 Wife and children to Heaven I take;
For my master was harsh, me, dear brother, believe,
 And no work, or a home can I find,
So my children I've poisoned, for them I can't leave
 To the cold world I've now left behind.

These words, too, he wrote, in the letter, you'll see,
 Ere on earth he gave up his last breath:—
Dear brother, three chances are now left to me—
 Starvation, the workhouse, or death;
The last one we choose, and may those that we love,
 When on earth we have ceased for to live,
For our crime here below, when we meet them above,
 Let us hope that our children forgive.

To the Station, a letter he also did write,
 To the house they did quick then repair,
The back window entered, and oh, what a sight!
 Met their gaze on the second floor there;
Poor Duggan he lay on his back in the bed,
 With the bottle and glass by his side—
The fatal word—poison—how soon it was read,
 Showed how that wretched father had died.

The mother and children then quickly was found,
 And calmly in death they did sleep;
This tragedy, sorrow has caused all around,
 And for them, now many will weep.
Such a tale may we never again have to read,
 And such deaths may we ne'er again hear,
Nor such misery cause manly hearts for to bleed,
 For those victims I pray shed a tear.

I

The tragedy occurred in the early hours of Monday, 28 June 1869. Father and mother were ages thirty-eight and thirty-nine; the six children ranged in age from one to thirteen. Surviving documents of the inquest, conducted on 30 June, include Duggan's two letters and testimony of ten people. Duggan's letters are postmarked the twenty-eighth. Reports in the *Daily News* and *West End News* say that he was seen posting them at 4:30 A.M. The letter to the police arrived at Smithfield Police Station three and a half hours later.

> 15 Hosier Lane
> Smithfield E.C.
> 27/6/69
>
> Sir,
> Your attendance will be required at the above address early this morning. A letter giving all particulars can be obtained from my Brother of 32 Milk Street Bristol. Posted same time as this.
> Yours truly,
> W. J. Duggan

Duggan's letter to his brother is headed and dated the same as the letter to the police. It is unsigned.

> Dear Brother,
> You are aware of Mr. Adams' harsh and hard course of action when he learned my lungs were affected which ended in his giving me 1 Months Notice to leave his employment, knowing as I told him I had no means of livelihood but the one week's wages I left with. His bearing & language has been thoroughly tyrannical from the very first moment he heard I was struck down and has been continued up till the last.
> And the cause of it all is that he had made a Miscalculation in Me. He had reckon'd he had a good sound servicable article in Me and when he discovered his mistake he was furious and showed his annoyance in ways that only a hard selfish narrow minded Man could.
> After the month expired, he allowed me after a great deal of solicitation to remain in the house, which is his, a week longer, while I looked for work and place to live in, which I had no opportunity of doing before. I have tried hard to obtain either or both, but can find no lodging or house for when they hear I am out of work and can give no reference they decline altogether. I asked Mr. Adams if he would allow me under the circumstances to name him as a Reference. He said he would have nothing to do in the Matter as he <u>may</u> have to pay. I asked what he thought I could possibly do. He said I could get a place somewhere if I liked and I must be out of his house at the expiration of the week or he would put my things into the Lane. I appealed to him for some consideration for My Wife and little ones, the Eldest he knew far gone in Consumption. I also asked if it were possible he could go to such extremes with me after being between 4 & 5 years in his employ and the long character he had with me and, up till the time of my health partially failing, had devoted My whole thought & energy to forwarding his interests. He took no notice of that, but said, he would not be trifled with and unless I was out of his

house he would act, so not to deceive myself in the Matter. So We have to face the alternatives of starving in the streets, the Workhouse or Death. We prefer the latter. We may have been able to surmount the difficulties of the position, if Mr. Adams had acted less unfeelingly, but he has shown scant Mercy, and if the same is Meted out to him in his extremity it will go hard with him for the blood of me and mine is on his hands, and will cling to him and his.

It is better to meet death as We have, than wait till he comes through want privation and Misery and would come with equal certainty for Me, Emma, and all the children are far from strong and must have quickly succumbed.

We are strongly attached to each other and separation alone would be as bad as death, and we love the Children dearly, too dearly to condemn them to utter wretchedness & want.

It is agony of mind almost passed endurance to think that the alternatives are so terrible, but we cannot shield them from one or the other.

Break the news gently to Mother. Tell her it is under the circumstances the best course, far better than the degradation & Want & disease before us which must have ended in the same way after all our sufferings.

Prussic acid was the thing used.

Pray undertake the funerals if you can. I think you will have enough things to pay expenses. Oh the horror of this night may it be visited upon the Man that forced it.

I can write no more for I am Nearly Mad Mad, so an eternal farewell to you all.
And May God Bless You
Farewell for ever

Starving in the streets—local authorities could deny assistance to anyone who refused to enter the workhouse
Separation alone—the Poor Law required separation of parents from children and husbands from wives within workhouses

Testimony at the inquest was imperfectly recorded. Within the documents quoted below I have bracketed additional or contradictory inquest testimony as reported in the *Times* and *Daily Telegraph*. Police officers at the inquest testified to receiving Duggan's letter at 8 A.M. on the 28th and to going to the house and finding the bodies undressed as for sleep and disposed as described in the ballad. Beside one of two bottles of prussic acid they found the family Bible with the names of the children inscribed in it. Pinned to the Bible was the marriage certificate of Duggan and his wife. There had been a fire in the grate, and charred papers lay there, unreadable. [*Times:* In a writing desk were letters to Duggan from his brother saying he would do what he could to help.]

Testimony of Duggan's mother:

I saw him at Whitsuntide—he was very desponding about his own health & that of his children—he said that he was in a consumption & his eldest boy also & that the rest would follow. That preyed on his mind very much. [*Times:* He also said his wife was getting very thin, and grieving much about the oldest boy.] He said he expected to leave his employment on account of his ill health. He was on very good terms with his wife. I had not seen him for some 3 or 4 years—he was greatly changed. He was a sober man. The wife was not a strong minded woman. [*Times:* I think she was extremely likely to be affected with the same feelings as her husband in all things. They never hinted at such a thing as this.]

Testimony of a neighbor living opposite the Duggans:

I knew the deceased persons. I saw them every day. [*Times:* She knew all the deceased persons by sight. . . . She had once spoken to Mrs. Duggan, but not recently.] On Sunday morning I saw the woman and some of the children at breakfast about eleven o'clock. They were drinking coffee. I did not see the man. I saw no difference in the appearance of the man or woman. They always appeared in a very deplorable state as far as their home & appearance went. I went out and returned late at night. I saw a light in the front room first floor at ten minutes past 12 on Monday morning. The blind was down. The gas was then burning as I could see the light thro' the blind. About ¼ before 4 I saw a flickering light as if a fire was burning. That was unusual. I saw nothing after that. I did not see anyone go out.

The neighbor's testimony as to the appearance of the family is not corroborated in any other inquest testimony, and is contradicted in the initial reports of the tragedy in the *Times, Daily Telegraph,* and *Daily News* on 29 June. The *Times* said that "the neighbours speak in touching terms of the unfortunate children, whose tidy appearance was creditable to the mother." The *Telegraph* said that Duggan was "spoken of as being a very steady, sober, and intelligent man," the wife was "very respectable," and the children were "always clean and apparently well fed." The *Daily News* said that the parents were "respectable persons of quiet and sober habits, and extremely fond of their children, whom they kept very clean and nicely dressed."

The publican of the Wheatsheaf tavern testified that he saw Duggan occasionally at his place and that at about eleven o'clock on Sunday night he sold a pot of ale to the oldest boy to take home. The chemist testified that he did not know Duggan and did not recognize the body. He had sold the prussic acid to another man. Other comment at the inquest and additional comment as reported in the *Times* suggest that the chemist was believed to be lying and had sold the acid illegally to Duggan.

Testimony of Duggan's personal physician:

He had disease of the throat. He came about 4 years back. He had had several bad attacks. He had [dried?] tonsils. He was very anxious about his chest. I told him that he need not trouble himself about his Chest. He was afraid that it was consumption of the throat & would gradually affect the lungs. That was between 3 & 4 years ago. I saw him several times since, the last time on Friday week, June 18th. He complained of his throat—that it was very bad. He was very low anxious & desponding. He told me it was all up with him. That he was [also?] losing his situation & that he was [several words unreadable, apparently having to do with Duggan's taking up itinerant silver work] & whether it would be conducive to his health—I told him it would. The wife always appeared to be remarkably affectionate to him & deeply sympathetic.

The police surgeon testified that the disposition of the bodies and of the poison, the quickness of action of the poison, and the apparent times of death indicated that the wife agreed to the poisoning. The poison was probably given to the children and wife as they slept. There were no signs of struggle. Wife and husband died some while after the children. Duggan's eyes and mouth were open. He may have taken the poison as late as 6 or 7 o'clock. The surgeon said further:

I saw the body of the eldest boy [the oldest of the children] in the bed by himself. He was on his back a little turned on his side. I saw two girls in the next cot, one about 12 years old & the other about 6. I examined the body of the elder girl. I examined the body of the mother—externally. No rigidity of death as in the children. The mother had not been dead so long I think as two or three hours. I examined the head of the man. The brain was nearly healthy. I found that consumption had begun. The lungs were diseased. It may have been of some months' standing. That would make a man less able to work, and depress him, and might act on his mind. [*Times:* He was ruptured on the left side and wore a truss.] The bodies were all well nourished.

Testimony of George Williams Adams, the head of the firm of Chawner & Co., silversmiths, who lived at 16, 17, and 18 Hosier Lane.

The deceased was in my employment. He was out of health—had been examined by a Doctor & on April 3rd he told me that he was ill & had had advice. I knew that he had had a cold. He then said, I am unable to continue my situation. I must leave it & seek outdoor employment. He said his lungs were affected. He said he had been to Dr. Powell a Homeopathic—that the doctor had told him what he told me. I reasoned with him. I told him that I had only a month for me to live in 1848 by the Doctors [because of having only one lung] & that I was alive now. I urged him to try & continue in his situation at all events for a time. I told him to take exercise & to consider his wife & children until he could get some employment. He said I am afraid I shall never be any better. Nothing more passed except he said "I can't continue, I must give it up."

He appeared to droop from that time—he did not work with energy. He had 35/- per week & was always paid. He lived quite rent free. He kept at his work as well as he could off & on. At Whitsuntide I advised him to go to Bristol. He went on the

Saturday morning & returned to his work on the following Wednesday. He seemed then as usual. He told me he could not get employment in Bristol. He kept saying he could not continue & on May 22nd he told me that he was not doing his duty by me & I said we had better arrange a time to part. I suggested that. I said I am in no hurry. Will a month suit you—this day 4 weeks. Which would expire on June 19th on which day he left off work. He was trying to get a place in London. He came in on Thursday last [the 24th] to say that he could not get a situation—nor had he found lodgings for the family. I told him I must have the house to do it up as I had another party to place in. On Friday morning [the 25th] he came in & told me that he had made all arrangements & should be out of the house by mid day on Monday. I said very well that will do. That is all that passed. That was the last time I saw him. I saw none of the family after. He did not thank me for what I had done.

[In response to questions:] He never asked me for a reference. Nor did I ever refuse him one. A week's notice was the usual time. [*Times,* apropos of Duggan's letter to his brother: Witness and deceased had always been on good terms, and he could not understand the letter, which to him as a gentleman was a most distressing return for his kindness to Duggan. A juryman said there was evidently no cause for such a letter.] [*Telegraph,* either reporting similar comment or perceiving the same comment differently: Some gentlemen in court said that the man was treated with great kindness by his employer, and that there was not the slightest grounds for such statements as those in the letter.] [*Times* again: Mr. Adams added that the deceased's duty was to receive and hand silver from and to the workmen, and to weigh it.]

The verdict as report in the *Times:*

The jury, after a few minutes' deliberation, returned a verdict "that Walter James Duggan and Emma Duggan murdered their children, and afterwards destroyed themselves while in an unsound state of mind." The Coroner said he entirely agreed in the verdict.

II

In such a way one family's anguish was officially concluded. The jurors apparently had no questions to consider among themselves, only agreement to confirm and record. The coroner was of like mind. In the course of testimony itself, there were few questions asked, and none of them were pursued. The chief gratuitous statement by a juror was the one in support of Adams's kindness. Many decades later it is easier to ask questions. Why did not the coroner call Duggan's brother to testify? Why did he not call any of Duggan's fellow workmen or a neighbor who knew the Duggans more than by sight? Why did he not ask for an autopsy on the oldest boy? A separate sheet among the documents of the inquest is headed "Witnesses." On it are eight of the ten names of people whose testimony is recorded, along with a further ten whose identities are unknown but for one. Jenkin Thomas is named in police testimony as the person who let them into the Duggan house. He is described further in the initial account in the *Daily Telegraph* as an engineer in the employ of Chawner's. He is perhaps the source for the *Telegraph*'s report therein that Duggan was an "exemplary employee." Some lines later the report says that Duggan is spoken of as "very steady, sober, and intelligent." Perhaps these words refer to Thomas's perception of him at work.

Might the coroner or jurors have asked Adams why he did not offer Duggan a reference if he felt kindly toward him? Why did Adams wait in vain to be asked? Why on Friday the 25th of June did his kindly feeling not extend to asking Duggan what lodging if not employment he had luckily found overnight? Who was the party Adams needed to put in the Duggan house, and how great was the need?

Such questions might not have exposed a hard and selfish man, but their absence suggests unwillingness by coroner or jurors to pursue troublesome or troubling matters. Why did the one juror feel the need to assert that there was no cause of the criticism of Adams in Duggan's letter? How did he—or the gentlemen attending the inquest—know of Adams's "great kindness" to Duggan, and of what did that great kindness consist? The *West End News,* one of two local newspapers to report the tragedy, said that the jurors were "city merchants." Was there a gentleman's agreement to succor a fellow gentleman in distress?

The harder questions that coroner and jurors did not face were whether Duggan could have been of sound mind when he acted as he did, and whether blame might attach to people other than Adams. It seems evident that Duggan was deluded to some large extent about the condition of the oldest boy. It may be that he made little effort to find other work and lodging. There is no doubt, though, that progressive deterioration of his health meant that sooner or later he would no longer be able to support his family. His illness was a clear threat to the health of everyone else in the family. What likely choice or fate lay ahead other than what he saw: death, starving in the streets, or workhouse? Would a loving husband and father of sound mind inevitably have chosen workhouse, with its enforced breaking up of family? Perhaps it might seem that coroner and jurors in 1869 could hardly be expected to address such questions. The tale told in appendix 2 of jurors in 1833 facing another murder suggests otherwise. Be that as it may, in 1834 when the new poor law was being enacted, the editors of the *Times* wrote that the act would "disgrace the statute book which contains Magna Carta and the Bill of Rights." In 1835 when Edward Lamborn yielded himself and family to Faringdon Workhouse, with enforced separation of himself, wife, and child, he wrote, "For those who made the poor laws they are the spawn of hell." When in either of those years John Embleton wrote a broadside called "The Poor Law Catechism," he foretold the Duggan tragedy as a crime of state. He gives there the sixth commandment of the poor law commissioners: "thou shalt commit murder by neglecting thy starving children, for we will give thee no assistance to get them food."

III

The *West End News* was a weekly paper, published on Saturdays, and it was able to report the case only after the inquest. It printed three apparently distinct and largely contradictory accounts of the tragedy in two adjacent columns. The presumed first in time to have been written occupies part of the third column of an inner page. It outlines the events, gives the opinion that Duggan "always appeared exceedingly fond of his wife and children," and says that he gave notice to leave Chawner's because the ceilings of the workrooms were too low and affected his head—an explanation that has no echo elsewhere among newspapers or documents of inquest. The other two accounts appear one below the other in the second column of the same inner page. Their headings imply they are two parts of a single account: THE SHOCKING TRAGEDY IN LONDON and INQUEST ON THE EIGHT BODIES. However, the first part is devoted to discounting unspecified rumors about the tragedy and to discussing the inquest with respect to the police surgeon's post mortem examinations and his conjectures as to times of death. The second part is mainly devoted to suggesting that one rumor is true, and it ignores the inquest except to name the coroner, provide the names and ages of the Duggan family, and give the verdict of the merchant-jurors. Of the wild rumors the first part says:

> The most wild and contradictory reports are in circulation as to the motives which led to the tragedy discovered in Hosier Lane on Monday morning, and the circumstances under which it was perpetrated, and every idle gossip of the neighbourhood has his or her version to give to eager listeners respecting the shocking catastrophe. But from reliable facts ascertainable and after careful inquiry, the only apparent reason for the conduct of the man Duggan is the fact that his dismissal from his situation, and being required to give up his house, had preyed upon his mind, already weakened by misfortune and illness, and being without any resources to maintain himself and family he resolved to put an end to his and his family's troubles in the way that he has done.

The second part says:

> The proceedings created great interest throughout the locality, as the deceased man was well known in the neighbourhood as foreman of the silversmith's in Hosier Lane, and it was believed that he had been discovered by his employer stealing some silver, and had been dismissed for doing so. He afterwards, it was said, returned to his wife and induced her to join him in poisoning their six children, and then he and she committed suicide.

None of the documents of the inquest gives the slightest hint of theft being an issue in the matter, nor do any of the five newspaper reports of the inquest that have been seen—*City Press* being the fifth. The *Daily News* reported theft as the cause in its initial report on 29 June. The *West End News* seems indeed to have had three separate accounts to assess in preparing its issue of 3 July, and the editors garbled the whole matter. What is significant is that the account which dismisses wild rumors is the only place in newspaper reports or in inquest testimony where impending destitution is a focus of discussion. The initial accounts in the *Times, Telegraph,* and *Daily News* piece together a sensational tale. The testimony elicited by the coroner, as recorded officially and as reported in the five newspaper accounts, has marginal concern for destitution. The only known serious public attention given to poverty (and by implication to laws on poverty) as cause of the tragedy was in the broadside ballad.

IV

The ballad was published by Henry Disley. It was his second ballad on the tragedy. His first, "Shocking Murder of a Wife and Six Children," could well have been published on the 28th itself and have been the first report of the tragedy by any press. The prose of this first sheet contains errors of fact that are not repeated in the second, notably that Duggan's letter to the police says that he has killed seven people and is about to slay himself and that Duggan's brother lives in Sheffield. (Both sheets give the family name as Duggin.) The verses say nothing of Duggan's character or the character of his employer, and make no mention of Duggan's looking for other work or lodging. Poverty is an explicit concern of only one stanza:

> He was discharged, and that we find,
> It preyed upon his anxious mind.
> Lest they should want, that fatal day,
> His wife and children he did slay.

The ballad ends with conventional piety about crime:

> Of such an heartrending affair,
> I trust we never more may hear,
> Such deeds they make the blood run cold,
> May God forgive their sinful souls.

The same broadside, with the same title, was also issued by W. S. Fortey, with the omission of a stanza that offers possible criticism of Adams:

> They happy lived, until of late,
> He appeared in a sad desponding state;

> At something he seem'd much annoy'd
> At his master's where he was employ'd.

V

A ballad of the eighteenth century or earlier, "A New Ballad Showing the Great Misery Sustained by a Poor Man in Essex," tells of a man who was prompted by the devil to kill his starving family, but charitable help arrived before the man could do the deed.[40] The true incidence of either fortunate or disastrous outcome to such distress can be better surmised than known. What seems evident from the research for this book is that very few cases of either sort were reported on broadsides. Among those few, several were issued by Harry Bonner of Bristol, the man who printed the false account of Charles Elliott's execution (pages 341–43). Whether he invented or reported truly in his starvation broadsides is not known. No trace of any of the supposed events could be found in the index to the *Times*. Bonner's titles include "A True, Full and Particular Account of the Melancholy Death of Mary Sawyers," which tells of a woman who threw herself and her starving children into the Thames at Richmond on 12 March 1819, "John Groves, a Poor Labourer of Ferrybridge in Yorkshire, Who Destroyed Himself and His Three Starving Children by Plunging with Them into a Bucket Well," undated, and "A True, Full, and Particular Account of Two Poor Children That Were Found Starved to Death," which tells that the two children were abandoned near Shirehampton and found on 15 October 1818.

Along with the Duggan broadsides, Henry Disley printed "Horrid Murder of Four Children at Capland Street, Lisson Grove," which tells a tale similar to the Duggan tragedy. The inquest was reported in the *Times* on 18 April 1872. C. Paul of 18 Great St. Andrew's Street printed "Copy of Verses on the Lamentable Death of Mr. and Mrs. Jessup," which tells of five children surviving murder and suicide of mother and father. The account of the matter in the *Times* says that the man had told his wife that he no longer had any work, but the *Times* gives more emphasis to testimony that the man was of violent disposition.

(The documents of the Duggan inquest are quoted by permission of the Corporation of London. I have regularized capitalization at the beginnings of sentences and also regularized end-punctuation, both of which uses are variable in Duggan's letters and in the records of testimony. I have left unchanged the use of capitals otherwise.)

4

People In and Out of Work

I

Employment for the working class in England in the nineteenth century was profoundly affected by revolutions in agriculture and industry, and by rapid increase in population—roughly from nine million in England and Wales in 1800 to eighteen million in 1850. The agricultural revolution, several centuries in the making, involved development of large-scale farms and farming, aided and abetted by enclosure; improvements in land drainage, fertilization, stock breeding, crops and crop rotation; and development of managerial skills. All these changes aimed in considerable part at maximizing profits. With efficient management, the great landowner and his large tenant farmers thrived. Wealth enabled them to survive bad harvests. Political influence ensured for many years a high price for their corn—through duties on imported cheap corn. The small farmer had difficulty competing. The farm laborer was worse off. Before enclosure, the farm laborer had rights in common fields, on common land; he had access to waste land. All such land provided food, shelter, and heat; it supplemented the income that he might earn from tilling a small strip of land belonging to the landowner. It afforded protection against bad harvests, high rents. It gave him a measure of independence. Enclosure robbed him of his common rights, and game laws and laws of trespass ensured that reassertion of those rights was hazardous. He became a landless hired hand, dependent upon wage, exposed to vagaries of cost of living, weather, employer. Add to these circumstances the fact that new farming meant greater yield with less labor, and that increase of population brought in more laborers. Overall, the situation of the farm laborer became precarious in a way it had never been before.

The revolution in industry was abrupt and dramatic. It was fed by invention that provided new material, power, production, transportation, and market. In 1760 the consumption of raw cotton by the textile industry was eight thousand tons. With inventions by Kay, Arkwright, Hargreaves, and others coming rapidly into use, consumption more than tripled in the next forty years, and by 1830 the triple figure had quadrupled to one hundred thousand tons. The first steam loom appeared in Manchester in 1806, and twenty-nine years later there were eighty-five thousand power looms in England. Such revolution brought appalling suffering. In part it was dislocation similar to that in agriculture: new methods throwing people out of work, with no independent resource for them to fall back upon. In part it was brutality of workplace, of brutal owners and managers who had fewer constraints upon them than their counterparts on the land. No long centuries of intimate relationship with workers had softened or cautioned them. Mills sprang up, and mines were dug, where no mill or mine had been the year before, and the paramount constraint was often profit, at whatever price in tragedy for workers.[1]

The 1832 parliamentary report on child labor in mills and factories took evidence of children being regularly worked twelve, fourteen, sixteen hours a day, sometimes with a single break for a meal, sometimes with no break at all, the children eating their food as they worked. Conditions were sometimes physically dangerous, polluted, cramped. Children were sometimes beaten for flagging at their task. An incapacitating accident might mean immediate stopping of wage. A child might earn three shillings a week for a twelve-hour day. The Children's Employment Commission in its report of 1842 examined conditions for both children and adults in coal mines. Children were employed as early as age five, commonly at age seven. At ages five and six in Bradford and Leeds, children earned two shillings and sixpence per week for a twelve-hour day. Adult life in the mines, said the report, brought "extraordinary muscular development, stunted growth, crippled gait, irritation of the head, back, etc., diseases, premature old age and death." A woman aged thirty-seven described her work:

> I have a belt round my waist, and a chain passing between my legs, and I go on my hands and feet. The road is very steep, and we have to hold by a rope, and when there is no rope, by anything we can catch hold of. . . . The pit is very wet where I work, and the water comes in over our clog-tops always, and I have seen it up to my thighs.[2]

Such tragedy was ameliorated chiefly by government intervention over a period of many years—against opposition sometimes on high principles of Benthamite and Malthusian economics.

What faced agricultural and industrial workers for whom the revolutions provided no work at all, or short-time work, or inadequate wage to support family? In 1842, when the population of England and Wales was just under sixteen million, the number of paupers receiving outdoor relief was 1,200,000. Another 221,700 were in workhouses.[3] These are the figures Thomas Carlyle refers to in the eloquent opening of *Past and Present* in which he likens the workhouse at St. Ives, Huntingdonshire, to Dante's Hell.

II

The precarious situation of ordinary laborers is described in two stanzas of a widely printed broadside ballad called "In the Days When I Was Hard Up":

> In the days when I was hard up for want of food and fire,
> I used to tie my shoes up with little bits of wire,
> When hungry, cold, cast on a rock, and could not get a meal,
> How oft I've beat the devil down for tempting me to steal.
>
> In the days when I was hard up I used to lock the door,
> For fear the landlady should say, You can't lodge here no more.
> From my own back drawing-room about ten feet by six,
> In the workhouse wall just opposite, I've counted all the bricks.

The special plight of farm workers, and the barren hope of land redistribution in redress for enclosure, is expressed in "Pity Poor Labourers":

> Some pity the farmers, but I tell you now,
> Pity poor labourers that follow the plough,
> Pity poor children half starving, and then,
> Divide every great farm into ten.

"The Tradesman's Complaint" speaks for factory trades people in the years after Waterloo:

> Come all you poor tradesmen, I pray lend an ear,
> Our trade it is lost, and I greatly do fear;
> Your mouth it is shut, and you cannot unlock it,
> The masters they carry the keys in their pocket.
>
> When there would be a peace, we did understand,
> That the rich with the poor would go hand in hand,
> But if you are starving they'll give no relief,
> You may eat what you will, instead of roast beef.

Among the most vulnerable of urban workers were street sellers, who by law depended on the sufferance of nearby shopkeepers and residents. The police could remove costermongers and their barrows upon complaint of noise or obstruction. "Pity the Poor Costermongers" of mid-century tells their tale:

> We are in a mess, Oh dear! Oh dear!
> What shall we do, where shall we steer.
> We'll all be starved to death, I fear,
>   All us poor costermongers.

> They have used us worse than any Turk,
> We must not sell, we must not work,
> They'd better pass an Act to Burke
>   All us poor costermongers.

To burke—to kill by suffocating.

Ballads of the unemployed are one of the larger groups of ballads in the great collections of nineteenth century broadside ballads. Insofar as they are among the less interesting ballads to collect, they may have been very numerous indeed in their time. Some purported to be the compositions of those who bore them to ask for charity, as with "John Taylor…, Cotton Spinner, Being Out of Employ," given below, and "The Tears of Pity…, Written by a Poor Framework Knitter." Others were common property, appearing in various guises. Six of the nine stanzas of "Staffordshire Nail-Makers Humble Petition" are the same as six of the twelve stanzas of "The Needle Makers' Lamentation of Redditch, Worcestershire," and the other three stanzas are the same as three stanzas of "Redditch, in Worcestershire, for the Master or Mistress." The two Redditch ballads share two other stanzas between themselves, and the second Redditch ballad is the same as "Cotton Spinners from Manchester, for the Master or Mistress," and these two ballads share lines with "The Mechanic's Lamentation on the Stagnation in Trade" (given on page 108) and "Mechanics' Lamentation" (Come listen, dear neighbours). These shared lines include the following quatrain.

> The oldest man now on earth,
>   Or living in the land,
> Can ne'er remember trade so bad,
>   Nor work at such a stand.

Another set of stanzas used repeatedly in large or small part are those of "The Tradesman's New Hymn," whose first stanza goes thus:

> When nature in the voice of pain,
>   Speaks of want or woe,
> The voice is heard—but heard in vain,
>   As our misfortunes show.

Some ballads have accompanying prose to describe the particular cause of unemployment. "The Manchester Cotton Spinner's Petition" says:

> There are upwards of 4000 of us thrown out of employment through the self-acting wheels, which run without the hands of man; and one of these wheels, containing

upwards of 4 or 500 spindles in a wheel, where, about five or six years since, we used to work about 40 spindles in a wheel, and each wheel taking from three to four men to work it.

"The Staffordshire Nail-Makers' Humble Petition," printed in Tipton, says:

The reason of our being out of employment is in consequence of the machines and foundries. They will cast and cut more nails in one day than 100 men can make in a week. Our Master (Mr. Woodhall in Tipton) failed and 100 men were thrown out of employment. We being so many in number were forced to leave our homes; our parishes being so much oppressed, could not give us employment, there being 500 out of employment there at this present time.

Such broadsides as these last two receive brief mention in the section on "Distressed Operative Beggars" in the fourth volume of *London Labour and the London Poor*. The author of the material, Andrew Halliday, provides several wonderful accounts of wonderful disguises undertaken by professional beggars to pass themselves off as unemployed gardeners, navvies, factory workers. He supposes that few people are thrown out of work by advances in machinery and that "the 'distressed weaver' is generally a spurious metropolitan production." He offers a supposedly spurious example:

My kind Christian friends,— We are poor workingmen from ——— who cannot obtain bread by our labour, owing to the new alterations and inventions which the master manufacturers have introduced, which spares them the cost of employing hands. . . .[4]

Halliday was an indifferent investigator, much of whose overall discussion of "Beggars and Cheats" was drawn uncritically from reports by the House of Commons Select Committee on beggary in 1816 and by the Mendicity Society in later years (see pages 299–300), and his observations here seem mainly to be absurd. One possible small piece of testimony against him is a copy of the ballad "Frame Work Knitters' Petition" ("Good people all attend awhile"), on which someone apparently wrote in hand at the time: "Singing in Sunderland streets by two frameknitters, June 24th 1826."

III

In "A Country Lad Am I" the country lad says that he will emigrate unless he can get a wage of more than eighteen pence a day. Until the 1850s he was unlikely to have had such a thought. Emigration in the 1820s stood at a yearly average of 22,000 for the whole of the United Kingdom. In the 1830s it tripled to an annual figure of 67,000, and in the 1840s that triple figure doubled to 149,000. In the first five years of the 1850s—when the ballad writer probably gave the country lad his words—the yearly average was 328,000.[5] How predominant poverty was as the cause for such figures is unclear. William Cobbett in *Rural Rides* says of emigration from Yorkshire in 1830: "It is not the *aged*, the *halt*, the *ailing*; it is not the *paupers* that are going; but men with from £200 to £2000 in their pocket."[6]

Emigration ballads on poverty take simple views, serious and light. A few warn against the venture. "The Emigrant" (Come all you gallant Englishmen) suggests that the ship might go down or that poverty awaits the emigrant in America. If he remains in England, friends will help, the times may mend, and in any event "the Lord he will provide." "'Tis Hard to Leave This Land" says that to leave England is to go from bad to worse. Rather more ballads dwell upon the sadness of departure. "The Lancashire Emigrant's Farewell" considers family and friends left behind:

> But when the vessel was in motion,
>   Loud shouts from shore did say farewell;
> To see our weeping friends and parents,
>   Would make your bosom heave and swell.

"The English Exile" considers a mother:

> Then give me thy blessing, dear mother,
>   Weep not, oh, weep not for me;
> Tho' stormy clouds hover o'er England,
>   There's fortune across the blue sea.

"Emigrant's Adieu" leaves a father behind. In "The South Australian Emigrant" a young man "borne down with poverty" leaves "my Mary Ann to mourn, / And tender parents, too." Unlike the three preceding ballads, this one progresses to the further shore:

> Young Henry found contentment
>   Upon that foreign land,
> And in a short time after,
>   He sent for Mary Ann;
> She landed safe and found
>   The bonny lad she did adore,
> They are married, and live happy,
>   On the South Australian shore.

Other ballads are preoccupied with religious or more broadly moral attitudes. A broadside entitled "Select Hymns for Christian Emigrants" offers Christian assurances:

> But with the Lord to guide my way,
> 'Tis equal joy to go or stay;

and:

> I can be calm and free from care
> On any shore since God is there.

This sheet, which has been seen in only one copy, makes no mention of poverty or any other cause for emigration. The widely printed ballad "There's Room Enough for All" is plain-spoken about England, idealistic about the foreign shore:

> From poison'd air ye breathe in courts,
>   And typhus-tainted alleys,
> Go forth and dwell where health resorts,
>   In rural hills and valleys.

The chorus for each of four stanzas repeats the title:

> Oh! fellow men, remember then,
>   Whatever chance befall,
> The world is wide where those abide,
>   There's room enough for all.

Ballads that concentrate upon the emigrant's new found land seem mainly to be comic. "California Gold" beckons both "high and low." Of British lasses it says:

> And when the British lasses to the land of riches go,
> And get among the shining stuff in California O,
> They shall have golden bustles, golden petticoats and smocks,
> And golden boots and trousers, and golden bantam cocks.

"California, or, Who Wants Gold!" carries on in similar vein:

> There's work for all without delay,
>   Men earn five hundred pounds per day,
> And gold may be had for taking away,
>   In the state of California.
> It's found in lumps both round and flat,
>   As thick as your leg—as big as your hat,
> Three feet square—like a hall door mat,
>   And often as big as a brewer's vat.

"Emigration" dilates upon the crocodiles, boa constrictors, kangaroos, and cannibals that await the poor emigrant to Australia.

Among all the ballads seen on emigration, very few give sustained attention to poverty. Two such ballads are "Emigrants' Farewell to Old England" and "The Emigrant's Farewell" (The shamrock and the rose I overheard conversing). The first speaks of "once dear and happy England" that is now torn "by false commerce's treacherous gale," where "more goods are made and sold than ever, yet work grows scarcer every day." It blames "Whig political economy" and hard-hearted manufacturers:

> Their coffers they have fill'd with gold, while daily in our streets we see,
> The poor man ragged and starved; Old England, now adieu to thee.

The second ballad speaks of "the dark cloud of poverty that set over Britain's isle." An Irishman first describes once happy Ireland "with hearts as light and minds as bright as the Shannon or the Liffey," now in "the chilling hand of famine," with "iron-hearted" and absentee landlords.

> Then up spoke a poor artisan, who England's rose did represent,
>   Whose sunken eyes and visage pale bespoke a heart o'ercharged with care:
> When I was for my labour paid, I gaily work'd in sweet content,
>   But now like you and thousands more I am driven to despair;
> Our tyrant task-masters grind us down, till by our trade we cannot live,
>   Such arbitrary systems no longer I'll endure,
> But seek employment where for a fair day's work a fair day's wage we'll receive,
>   And strive to live in happiness on fair Australia's shore.

England for him is "pride-tainted Babylon," with money swept into "large heaps, / And its keepers with a miser's eye watch it with a jealous care." Could any man, he says, "hear his children cry for bread when no relief was near" and be sorry to leave such an England?[7]

Turn the Carpet; or the Two Weavers

> As at their work two Weavers sat,
> Beguiling time with friendly chat,
> They touch'd upon the price of meat,
> So high, a Weaver scarce could eat.
>
> What with my brats, and sickly wife,
> Quoth Dick, I'm almost tir'd of life;

So hard my work, so poor my fare,
'Tis more than mortal man can bear.

How glorious is the rich man's state!
His house so fine! his wealth so great!
Heaven is unjust you must agree,
Why all to him, why none to me?

In spite of what the Scripture teaches,
In spite of all the Parson preaches,
This world (indeed I've thought so long)
Is rul'd, methinks, extremely wrong.

Where'er I look, howe'er I range,
'Tis all confus'd, and hard, and strange;
The good are troubled and oppress'd,
And all the wicked are the bless'd.

Quoth John, our ign'rance is the cause
Why thus we blame our Maker's laws;
Parts of his ways alone we know,
'Tis all that man can see below.

See'st thou that Carpet, not half done,
Which thou, dear Dick, hast well begun?
Behold the wild confusion there,
So rude the mass it makes one stare!

A stranger, ign'rant of the trade,
Wou'd say, no meaning's there convey'd;
For where's the middle, where's the border?
Thy Carpet now is all disorder.

Quoth Dick, my work is yet in bits,
But still in every part it fits;
Besides, you reason like a lout,
Why, man, that *Carpet's inside out.*

Says John, thou say'st the thing I mean,
And now I hope to cure thy spleen;
This world, which clouds thy soul with doubt,
Is but a Carpet inside out.

> As when we view these shreds and ends,
> We know not what the whole intends;
> So when on earth things look but odd,
> They're working still some scheme of God.
>
> No plan, no pattern can we trace,
> All wants proportion, truth, and grace;
> The motley mixture we deride,
> Nor see the beauteous upper side.
>
> But when we reach that world of light,
> And view these works of God aright;
> Then shall we see the whole design,
> And own the workman is divine.
>
> What now seem random strokes, will there
> All order and design appear;
> Then shall we praise what here we spurn'd,
> For then the *Carpet shall be turn'd.*
>
> Thou'rt right, quoth Dick, no more I'll grumble,
> That this sad world's so strange a jumble;
> My impious doubts are put to flight,
> For my own Carpet sets me right.

"Turn the Carpet" is one of the best of the broadside ballads produced in the late 1790s by Hannah More (1745–1833) and her friends. Mrs. More wrote it in 1796. It seems to have had a more substantial life than most of the other ballads produced by the group. How much of an appeal it made is another matter. It was greatly outnumbered by ballads aiming to show a carpet badly made and wanting mending. More especially it had to contend with ordinary grim facts such as those alluded to by Dick and with further grim facts impending in the weaving trades. While Dick and John were beguiling time in 1796 with friendly chat, other workers were rioting, and presently Dick and John were thrown out of work by the power-loom and engaged in the Luddite violence in the years from 1811. Mrs. More's thoughts about the 1796 riots were expressed in her ballad "The Riot; or, Half a Loaf is Better Than No Bread." Rash Tom says at the outset, "I am hungry, my lads, but I've little to eat, / So we'll pull down the mills, and seize all the meat"; but by the end of the ballad he has learned from wise Jack: "And when of two evils I'm ask'd which is best, / I'd rather be hungry than hang'd, I protest."

Hannah More's advice to the poor was much the same as that of her friend Anna Barbauld in her poem "To the Poor":

> Bear, bear thy wrongs, fulfil thy destined hour,
> Bow thy meek neck beneath the foot of power!⁸

See page 410 or Eliza Cook's similar view. For other discussion of Mrs. More and her Cheap Repository Tracts see the General Introduction.

Joan o' Grinfield!

I'm a poor cotton weaver, as many a one knows,
I've nowt to eat ith house and I've worn out my clothes,
You'd hardly give sixpence for all I've got on,
My cloggs they are bursten and stockings I've none,
    You'd think it wur hard to be sent to the ward,
    For to clam and do best that you can.

Our church Parson kept telling me long,
We should have better times if I'd but hold my tongue,
I've holden my tongue till I can hardly draw breeoth,
I think in my heart they mean t' clam me to death,
    I know he lives weel by backbiting the deel
    But he ne'er pick'd o'er in his life.

I tarried six weeks, thought every day was the last,
I shifted and shifted till now I'm quite fast,
I liv'd upon nettles while nettles were good,
And Waterloo porridge was t' best of my food,
    I'm telling you true I can find folks enow,
    That are living no better than me.

Old Bill o' Dans sent bailiffs one day,
For a shop-score I owed him which I could not pay,
But he was too late for old Bill o' Bent,
Had sent tit and cart and ta'en goods for th' rent,
    We'd nowt but a stoo that was seats for two,
    And on it keawred Margit and me.

The bailiffs look'd round as sly as a mouse,
When they saw all things wur ta'en out oth house,
Says one to the other all's gone thou may see,
Sed I, never fret lads your welcome to me,

They made no more ado but nipt up th' old stoo,
And we both went wack upon th' flags.

I geet hold of Margit for hoor stricken sick,
Hoo sed hoo ne'er had such a bang sin hoor wick,
Then the bailiffs scour'd off with th' old stoo o' their back,
They would'n a cared had they broken her neck,
    They'n mad at old Bent he'd ta'en goods for rent,
    They was ready to flee us alive.

I sed to our Margit as we lay on the floor,
We ne'er shall be lower in this world I'm sure,
But if we alter I'm sure we mun mend,
For I think in my heart we are both at far end,
    For meat we have none nor looms to weave on,
    Egad they're as good lost as found.

Then I geet up my piece and I took it 'em back,
I scarcely dared speak master looked so black,
He said you were o'er paid the last time you coom,
I said if I was 'twere weaving bout loom,
    In the mind that I'm in, I'll never pick o'er again,
    For I've woven mysel to th' far end.

Then I coom out of th' house and left him t' chew that,
When, thought at it again I was vex'd till I sweat,
To think of I mun warch to keep him an uwth set,
All the days of my life and still be in their debt,
    So I'll give over trade and work with a sped,
    Or go and break stones upon th' road.

Our Margit declared if hoo'd cloose to put on,
Hoo'd go up to London to see th' great mon,
And if things wur not altered when she had been,
Hoo swears hoo would fight blood up to the een,
    Hoos nowt agen th' King but hoo likes a fair thing,
    And hoo ses hoo can tell when hoos hurt.

Clam—starve
Deel—devil

Pick'd o'er—wove
Waterloo porridge—porridge made with water
Shift—make do
Tit—horse
Wick—alive
Flee—flay
Bout—without
Uwth set—all his set

The spellings and words of the ballad vary from printing to printing. I have made three slight changes here in accordance with another printing. In *Ballads and Songs of Lancashire* (1875), John Harland and T. T. Wilkinson give the first lines thus:

> Aw'm a poor cotton-wayver, as mony a one knaws,
> Aw've nowt t' ate i' th' heawse, un' aw've worn eawt my cloas,
> Yo'd hardly gie sixpence fur o' aw've got on,
> Meh clogs ur' booath baws'n, un' stockins aw've none;
>   Yo'd think it wur hard, to be sent into th' ward
>   To clem un' do best 'ot yo' con.

They date the ballad just after the battle of Waterloo, when, they say, hand-loom weavers' wages were falling from £3 to 21–25 shillings a week.[9] The date is generally agreed upon by commentators, but Roy Palmer in *A Touch on the Times* (1974), gives wages of about 18–25 shillings between 1800 and 1814, with a steep decline to 8 shillings by 1820.[10] Harland and Wilkinson remark that the last three lines of the ballad became household words in Lancashire, and remained such.

Joan o' Grinfield (also Jone / John / Johnny / Grinfilt / Greenfield / Green) is one of the few substantial characters who appear in nineteenth-century broadside ballads. The present ballad, by an unknown author, is second in a line of at least nineteen broadside ballads about him. The first one, usually called "Jone o' Grinfilt," is more concerned with Jones's comical effort to enlist in the French wars than with the poverty that spurs him. The origin of this first ballad was in dispute for many years. It seems fairly certain now that the author was Joseph Lees of Glodwick, a hamlet south of Oldham. He was a weaver and later a schoolmaster there, and he wrote a number of songs that were popular in the district. He is said to have written his Jone ballad in 1805 and to have sung it for the first time at a Christmas party in the same year. Some time later it was supposedly sung with great success before the king by a local musical society. Harland and Wilkinson say that it became the most popular of all songs in rural Lancashire.

Harland and Wilkinson themselves rely upon the chief alternative account of the origin of the ballad, that transmitted by Samuel Bamford in *Walks in South Lancashire* (1844).[11] Bamford recalls hearing the ballad sung by a cripple during the wars, and of years afterwards meeting the man and learning from him of the making of the ballad. In the cripple's version the ballad was a collaborative effort between Lees and Joseph Coupe (or Coop), a barber, tooth-drawer, blood-letter, spinner, and rhymester from Oldham. The two men were returning together from Manchester, penniless from hard drinking, and they decided to compose a song to sing at a succession of pubs on the way home and thereby sustain themselves. Composition took three days, with Coupe composing the first stanza, Lees the second, and so forth. Bamford himself had earlier believed that the ballad was written by a poet named James Butterworth, author of a poem called "Rochervale"; but he accepted the cripple's tale. Four years after the appearance of Harland and Wilkinson's book a series of exchanges appeared in the *Oldham Chronicle,* 25 January to 22 February 1879, with one correspondent, identified as Jerry Lichenmoss, providing argument and evidence that the ballad was solely the work of Lees, writing in 1805. Lichenmoss says that Coupe never claimed to be the author and that any verses Coupe might have written would have been inferior additions to the completed ballad by Lees. For further information see the endnote.[12]

In broadside form, the present ballad seems to have been much more popular outside Lancashire than the first ballad. It is one of very few dialect broadside ballads of the century to have been printed widely around England. Later Jone ballads, which took him in the 1830s to see the Manchester railway and in the 1850s to the Crimean War, seem to have aroused little general interest.

Four other Jone ballads that touch upon poverty are given in the endnote.[13]

The Occasion of These Verses Being Written Was the Writer John Taylor, Cotton Spinner, Of Manchester, in the County of Lancashire, Being out of Employ, and His Goods Were Sold for Rent

> O friend of sinners hear my cry,
>   To thee I raise my heart;
> Oppress'd I am by great distress;
>   O bid my grief depart.
>
> Thy word assures that all things shall
>   Together work for good;
> O let thy ways of dealings, Lord,
>   By me be understood.
>
> No home have I, nor yet a friend,
>   To take me by the hand;

A stranger I am now become,
    In my own native land.

Through towns and villages I rove,
    To seek my daily bread;
No place have I, or shelter for
    To screen my naked head.

I call to mind the former times,
    When comforts I enjoy'd;
When peace and plenty from thy hand,
    Thy goodness ne'er denied.

Then I had work, and took delight
    My duty to perform;
Not fearing then the ills I met
    In life's tempestuous storm.

My earnings then I did divide,
    With those who stood in need;
Freely partaking of the woes
    Of Adam's helpless seed.

But now my labour it is stopp'd;
    I have no work to do:
O let thy loving kindness, Lord,
    Compassion on me show.

My helpless babes require some food,
    Their nature to sustain;
My wife she hears their piercing cry,
    Which makes her to complain.

Lord, undertake and work afford,
    For this I humbly pray;
So will I own thy sentence just:
    And homage to thee pay.

Then shall my feet thy statutes tread;
    My life thy word obey;
I'll strive to glorify thee, Lord,
    In all I do or say.

The man is blest, that careful is,
   The needy to consider;
For in the season perilous,
   The Lord will him deliver.

Please deliver this to no person but the said John Taylor, who left it.

No printer is given on the single copy I have seen of the ballad. The character of the ballad suggests that it came earlier in the century rather than later. Possibly the year was 1827, when there was severe economic depression in Manchester.

Bill Bounce, the Swell Cove out o' Luck

In London town there once did dwell,
A broken kneedy thread-bare swell,
He was well known to high and low,
The shickery gent of Rotten-row;
Fate like a ball knock'd him about,
As if to put him in mind of Clout!
In truth he was a sorry buck,
Bill Bounce the swell cove out o' luck.

    Cadgetty cringe and foodlem fum,
    Gripe O, grab O, brevit O, rum;
    Pontickey, cheap O, hand me down,
    Sneakery, cheekery, rum ti tum.

His seedy coat once best of cloths,
Had been a cook-shop to the moths,
For his Uncle when it was in good trim,
Had had its use much more than him;
His funny bones—once laugh'd in their sleeves,
But now they look'd out, but to grieve,
In truth he look'd a decoy duck,
Bill Bounce the swell cove out o' luck.
                    Cadgetty &c.

And then had you but seen his hat,
'Twas worth its weight I'm sure in fat,
And his tattered shirt, he dar'd not doff,

'Cause it wouldn't go on again if it came off.
His stocking feet were coax'd and crush'd,
That the taters from their windows blush'd,
And his shoes like shovels scoop'd the muck,
Bill Bounce the swell cove out o' luck.
Cadgetty &c.

The seatless pantaloon he wore,
Like harlequin's dress, look'd much more,
With large straight stripes an inch apart,
He wanted stripes to make him smart;
'Twere shame to rig so sad a wight,
But he wanted rigging—so then it's right,
Poor in purse and panum struck,
Bill Bounce the swell cove out o' luck.
Cadgetty &c.

Where'er he went the girls would grin,
His winning ways were sure to win,
Like clustering cobwebs hung his hair,
A bare-faced man, and quite a bear;
The cry was raised by all the wags,
"There goes a walking bundle o' rags!"
But still he bore it all with pluck,
Bill Bounce the swell cove out o' luck.
Cadgetty &c.

A third hand cloak he bought one day,
A sort of dandy russet grey,
He march'd about a swaggering pup,
Like a dirty joke he was well wrapt up;
He could make a pun and laugh himself,
He'd victimise if he met an elf,
At concert-room he'd drink your suck,
Bill Bounce the swell cove out o' luck.
Cadgetty &c.

But mark his pride it did come down,
To Macadamise stones about the town,
A wanton proof of fortune's freak,
His wages seven bob a week;
But yet the fall his pride ne'er broke,

> He thump'd away still in his cloak,
> And now he drags about a truck,
> Bill Bounce the swell cove out o' luck.
> Cadgetty &c.

Bounce—cheeky swindler
Shickery—shabby
Clout—mythical boxer?
Pontickey (pontic)—on credit
Uncle—pawnbroker
Panum struck—without bread
Suck—strong drink
Macadamise—London roads began to be macadamized in the late 1820s; after John McAdam, 1756–1836

The ballad is by James Bruton, prolific songwriter and professional singer. His work appears in a number of song collections from about 1830 to 1870. That he ever wrote directly for the street seems doubtful, but at least a few of his ballads attained some popularity there, including the present one, "Quarter Day" (given in volume 1 without his name), "Happy Land" (quoted on page 132, and "Such a Getting out of Bed." He was also a writer of farces, at least seven of which survive, and he edited a song collection, *National Melodist,* published in London by William Strange in about 1845. He himself is represented there by more songs than anyone else, with J. E. Carpenter (mentioned elsewhere in these pages) in second place.

Bruton's dates are customarily given as 1815–67, and are so given in volume 1, but the fact that "Bill Bounce" is listed in Catnach's 1832 catalogue suggests that the birth date is wrong. The ballad appears on page 116 of *London Melodist,* published by the firm of Diprose and datable by various internal evidence to about 1831. The British Library dates the collection uncertainly at 1835. That date itself would be early for a ballad of the "Bill Bounce" sort written by someone born in 1815.

I have printed the ballad from a broadside that shows negligible differences from the printing in the song collection.

In a sequel, "Bill Bounce the Swell Cove Now in Luck," Bill helps to rob a shop, and "with his share of the swag he bought toggery gay, / Like a lord up Regent Street struts every day." Then when cash begins to run low again, he takes up with a rich woman (Miss Tuck, to rhyme only with luck):

> All you coves who are hard up—follow Bill Bounce's plan,
> He'll suffer no more for he's turned fancy man.

The Dead Alive

A man at an alehouse was sitting one night,
Both his purse and his cloaths were in very poor plight,
He was forming a plan for a dinner next day,
And thought half-a-crown would his score nicely pay:
He saw there a fellow laid drunk on the bench,
Whose cascading created a terrible stench;
So says to the landlord "my good friend I wot,
"You feel much desire to get rid of this sot?"
"'Pon my soul, and I do," cries the man, "but what then,
"Nobody can move him, he's a load for two men."
"Well, never mind that, but inform me, I pray,
 "What I am to have if I take him away."
The landlord replied, "you shall have half-a-crown."
"I thank you good Sir, will you please put it down,
"And get me a sack"; this quickly was done,
And his putting him in it created much fun.
With the man on his back, he now trudged away
To an anatomist's house, hoping there to get pay;
He knock'd at the door, and a voice cried "who's there?"
"I have brought you a *Subject,* a good one I'll swear;
"Come give me my fee, and think it no sin:"
The money was paid, and the sack taken in;
Which, with its contents, in the surgery was plac'd,
And the fellow set off in a devil of a haste.
Now this moving so quick nearly made the man sober,
 (This adventure took place, I believe, last October)
And he strove to get out; this the surgeon espied,
Who at being thus cheated, could almost have cried.
He ran after the other, and collar'd him quick.
"Why, you dog, he's alive, and had I a stick,
"I would handsomely baste you:" "My friend," cries the man,
"To bring you him living I thought the best plan,
"That he'll keep very well while alive must be granted,
"So you've only to *kill him whenever he's wanted.*"

    The killing of people, usually nameless wayfarers, to sell to anatomists was most notoriously the enterprise of William Burke, who was hanged in 1829. He and his accomplice, William Hare, killed fifteen or more people, chiefly by smothering to avoid bruising and wounding. They sold the bodies for £7.10s. to the surgeon Robert Knox for his School of Anatomy.

The ballad is listed in Catnach's 1832 catalogue. I have seen only one copy of it, printed by S. Bailey, 50 Bishopsgate Within. I have corrected and supplied punctuation and quotation marks.

A broadside ballad about a gang of body snatchers, "Not a Trap Was Heard," written as by one of them, was quite popular. It parodied "The Burial of Sir John Moore," itself popular in broadside form as "Not a Drum Was Heard," by Charles Wolfe (1791–1823).[14] Wolfe's poem was apparently first published in a Newry newspaper in 1817.

The Pitman's Widow's Lament
Or, the Poor Trapper Boy

Ventilation of coal mines is conducted by numerous doors, named trap doors, double doors, &c, to which free ingress and egress must be had. These doors of life and death are kept by children of tender ages, from 5 to 10 or 11 years. The hours they have to attend them are from 12 to 14 (sometimes more). Any neglect of these doors is attended with fatal consequence; the air of the mine becomes stagnant (or as it is termed, *Laid Dead*); the first light that comes in contact with it, an explosion takes place, which often destroys the greatest part of the workmen; thus from avarice, children are made the instruments of destruction to human life, to their parents, and to themselves. Spare a penny, is an appeal to the consumers of coals, to allow an advance of one penny per chaldron on the London or single chaldron of 86 bushels (to be forever called the mercy penny) and one halfpenny per fother, or cart of coals consumed in these districts. To indemnify the coal owners for placing proper persons in trust of the workmen's lives, this estimate was made from the quantity of coal shipped on the River Tyne in 1826, and from the number of trappers then employed (this estimate is for the Tyne only). This sum, added to the tenpence per day now paid to the trappers, is equal to two shillings per day. To the aged pitman no longer able to wield the pick, to the numerous cripples daily mutilated in the coal mines, this would prove a comfortable maintenance; these doors of life and death would then be attended by men of experience—the workmen in the mines would be secured—the children of tender years (now employed) would receive that education so necessary to form them into good and useful members of society, fitting them for the various stations in which providence may place them—the parochial rates would be reduced, and those fatal catastrophes which have so long separated husbands from their wives, parents from their children, and children from their parents, would then cease.

At Harraton colliery, June 13, 1817, ten persons of one family named Hills, were killed by the explosion, viz:— the grandfather, 2 sons, and 7 grandsons. On the 3rd of August 1830, an explosion took place at Jarrow, when upwards of 40 lives were lost.

O hearken unto our prayer, and let the cries of the widows and the fatherless enter your house.

> In the dark gloomy mine,
>   Where horror is reigning,
> The poor trapper boy,
>   Forlorn, sits complaining;
> Behind the trap door
>   He is doom'd there to sit
> For twelve hours, oft more
>   In the gloomy coal pit.
>
> Spare, spare a penny,
> Spare, spare a penny,
> One penny a chaldron.
> Save the poor trapper boy.
>
> My father and brothers,
>   And kindred so brave,
> By the blast of the mine
>   Lie low in one grave:
> My mother's a widow,
>   A stranger to joy,
> No comfort has left
>   But her poor trapper boy.
>   Spare, spare, &c.
>
> Coal owners are cruel,
>   Coal viewers much worse;
> Upon their fell av'rice
>   Hang heaven's dire curse,
> For placing with children
>   The power to destroy
> Fathers, brothers, and kindred,
>   And the poor trapper boy.
>   Spare, spare, &c.
>
> Ye of Britain's fair isle,
>   Humanity's dwelling,

To relieve the oppress'd
    All others excelling:
The poor climbing sweep
    You no longer employ,
O! dry up the tears
    Of the poor trapper boy.
        Spare, spare, &c.

From the rude northern blast,
    And the stormy winds blowing,
From the cold pinching frost,
    Hail, sleeting, and snowing,
By a warm fireside,
    Your friends you enjoy,
Feel, feel, for the colliers,
    And the poor trapper boy.
        Spare, spare, &c.

Ye rulers of Britain,
    Who set the slave free,
When sitting in judgment
    Have mercy on me,
The God that you worship
    Forbids to destroy
Fathers, brothers, and kindred,
    And the poor trapper boy.
        Spare, spare, &c.

But on that dread day,
    When all shall assemble
Before the great judge
    How the guilty will tremble,
Who, for lucre, gave children
    The power to destroy
Fathers, brothers, and kindred,
    And the poor Trapper Boy.
        Spare, spare, &c.

The 1842 report of the Children's Employment Commission noted that in South Staffordshire children as young as seven were employed in mines, in South Wales children as young as four. Of trapper-children the report said:

The trappers sit in a little hole scooped out for them in the side of the gates behind each door, where they sit with a string in their hands attached to the door, and pull it open the moment they hear the corves (i.e. carriages for conveying the coal) at hand, and the moment it has passed they let the door fall to, which it does of its own weight. . . . They have nothing else to do; but, as their office must be performed from the repassing of the first to the passing of the last corve during the day, they are in the pit the whole time it is worked, frequently above twelve hours a day. They sit, moreover, in the dark, often with a damp floor to stand on, and exposed necessarily to drafts. It is a most painful thing to contemplate the dull dungeonlike life these little creatures are doomed to spend—a life, for the most part, passed in solitude, damp, and darkness.[15]

The explosion at Jarrow in 1830 was one of many such catastrophes to be reported in broadsides. Four years earlier another explosion there killed thirty-four people. It too was reported in a broadside.[16]

Abolition of slavery in the British Empire began in 1833. In 1834 legislation was passed to fine anyone who forced or allowed a child under the age of ten to climb and sweep chimneys.

The printer of the ballad is identified only as Kay. C. J. Hunt gives Thomas Kay active in Newcastle in 1829–30, four or so years earlier than the presumed date of the ballad. I have made a few changes in punctuation of the prose.

The White Slave;
Or, the Factory Girl's Last Day

Four or five months back there was a girl of a poor man's that I was called to visit; it was poorly; it had attended a mill, and I was obliged to relieve the father in the course of my office (that of assistant overseer,) in consequence of the bad health of the child; by-and-by it went back to work again; and one day he came to me with tears in his eyes. I said, "What is the matter, Thomas?" He said, "My little girl is dead." I said, "When did she die?" He said, "In the night; and what breaks my heart is this. She went to the mill in the morning, she was not able to do her work, and a little boy said he would assist her if she would give him a halfpenny on Saturday; I said I would give him a penny." But at night when the child went home, perhaps about a quarter of a mile, it fell down several times on the road through exhaustion, till at length it reached its father's door with difficulty, and it never spoke audibly afterwards; it died in the night. I judge she might be ten years old.

'Twas on a winter's morning,
The weather wet and wild,

Three hours before the dawning,
    The father roused his child;
Her daily morsel bringing,
    The darksome room he paced,
And cried, "The bell is ringing,
    My hapless darling, haste!"

"Father, I'm up, but weary,
    I scarce can reach the door,
And long the way and dreary,
    O carry me once more!
To help us we've no mother,
    You've no employment nigh,
They killed my little brother,
    Like him I'll work—and die!"

Her wasted form seemed nothing,
    The load was at his heart;
The sufferer he kept soothing
    Till at the mill they part.
The overlooker met her,
    As to her frame she crept,
And with his thong he beat her,
    And cursed her as she wept.

Alas! what hours of sorrow
    Made up her latest day;
Those hours that brought no morrow,
    They slowly passed away;
It seem'd, as she grew weaker,
    The threads the oftener broke
The rapid wheels ran quicker,
    And heavier fell the stroke.

The sun had long descended,
    But night brought no repose;
Her day began and ended,
    As cruel tyrants chose.
At length a little neighbour,
    Her halfpenny she paid,
To take her last hour's labour,
    While by her frame she laid.

> At last, the engine ceasing,
>   The captive homeward rush'd;
> She thought her strength increasing—
>   'Twas hope her spirit flush'd:
> She left, but oft she tarried,
>   She fell and rose no more,
> Till by her comrades carried,
>   She reached her father's door.
>
> All night, with tortur'd feeling,
>   He watched his speechless child;
> And close beside her kneeling,
>   She knew him not nor smil'd.
> Again the factory's ringing,
>   Her last perceptions tried;
> When from her straw-bed springing,
>   *"'Tis time!"* she shrieked, and died!
>
> That night a chariot pass'd her,
>   While on the ground she lay;
> The daughters of her master
>   An evening visit pay—
> Their tender hearts were sighing
>   As Negro wrongs were told;
> While the white slave was dying,
>   Who gain'd their father's gold!

Nothing is known of the origin of the ballad. The named printer in copies I have seen was Thomas Ford of Chesterfield. He was active as a printer from 1830 to 1840, printing from Irongate, the address for "The White Slave," from 1833 onward. He was the publisher of a satirical magazine, *Figaro in Chesterfield*, and of a history of Chesterfield. I have changed punctuation slightly in the ballad.

In another printing, under the title "The Factory Girl's Last Day," the ballad was used as an offering by people asking for charity. The verses were followed by an appeal:

> Friends—It is with feelings of the deepest regret that we are at present compelled, for the support of ourselves and families, to offer these few but simple verses to your notice, trusting, at the same time, you will be pleased to purchase this paper, it being the only means left at present to support the tender thread of our existence, and keep us and our families from the utter starvation which at present surrounds us.

The term "white slave" drew upon the concern over Negro slavery. It was especially associated with Richard Oastler, the leader of the "ten-hours movement" to limit the hours of work for children to that time. In a letter to the *Leeds Mercury* in 1830 he spoke of "the little white slaves of the factories." His enemies among factory owners, managers, and politicians called him "the king of the factory children." He accepted the sobriquet. In the middle 1840s, upon his release from imprisonment for debt, a broadside ballad used the title to celebrate him and his work. See the endnote for slight added information on him.[17] Negro slavery in the British Empire began to be abolished with the Emancipation Act of 1833, and the first significant act in the amelioration of industrial slavery came with factory legislation in the same year. The essential truth of the narrative of "The White Slave" is indicated in the government reports mentioned in the introduction to this section.

Naked Truth

Tax-gatherers now how thick they swarm,
Around the man who rents a farm,
Like hungry wasps when one is fled,
Another flutters round his head;
The overseer first haunts the door,
I want some money for the poor,
Steam engines now their work can do,
And they must be maintained by you.
Scarce has he turned his back before
Some other person raps the door,
The church has been repaired of late,
And there is now a larger rate;
Next quarter day appears in view,
Presenting rates and taxes new,
The holy priest brings up the rear,
Waiting the farmer's back to shear,
Rent day is fix'd, the farmer goes,
And tells the landlord all his woes;
The landlord hears but feels no more
Than flinty rocks when tempests roar,
Well farmer if you cannot pay,
I would not wish for you to stay,
For other people can be found,
That would be glad to have the ground.
The farmer now with heavy heart,
 Presents his landlord but a part,

The landlord grumbling waits awhile,
The farmer spends his days in toil,
The night affords him no relief,
He sleepless lies in pain and grief;
On the rising sun new troubles are seen,
Money he wants for church or queen.

The farmer like a horse once good,
Has tried and struggled all he could,
But still the heavy burden galls,
Till tired and weary down he falls.
His masters now around him stand,
But none will lend an helping hand,
Nor take away the heavy yoke,
But each with whip will give a stroke,
The landlord first the whip applies,
Get up you lazy wretch he cries,
Your burden once with ease you bore,
And paid your landlord, queen and poor;
The parson in a milder tone,
Gives the next whip and cries you drone,
Don't in the mire there struggling lie,
For if you do you'll surely die,
The poor old horse now tries in vain
To stand upon his legs again:
But weighty burdens press him round
And keep him prostrate on the ground;
The landlord cries what shall we do,
I'll have his hide and carcase too;
The parson cries, dead or alive
I swear I will not lose my tythe.

But now in plainer terms to speak,
What could a farmer do but break,
When all his corn, cattle and hay
Will not the rent and taxes pay.
How can the farmer's house be fed?
How can the tradesmen's bills be paid?
If trade continues to decay,
And goods grow cheaper every day.
The bailiff then like a cruel bear
Seizes the stock, nor does he care

> If every farmer was the same,
> Distress and misery are his game,
> The auctioneer without remorse,
> Sells every sheep, and cow, and horse,
> And if the stock the rent wont pay,
> The very beds he takes away.
> Thus after spending years in toil,
> The landlord bears away the spoil,
> The farmer he turns out of door,
> Nor cares to see his face no more.
> So like a landlord in the town,
> Who keeps the Lamb, or Bear, or Crown,
> When the last penny he has got,
> Turns out of door the drunken sot.
>
> Printed for T. Johnson, Hull

T. Johnson of Hull has not been identified. Assuming that he is the author, he took his ballad seriously and revised it at least once over a period of some years. An earlier version, entitled "The Times" (Tax gatherers . . .) was written while William IV was still on the throne. Its sixteenth couplet says:

> The rising sun new troubles bring,
> Money he wants for church and king.

The succeeding two couplets in "The Times" likewise involve the king, and are abandoned in revision.

The major difference between the two versions is that "The Times" begins and ends the horse simile within four lines, whereas in "Naked Truth" the same four are the start for twenty-four lines. Following the line "And goods grow cheaper every day," "The Times" has eight lines that are rejected in revision:

> The landlord like the Egyptian king,
> Wishes the farmer all to bring;
> Gather the straw where e'er he will,
> The tale of brick he must fulfill,
> And if the rent cannot be found,
> He sends the cruel bailiffs round,
> At once to seize upon the stock,
> Horses and cows and corn and flock.

Lastly "The Times" finishes weakly, without the new comparison in the last four lines of "Naked Truth" and with "hopes" instead of "cares" in the last line: "And hopes to see his face no more."

I have taken the liberty of separating "Naked Truth" into three parts. "The Times" is printed as quatrains. I have also made a few changes in punctuation, and in the sixth couplet from the end I have substituted "remorse" for "reserve," following the rhyme in "The Times." "The Times" was printed in Highworth, Wiltshire. No printer is given for "Naked Truth."

The Lucky Factory Boy

The sun had set behind yon hill,
    Across the dreary moor,
When, weary and lame, a boy there came,
    Up to a Factory door;
Can you tell me if there may be
    One that will me employ,
To strip or grind, or weave or wind,
    Or be a factory boy.

My father's dead, my mother's left
    With six children very small,
But what is worse for mother still,
    I'm oldest of them all;
Though little I am, I'll work like a man,
    If I could get employ,
To strip or grind, or spin or mind,
    Or be a factory boy.

And if that you no boy do want,
    One favour I've to ask,
If you'll shelter me till break of day,
    From this cold winter's blast,
At break of day I'd trudge away,
    Elsewhere to seek employ,
To strip and grind, to weave and wind,
    And to be a factory boy.

The master's wife cried, "Try the lad,
    Let him no further seek."
"O do, O do," the daughter cried,
    While tears ran down her cheek;

"For those who'd work it's hard to want
    And wander for employ,
Don't let him go, but let him stay,
    And be our factory boy."

The factory boy grew up a man,
    This good old couple died,
And left the boy with the mill they had,
    And their daughter for his bride;
The boy that was, now the master is,
    Oft thinks and smiles with joy,
On the lucky day he came that way,
    To be a factory boy.

The factory boy was as lucky in ballad history as he was in life. Before he was a factory boy he was a farmer's boy, and he came up to the farmer's door seeking "to plough and sow and reap and mow / And be a farmer's boy." Often his mother had five children instead of six, and he promised that "though little I'd work as hard as a Turk." "The Lucky Farmer's Boy (or "The Farmer's Boy") remained popular as a broadside at least through the 1850s.[18]

S. Baring Gould in *English Minstrelsie* says that "The Farmer's Boy" was "one of the most popular and widely known folk songs in England."[19] Robert Bell in *Ancient Poems, Ballads, and Songs of the Peasantry of England* (1857), offers the opinion that it was probably written in the beginning of the 1700s.[20] In what year an enterprising broadside printer substituted "factory" for "farmer" is not known. *Oxford English Dictionary* gives first use of "factory" in the attributive sense as 1802. It seems unlikely that "The Lucky Factory Boy" emerged before the 1830s. The printing used here is by Harkness of Preston, who was printing from 1840 to 1866 (Neuburg).

The same progress from farm boy to factory boy seems to have occurred with "Rosetta and Her Gay Ploughboy" and "Mary and the Handsome Factory Boy." Harkness is the one noticed printer of the ballad under the latter title.

The Factory Child

I hear the blythe voices of children at play,
And the sweet birds rejoicing on every green spray;
On all things the bright beams of summer hath smil'd,
But they smile not on me the poor Factory Child.

> The gay spirits of childhood to me they deny,
> And the fair path of learning, I never must try,
> A companion of creatures whom guilt hath defiled,
> Oh! who does not pity the poor Factory Child.
>
> Oh! who would not mourn for a victim like me,
> A young heart-broken *slave* in the land of the free,
> Hardly tasked, and often beaten, oppress'd and revil'd,
> Such, such is the fate of the poor Factory Child.
>
> In the dead of the night, when you take your sweet sleep,
> Through the dark dismal street to my labour I creep,
> To the din of the loom till my brain seems wild,
> I return an unfortunate Factory Child.
>
> The bright bloom of health has forsaken my cheek,
> My spirits are gone, and my young limbs grown weak;
> Oh! Ye rich and ye mighty, let sympathy mild
> Appeal to your hearts for the poor Factory Child.
>
> Oh! Pity my sufferings ere yet the cold tomb
> Succeed my loathed prison, its task and gloom,
> And the clods of the valley untimely are piled
> O'er the pale wasted form of the Factory Child.

On a recently seen broadside printing, issued by H. Wardman of Bradford, the author of the ballad is named as "Miss A. Strickland," and the ballad has been "received from George Strickland, Esq., M. P. for the West Riding." Sir George Strickland (later Cholmley, 1782–1874) represented the West Riding from December 1832 to June 1841. He and his wife Mary were childless, and Miss Strickland was perhaps a niece. Wardman is known to have printed in the 1840s, and the printing used here, by Harkness of Preston, could not date earlier than 1840 when Harkness began printing. The ballad presumably dates from 1840–41.

Strickland was the author of a small book, *Discourse on the Poor Laws,* published in 1827. He took there a sternly realistic and religious view of the laws, quoting Deuteronomy, "the poor shall never cease out of the land," and Thessalonians, "that if any will not work neither shall he eat." He was very much concerned that the poor rates borne by the rich should not be insupportable. Perhaps his views mellowed in succeeding years, or perhaps they were equally stern about insupportable factory conditions for child labor.

The title of the ballad as printed by Wardman is "The Factory Child's Complaint" and line 3 gives "have" instead of "hath."

Stitch Goes the Needle!

Females work too hard I'm told,
    Stitch goes the needle;
A tale or two I will unfold,
    Stitch goes the needle.
At the East and the West,
I'm told it is the same, sirs,
That females work and get no rest,
    Stitch goes the needle.
Females work too hard I'm told,
    Stitch goes the needle;
A tale or two I will unfold,
    Stitch goes the needle.

The milliners just o'er the way,
    Stitch goes the needle.
They work by night and work by day,
    Stitch goes the needle.
With sallow cheek and sunken eye,
To earn a scanty living try,
'Tis thus they slave until they die,
    Stitch goes the needle.
            Females work, &c.

Ladies must dress for the ball,
    Stitch goes the needle.
Or else they would not go at all,
    Stitch goes the needle.
Thus it is to dress the gay,
They have to toil and labour,
For which they get such horrid pay,
    Stitch goes the needle.
            Females work, &c.

Shame upon employers all,
    Stitch goes the needle,
That starve or make the virtuous fall,
    Stitch goes the needle.

> On what they earn their lives depend,
> And the pay is so much cut down,
> That death creeps in and there's an end,
> Stitch goes the needle.
> Females work, &c.

In *Hard Times, Social Realism in Victorian Art* (1987), Julian Treuherz says that the sempstress was "the most commonly depicted social realist subject in Victorian painting," a fact owing immediately, he says, to the success of Richard Redgrave's painting of a sempstress in 1844.[21] Redgrave's painting was inspired in part by Thomas Hood's "The Song of the Shirt," and Hood's poem was inspired by press accounts in 1843 of a woman named Biddell who had been charged with pawning articles belonging to her employer. In the course of proceedings against her it was disclosed that she received sevenpence a pair for making trousers (rather than shirts) and that the most she could earn in a week of working fourteen hours a day was seven shillings—£18 a year. She had herself and two children to support, her husband having died the previous January.[22] Her seven shillings was less than the starvation wage condemned in the contemporary ballad "The Present Times, or Eight Shillings a Week" (quoted on page 251). On 27 October the *Times* had a blistering leader on the subject, *Punch* took up the matter, and Hood published his poem in the Christmas issue of the latter journal. Given the immense popularity of Hood's poem, it turns up much less frequently in broadside ballad collections than one might suppose it would. It was occasionally imitated, as in "The Song of the Truck" ("truck" referring to factory payment in goods, often of inferior quality and exorbitant price, in lieu of wages) and "The Song of Work" (a hymn to the nobility of labor, written by John Parnell, a man connected with a polite literary society and with a printing firm named Parnell).

The date of the present ballad is unknown. No printer is given on the single printing seen. Another ballad, "The Distressed Sempstress," dating from 1845 or earlier, is prefaced in one or two printings with the words, "A great number of these young women (after twelve hours hard labour) being without friends, are compelled to walk the streets at night, in order to make out a miserable existence." Another, "White Slaves of England," says that missionary work properly begins at home. It begins thus:

> O England that boasts of her riches so rare,
> And every country braves,
> Where is thy boasted freedom now
> When women are thy slaves.

The Hungry Army

When I was young and in my prime,
I thought I'd go and join the line,
And as a soldier cut a shine,
   In a lot called the hungry army;
Said the sergeant you are just the chap,
And placed a knapsack on my back,
Then sent me off to Ballarat,
   To fight in the hungry army.

    Sound the bugle, blow the horn,
    Fight for glory, night and morn:
    Hungry soldiers, ragged and torn,
       Just returned from the army.

March, boys, march, the way is on before us,
Shout, boys, shout, and join me in the chorus,
March, boys, march, the foe is still advancing,
   Cheer, boys, cheer, for the new and happy land.

I went to drill on one fine day,
The wind was rather strong that way,
In fact it blew the lot away,
   This glorious hungry army;
I've got a medal as you see,
The workhouse presented it to me,
For hanging fast to a rotten tree,
   When the wind took the hungry army.

They cut my hair with a knife and fork,
And curled it with a cabbage-stalk,
And fed me on some cabbage broth,
   To fight in the hungry army;
They served it out in a large tin can,
A tea-spoonful to every man,
I got so fat I couldn't stand
   To fight in the hungry army.

They sent me out to drill recruits,
But they kick'd me with their hob-nail'd boots,
Oh take, oh, take away these brutes,
    Of this glorious hungry army;
Now, kind friends, I must be off,
I think I smell the cabbage broth;
Here comes old general Howl and Scoff,
    The head of the hungry army.

Ballarat—city in Victoria Province, Australia, where gold was discovered in 1851; fresh troops were sent out from England in 1854 in consequence of armed conflict between miners and legal administrators

The last line of the chorus, "cheer, boys, cheer, for the new and happy land," comes from Charles Mackay's emigration ballad "Cheer, Boys, Cheer"; see pages 409–10. As a whole the ballad draws upon an Irish ballad of the same title. In the latter ballad a farm worker who joins the hungry army is at first flattered and cajoled, but presently floggings begin, and on the troopship to the wars he and the other soldiers are stifled and starved. Soon enough he is wounded, and then discharged, and he thinks he is likely to end in the workhouse. He will always remember the day "when I went to enlist in the hungry army."[23] "The Beggar" on page 304 comments on the hungry army.

God Speed the Good Ship; Or, the English Emigrant!

God speed the keel of the trusty ship
    That bears you from our shore,
There is little chance that you'll ever glance
    On our chalky sea-beach more:
You are right to seek a far off earth,
    You are right to boldly strive,
Where labour does not pine in dearth,
    And the honest poor may thrive.

God speed ye all, ye hopeful band,
    O'er your boundless path of blue,
But you'll never forget your English land,
    Though wealth may gladden the new.

You'll sometimes think of the hawthorn leaves,
   And the dog-rose peeping through,
And you'll sometimes think of the harvest sheaves
   Though the wheat was not for you;
You'll sometimes think of the busy plough,
   And the merry beating flail,
And you'll sometimes dream of the dappled cow,
   And the clink of the milking pail.

You'll call to mind good neighbour Hind,
   And the widow down the lane,
And you'll wonder if the old man's dead,
   Or the widow wed again:
You'll sometimes think of the village spire,
   The churchyard green and fair,
And perhaps you'll sigh with drooping eye,
   If you've left a loved one there.

Perhaps you leave a white-haired sire,
   A sister or a brother,
Perhaps your heart has dared to part
   For ever from a mother;
If so, then many a time and oft
   Your better thoughts will roam,
And memory's pinion strong and soft,
   Will fly to your English home.

The ballad is by Eliza Cook (1812–89), author of much sentimental verse. She was born in London, the youngest of eleven or more children of a brazier there. During her childhood the family moved to Sussex, and her father farmed. She was said to be self-educated. She had early success writing poetry, and in her middle years she was widely known. From 1849 to 1854 she edited *Eliza Cook's Journal*, a family paper. A number of her poems were taken up by broadside printers. They include "I'm Afloat," "Mother Be Proud of Your Boy in Blue," "The Old Arm Chair," and "Song of the Haymakers."[24]

"God Speed the Good Ship" was omitted from collections of her poetry in the late 1850s, early 1860s. It is given under the title "On Seeing Some Agricultural Emigrants Embark" in her *Poetical Works* (1870). It was written in the 1850s, very likely in response to Charles Mackay's ballad "Cheer, Boys, Cheer!" The two ballads, both apparently very popular as broadsides, show two faces of emigration, one looking backward, the other forward. The verses of Mackay's begin thus:

> Cheer—boys—cheer, no more of idle sorrow,
>   Courage, true hearts shall bear us on our way,
> Hope points before and shows the bright tomorrow,
>   Let us forget the darkness of today.

Sheet music for the Mackay ballad came in 1852 or earlier, with music by Henry Russell; that for the Cook ballad came in 1855, with music likewise by Russell. Russell wrote music for two other emigration ballads, and in the 1840s he and Mackay collaborated on a cheerful entertainment called *Far West, or the Emigrant's Progress*. It seems altogether likely that "Cheer, Boys, Cheer!" made its first appearance there. Russell set other of Eliza Cook's poems to music, including her most famous poem, "The Old Arm Chair," and "The Old Clock."

Eliza Cook's concern for the poor is evident in many poems. In "Song of the Spirit of Poverty" she describes the boy of withered spine and the girl of hollow staring eyes, and thinks that wealth and care would have made them different. The spirit sees the well-fed, easeful woman:

> If I'd held your cheeks by as close a pinch,
>   Would that flourishing rose be found?
> If I'd doled you a crust out, inch by inch,
>   Would your arms have been so round?

Eliza Cook wanted change, but without upheaval, and she relied upon God in the same manner and in fairly much the same sense that Charles Mackay relied upon courage, true hearts, and hope. In "Stanzas to My Starving Kin in the North," she wrote:

> Women and men of this brave old soil!
> I weep that starvation should guerdon your toil;
> But I glory to see ye—proudly mute—
> Showing *souls* like the hero, not *fangs*, like the brute.
> Oh! keep courage within; be the Britons ye are;
> He who driveth the storm hath His hand on the star!
> England to England's sons shall be true,
> And "God and the People" will carry ye through!

The poem was written on 3 January 1863 in aid of the Fund for the Relief of the Distressed Operatives in the Cotton Districts.[25] The immediate cause of the distress was the naval blockade by the North in the American Civil War.

As printed in *Poetical Works*, "God Speed the Good Ship" has a number of minor differences from the broadside form used here. Occasional words and phrases differ, as with "often think of the blackthorn leaves" in stanza 2. The chief difference is that the four stanzas are twelve lines each, with the four-line refrain constituting lines 9–12 in each stanza. Line 3 of the refrain is, "But you'll never forget your own, Old land."

5

Maidens and Lovers

I

If nineteenth-century broadside ballads about maidens and lovers have any special characteristic, it is that they more often involve ordinary believable life, including poverty, than did their predecessors and that—perhaps less certainly— their language tends to be plainer. Up through the eighteenth century, tales of knightly, courtly, and pastoral love abound, unconcerned with poverty. There are exceptions, notably in ballads that tell of the king, nobleman, knight, or squire who takes a poor girl for his bride: "King Cophetua and the Beggar Maid," "Patient Grissel" (who marries a marquis), "The Beggar's Daughter of Bednall Green" (who wins a knight before even she learns that her father is a man of wealth and honor), and "The Virtuous Milk-Maid" (who marries a squire).[1] But the first three of these are in the way of being amazing tales, and the fourth is a very pretty one. It may be the case that "The Beggar's Daughter of Bednall Green" survives into the nineteenth century (in severely truncated form) because beggary and Bethnal Green were increasingly harsh realities. It is certainly the case that "The Virtuous Milk-Maid" survives only with its prettinesses about kings and princes and Venus and Cupid stripped away, transformed into "Squire and Milkmaid" given below. To the very end of the eighteenth century, broadside balladry was strewn with tales of Strephon, Chloe, Sylvan, and Phyllis, whose only pains are the pains of love.[2] Their replacements show a difference.

The difference sometimes seems small enough. Together such titles as "The Lady and Weaver," "Lady Who Fell in Love with a Prentice Boy," "The Lady's Loyalty to Her Bonny Labouring Boy," "The Lady Lov'd Her Father's Groom," and "The Blooming Lady Worth £500,000 and Her Footman" hardly suggest ordinary life. But the lady with the groom is a parson's daughter, and she and her young man delight in jumping Jim Crow together—in allusion to the song that the American Thomas Rice brought to England in the 1830s, and she hopes to enjoy married life in a small cottage in Woking. And the blooming lady is a real woman, wife of a Norfolk M.P., who is identified by initial in the ballad, with his name completed by hand by an interested reader of one copy of the ballad.

It is often the case that the narratives of such nineteenth century relationships are still fairly amazing. In John Morgan's "The Farmer's Daughter and the Gay Ploughboy," father has violent prejudice:

> He fixed his eyes to her surprise,
> And swore by all the powers,
> That he was told the strumpet bold,
> Along with poverty did toy.

He locks daughter in the cellar for fifteen months and feeds her on bread and water. Then luckily he dies, and she inherits, and she and her ploughboy live happily ever after. But alongside this ballad stands "William and Dinah," another amazing tale. It undergoes amusing transformation. It tells of a double suicide the romantic melodrama of which is insufficiently leavened by plain and common names for the two lovers and by the fact that Dinah's father is a liquor merchant who wants a mere moneyed man "worth ten thousand a year" for her.

> Dinah wrote her love a letter with all haste and speed,
> And told her sweet William what her father had said,
> Farewell, my sweet William, for ever farewell,
> How dearly I loved you there is no tongue can tell.
>
> As William was walking the groves all around,
> He found his dear Dinah lay dead on the ground,
> With a cup of strong poison, and a note lying by,
> 'Twas my cruel father that caus'd me to die.
>
> He kiss'd her cold lips as she lay on the floor,
> And he call'd her his jewel ten thousand times o'er;
> Then he drank up the poison like a lover so brave,
> There's William and Dinah both lie in one grave.

Thus the ballad stood as published perhaps in the 1820s. Catnach listed it in his 1832 catalogue. The effective shift in the melodrama was, presently, to make it funnier than it already was. The poet and dramatist E. L. Blanchard (1820–89) wrote a Cockneyfied version, "Vilikins and His Dinah," for Henry Mayhew's brief farce *The Wandering Minstrel*, probably for the revival of the piece in 1853. Not counting the moral that he tacks on at the end, the last three verses go thus (the verses are sung, the italicized lines are spoken):

> *This is what the indignant parient replied, —I represent the father.*
> Go, boldest daughter, the parient replied,
> If you don't consent to be this here young man's bride,
> I'll give your large fortune to the nearest of kin,

        And you shan't have the benefit of one single pin.
           Singing Too-ral-loo, &c.

Now comes the epiflabbergastrinum of the lovier.
        As Vilikins vas valking the garden around—
The aforesaid front garden,
           He espied his dear Dinah, lying dead upon the ground,
           A cup of cold pison it lied by her side,
           And a Billy Dux stating 'twas by pison she died!
Taken inwardly.   Singing Too-ral-loo, &c.

This is what the lovier did.
        Then he kissed her cold corps a thousand times o' er,
        He called her his dear Dinah—although she vas no more!
        He swallowed the pison, like a lovier so brave—
        And Vilikins and his Dinah, lies buried in one grave!
Both on 'em,   Singing Too-ral-loo, &c.

The ballad was a very considerable success on both stage and street. John Ashton says in *Modern Street Ballads* that it was "as popular as any street song I remember."[3]

II

One aspect of rich man/poor girl that was of special interest in the nineteenth century was prostitution. The authors of the discussion of prostitution in London in Mayhew's *London Labour and the London Poor* accepted the opinion that there were eighty thousand prostitutes in London in the middle 1850s. The estimate was generous enough to include all kept women; and with a city population not much above two million, it thus labelled as prostitute one female in ten above about age eight. The figure was much disputed, but what was not in dispute to many observers both native and foreign was that prostitution in London had long since become a scandal.[4] The subject as social phenomenon, social scourge, is itself rarely the central issue of a broadside ballad, the only example I have noted being "Burning Them Out," which speaks with moral enthusiasm of assaults by a mob on a number of London brothels in the 1830s.

Even those ballads that depict individual prostitutes seem fewer in number than one might expect. Where there is condemnation, it is more likely to be directed against the man than against the woman. One ballad that takes a stern view of the prostitute is "The Story of Sinful Sally," written in about 1796 by a woman named Sally—Sally More, sister of Hannah More. It tells of a modest village maiden who marries modestly and who then succumbs to the temptations of rich Sir William.

He sets her up in London, and presently she sinks into indiscriminate prostitution, thievery, and disease, and then she begins to turn to God. Copies of this ballad were probably given away in their thousands, and perhaps it sold well; but it rarely appears in broadside collections, and it may not have made much appeal.[5] In contrast is "The Village Beauty," given below, which tells much the same tale, directs its anger in first line and last against the aristocratic villain, and seems to have sold widely and well.

One of the most badly written ballads on any subject, and yet in its way quite affecting, is the rarely seen "Found Dying in Our Streets." The title is the refrain for four of the eight stanzas. The ballad tells of a poor milliner, overworked ("Hard work is killing her, poor girl"), and sole support of her mother.

> There came one rich and wealthy too
> Who deceived her with his smile
> He won her from her mother's side
> He'd no pity for her child
> She was tempted by his flattery
> He spoke with words so sweet
> There is many a poor fond sister dear
> Found dying in the street.

He abandons her, and apparently after some months of prostitution she dies in childbirth.

Other ballads on prostitution are unconcerned with the wealth of the man involved. "Murder at Cambridge" tells of a poor prostitute murdered there. It sees that poverty drove her into prostitution, and it commiserates with her. Another ballad of the sort, "Copy of Verses on the Dreadful Murder at Finsbury," offers a general thought:

> There are many poor girls in the streets of London
> Who are neglected when they are young
> They would have made as bright a woman
> As ever shone beneath the sun.

Ballads on seamstresses suggest that wages for them are so low that they turn to prostitution as additional or sole support (see pages 405–6). Still other ballads such as "The Fancy Lad" and "Artichokes & Cauliflowers," both given below, and "Sally Carter," are neutral or lighthearted in their treatment of prostitution in relation to poverty.

Of all sorts of ballads about maidens and lovers, whether concerned with highborn/lowborn or solely with the poor or the presumed poor, the sort least likely to deal directly with poverty is the racy or bawdy one. In contrast to "The Lady and the Welsh Ploughboy," given below, is "The Old Lady & the Page."[6] The first lady laments that difference in status, expressed in the ballad in economic terms, should be a barrier to love and marriage. The old lady uses difference in status, measured by what money can buy, to provide sexual pleasure for herself and something else for the page. In the second ballad, difference in status is merely a piquant aspect of irregular sexual conduct. In "Poverty's No Sin" and "The Crossing Sweeper," the first given below, the impoverished situations of the chief characters are settings for true love. In any number of racy ballads about hiring fairs, the young men and women who nominally go to the fairs to hire themselves out are preoccupied with easy sexual conjunctions. Poverty is an appropriate background—if riskily sentimental or melodramatic—to show off true love or to expose false; it is mainly ignored or forgotten in tales of sexual jollities outside marriage. A late-noted exception to the rule is "The Dairy Maid," a mildly racy ballad printed in 1791. The once innocent young woman is thrown on the street by her master when she gives him the clap:

> Then from a quid to half a crown,
> With dirty fellows must lay down,
> Tho' much against my will.

Squire and Milkmaid; or, Blackberry Fold

> It's of a rich squire in Bristol doth dwell,
> There are ladies of honour that love him well,
> But all was in vain, in vain was said,
> For he was in love with a charming milkmaid.
>
> As the squire and his sister did sit in the hall,
> And as they were talking to one and to all,
> And as they were singing each other a song,
> Pretty Betsy, the milkmaid, came tripping along.
>
> Do you want any milk? pretty Betsy did say,
> O yes, said the squire; step in, pretty maid.
> It is you, fair body, that I do adore,
> Was there ever a body so wounded before?
>
> O hold your tongue, squire, and let me go free,
> Do not make your game on my poverty;
> There are ladies of honour more fitter for you,
> Than I, a poor milkmaid, brought up from the cows.

A ring from his finger he instantly drew,
And right in the middle he broke it in two;
And half he gave to her, as I have been told,
And they both went a walking to Blackberry Fold.

O Betsy, O Betsy, let me have my will,
So constant a squire I'll prove to you still;
And if you deny me, in this open field,
Why, the first time I'll force, and make you to yield.

With hugging and struggling, poor Betsy got free,
Saying, you never shall have your will of me;
I'll protect my own virtue, as I would my life,
And drew from her bosom a large dagger knife.

Then with her own weapon she run him quite through,
And home to her master like lightning she flew,
Saying, O, my dear master, with tears in her eyes,
I have wounded the squire, and I'm afraid dead he lies.

The coach was got ready, the squire brought home,
The doctor was sent for to heal up the wound,
Poor Betsy was sent for—the gay maiden fair—
Who wounded the squire, drove his heart in a snare.

The parson was sent for, this couple to wed,
And she did enjoy the sweet marriage bed;
It's better to be honest if ever so poor,
For he's made her his lady instead of his whore.

I

The ballad is one of the most impressive of an old-fashioned sort among nineteenth-century broadside ballads, and it is also one of the most varied in its verses. The two earliest printings noticed are those by Theophilus Bloomer of Birmingham, who printed in the years 1817–25, and John Pitts, who issued his version (under the title "Young Squire") in the years to 1819 when he was at 14 Great St. Andrew's Street. Both printings are notably careless, and apparently derive from individually careless sources. Later prints display similar faults. No apparent path leads to the most satisfactory printing seen, the late one used here, issued by Henry Disley from 57 High Street, St. Giles's, sometime in the years 1860–78.

The virtues of Disley's printing over other versions are readily apparent. The second couplet in the first stanza is sometimes printed thus, losing its rhyme:

> But all was in vain, O it all was vain,
> For he was in love with a charming milk-maid.

Or it goes thus in a printing by Williams of Portsea, who printed in the 1820s and later:

> But all was in vain as I do declare,
> For he fell in love with a milk maid so fair.

Other printings do not give all of stanzas 7 and 8. Sometimes the printing is obviously defective, making a five-line stanza that begins with the first line of stanza seven and then goes on with stanza eight. In other versions the printer makes a more or less passable four-line stanza from the two stanzas. Bloomer's is one of the less passable. The Williams printing goes thus:

> With hugging and struggling poor Betsy got free,
> And with his own weapon she pierced his body,
> And with his own weapon she pierced him thro',
> So home to her father like lightning she flew.

Betsy's weapon in this printing is the squire's rather than her own, and here though not elsewhere his weapon is identified as a "glittering sword." In Bloomer's version she wields a pair of scissors.

Two interesting variations occur with the last lines. The Williams printing avoids the word "whore."

> So he made her his lady he did adore,
> It's best to be virtuous if ever so poor.

Other printings give "w——" or "w——e." The last lines in Bloomer's version have the virtue of making some kind of sense of the squire's contradictory conduct in Blackberry Fold. In them the ballad proper ends with the quatrain in which Betsy is sent for. The quatrain is little different from the next-to-last stanza given here. Bloomer then provides a couplet in smaller type in which the sententious conclusion of most versions is replaced by a blunt explanation by the squire of his conduct.

> Now as she is honest, tho' ever so poor,
> I'll make her my wife instead of my whore.

One minor variation in some other printings that is better than Disley's version is the use of "lover" instead of "body" in the fourth line of the third stanza.

In 1904 Cecil Sharp recorded a much reduced, much altered version of the ballad from the singing of Mrs. Overd. In it "the young squire began to be rude" in the last line of stanza two, and Betsy shoots him with her pistol in the first line of stanza three. At the end of the sixth and last stanza, eleven years later, the squire has died and "left three small children by sweet Betsy's side." In 1906 Eva Ashton recorded a version in forty-four lines from the singing of Edmund Pack. The language is generally more slack than in Disley, and the ninth stanza in Disley becomes two four-line stanzas. Ashton offers the ballad as a Sussex song. In *Six Suffolk Folksongs* (1932), F. J. Moeran printed a truncated version of the ballad from the singing of two men. Here the ballad has become an altogether polite song. The squire protests his love, and Betsy thinks he is making game of her poverty; but he breaks the ring in two, and they send for the parson. The word whore is absent from all three recordings.[7]

II

"Squire and Milkmaid" had its origin in a mediocre eighteenth-century ballad called "The Virtuous Milk-Maid," known from garlands rather than from broadsides. In the printing quoted from here, "The Virtuous Milk-Maid" has twenty-six stanzas instead of Disley's ten, and it has a slightly incremental three-line refrain for each stanza.[8] It begins thus:

> Draw near you young lovers, and I'll let you know,
> That love it will creep where it dare not to go;
> Young Cupid and Venus together dost play,
> One wounds, and the other steals poor hearts away,
>   Crying, Ah! Ah! young Cupid,
>   Forbear to wound a squire, I am catched in a snare.
>   For love has entangled me I do declare.

The squire in the ballad is from Bloomsbury Square rather than from Bristol, and he and Nan rather than Betsy go walking to Blackmary's Hole rather than to Blackberry Fold. Nan runs the squire through with his rapier. The printer is not afraid of the word whore, and has Nan cry out, "I'll ne'er be whore, I will first lose my life." The final refrain offers the moral:

>   Crying, Ah! Ah! young virgins you see,
>   If you virtuous be, with right honesty,
>   You may be advanced to some high degree.

It would seem that "Squire and Milkmaid" is a rewriting of "The Virtuous Milk-Maid" by someone with the conscious intention of extracting a good ballad from an indifferent one, in considerable part by cutting out prettinesses and excessive dialogue. The narrative is the same, and some stanzas and couplets are little altered. The second and ninth stanzas of "The Virtuous Milk-Maid" go thus:

> There was a young squire in Bloomsbury Square,
> And many young ladies that loved him dear,
> Yet all their affections were nothing, 'tis said,
> For he was in love with a charming milk-maid.
> > Crying, Ah! Ah! &c.
>
> As he was making his pitiful moan,
> The damsel came by with a pretty soft tone,
> Do you want any milk, Mrs. Betty, she said,
> Yes, yes, said the squire, come in pretty maid,
> > Crying, Ah! Ah! . . .

Couplets from stanzas fourteen, nineteen, and twenty-one go thus:

> A ring from his finger he immediately took,
> And just in the middle the same he straight broke.
>
> And with it she pierc'd the young squire through,
> Then home to her master like lightning she flew.
>
> His coach was got ready, and soon was brought home,
> And surgeons were sent for to dress up his wound.

Such repeated material goes to make up about a third of the later ballad. Individual lines and phrases reappear as well.

It seems fairly certain that the transformation of "The Virtuous Milk-Maid" into "Squire and Milkmaid" was accomplished at a stroke. It also seems clear that subsequent small changes in "Squire and Milkmaid" were made— whether for good or for ill—without backward glances to "The Virtuous Milk-Maid." Bloomer's early version and others do preserve two rather good lines from "The Virtuous Milk-Maid" that are lost to Disley. When Nan flies home, she tells her master:

> Upon my poor body he grew very bold,
> I left him a bleeding in Blackmary's hole.

Bloomer gives:

> For on my fair body he began to grow bold,
> So I left him a bleeding in Blackberry Fold.

It does seem possible too that Bloomer's concluding couplet in reduced type is an echo of the italicized refrain that ends every stanza of the earlier ballad. The couplet is an intelligent variant that has not been seen in any other printing, and it sits oddly in a printing that in several respects is careless and unintelligent. Perhaps the capable transformer of the earlier ballad made two endings: Bloomer's couplet that echoes the use of refrain and the sententious quatrain that derives from the final refrain as quoted above.

Two early printings of "The Virtuous Milk-Maid" are held by the British Library and Cambridge University Library, and are provisionally dated 1760 by the libraries. They appear to be in some part garbled printings from a true or truer text, with the Cambridge version slightly more garbled than the British Library version and perhaps printed from it. Three later printings are held by the British Library. The first two are provisionally dated 1765 and 1780 by the Library—though to ordinary inspection they appear to be the same printing; the third is provisionally dated 1780 and varies slightly from the other two. These later printings correct several of the mistakes in the earlier printings, but they themselves fall into confusion in the stanzas of reconciliation at the end. Amid unsuccessful efforts to restore order, they do introduce a new good line in which Nan makes an initial disbelieving response to the squire's apology, saying, "And make not your pastime of my poverty." In "Squire and Milkmaid" this line becomes "Do not make your game on my poverty" and appears towards the beginning of the ballad.[9]

It is worth noting that Blackmary's Hole was a real place—sometimes called Blackmary's Well—situated near the Fleet River to the east of the road to Hampstead. It was about a mile from Bloomsbury Square, and in the eighteenth century it was in open country. In 1818 it was covered, and houses were built on the site. Henry Wheatley in *London Past and Present* (1891) says that the most likely explanation of the name was that a black woman named Mary Woolaston lived there in a hut in 1680 and rented water to people.[10]

III

Milkmaids were a popular subject of eighteenth- and nineteenth-century balladry. Along side "The Virtuous Milk-Maid" in the eighteenth century stood "The Milk Maid," "The Bonny Milk-Maid," "The Pretty Milk-Maid," "The Pretty Maid Milking Her Cow" and "The Milk-Maid and Squire!" (no relation to "The Virtuous Milk-Maid").[11] In the 1820s and 1830s James Catnach had at least four broadside ballads about milkmaids for sale: "The Milk-Maid," "Pretty Maid Milking Her Cow" (the same as the eighteenth century ballad), "Milk-Maid Coming from the Wakes," and "Squire and Milkmaid" under the title "Milkmaid of Blackberry Fold." This last one is given in his 1832 catalogue, but has not been seen in his printing.[12] In his ballad "The Cruel Sea-Captain and Nancy of Yarmouth," issued some time in the years 1833–38, George Brown plagiarizes from "Milkmaid of Blackberry Fold"; see pages 46–47.

Poverty's No Sin

Poor Kate with nosegay basket trim,
    Sent forth a plaintive cry,
Her varied flowers round the brim,
    She bids each traveller buy;
But heedless pass the giddy throng,
    In vain she hop'd to win,
She sighed and held her basket low,
    Sure poverty's no sin.

She silent grieves but perseveres,
    By hunger pinch'd and cold,
A brute who saw her falling tears,
    Grew impudent and bold;
By force he prest this modest maid,
    Who pity wish'd to win,
Who struggled, blush'd and frowning said,
    Sure poverty's no sin.

Tom Truelove flush'd with golden ore,
    His constant girl he knew,
Just cry'd 'tis lucky I'm on shore,
    To her relief he flew;
His cudgel laid the assailant low,
    While Tom did thus begin,
D'ye mind me lubber don't ye know,
    That poverty's no sin.

Then bore his prize with love and pride,
    Beneath his conq'ring arm,
And swore he'd keep her by his side,
    And shield her safe from harm;
Thy sails says Tom shake in the wind,
    Thy cheeks look pale and wan,
But cheer my lass the breeze is kind,
    For poverty's no sin.

Kate told him all her friends were dead,
    And she distrest and low,

> Avast he cry'd enough is said,
>   His heart felt all her woe;
> Here take this gold 'tis all your own,
>   'Twas you made me to win,
> I've fought for you and you alone,
>   Why poverty's no sin.
>
> Rigg'd like a lady Kate next day,
>   Was made by Tom a wife,
> And cheerly passes life away,
>   They know no care or strife;
> To her the needy tell their grief,
>   Who asks is sure to win,
> She says and always gives relief,
>   That poverty's no sin.

Crime, prostitution, and drunkenness were visibly associated with poverty in London, and the poor were often regarded as their own worst enemies. In *Life in London,* which he thoughtfully and with permission dedicated to George IV, Pierce Egan has his hero Tom give an account of the "rascality, wickedness, and deceit" of the cadgers of London. Presently Tom and friend Jerry enter one of the haunts of cadgers in St. Giles's, and soon enough Peg the ballad singer, in particolored rags, leers at Tom and sings "Poverty's No Sin" at him, "in hopes to procure a new fancy man."[13] See the drawing of the haunt and the identification of its denizens on pages 309–10. That the ballad was usually sung in such fashion as is described in the book may be doubted. Its apparent popularity on the street suggests that ballad singers who did not leer at their audience found buyers among people who did not think that poverty was a sin.

The earliest printing of the ballad that I have seen is in a garland published by John Pitts in the years when he was at 14 Great St. Andrew's Street: c. 1797–1819. The British Library gives a provisional publication date of 1815. The garland, "Lovers' Jubilee," is "an entire new choice collection of the most admired songs sung at the theatres and all public places."

In "Fortunate Factory Girl," the girl says to the squire, "though poor I am, poverty is no sin." The squire presses his suit honorably, and the girl becomes a lady.

The Fancy Lad

> When first I came to town,
>   They call'd me lovely Nancy,

But now they've chang'd my name,
    And call me the soldier's fancy.

    CHORUS
Go along, go along Bob,
    Go along Bob's a dying,
Go along, go along Bob,
    Your fancy girl's a crying.

I will buy my love a coat,
    Silver buttons to it,
I will let them see
    I am the girl can do it.
        Go along Bob, &c.

Now when my love comes home,
    I will roll in riches,
And I will buy my love
    A pair of buck-skin breeches.
        Go along Bob, &c.

I for beef and pork,
    You for peas and pudding;
Put a pair of clean sheets on the bed,
    For the fancy lads are coming.
        Go along Bob, &c.

When first I came to town,
    I had not a smock to wear O,
But now I have nine or ten,
    For the fancy lads to tear O.
        Go along Bob, &c.

O once I had a bed,
    But now I am forc'd to plank it,
Hang and take the jade,
    She stole my bed and blanket.
        Go along Bob, &c.

Then in comes merry Peggy,
    Hang her ragged fortune,

>
> She pawn'd her Holland smock,
> To raise her lad a quartern.
> Go along Bob, &c.
>
> My fancy lad's in quod,
> I am free and willing,
> To turn out at night,
> And get an honest shilling.
> Go along Bob, &c.

Peas and pudding—poor fare, workhouse fare
Quod—prison

The ballad has been seen in one copy, issued by Bloomer of Birmingham, who is known to have been in business in the years 1817–25. He died in 1827. He describes the ballad as a new song.

The Dogs-Meat Man and Miss Dorothy. By permission of the St. Bride Printing Library.

The Dogs-Meat Man

DOGS-MEAT MAN. Good morning, Miss Dorothy; how does this frosty weather agree with you? Why, you look as fresh and tempting as this here bunch of dogs-meat!

WOMAN. O dear Mr. Barebones, how you flatter me.

HE. Not at all, Miss Dorothy, I like you better than all the dogs-meat and cats-meat in my barrow!

SHE. Dear Sir, I almost blush! You men are coaxing fellows, and know how to flatter poor girls like me! But what's your best news this morning, Mr. Barebones?

HE. Why, I've just heard how that one of my customers was popp'd into *quod* last night, through which I shall lose a matter a' twelve *bob*— It is *exprising* how much good-natured folks like me are *supposed* upon now-a-days!

SHE. I would have them every one hung that would cheat such good-looking fellows as you!

HE. Aye, and cut up for dogs-meat! Wouldn't that be *sarving* them out in style? But you can't guess what I dreamed last night.

SHE. What did you dream about, Mr. Barebones?

HE. Why, I dreamed as how you lent me five pounds to set me up in a tripe-shop near the 7 Dials; and that we were married in St. Giles's church; and that we went to the *Delphi* and saw GREEN IN FRANCE; and that I treated you with apples and ale, and a drop of something short; and as how some *chaffing cove* had *deposed* a Song about us, calling me the "DANDY DOGS-MEAT MAN," and that it was chaunted before your door—and when I had done dreaming all this, I awoke.

SHE. Oh! what a charming dreamer! Pray, my dear Barebones, have a little gin and cloves—'tis a cold morning!

* * *

Well, the gin was drank, the matrimonial bargain was struck, the five pounds was lent him—they went at night to the Adelphi, and he treated her to some halfpenny dumplings and red hot grey pease, near St. Clement's Church, on their way to the Theatre. After the performance they supped on Alamode Beef, and on their way home they drank to the prosperity of the tripe-shop in such repeated potions of *daffy's elixir,* that the Dogs-Meat man became fightable, swore he could act Tom and Jerry to the life, and that he would floor the first charley he met. Accordingly in Drury-Lane he made an attempt to upset a watch-box, but was instantly seized by the watchman, —he resisted but in vain, and after losing a *bra'* new hat, and getting a sound drubbing, he was dragg'd neck and crop to the watch-house and locked up for the night. In the meantime the disconsolate Miss Dorothy, half-dead with gin, fright, and vexation, staggered home the best way she could, and at four in the morning arrived at her mansion without either cloak or bonnet, and her pockets cut off. On entering her bed-room her foot stumbled against a stool and her head went bang through a pane of glass, which cut her face so sadly that she is now confined to her house. She has not seen the Dogs-Meat Man since the fatal night in question and was informed yesterday that he has a wife and 7 children. We are informed that she bears her disappointment with Christian fortitude, and by way of solacing her grief, has recorded the history of her unfortunate courtship in the following song:—

The Dogs-Meat Man

In Grays Inn Lane, not long ago,
An old maid liv'd a life of woe:
She was fifty-three with a face like tan,
And she fell in love with a dogs-meat man.
Much she lov'd this dogs-meat man,
He was a good-looking dogs-meat man,
Her roses and lilies were turned to tan
When she fell in love with a dogs-meat man.

Every day when he went by,
Whether the weather was wet or dry,
And hoppersite her door he'd stand,
Crying dogs-meat, did the dogs-meat man;
When out ran the cat to the dogs-meat man,
And rubb'd 'gainst the barrow of the dogs-meat man,
As hoppersite her door he'd stand,
And cry'd dogs-meat did this dogs-meat man.

One day she kept him at the door,
A talking a matter a' hour or more,
For you must know that 'twas her plan
To have a bit of chat with the dogs-meat man;
Times are hard says the dogs-meat man,
Folks get in my debt, says the dogs-meat man;
Then he took up his barrow and off he ran,
And cried dogs-meat, did the dogs-meat man.

He plainly seed how the cat did jump,
And his company he offer'd plump;
She couldn't blush, 'cause she'd no fan,

So she sat and grinned at the dogs-meat man.
If you'll have me, says the dogs-meat man,
Why! I'll have you, says the dogs-meat man,
For a quartern of peppermint then she ran,
And she drink'd a good health to the dogs-meat man.

That very evening he was seen,
In a jacket and breeches of welweteen;
To Bagnigge-Wells then in a bran
New gown she went with the dogs-meat man;
She'd biscuits and ale with the dogs-meat man,
And walk'd arm in arm with the dogs-meat man,
And the people all said that round did stand,
My eyes! what a dandy dogs-meat man.

He said his customers, good lord!
Owed him a matter of two pounds odd;
When, said she, that is a wicked plan,
To cheat such a good-looking dogs-meat man.
If I had but money, says the dogs-meat man,
I'd open a tripe-shop says the dogs-meat man,
And marry you tomorrow. She admired his plan,
So a five pound note she lent to the dogs-meat man.

He pocketed the money, and then went away,
She waited for him all the next day,
But he never comed; so she then began,
To think she was diddled by the dogs-meat man,
She went to seek the dogs-meat man,
But she couldn't find the dogs-meat man!
And somebody gee'd her to understand,
He'd a wife and seven children, had this dogs-meat man.

So home she went with sighs and tears,
As her hopes were all turned to fears,
And her hungry cat to mew began,
As much as to say, where's the dogs-meat man!
She couldn't forget the dogs-meat man,
The handsome swindling dogs-meat man;
So you see in one day's short span,
Her heart was lost, her five pound note, and the dogs-meat man.

The Answer

O sure you've heard sung thro' every street,
How that an old maid was diddled complete,
And eas'd of a five pound note out of hand,
All by a Dandy dogs-meat man,
An amorous Dandy dogs-meat man,
A good-looking Dandy dogs-meat man,
And how her heart he did trepan,
Then left her in the lurch did the dogs-meat man.

Now this old maid as you all must know,
To seek this dogs-meat man would go,
For days and nights her thoughts still ran,
On her five pound note and the dogs-meat man,
Her swaggering Dandy dogs-meat man,
Her five pound note and the dogs-meat man.
Says she I'll go and if I can,
I'll find out this villain of a dogs-meat man.

So away she went lamenting her loss,
And was told he lived hard by Cow-Cross,
Immediately away she ran,
To ring a peal in the ears of the dogs-meat man,
To blow up her Dandy dogs-meat man,
The shuffling, knavish dogs-meat man,
She swore in her garters she'd rather hang,
Than thus to be served by a dogs-meat man.

Near Smithfield market she did him meet,
And he kindly ask'd her to take a treat,
But she in a rage at him began,
And call'd him a swindling dogs-meat man.
She call'd him a bilking dogs-meat man,
A wicked dissembling dogs-meat man,
She said all London should understand,
What a rogue in grain was the dogs-meat man.

So fast on him her tongue did run,
That the people all laughed to see the fun,
And the boys all said that around did stand,
Success attend the dogs-meat man,

Long life to the Dandy dogs-meat man,
The charming Dandy dogs-meat man,
And this old maid may recover if she can
Her five pound note from the dogs-meat man.

Green in France—one of several dramatizations concerning Tom and Jerry, the swells of Pierce Egan's *Life in London;* this one tells of their rambles in Paris; it showed at the Adelphi Theatre in 1823; Catnach issued a sheet on the subject, with thirteen cuts, that supposedly went through at least eight printings, Catnach advertising the eighth printing on his printing (used here) of "The Dogs-Meat Man" itself[14]
Daffy's elixir—gin
Charley—night-watchman, characteristic enemy of Tom and Jerry; the Dogs-Meat Man was imitating boxers Tom and Jerry to the life in becoming fightable
Cow-Cross—a lane (slum) just off what is now the Farringdon Road at Farringdon Underground Station

According to John Morgan, as quoted by Charles Hindley in *The History of the Catnach Press*, the tale of the dogs-meat man and Miss Dorothy was based upon an actual affair.[15] Catnach printed the tale and verses on a sheet thirteen by ten inches at the time that *Green in France* was showing. The ballad seems to have been deservedly popular for a good many years. Thomas Hood refers to the chaunting of it in his topical piece "The University Feud" of 1842.[16]

There was a sequel, "The Dandy Cats-Meat Lass," likewise issued by Catnach and described by him with some humor as having been "sung with great applause at public dinners." In it the cats-meat lass takes up with a recently bereaved husband who has offered her a pound. While they are snuggling, some cats run off with her meat. But she nails her man. Another ballad, "Kitty the Cats Meat Woman," concerns miscegenation.[17]

Whether Catnach pirated or paid for "The Dogs-Meat Man" is unknown. The author of the first eight stanzas (to "The Answer") was Thomas Hudson, who published them in *Comic Songs, Collection the Fourth* in early 1823.[18] Hudson was born in 1791—according to Harold Scott in *The Early Doors* (1945)[19]—and he issued fourteen or more comic songbooks from 1818 to about 1832, the last one with a date on it coming in 1831. In the same years and later he was a stationer, grocer, tea dealer, and music seller at a variety of addresses. And for perhaps ten years, from 1821 or a year or two before, he kept a well-known tavern, the Kean's Head, in Russell Court, Covent Garden. Hindley has a note on Hudson and the tavern in his *True History of Tom and Jerry*.

> It had previously been called the O.P. and P.S. but re-christened in *honour!* to the celebrated tragedian—then in the zenith of his fame, the late Edmund Kean. . . .

The tavern was much frequented by all persons directly and indirectly connected with the theatrical profession. And was at one time kept by Tom Hudson, a jolly *bon vivant*, and famous comic song writer and singer, of whom Pierce Egan wrote—"his facility in producing songs is astonishing—he also sings them with a peculiar *naivete* and tells his 'story' to his company better than most men who are not regular performers. In his line, he is a second Charles Dibdin Sr. . . ."

It was Tom Hudson who altered the sign of the tavern to the Kean's Head: a remarkable likeness of the great tragedian was hung over the fireplace, and he was wont to visit Tom and take a drink after the fatigues of the night's performance. The mere rumour of this attracted many to the house. A capital harmonic meeting took place late at night—or rather early in the morning, which was supported by a mixture of professionals from the theatres, and amateurs of talent and celebrity. Vain endeavours were seldom entered upon at Tom Hudson's; a pretender was soon coughed down.[20]

Harold Scott remarks that Hudson was a favored singer at other taverns, notably the Coal Hole and the Cider Cellars (Thackeray's Cave of Harmony). Sheet music for the first version of "The Workhouse Boy," issued in about 1837, speaks of it as "a celebrated ballad sung by Mr. Hudson" (see page 168). Hudson's own ballads are occasionally of a sort that Colonel Newcome would have found—and Harold Scott did find—"tainted with licentiousness." One such ballad of his (a parody) appears in George Speaight's *Bawdy Songs of the Early Music Hall* (1975)—"Follow the Drum," which concerns young women who follow the drum for the drumstick.[21] Hudson's very active life seems to have diminished with the 1830s. Perhaps his last ballad was "Her Majesty's Monkey," published in issue number 53 of *London Singer's Magazine* probably in 1841–42. It is described there as a "celebrated comic pathetic song, written and sung by Mr. T. Hudson at public dinners, etc."[22] The ballad tells of the death of a monkey of which Victoria was very fond, of how Lord Melbourne and others sought unavailingly to console her with a pair of cats, and of how they presently succeeded by turning her attention upon Albert of Saxe-Cobourg:

> He has come over—these are facts—
> In her heart and throne to go snacks—
> . . . .
> And though dead pug has got a place,
> Stuffed like life in a grand glass case,
> Victoria looks up in Albert's face,
>   And never thinks of the monkey.

Hudson died in 1844. W. Macqueen Pope in *The Melody Lingers On* (1950) says he died poor—though how poor is unclear. Macqueen Pope adds that a benefit for his widow and children was held at the old Princess's Theatre in Oxford Street, and that it was supported by the duke of Cambridge, the lord mayor, members of Parliament, and stars of the theatre.[23]

The overall unity of the prose and verse for "The Dogs-Meat Man" in its broadside form might suggest that Hudson elaborated his original song for Catnach. However, Catnach was a known pirate, and in any event there is evidence of another accomplished hand at work. Firstly the narratives of prose and verse do not quite jibe. Secondly the broadside verses add a few Cockney touches to the text in Hudson's songbook: "vent," "hoppersite," and so on. All the same, the verses in the songbook do give "drink'd," "so she sot and grinned at the dogs' meat man," and "she'd biscakes and ale with the dogs-meat man." There are also changes in phrasing that it seems unlikely Hudson himself would have made. The songbook gives:

> One morn she kept him at the door,
> Talking half an hour or more.
> . . . .
> And she replied it was quite scan-
> -dalous to cheat such a dog's meat man.

Lastly there is a difference in rhyming. All the rhymes in the songbook are perfect. Where "stand," "brand," and "understand" are used, an apostrophe is given in place of "d," and the first line of the sixth stanza gives "good lod" to rhyme with "odd." The broadside version is content with imperfect rhyme in both sets of verses.

Perhaps the chief clue, though, is that on an otherwise blank page at the front of *Collection the Fourth* Hudson prints in large type: "Pirates Beware!" And in *Comic Songs, the Eleventh Collection* (1830), he writes, "T. Hudson, having been injured very materially by men calling themselves publishers printing his songs, is resolved to prosecute any party publishing or vending pirated copies in future." Whatever Catnach may have done about "The Dogs-Meat Man," it seems certain enough that he and many other broadside printers pirated Hudson's songs freely. Hudson's songs abound in broadside collections. Among familiar titles are "The Bailiffs Are Coming," given elsewhere here, and other songs touching on poverty: "The Back and the Belly," "Pawnbroker's Shop on a Saturday Night," and "Polly Cox's Party." Three of these titles, and several other Hudson titles, are advertised in Catnach's 1832 catalogue. They also appear in certain of the more lively song collections of the time: *Corinthian*, 6th edition, c. 1833, *London Singer's Magazine* (1838–45?), and J. Sharp's *Vauxhall Comic Song-Book*, first series (c. 1847). Had there been better protection against piracy, and had there been a royalty system in place, Hudson—like John Morgan—would probably have been a wealthy man.

In his note on "The Dogs-Meat Man" in *Collection the Fourth*, Hudson says that the ballad is to be sung to the tune of "The White Cockade." In the latter ballad, dating from about 1790, a woman in love speaks the verses, saying that she will follow her army captain wherever he goes. Words and tale have no connection with Hudson's ballad except possibly in a single line: "Whose bonny, smiling face did my heart trepan."[24]

John Morgan in his comments to Hindley about "The Dogs-Meat Man" quotes four stanzas approximately as Hudson wrote them. Presumably he is remembering another printing by Catnach. The British Library holds a third Catnach printing (solely of Hudson's verses) with some but not all of the changes in the printing given here.

The Weaver's Daughter

Across the fields one sweet May morn,
    As I walked out quite early,
A lovely lass came tripping by,
    As light as any fairy,
Where are you going pretty maid said I
    As by the hand I caught her,
I asked her name, she blushed and said,
    I'm a poor old weaver's daughter.

Sweet maid, said I, if you'll be mine,
    I've gold and riches plenty,
I'll make you when away a lady gay,
    Kind sir said she I thank you,
Her mother she said who was dead and gone,
    An early lesson had taught her,
To marry for love and not for gold,
    Tho' a poor old weaver's daughter.

My father sir, is nearly blind,
    And now gone past his labour,
It would break his heart from me to part,
    Cried the poor old weaver's daughter,
Parted from me he never shall be,
    For he has been a good and kind father,
Until he's in his peaceful grave,
    Cried the poor old weaver's daughter.

Farewell sweet maid, said I, farewell,
    May you happy be united,

> May the lad that you love—constant prove,
>   And your prospect never be blighted,
> For friendship sake this gold ring take,
>   So lovely a girl I thought her,
> That while I live I shall never forget,
>   The poor old weaver's daughter.

I have changed the fourth line in the second stanza from "Kind sir, then said she, I thank you," in conformity with another printing, which itself suffers from an unfortunate fourth line in the last stanza, "And your prosperity ne'er be slighted." The ballad was apparently popular. The present printing is listed in Catnach's 1832 catalogue, and very likely it is the same "Weaver's Daughter" that appears in the catalogue of R. Hook of Brighton, issued perhaps in 1824. In another ballad, "The Village Maid," the girl prefers her farm lad to the rich suitor. These and similar ballads seem to suggest that poverty—helped by idyllic rural setting—is the best basis for love and happiness. See for example "Mary of the Lowly Cot" and "The Answer to Why Did She Leave Him." The latter ballad is a reply to "Why Did She Leave Him, Because He Was Poor," which tells of how the poor but beautiful girl grew up to spurn her poor lover, being able to marry wealth, and of how she is now unhappy and laments her loss. "The Answer" describes the marriage she missed:

> We think it a blessing that we have not riches,
>   For they cannot make the mind happy at last,
> For wealth in most cases wickedness teaches,
>   May our little future be like the past,
> My toil it seems light as I return from labour,
>   My wife runs to meet me at the cottage door,
> With sweet blooming cheeks and a smile she does greet me,
>   She loves me the better because I am poor.

The pair of ballads seem to have been very popular. Further comment on poverty and contentment appears in the introduction to "Scenes of Mirth and Contentment."

Advice to Country Maidens on the Poor Law Bill

> Come all you bucksome men and maids,
>   Tom, Jenny, Bet, and Will,
> I have a little ditty here
>   About the Poor Law Bill.

What's occurred since that took place,
    To please you I have penned—
From "Johnny Groat's" in Scotland,
    All the way to the land's end.

So pretty maids take my advice,
    Or you may cry your fill,
If once you get entangled
    With the cursed Poor Law Bill.

There was a farmer's daughter
    One day to market went;
She in a village did reside,
    Near Maidstone town in Kent;
She with the ploughman kiss'd and toyed,
    And played a pretty rig,
And in nine months time she brought to town
    A little Br——'s wig,

The dairy maid went out one evening,
    For to milk the cow;
She met with Ned the thrasherman
    A coming from the plough;
They rolled together on the grass—
    They could not keep long still,
Till she learnt the 57th clause
    Of Br——m's Poor Law Bill.

A cobbler had a daughter, who
    Was fond of mirth and fun;
She forgot the cursed Poor Law Bill,
    And courted tailor Tom;
It did her father sore enrage,
    And greatly him perplex;
She brought to town two cabbage leaves,
    And a little ball of wax.

At Farmer Giles' across the road,
    There lived a blooming maid;
She learnt the Poor Law Bill by heart,
    Before she long had stayed:

Two little sons she brought to town,
    Which caused a pretty row,
For one was marked with a milk pail,
    And the other with a plough.

If you have a wife and family,
    To put you in a rage,
They will put the father in the stocks,
    And the mother in the cage,
And send the children far away—
    It nearly makes me jump—
I wish Br——m had his Poor Law Bill
    A sticking in his ———.

Now all young men take my advice
    If you would banish strife,
Kiss and toy with all you can,
    And never marry a wife;
Court Polly, Betsy, Jenny, Kit,
    And Sally if you will,
Till they've learnt the 57th clause
    Of Br——'s Poor Law Bill.

So you pretty maids beware
    When you go out to milk the cow,
Or you may have a little son
    Just fit to drive the plough;
And in the sun pray do not roll,
    Among the new mown hay,
Or it's two to one but you may get
    In a very curious way.

I heard a pretty maiden cry,
    Oh, cursed be the laws!
Bad luck to Mr. Br——m
    For his 57th clause;
For I am in a pretty mess
    Since I have played with Will,
For I rock the cradle day and night,
    Singing, oh the Poor Law Bill.

                              J. Morgan

Lord Brougham (Henry Peter Brougham, 1775–1868), Whig politician, moved the second reading of the new Poor Law Bill in the House of Lords on 21 July 1834. His biographer, A. Aspinall, speaks of his "lifelong advocacy of Poor Law reform."[25] Brougham's general view was that the old poor law encouraged idleness and wastefulness among the poor. The aim of the new law was to provide a harsher regime. Among its features was the enforced separation of husbands and wives and parents and children in the workhouse. The "cage" was a punishment cell. The clause relevant to single young women in the ballad was—in the law as enacted—the 69th rather than the 57th. It revoked part of an earlier act that enabled a single woman to charge a man with having got her pregnant. The implication was that if she could not support the coming child herself, both she and the child might be forced into the workhouse. For a note on stocks see page 468.

Artichokes & Cauliflowers

An old woman there lived at Rumford,
And she was a gay old lass,
And many an honest penny got,
By selling sparrow-grass:
She with her barrow loaded well,
From street to street did pass,
Saluting all her customers with
Who'll come buy my artichokes.

CHORUS
Artichokes and cauliflowers come buy, come buy of me, &c.

This old woman had a daughter sweet,
The girl her name was Cis,
And she went into the garden
Every morning for to pick
Some parsley, thyme, and sage,
Likewise some sparrow-grass,
For to decorate her barrow, when
She cried who'll buy my artichokes.

This old woman had a lodger, too,
Who used to bed and board,
And she resolv'd one morn to treat him
To a good brown rousing turkey,

She boil'd some cauliflowers,
Likewise some sparrow-grass,
For she had made a lucky hit,
And sold her precious artichokes.

This put the lodger in a rage,
Says he, my queer old lass,
If you give me further impudence,
I'll kick your precious artichokes,
And tender cauliflowers,
From your barrow as you pass:
No, no, you must not touch me,
Nor my daughter's precious artichokes.

Now if you will wed my daughter Cis,
I swear now with the lass,
Five hundred pounds I will pay down,
Which I've got all by my grass;
Then she may be a lady gay,
And visit every opera, ball, and farce,
And never mind what people say,
About her old mother's artichokes.

This was not to be resisted,
So he pocketed the cash,
And he, not being close fisted,
Resolved to cut a dash,
He had parties every day to dine,
Made each guest fill up his glass,
And the first toast he gave in a bumper,
Here's success to her old artichokes.

Turkey—the word meant is turd

The printing does not indent with the rhyme and failed rhyme as other printings do.

The ballad, also known as "The Old Woman of Rumford," seems to have been one of the most frequently printed of bawdy ballads. Along with a number of similar ballads such as "The Maiden's Bantam Cock," "The New Bury Loom," and "Nine Times a Night," it apparently sold freely or fairly freely.[26] More bluntly bawdy ballads often or usually omitted the printer's name and were sometimes or customarily sold clandestinely. As a whole, bawdy ballads are among the most interesting nineteenth-century broadside ballads, usually having more literary inventiveness and energy than ballads on beggar children, naval heroes, prizefights, and a host of other common topics.

John Holloway and Joan Black in *Later English Broadside Ballads* (1979) suggest—on what basis is unknown—that "Artichokes & Cauliflowers" is a disguised skit on the duke of Clarence's mistress.[27] The duke (William IV in 1830) separated formally from his mistress in 1811 after a relationship lasting some twenty years. Printings of the ballad that I have seen date from the middle or late 1830s.

Rigs and Flares-Up of the Fair

———— Fair is come, without delay,
　　The lads and lasses haste away,
Drest in their best, they do repair
　　To see the rigs of ———— Fair.
　　　　With their dumble dum deary, &c.

Johnny leads his blooming girl along,
　　A-crowding, pushing thro' the throng,
Shows her cakes and comforts going thro',
　　And a pair of cock and breeches, too.
　　　　With his dumble dum deary, &c.

He gives her ale, he gives her beer,
　　He gives her something nice and queer,
For Molly from Johnny will something crave,
　　And perhaps in 9 months she will have
　　　　A dumble dum deary, &c.

In pleasure they walked about all day,
　　And Jenny to her love did say,
Dear William, sing a pretty song,
　　For that, and nothing else I long
　　　　But your dunble dum deary, &c.

And when the evening does advance,
　　Like devils they begin to dance,

To drive all sorrow and drown dull care,
    They have a game at ——— Fair.
        With dumble dum deary, &c.

When the day is o'er, then off they roam,
    Cries Bet before we do go home,
It's a lovely night and charming weather,
    So we'll lay down and pig together.
        With our dumble dum deary, &c.

Before the night is gone, I ween,
    John gives her an elegant gown of green,
And as she rises from the ground,
    She cries, I thought the world went round.
        With your dunble dum deary, &c.

Oh then a loving tale they tell,
    Says Johnny, did I please you well?
Oh yes, says Bet, but, love, I'd fain
    To see the world go round again,
        With your dumble dum deary, &c.

Then both being tired, they homeward raced,
    John with his arm round Betsy's waist.
For a doctor and nurse poor Bet will send,
    Her stomach to cool at the 9 months end.
        With a dumble dum deary, &c.

So lasses all, if you repair
    To see the rigs of ——— Fair,
At night when you are homeward bound,
    Don't wish to see the world go round.
        With a dumble dum deary. &c.

Forget the styles or you will rue,
    Forget the cocks and breeches too,
For if once the world goes round I fain
    You'd wish to see it go round again.
        With a dumble dum deary, &c.

                                  J Morgan

World go round—familiar expression for female ecstasy in intercourse
Styles—stiles

The ballad was printed by W. Taylor in his last year of publishing, 1837, when his address was "near the Victoria Theatre." The indenting of lines in the ballad goes against the rhyme; I have left it unchanged. I have amended punctuation and abandoned inconsistently used quotation marks.

Morgan wrote several other ballads of similar lightly sexual character, among them "New Rigs of the Races," "Rigs and Flares-Up of Greenwich Fair," and "Blow the Candle In." The first of these is an answer to the present ballad in being a warning to young men, the third was widely printed for a number of years. Morgan is possibly the author of the bawdy ballad "The Beautiful Muff," though he is identified only as the seller of it on the copy that bears his name.[28] Like "Rigs and Flares-Up of the Fair," it is to the tune of "Dumble Down Deary." The first lines go thus:

> A buxom young damsel on a cold winter's day
> Abroad from her dwelling she chanced for to stray,
> She was muffed up warm, in a boa rather ruff,
> At her front she display'd a most beautiful muff.
>
> It's mine and I wear it, so do not come near
> To damage and tear it, my beautiful muff.
>
> Now this muff was the finest that ever you saw,
> And all the young men their attention did draw;
> It was lined with red silk tho' the outside was ruff,
> And as warm as a toast was this beautiful muff.

She meets a young man who is stiff with the cold, and wants to be warmed by her beautiful muff. Presently he damages it, and the ballad ends with a warning to young damsels against young sparks:

> They will tell you fine tales and a parcel of stuff,
> And will try to disfigure your beautiful muff.

The Lady and the Welsh Ploughboy

> All in the month of May,
>   When flowers were springing,
> I went into the meadows
>   Some pleasure for to find.

I went into the meadow,
    I turned myself around,
There I saw a pretty Welsh lad,
    Ploughing up the ground.

Now as he was a ploughing,
    His furrows deep and low,
Cleaving his clods in pieces,
    His barley for to sow,

It is the pretty Welsh lad,
    That runs all in my mind,
And many hours I wander,
    My Welsh boy for to find.

An old man he came courting me,
    A man of birth and fame,
Because I would not have him,
    My father did me blame.

It is the pretty Welsh lad
    That runs all in my mind,
A most distressed lady,
    The Welsh lad for to find.

An old man I do disdain,
    His wealth and all his store,
O! give me to my ploughboy,
    And I will ask no more.

He is the flower of this country,
    A diamond in my eye,
It is for the pretty Welsh lad
    That I for love must die.

I wish the pretty sky lark
    Would mount up in the air,
That my pretty ploughboy
    The tidings might hear.

Perhaps he may prove true to me,
    And ease my aching heart,

> It is for the pretty Welsh lad,
>   That I do feel the smart.
>
> I will wait until I see him,
>   To tell him my mind;
> If he will not relieve me,
>   I shall think him unkind.
>
> If he will not give me his love,
>   Then distracted I shall be,
> Into some grove I'll wander,
>   Where no one shall see me.

Along with obvious defects, the ballad has unusual virtues. The latter qualities suggest a problem in date of composition. The defects are visible in the line "My father did me blame," where the presence of "did" serves merely to obtain dull rhythm and rhyme. The first of the virtues is that, unlike most nineteenth-century broadside ballads on the same subject—rich girl/poor boy, and vice versa—it is more lyric than narrative. Other ballads move their tales rapidly to happy or unhappy conclusions. The second virtue is a fair degree of lyric skill. Certain phrases repeat themselves in easy rhythm: "went into the meadow," "runs all in my mind," "Welsh boy for to find." "Ploughing up the ground" completes stanza two, but it is then repeated in the first line of stanza three, and the image is elaborated in the next lines. Stanza five introduces the minor subject of the old man, but stanza six returns to three lines of stanza four, and then stanza seven concludes the thought on the old man. The ballad is a lyric meditation whose material "runs all in the mind" of the lady. This last phrase helps to qualify the character of the meditation: it is active rather than passive. The lady sees that "the flowers were springing," and "turned myself around"; she is "a most distracted lady," but "an old man I do disdain," and the Welsh lad is "a diamond in my eye."

Notwithstanding these virtues, the ballad is familiar old-fashioned lover's plaint. It is pastoral, with meadow, skylark, and grove, in the month of May, and with characteristic thought of dying for love. The language shows old-fashioned idioms: "all in the month of May," "pleasure (and Welsh Lad) for to find," "an old man he came courting me." In sum, one might think that the ballad was an original composition of some merit, written early in the century, instead of being—as more tangible evidence suggests—an elaboration written in 1840 of the first part of an inferior ballad.

Only two printings are known. The one used here was issued by Harkness of Preston, who printed in the years 1840–66 (Neuburg). The other, without stanzaic division, bears no printer's name, but the purchaser kindly wrote at the bottom of the sheet, "B't at Worcester, Dec. 1840." At least eight years earlier, James Catnach issued a ballad entitled "Cupid the Pretty Ploughboy," giving the title in his 1832 catalogue. The first two of six stanzas go thus:

> As I walked out one May morning,
>   When May was all in bloom,
> I went into a meadow so sweet,
>   To taste the sweet perfume.
> I went into a flowery field,
>   I turned my head awhile,
> When I saw Cupid the ploughboy,
>   Who did my heart beguile.
>
> As this young man was ploughing,
>   His furrows deep and low,
> Breaking his clod to pieces,
>   Some barley for to sow,
> I wish this pretty ploughboy,
>   My eyes had never seen,
> 'Twas Cupid the pretty ploughboy,
>   With his arrows sharp and keen.

Some of the phrases of "The Lady and the Welsh Ploughboy" are here, along with similar repetitions, and the grammatical disjunction between the two quatrains of the second stanza is the same as that between stanzas three and four in "The Lady and the Welsh Ploughboy." But overall language, rhythm, and feeling are inferior, and most of the rest of the ballad is clumsy narrative. In stanza three the lady thinks she might reveal her desire in a letter to the ploughboy, but imagines that "he'll take it scornful." Stanza four says that "a worthy rich young gentleman" courted her but was rejected. Stanza five tells of the ploughboy overhearing the lady's plaint and crying out, "I, my dearest jewel, / I will ease you of your pain." In stanza six they agree to marry.

> So now they live in pleasure,
>   For they have gold in store,
> The lady and the ploughboy,
>   Each other do adore.

The chief point at which these later stanzas resemble "The Lady and the Welsh Ploughboy" is with the parents' response to the lady's refusal of the worthy rich young gentleman: "my parents did me blame."

Is indeed the often skillful lyric meditation of "The Lady and the Welsh Ploughboy" the result of tinkering with an inferior model, or is it the result of an original sustained impulse? The latter case seems more likely to me, but insofar as the evidence is highly problematical, I have left the ballad in the chronological position in which I first placed it. One incidental odd element of the ballad is the absence of rhyme in the first stanza.

In the printing used here, lines four and five of the ballad are divided by a period. I have substituted a comma to link them, following the other printing.

Both printings are accompanied by another ballad of the same length entitled "The Welsh Boy's Answer," a piece with none of the virtues of its partner and all the defects of "Cupid the Pretty Ploughboy." It begins:

> The Welsh boy overhearing
> The lady in distress,
> Boldly stepped up and said—
> I grant you your request.
>
> My hand and heart for ever
> To you I freely give!
> It is to me, fair lady,
> Can save you from the grave.

He doubts that parents and friends of the lady will have him; and if they will not, he will cross "the raging ocean." However, father capitulates: "If your delight is a Welsh boy / Then married you shall be." And that is that. The author of "Cupid the Pretty Ploughboy" could well have written the piece.

Other tales of rich girl and poor boy include "The Lady who Fell in Love with a Prentice Boy," "A Lady's Love and Loyalty for Her Sweetheart," "The Lady Lov'd Her Father's Groom," and "The Blooming Lady Worth £500,000." In the first ballad the parents get the youth transported, but he returns successfully after rising to be a butler and then winning a fortune in a lottery. In the second the young man is likewise transported, and the lady tries to follow him. She is intercepted by father and locked up for five months. She leaves again, and this time she joins her young man in Van Dieman's Land. The other two tales apparently have some basis in fact. The young lady who loves her father's groom is not to be denied, nor is her lover. Their marriage is reported in a further ballad, "Marriage of the Blooming Lady and the Groom." The married lady of the fourth ballad has the good luck to possess £500,000 in her own name. She does as she pleases:

> Give me says she my servant man,
> He is my only joy,
> Then with my bonny footman,
> I will sweetly kiss and toy.

As for the footman:

> Oh the lucky lucky footman,
> He has done the trick so brown,

Got his master's lovely lady,
    And five hundred thousand pounds.

And as for Members of Parliament such as the husband:

You British Members of Parliament,
    If you wish to banish strife,
When you go out on business,
    In the cupboard lock your wife.

The Village Beauty

See the star breasted villain to yonder cot bound,
Where the sweet honeysuckle entwines itself round,
Yet sweeter, far sweeter, than flower e'er seen,
Is the poor hedger's daughter, the pride of the green.
But more, never more, will she there please all eyes,
Her peace of mind withers, her happiness flies!
She pauses, sighs, trembles!—and yet dares to roam,
The village born beauty, seduced from her home.

From a post-chaise and four, she's in London set down,
Where robb'd of her virtue, she's launched on the town,
Her carriage, her servants, and jewels so gay,
Tell how she is kept, and o'er all bears the sway!
At the opera, the playhouse, the parks, and elsewhere,
Her beauty outrivals each beauty that's there;
And while big with envy, her downfall they tell,
The village born beauty o'er all bears the bell.

But soon from indifference, caprice, and what not,
She's turned on the world, by her keeper forgot;
Yet fond to be flattered, and fettered in vice,
She's this man's or that as he comes to her price:
At length growing stale, all her finery sold,
In the bloom of her youth, through disease looking old,
Forsook by her lovers, and sought for no more,
The village born beauty becomes a street whore.

Up lanes and through alleys she now stalks her way,
Exposed to all weather, by night and by day,

THE VILLAGE BEAUTY.

See the star breasted villain to yonder cot bound,
Where the sweet honeysuckle entwines itself round,
Yet sweeter, far sweeter, than flower e'er seen,
Is the poor Hedger's Daughter, the pride of the green,
But more, never more, will she there please all eyes,
Her peace of mind withers, her happiness flies!
She pauses, sighs, trembles!—and yet dares to roam,
The village born beauty, seduced from her home.

From a post-chaise and four, she's in London set down,
Where robb'd of her virtue, she's launched on the town,
Her carriage, her servants, and jewels so gay,
Tell how she is kept, and o'er all bears the sway!
At the Opera, the Playhouse, the Parks, and elsewhere,
Her beauty outrivals each beauty that's there;
And while big with envy, her downfall they tell,
The village born beauty o'er all bears the bell.

But soon from indifference, caprice, and what not,
She's turned on the world, by her keeper forgot;
Yet fond to be flattered, and fettered in vice,
She's this man's or that as he comes to her price:
At length growing stale, all her finery sold,
In the bloom of her youth, through disease looking old,
Forsook by her lovers, and sought for no more,
The village born beauty becomes a street whore.

Up lanes and through alleys she now stalks her way,
Exposed to all weathers, by night and by day,
Cold, houseless, and shivering, and wet to the skin,
With glass after glass drowns her sorrows in gin;
Distressed, sore, and ragged, sad, friendless and poor,
She's borne to some garret, or workhouse obscure,
Breathes a prayer hope to Heaven—a sinner to save,
When the village born beauty is laid in the grave.

Then pity, ye fair ones, nor be too severe,
And give a frail sister the boon of a tear,
When prone to condemn them—reflect, think awhile—
That the heart often bleeds, when the face wears a smile,
Think too that through beauty they oft owe their fall,
And what may through vice, be the fate of you all;
And oh, while sweet innocence bears a proud sway,
May hell seize the villain that smiles to betray

"The Village Beauty." By permission of the Syndics of Cambridge University Library.

Cold, houseless and shivering, and wet to the skin,
With glass after glass drowns her sorrows in gin;
Distressed, sore and ragged, sad, friendless and poor,
She's borne to some garret, or workhouse obscure,
Breathes a prayer hope to Heaven—a sinner to save,
When the village born beauty is laid in the grave.

Then pity, ye fair ones, nor be too severe,
And give a frail sister the boon of a tear.
When prone to condemn them—reflect, think awhile—
That the heart often bleeds, when the face wears a smile,
Think too that through beauty they oft owe their fall,
And what may through vice, be the fate of you all;
And oh, while sweet innocence bears a proud sway,
May hell seize the villain that smiles to betray.

The straightforwardness of the ballad compares favorably with the sentimental blurring in Thomas Hood's "Bridge of Sighs" and the evasions and condescension of D. G. Rossetti's "Jenny." Even so, it is some distance from the bluntness of a badly written ballad called "The Poor Whores Complaint" that dates from about 1790. Several whores complain about their situation:

> Says Sally I think I've the worst luck of you all
>   Since I have known whoring,
> I ne'er in my life before went without a smock,
>   Altho' it was ne'er such a poor one.
> Altho' I'm trudging the streets all night in the cold,
>   My rags men are pulling and hauling;
> Old Nick I'm sure would not be a whore,
>   It is grown such a devil of a calling.
> Straightway young Nelly replied,
>   What signifies complaining,
> You know you're all poxt, and so am I,
>   And that indeed's our failing,
> We swarm like bees at every street end,
>   Catching at every fellow,
> Let him be ever so poxt or clean,
>   We are always ready him to follow.

The present ballad dates from the 1840s or 1850s. It seems to have been moderately popular. The last two lines of the fourth stanza are printed variously. Sometimes a hyphen joins "prayer" and "hope" or sometimes "hope" is omitted; sometimes the dash after "Heaven" is omitted; sometimes "When" is "And" or "While." The title is sometimes "The Village-Born Beauty."

A ballad of about 1799 that tells very much the same tale is "Blue Ey'd Mary." Two similar broadsides—one verse, the other prose—that purport to be true are "A Copy of Verses on the Life and Death of Miss Sophia Wright" and "The Wicked Life and Alarming Death of Jane Wilson."

Oh, Ain't I Nuts on Sarah

One evening, going thro' the market place
I saw a girl with a laughing face,
            At a stand, at a stand.
She was not dress'd in satins or silks,
But selling oysters mussels and whelks,
            At a stand, at a stand.

    Oh, ain't I nuts on Sarah, oh, heighho,
      In a parlour high, that's next the sky,
        Oh, ain't I nuts on Sarah.

She'd no flounced petticoats nor Balmorals,
No fine feathers, nor such fal de rals,
            At a stand, at a stand.
No pork-pie hat nor knickerbocker,
But everything slap, right up to the knocker
            At the stand, at the stand.
        Oh, ain't I nuts on Sarah, &c.

She'd a jolly red face without ever a speck,
And a yellow belcher loose round her neck,
            At the stand, at the stand.
No signs of her buying a bun I espied,
For she'd got a plate of sassinger fried.
            At the stand, at the stand.
        Oh, ain't I nuts on Sarah, &c.

Being fond of oysters, said I "if you please,
Just open me sixpen'orth of these."
            At a stand, at a stand.
Six dozen I swallowed, soon d'ye see,
I wink'd at her, and she laughed at me.
            At the stand, at the stand.
        Oh, ain't I nuts on Sarah, &c.

She fetched me bread, she fetched me beer,
And then politely handed her chair,
    At a stand, at a stand.
I had my supper, and paid my tin,
And then invited her to have a drop of gin,
    At the stand, at the stand.
  Oh, ain't I nuts on Sarah, &c.

She said at first, "she was afeard,"
But a half-pint soon disappeared,
    At the stand, at the stand.
I found her single, so I asked her hand,
Says she, "it's rayther sudden, but it's yours at command,"
    At the stand, at the stand.
  Oh, ain't I nuts on Sarah, &c.

We've been married three weeks, I've no cause to fret,
We don't want a nurse, nor a cradle yet.
    At the stand, at the stand.
So you dashing girls of the west step forth,
We've dashing girls in the south, east, and north.
    At a stand, at a stand.
  Oh, ain't I nuts on Sarah.

Belcher—spotted handkerchief
Sassinger—sausage
Tin—money

Balmorals, porkpie hats, and knickerbockers came into fashion in the late 1850s, early 1860s.

Polly Perkins, of Paddington Green

I'm a broken hearted milkman, in grief I am arrayed,
Through keeping the company of a young servant maid,
Who lived on board wages, to keep the house clean,
In a gentleman's family near Paddington Green.

CHORUS
She was as beautiful as a butterfly,
   And as proud as a queen,
Was pretty little Polly Perkins
   Of Paddington Green.

Her eyes were as black as the pips of the pear,
No rose in the garden with her cheeks could compare;
Her hair hung in ringlets so beautiful and long,
I thought that she loved me, but I found I was wrong.
                She was, &c.

When I'd rattled in the morning and cried, "Milk below,"
At the sound of my milk-cans her face she would show,
With a smile upon her countenance and a laugh in her eye—
If I thought she'd not love me I'd lay down and die.
                She was, &c.

When I asked her to marry me, she said, "Oh! what stuff,"
And told me to drop it for she had quite enough
Of my nonsense—at the same time I'd been very kind,
But to marry a milkman she did not feel inclined.
                She was, &c.

"Oh! the man that has me must have silver and gold,
A chariot to ride in, be handsome and bold.
His hair must be as curly as any watch spring,
And his whiskers as long as a brush for clothing."
                She was, &c.

The words that she uttered went through my heart,
I sobbed, I sighed, and from her did depart,
With a tear on my eyelid as big as any bean,
Bidding goodbye to Polly and Paddington Green.
                She was, &c.

In six months she was married—this hard-hearted girl—
But it was not a wiscount, and it was not a "nerl,"
It was not a baronite, but a shade or two wus,
'Twas a bow-legged conductor of a twopenny 'bus.
                She was, &c.

The ballad was perhaps more popular in the parlor than on the street, though it is not rare in broadside collections, and it inspired a sequel, "Polly Perkins' Answer," which likewise sold on the street. In her answer Polly Perkins ridicules the milkman ("Chalk-and-water" to her), denies that her husband Tickle has bowlegs (rumor doubtless spread by Chalk-and-water), says that she has had three children by Tickle in three years, and avers that she remains as beautiful as a butterfly. Three other ballads quite similar to "Polly Perkins" in substance and character are "Polly Brindle," "The Broken-Hearted Gardener," and "Mr. Walker, the Twopenny Postman."[29] In the last named, which was written in about 1824 by Thomas Hudson, a young woman falls for a twopenny postman. She happens to be married, and she and Mr. Walker cuckold her shoemaker husband. Mr. Walker brings shoes for the husband to repair, and the wife brings him a boy, "the image exact, / Of Walker the twopenny postman." The tale is supposed to be true.

"Polly Perkins," words and music, was written by Harry Clifton (1832–72), and was published in 1865. It is generally reckoned to be his best composition. He was born in Hoddesdon, Hertfordshire, and educated at the nearby town of Cheshunt. He was orphaned, apparently at about age twelve to fifteen, and presently apprenticed himself to a circus proprietor, who taught him riding and clowning. He then turned to concert room and music hall, and achieved great success as singer and lyricist-composer. He was notable for his "motto" songs—songs of advice with such titles as "Always Put Your Shoulder to the Wheel," "Act on the Square," "Paddle Your Own Canoe," and "Work, Boys, Work, and be Contented." These ballads apparently ensured that he was as popular in drawing rooms as on the halls. I have noticed only the last two as broadsides. His obituarist in *Era* (London), 21 July 1872, remarks that his songs "are pure, and each has a moral tendency," an expression of approval echoed as late as 1965 in Mander and Richardson's comment in *British Music Hall* that everyone could sing his songs "without a blush of shame."[30]

6
Husbands and Wives

Of all the familiar subjects of life, one of the most distinctive in nineteenth-century broadside ballads is that of husbands and wives. Search through parlor, concert, and theater songs of the age and see first of all that the subject is occasional rather than omnipresent, and second that it is dealt with mainly in sentimental or lightly comic vein. Characteristic music hall songs from late in the century are of these sorts: "My Old Dutch," "It's a Great Big Shame," and "John Willie, Come On." In broadside ballads husbands and wives are a frequent topic, and though there is sentiment and light comedy in good measure, there is equally harshness, grim comedy, and sensuality. The broadside ballads are as a whole much closer to ordinary life, and the picture many of them paint is hardly suggested by the word Victorian.

A number of ballads consider the desirability of marriage. Some would do well for the parlor. In "Nobody Coming to Woo," the impatient maid says, "Come handsome, come ugly, come old, / Come and fetch me away." She does not say, "Come poor," and one suspects that she is a nice middle-class girl. Some of her words echo the refrain of the Roxburghe ballad "The Wooing Maid."[1] Another young maiden is more reckless. "Oh dear, how I long to get married," says she in title and refrain:

> I would marry a tinker or sweep,
>   A weaver, a cobbler or tailor,
> A coalheaver, a butcher or baker,
>   A spinner, a soldier or sailor;
> If he'd never a shirt on his back,
>   Or a nose to his face, I'd him carry
> To church any day in a crack—
>   Oh dear, how I long to get married!

And why?

> When I go to my bed every night,
>   I, like an old witch, begin grumbling;
> I kick, toss and caper about,
>   A-mumbling, a-tumbling and fumbling.

The ballad is a rewriting of an entirely polite song called "Dear Me! How I Long to Get Married!" written by Charles Dibdin in about 1767. The most interesting ballad of this sort is a rare one called "The Old Woman's Wish," which dates from the middle 1850s or before. Its central stanza calls to mind the woman young and old of Yeats:

> Fourscore years of age I am,
>   With scarcely a tooth in my head,
> Yet I long to play the game I played,
>   When I lost my maidenhead.

She has forty shillings between her and destitution, but she would "part with it for the charms of love, / That bliss to womankind." Young men and old men feel similarly. In "The Bachelor's Complaint," by John Morgan, the young man thinks he would say yes to whatever his wife wanted: "I would rise with delight, in the dead of the night, / For whatever she'd ask, I'd say YES!"[2] In "The Bachelor of Sixty-Two," the old man thinks, "alack, / No wife have I to warm my back."[3] Neither of these two ballads explicitly concerns poverty, but their overall character suggests humble rather than easeful life. Wholly unconcerned with poverty but worth mentioning for their special subject are three ballads about Queen Victoria at the time of her marriage. In the first, "I am Going to Be Married," Victoria echoes the language of the girl in "Oh Dear, How I Long to Get Married":

> I am like a mouse on an empty shelf,
> When I get in bed by myself,
> I kick and tumble about all night,
> Oh! give me the joys of a wedded life.

She looks forward to making "Prince Albert skip and jump, / And play the tune of tiddle-de-bump." Her dream is fulfilled in "I am Married at Last" and "I was Married on Monday!" The latter ballad says:

> For my dear Albert I propose,
> To buy him a suit of scarlet clothes,
> And a sword as long as Wellington's nose.
> . . . .
> My wedding story I will tell,
> And view ladies in Pall Mall,
> I like a German sausage well.
> . . . .

> I will buy him a gun as big as a pump,
> I into bed will quickly jump,
> Singing moll in the wad and tiddle-de-bump.
> . . . .
> Pretty maidens gay and kind,
> Don't live single, change your mind,
> Think what pleasure I shall find,
>   For I was married on Monday.[4]

"Moll in the Wad" was a lively Irish dance, dating from before the turn of the century. The immediate reference may be to a broadside ballad known in one form as "Moll in the Wood," dating from some years later, in which Moll takes up with a drummer and "learnt him to beat on her rub-a-dum-dum."[5] Perhaps poor people reading such ballads about Victoria thought of the cramped quarters, cold, dirt, hunger, and disease that must so often have hindered for them the pleasures of sexual love. Perhaps also they thought of one nation.

The desire for marriage was matched by disdain of it. A young man who got the publican's daughter and other young women pregnant ("The Batchelor's Lesson") does not intend to marry and be cuckolded.[6] An old woman who has resisted men's wiles all her life ("I'm Ninety-Five") supposes that marriage brings only strife, a half dozen brats, washing and mending, and finally desertion by the husband.[7] These two ballads have tenuous connections with poverty. Others of the sort—"A Single Life For Me" and "What Do People Marry For?"—have none.[8]

Poverty is more clearly and more often present in ballads about marriage itself. Arrayed on one side are ballads extolling the virtuous wife or husband. They include "The Blessings of a Good Little Wife," given below, "Dear Woman is the Joy of an Englishman's Life," and "The Good Husband." In the second of these the author sees that the single man is "like a poor tool that is of no use," whereas a happily married man "can appear like a king." His wife not only provides comfort and convenience but also offers good sense and prudence:

> If home you go tipsy, and at her do bawl,
> It will make her unhappy, no wonder at all,
> And think that a woman is right for to speak,
> She knows the bread must go short the next week.

The third ballad gives a stanza to the bad husband, the rich man who squanders his money on a whore, and it then turns to the good husband:

> If poverty comes to invade you,
>   O never deem it a curse,
> Remember the promise you made,
>   'Twas to marry for better, for worse.

> Then join your affections together,
> Let strife never enter your head,
> You'll find that you're richer than ever,
> Tho' you have but a morsel of bread.

Such an agreeable view of good little wives and husbands making a good thing of poverty is hardly the main view that the ballads offer. They are more often preoccupied with poverty as an accompaniment of scolding wives and drunken husbands, of husband-beaters and wife-beaters, of sexual discontent and adultery, of general unhappiness. Some of the ballads given below are of this sort. It is noteworthy that many such ballads are written either as by a woman or from a woman's perspective and that a large proportion of them show the woman dominating the marriage, abusing her husband verbally and physically. What is to be made of these two circumstances? There is no evidence to suggest that women wrote many broadside ballads, though they wrote a good deal of other verse in the century. And those women whose names can be put to broadside ballads—Eliza Cook, Jane Harvey, Hannah More, Miss Strickland—wrote as Christian moralists rather than as realists or satirists. It was a man who wrote "I'll Be No Submissive Wife":

> I'll be no submissive wife,
> No, not I—no, not I;
> I'll not be a slave for life,
> No, not I—no, not I.
> Think you, on a wedding day,
> That I'd say as others say,
> Love, and honour, and obey,
> No, no, no—no, no, no—not I.
>
> I to dulness don't incline,
> No, not I—no, not I;
> Go to bed at half past nine!
> No, not I—no, not I.
> Should a humdrum husband say
> That at home I ought to stay,
> Do you think that I'll obey?
> No. no, no—no, no, no—not I.[9]

The man was Thomas Haynes Bayly (1797–1839), known today chiefly as the composer of "Long Long Ago." He was a prolific and popular dramatist and songwriter, whose other songs appearing as broadsides include "I'd Be a Butterfly," "Fly Away Pretty Moth," and "She Wore a Wreath of Roses."[10] It seems reasonably certain too that a man wrote Victoria's ballads for her. In the main it seems probable that imaginative men (sympathetic, vindictive, perverse) were responsible for the sometimes confident and defiant, sometimes bitter and brutal, female voices one hears in broadside verse. Often enough the efforts seem reasonably successful, as in "I'll Be No Submissive Wife" and in the dialogue that the wife shares with the husband in "Struggle for the Breeches" given below.

The large presence of the dominating, often truculent and violent wife is another mystery, complicated by elements of exaggeration, humor, irony, and fantasy. It is certainly the case that one of the opposing figures, the patriarchal husband of Victorian legend, makes only the rarest of appearances—if any appearance at all. I have not noticed him in broadsides of the day specifically concerned about husbands and wives. One husband or another in the ballads sees himself doing most of the housework, lighting the fire, putting the kettle on, running errands, taking care of the children, putting the children to bed—with never a penny of the money he has earned to call his own ("The Man Who Wished He'd Never Got Married"). Sometimes the husband thinks he is little more than a body servant, lacing his wife's stays, tying her shoes, washing her smock, curling her hair—amid threats of being knocked about ("The Henpeck'd Husband").[11] Other husbands dwell upon their wives' shrewish characters and disgusting habits ("Termagant Wife" and "The Pensioner's Complaint"). In the first of these the husband says:

> When supper is over, and to bed we are going,
>   She takes up the candle and leaves me behind,
> When into bed we are got she turns her back to me,
>   And she f——ts like a pig, and says it's the wind,
> I repent of the day that I joined in wedlock,
>   Or to such a jade I was ever made fast,
> With scolding and brawling, and souring and f——ting,
>   I wish from my heart she had f——ted her last.[12]

In "That's the Way She Sarves Me Now" the husband says that "she wops me till I'm black and blue," keeps a fancy man, eats the best food in the house, and ignores the children.[13] In "The Fire Shovel" the several stanzas are mainly given over to the violence inflicted upon the husband:

> Then tables, chairs, and poker like fury she let fly,
> With her nails she scratch'd my face, with the bellows
>   black'd my eye,
> She tore my shirt in pieces, broke my smeller with the broom,
> Then bang'd me with the frying pan all up and down the room.[14]

Ballads from the wives' standpoints are sometimes more lighthearted. In "A Wife's Resolution to Find Her Husband Full Employment" the wife demands that the husband light the fire, sweep the house, get the breakfast, go to work for the day, make the bed when he returns home, and then come to bed and give her a kiss. "You rogue" and "you dog" she says to him at every turn except the last two.[15] In "My Husband Was a Good for Nothing Man" and "New Way to Make a Good Husband" the wives tame their spendthrift and violent husbands. After she wins a knockdown fight, the wife in the first of these two ballads calls the police and has her husband locked up. In "The Woman That Conquered a Man"[16] and "Pop Him into Limbo," the wives advise violence against the husband from the outset. The second says:

> Wop him with the rolling pin, and whack him with the ladle,
> Pop your husband in the eye, and smash him with the table;
> He must not fight, or dare to strike, or he will be a croker,
> Wop him with the bellows well, and pop him with the poker.[17]

About half of these named ballads on dominating wives give some hint of poverty in their settings. What is to be made of social class in the others is unclear, except that only rarely do they describe an obviously well-to-do or wealthy household. And what the role of poverty is in such general unhappiness is equally unclear. It is never offered as a cause and only rarely as a possible consequence, as in "New Way to Make a Good Husband." In any event the plenitude of dominating wives can perhaps be seen as a nineteenth-century male answer to an old male question: what do women most desire? Chaucer offered the example of the Wife of Bath and the presumed knowledge of Queen Guinevere: women desire the mastery. The nineteenth-century broadside ballad writers characteristically dealt with humbler life, but in 1837 they found themselves with a royal example, and they wrote a number of ballads with such titles as "Petticoat Government," "Petticoats Forever," and "Petticoats is Master."[18] In each of these ballads, and in "Pop Him Into Limbo," Victoria's sovereignty is a spur to humble women. The first ballad, by John Morgan, goes thus:

> An old tailor slap over the way was dancing and hopping so nimble,
> Then he pack'd up his sleeve-board and shears, his needle, his bodkin and thimble,
> 'Cause his wife in à terrible rage did wop him about for all devilment,
> While she shouted, Victoria huzza! we are all under Petticoat Government!

It may not be amiss, then, to conclude with two examples that do concern rich young women. "My Mama Did So Before Me" concerns a young lady who possesses fine brocades and diamonds, who entertains herself at parks and plays, and who expects to marry a suitable beau.

> Well I will manage when I'm wed
> My husband to perfection,

>And as good wives have often said,
>   Keep husbands in subjection,
>No snarling fool shall o'er me rule,
>   Nor e'er eclipse my glory,
>I'll let him see I'll mistress be,
>   Mama did so before me.[19]

The other woman is Victoria, as seen by Albert in "Prince Albert in England":

>She says now we are wed,
>   I must not dare to tease her,
>But strive both day and night,
>   All e'er I can to please her.
>I told her I would do
>   For her all I was able,
>And when she had a son
>   I would sit and rock the cradle.[20]

Love and Liver

>My toggery I took out of pawn,
>And gave my donkey a feed o' corn,
>Then mounted him—a good 'un to go,
>And off he trotted, ke marp, ge woh!
>   Singing, dumble dum deary, &c.

>Come up, says I, come up, my flower,—
>He went about ten yards an hour;
>I hit him and kicked him, and made him groan,
>Now, can't I do as I like with my own.
>   Singing, &c.

>I fell in love with a nice young dame,
>A fortune she had, although she was lame,
>Her fortune for me, it proved a bad lot,
>For Bet she was a drunken sot.
>   Singing, &c.

>Now Bet and I did jump the broom,
>We took a cock-loft for the room:
>Tin kettles the boys began to play,

But with hot suds I sent 'em away.
              Singing, &c.

Somehow things took a different turn,
Bet took to drinking things that burn;
She pawn'd my clothes and often spent
The money I saved to pay my rent.
              Singing, &c.

One night I bought some liver to fry,
And carried it home upon the sly;
But when I knock'd and kick'd the door,
I heard a most tremendous snore.
              Singing, &c.

I opened the window and got inside,
And then, sirs, what do you think I spied?
I spied a bottle of old black strap,
And Bet asleep on a chummy's lap.
              Singing, &c.

At the chummy's mug I soon let fly,
And hit him bang upon the eye;
Then told him I had not done yet,
So with the liver I wollop'd Bet.
              Singing, &c.

I beat 'em both my rage was sitch,
That no one could tell which was which;
So I rode my donkey off in the rain,
And now I'm here myself again.
              Singing, &c.

Black strap—"pejorative for thick, sweet port" (Partridge)
Chummy's—chimney sweep's

I have imported stanza 3 and made other slight changes from another printing entitled "Go It Neddy." The present printing is otherwise more satisfactory.

The earliest printing I have seen is by T. Batchelar, Hackney Road opposite the Refuge, who printed there from 1828 to 1832 (Todd).

Struggle for the Breeches!

HUSBAND. —About my wife I mean to sing a very funny song,
WIFE. —I hope that you will tell the truth, be it right or wrong.

My wife she is an arrant scold both out of doors and in,
I knew it was untrue you brute before you did begin;
You are inclined I now do find the breeches for to wear,
No dear not I, but I will die, or I will have my share.

Every morning I must rise before the day does break,
It is to the door I suppose, your water for to make,
No, it is to light the fire and have the breakfast by,
You've such a craving appetite in bed you cannot lie.

Don't contradict me now you jade, nor let my passion rise,
You stupid sot, I heed you not, because you are not wise,
I tell you for to hold your tongue, your temper I can't bear,
You ass! if I should hold my tongue my fingers I'd besmear.

You promised when I married you that you would me obey,
You promis'd for to cherish me—but then you went astray;
Women's made of crooked mind, and formed on the sixth day,
Yes, they are made of pure stuff, but men are made of clay.

Keep silence now, or I will tell your faults to all around,
You silly fool do all you can for I will stand my ground,
King Solomon says of virtuous maids he could but find a few,
You lie to say that he was wise, he was a fool like you.

Since you provoke me now, I'll let the truth be known,
I know well my faults you tell, but pray first tell your own,
Either in or out of bed I have no peace with you,
You simpleton don't talk of bed—it's little there you do.

Before that you get out of bed there is your dram for you,
You share it, out of three glasses you have two,
And when at breakfast you do sit your tongue it goes along,
Because you eat a butter'd toast, and I eat a dry one.

I have the young one for to nurse, and rock the cradle too,
For fear that you do something worse, I give you that to do!
There in an honest publican's you go and sit you down,
You sot where I spend sixpence, you spend half-a-crown.

When it draws near dinner time, to me you show your face,
It's true but I could show a droller looking place,
And when you do to dinner sit, there you sigh and groan,
That's because you eat the meat, and leave me the bare bone.

And when the tea time is come, then you take the pot,
I look for a strong cup of tea, but the devil a drop I get;
And when we go to bed at night you'll not agreeable be,
Because you act not like a man, but turn your back on me.

You know I've acted like a man since you and I were joined,
The devil a bit of manhood in you I ever find,
If in any part I've acted wrong, explain it to me now,
A many men do harrow what other men do plough.

My father was a wealthy man, had horses, ploughs, and carts,
Your father's fowls had wings of gold, we hear from you in part,
My mother was a lady gay—that's known to be true—
I wish that she had broke your back—or made a man of you.

Several versions of the ballad exist, one under the title "Hard Struggle for the Breeches," and they show a bit of a struggle themselves over its alternating clumsiness and straightforwardness. Few of the variations are of interest. Line 8 sometimes goes "Unto the door I do suppose your notice for to take" or "It is to the door, I suppose, you want for to make." In the latter printing the wife eats "a dry scone," she squanders money on drink "in that honest publican's," and she says more clearly scornfully in the last stanza, "Yes, feathered fowl have wings of gold, we hear, in foreign parts." The ballad seems to have been the most popular ballad of the "struggle for the breeches" sort. The earliest printing I have noted was issued by Catnach, probably between 1832 and 1836.

The Blessings of a Good Little Wife

Some people 'gainst women are railing,
And say that to tease is their plan,

But without them we would be bewailing
    For a woman's a pleasure to man.
A virtuous woman's a treasure,
    Her smile quickly banishes strife,
And that man is a stranger to pleasure,
    Who has not got a good little wife.

The man who is lonely and single,
    Is at best but a poor wretched elf;
With the drunkard he daily does mingle,
    And wastes both his health and his pelf.
He has nothing to make him be careful,
    No partner to sweeten his life;
But his time passes happy and cheerful,
    When he's blest with a good little wife.

A single man's troubles are plenty,
    To molly about is his doom;
The slops in his pail he must empty,
    And sweep up and scour the room.
He must wash his own shirts—light the fire,
    And mend his own clothes 'pon my life,
But he's as happy as a man can desire,
    When he's blest with a good little wife.

A single man's life is distressing,
    In a garret he's stuck all alone,
It's always a deuce of a mess in,
    As cheerless and cold as a stone.
His bed, too, is wretched and lonely,
    Scarce made once a month 'pon my life,
But no bed looks so pleasant and homely,
    As the one that contains a good wife.

A woman is man's sole enjoyment,
    In sickness and woe she's his friend.
To comfort him is her employment,
    And the cares which oppress him to mend.
When sickness brings sorrow and sadness,
    Though with pain he is ever so rife,
He'll find nought can yield him such gladness
    As the smiles of a good little wife.

At night when from labour retiring,
    He finds a good supper prepar'd,
Such pleasures who'd not be admiring,
    But those who such pleasures ne'er shar'd.
Then wedlock he finds a blessing,
    He sits down devoid of all strife,
On his knee he's his children caressing,
    By his side sits his good little wife.

Then you that in pleasure would mingle,
    Get married—for that's your best plan,
They are fools who resolve to die single,
    For woman's an angel to man.
In fact she's his sole consolation,
    The pleasure that cheers him through life,
And the brightest of gems in the nation,
    Is that jewel—a good little wife.

The ballad is known also under the title "The Charms of a Good Little Wife," from which I have taken stanza division. The earliest printings I have seen date from the middle 1830s.

The Wives Lamentation

Ten years ago I married a man who's such a drunken sot,
That since the day I'm sorry to say, my things are gone to pot.
In a public house from morn till night getting drunk is he,
And I not a penny to buy a roll or get a bit of tea.

CHORUS
Drunk, drunk from morn till night in a public house is he,
Smoking, drinking, then at night comes home and wollops me.

I've children five, they're all alive and all are young and small,
They are half-starved, clothed in rags, not a shoe amongst them all,
When they ask for bread it drives me mad to hear them squall and bawl,
While all the money their father gets goes up against the wall.

The other night he came home, kick'd up the devils own rout,
Because that I had gone to bed and put the candle out.
And in the night all in a fright, if one of the children squall,
He out of the window swears he'll throw me, children and all.

Now he can get two pounds a week, if he would only work,
But if I only tell him so he bangs me like a Turk.
It's many a month since a week's work he's done, you see,
Nor will he do a single job when he's at home for me.

To raise some money to get drunk what do you think he done,
My flat iron pawned and tinder box all for to get some,
And when no snuff was in his box, nor in his pocket money,
My mop he went and sold for rags, to a rag shop for a penny.

When he comes home at twelve at night into bed he'll pop,
So stupid drunk before he gets in, he cannot reach the pot,
Then in the morning when he wakes and raises up his head,
He raves and roars and loudly swears, the child has —— the bed.

Now if you meet him in the street I'll tell you how he's drest,
His coat it is in five hundred holes, and that coat is the best,
His breeches are so worn and torn they're almost gone to pot,
That's why he wears an apron to cover what little he's got.

I wish I was a maid again, as I was ten years ago,
I would not marry the finest man that ever stept in a shoe,
I'll here agree with any wife that's plagued with such another,
To give old Nick one of them, to run away with the other.

Goes against the wall—goes to settle the score for drink, totted up on the wall of the bar

The ballad tells its unhappy tale with mixed vigor and clumsiness. I have imported stanza 5 from another printing, along with several other words and phrases that seem to serve the ballad better than the equivalents given in this one. Some other versions of the ballad do not make the derogatory sexual comment in the latter half of the last line in stanza 7, giving instead, "and no shoes to his feet he's got."

Drunkenness is a common topic of nineteenth-century broadside ballads. The more serious attacks on it are often from religious standpoints. One of the Cheap Repository Tracts of the 1790s, Hannah More's "Hard Times" (We say the times are grievous hard), suggests that hard times are mainly the result of drunkenness. Another Cheap Repository title is "The Gin-Shop; or, a Peep into Prison." With the coming of the railway in the 1830s came "The Railroad to Hell" (which followed hard upon "Railway to Heaven"):[21]

> You've nothing to do but guzzle and swill,
> As long as the landlord is willing to fill,
> For this is the line and the railroad to hell,
> Where drunkards and devils for ever must dwell,

Another religious ballad, "A Laughable and Interesting Picture of Drunkenness," observes that there are 50 places of worship in town (Preston) and 245 places licensed to sell strong drink.

At some point gin shops turned into gin palaces. An article on the streets of London in *Chambers' Journal* (1845) says that four of the seven houses that form the angles of Seven Dials are occupied by gin palaces, outdoing in splendor the jewellers' shops of better districts. They are, says the writer, the only sort of splendid shop that welcomes the poor.[22] Ten years earlier, John Morgan touched upon the splendor in "A True Picture of the London Gin Palaces":

> Like palaces the doors afar, sir,
> And a lamp as big as Temple Bar, sir,
> A slashing clock, and that's not all, sir,
> Quite as big as the dome upon St. Paul's, sir.[23]

By and large, poverty is a side issue, a threat, or a single consequence among several consequences in ballads about drunkenness. Two teetotal ballads that dwell upon drunkenness and poverty are "The Drunkard's Looking Glass" and "The Reformed Drunkard's Children's Song." The latter ballad says:

> Our fathers were sots, they had drunken of ale,
> Our mothers were ragg'd and their faces were pale,
> The teetotal breeze blew their rags all away,
> Teetotal forever, teetotal huzza.

Three other ballads linking drunkenness and poverty are "Rag Bag," "The Snob and the Bottle," and "The Snob's Confession."

The earliest printing I have seen of the present ballad is by Catnach at 2 Monmouth Court, presumably dating from 1832–36. It does not appear in his 1832 catalogue.

Mrs. Johnson

Oh, I have got a charming bride,
Thro' life we both so sweetly glide,
She's really worth the world beside,
    Her name is Mrs. Johnson!
We both agree in every frame,
So one another we ne'er blame,
I'm humpty, bandy—she's the same,
    Oh, lovely Mrs. Johnson.

CHORUS

So I've got a charming bride,
Thro' life we both so sweetly glide,
She's really worth the world beside,
    Oh, pretty Mrs. Johnson.

I to the gin-shop go each day,
A dozen drops I stow away,
I after that at skittles play,
    And so does Mrs. Johnson!
I beat the chaps with great delight,
And put the gatter out of sight,
Then stagger home dead drunk at night,
    And so does Mrs. Johnson!

To free and easy's I repair,
My name is famous everywhere,
I very often take the chair,
    And so does Mrs. Johnson!
Do you think I pay my penny? No!
I chaunts "The Bay of Biscay O!"
And like a lord my backey blow,
    And so does Mrs. Johnson.

At dancing I am quite a don,
To twop'nny shops I often run,
And I can shuffle, too—like fun,
    And so can Mrs. Johnson!

At fighting I can take my share,
I am a match for any here,
A fighting man I am they swear,
    And—so is Mrs. Johnson.

Among the girls I sometimes roam,
'Bout which she does not stamp or foam,
I often take a lover home,
    And so does Mrs. Johnson!
In getting children I'm not shy,
For modesty is all my eye,
I've got four young 'uns on the sly,
    And so has Mrs. Johnson.

'Bout dress I do not care a jot,
Tho' once of clothes I had a lot,
I've pawned all but the suit I've got,
    And so has Mrs. Johnson!
Of trouble I have felt the shocks,
And 'cause I gave a cove some knocks,
I twice have been put in the stocks,
    And so has Mrs. Johnson.

So all who are to wedlock prone,
If you its joys would have alone,
Select a temper for your own,
    As I did Mrs. Johnson!
For if your ways bring misery,
So long as you can both agree,
As blest as turtle doves you'll be,
    Like me and Mrs. Johnson.

Humpty, bandy—dumpy, bandy-legged
Gatter—beer
Free and easy—more or less informal gathering for drink and song at pub or tavern; forerunner of music hall
Bay of Biscay—popular song from the end of the eighteenth century
Don—an adept
Twopenny shop—pawnbroking intermediary
Shuffle—scrounge

The ballad is by Thomas Peckett Prest, and appeared under his name in the twenty-fifth number of *Singer's Penny Magazine and Reciter's Album,* which Prest himself edited. The date would have been about December 1834. The ballad seems to have been fairly popular on the street, and apparently was Prest's most successful ballad there. No broadside printing I have seen bears his name. For comment on Prest and *Singer's Penny Magazine and Reciter's Album* see pages 511–14.

I have printed from a broadside. It shows negligible differences from the magazine version aside from a defective line in stanza 5. I have made correction from the magazine.

How likely it was that anyone in 1834 would have been put in the stocks is unclear. In 1872 the *Times* reported as an extraordinary event that a man had been put in the stocks at Newbury for drunken and disorderly conduct, noting that the stocks at Newbury had not been used for the previous twenty-six years. Leon Radzinowicz's *History of English Criminal Law,* volume 4, 1968, says that "the punishment of the stocks began to be disused about the beginning of the nineteenth century, but has not been expressly abolished."

A Week's Matrimony

On Sunday morning I went out for a spree,
And met a maid as fair could be;
An angel quite in every part,
And Cupid pierced me with his dart.
I walk'd up to her, and made a bow,
 And told her that I hop'd as how,
My arm and company she'd partake—
To which she did a curtsey make.
We walk'd about from place to place;
She prais'd my wit, and I prais'd her face;
I treated her, made all things right,
And courted her on Sunday night.

On Monday morning I met her again;
I think the place was Drury-lane,
We pass'd an hour in harmless chat,
Talking of wedlock and all that.
She vow'd she for a husband sigh'd;
Said I, "I sadly want a bride —
How blest I'd be if you I had!"
"Oh dear!" said she, "you're just the lad."

We both agreed as quick as thought,
That hour the ring and license bought;
And then got swish'd all right and tight—
So married I was by Monday night.

On Tuesday I got up with glee,
No one could feel more joy than me;
A party had so fine and gay,
And cheerfully we pass'd the day.
A man, who at the table sat,
With my wife cut it rather fat;
He tipp'd her on the sly a kiss—
She seem'd to think it not amiss;
My mind at that soon caught alarm,
But he declared he meant no harm;
While she wink'd at him out of spite,
So jealous I was by Tuesday night.

On Wednesday morning I look'd blue,
My wife was cross and snappish too;
I soon found out she had a tongue,
And we went at it both ding dong,
Vexation on vexation rose—
Abuse came first and then came blows,
She tore my hair and scratched my face,
And in return I smash'd the place.
"She'd quickly conquer me," she said,
Then with the tongs she broke my head,
So I went at her left and right,
And we mill'd each other by Wednesday night.

On Thursday morning I went out,
To take the air and walk about;
Without my plague I wished to roam,
So left my wife in bed at home.
To soothe my cares and drown my pain,
I took at every shop a drain,
Till I had swigged a decent stock,
Then staggered home at ten o'clock.
But when to bed I did repair,
Another man, quite happy there,
In bed with her soon caught my sight,
So cuckold I was by Thursday night.

On Friday we agreed to part,
So I went and hired a horse and cart,
Pack'd up my goods without delay,
And bore them every one away.
My wife at this began to grieve,
And said without me she'd not live,
But I made answer with a frown,
And then politely knocked her down.
I soon found out she had not lied,
Her neck she in her garters tied;
Then to a nail she fix'd them tight,
And scragg'd herself by Friday night.

On Saturday morning I hired the ground,
Then bought her coffin tight and sound,
I next with onions rubb'd my eyes,
And gammoned a lot of tears and sighs.
I took a stroll about the town—
Went home, and seen her fasten'd down—
Thank'd my stars she was now at peace,
And own'd it was a happy release.
To blow my clay and take a drop,
I hasten'd to a daffy shop—
Ten goes of max put out of sight,
And got drunk for joy on Saturday night.

On Sunday morning I looked sad,
Although in secret were more glad,
The mourners came in dark array,
With men to bear the corpse away.
The undertakers bore her out—
Relations, friends all flocked about,
They cried themselves till nearly blind,
I hid my face and laughed behind.
The parson read the funeral prayers,
I gave a few more sighs and tears,
Then saw her in the grave, all right,
And made love to another on Sunday night.

Drury Lane—Among other uses, a place for prostitutes

Mill'd—fought
Scragg'd—hanged
Gammon'd—feigned
Clay—clay pipe
Daffy—gin
Max—gin

Another ballad that tells much the same tale is "Woeful Marriage." In a third ballad of the sort, "Johnny Raw and Polly Clark," the wife leaves with the other man.

The present ballad is not in Catnach's 1832 catalogue but was printed by him from 2 Monmouth Street, and presumably dates from 1832–36. A printing by W. Taylor was issued in 1837, just after Victoria ascended the throne and just before Taylor disappeared from business. His address is given as "14 Waterloo Road near the Victoria Theatre (late Coburg)." I have used some punctuation here from the Taylor printing. The ballad seems to have been fairly popular.

The Drunken Husband
A New Comic Song, Written by John Morgan

You married women draw near awhile,
I will tell you a tale will make you smile,
Concerning a man and his wife, d'ye see,
Who after they married could never agree.

CHORUS
So women I hope you will follow this plan,
If you should be plagued with a drunken man.

This couple got married for better or worse,
But the wife had reasons the man to curse,
For never could he give her a good word,
But came home of a night as drunk as a lord.

One morning a scheme came into her head,
While he was drinking she pawned the bed,
When he came home he began to rant and roar,
For that night he was forced to lay on the floor.

Next morning early she went in a flirt,
And pawned his waistcoat, breeches and shirt,

And before she returned again to him,
She spent three-parts of the money in gin.

He put on his rags and went afloat,
She went and sold his hat and his coat,
She went where he was and he did her abuse,
Then she went and spouted his stockings and shoes.

He came home at night in a terrible rage,
But she was ready the foe to engage,
She picked up her spirits, —he did begin,
But she knocked him down with the rolling-pin.

I will serve you out, to her he then said,
She up with the poker and cracked his head,
She cried, you villain, I'll serve you out,
Then wollop'd him well with a dirty clout.

He hollow'd aloud—she tore his clothes,
She blacked his eyes and broke his nose,
You villain! she cried, no more of your airs,
Then slap she bundled him over the stairs.

Dear wife! dear wife! he then did say,
On your husband have compassion I pray,
And if my dear you'll me forgive
I will never get drunk as long as I live.

Together we will contentment seek,
My wages I'll bring you every week.
Then on him she looked with great disdain,
And said—I'll try you once again.

I'll forgive you, she cried, then opened the door,
If you'll promise to never get drunk any more,
He swore an oath and she found him right,
And now they live happy like man and wife.

He never gets drunk,—his wife he loves,
And they live together like turtle doves,
So women you'll find this an excellent plan,
If you wish to reform a drunken man.

The ballad dates from 1836–37 when the printer, W. Taylor, 14 Waterloo Road (sometimes 16), was on the verge of going out of business and was in association with a ballad seller and printer named Martin (presently Hillatt and Martin, printers), 13 Little Prescott Street, Goodman's Fields, Minories. I have deleted sporadically used quotation marks. Lines 3 and 4 in the third quatrain appear to be defective. Other printings, not bearing Morgan's name, omit the third from last stanza.

The ballad seems to have been popular for a number of years. It has a counterpart in "The Drunken Wife." In the latter ballad the husband is forbearing, though he considers leaving the marriage. Meanwhile the wife pawns his goods to sustain her vice. He sleeps on straw and thinks that "a drunken wife is a poor man's plague." Whether this ballad is also by Morgan is unknown. Of Morgan's nine known ballads on marriage, five describe its joys (all from the man's standpoint), and four describe its woes (two from the man's standpoint, two from the woman's). In one of the last group, "The Good Looking Man," the wife smashes her philandering husband's face with rolling pin and poker.[24]

The Woman That Wished She'd Never Got Married

Young ladies, have pity on me,
    Let me in your company mingle;—
I once was a maiden so free;
    Like you I was happy and single:
My mother advised me to wed,
    When till seventeen I had tarried;
To church I set off in a trice,
    With a man, lack-a-day! to be married.
        Rite fol de rol, &c.

A short time he loved me sincere,
    And used me both kindly and civil;
But the honeymoon scarcely was over,
    When my husband turned out a mere devil:
The bellows he threw at my head,
    My clothes to the pop-shop he carried:
I often have wished I'd been dead,
    Before I had ever been married.

One night he came home in a pet,
    And burnt my new boots to a cinder,

The cat he kicked under the grate,
    And the table threw out of the window;
The bed he took up on his back,
    And off to the brokers he carried;
He sold both the poker and tongs;—
    Oh! I wish I had never been married.

He has but one shirt to his back:
    To the ginshop he likes to be dashing.
Sunday all day he lays in the bed,
    While his shirt and his socks I'm washing;
His trousers are all full of holes:
    Long my apron before him he's carried:
He grunts and he snores like a pig:
    Oh, I wish I had never been married!

My husband's a comical man,
    He is a regular out-and-out nipper;
He lays out his money himself,
    In tea, sugar, candles, and pepper.
Sometimes for a ha'p'orth of starch,
    A week or a fortnight I've tarried;
I'm pothered to death and half starved:
    Oh! I wish I had never been married.

Whenever he buys any meat—
    Once a month, or I'm greatly mistaken—
It is only a sheep's head and pluck,
    Or a small bit of liver and bacon.
He says bread and butter is dear,
    And times are most shocking and horrid;
I drink water while he drinks strong beer:
    Oh! I wish I had never been married.

To the landlord the rent he won't pay,
    Because, he declares, he's not able;
He has nought to be taken away
    But two broken chairs and a table;
For the bedclothes, the kettles, and broom,
    And washing tubs, off he has carried:
May old Nick fetch him off very soon!
    Oh! I wish I had never been married.

I should be happy and joyful once more
    If I could but just see it all right:
May old Nick come and whip him away
    Some morning before it is day light.
While you ladies do single remain,
    By a tyrant you'll never be harried:
If I was but single again,
    Oh! by jingo I'd never be married.

Pop-shop—pawnshop

The printing used here is the earliest one I have seen of the ballad. It was issued by James Paul at 2 & 3 Monmouth Court in the early 1840s. He worked there jointly with Anne Ryle for some years after Catnach's death. Paul also issued "The Man Who Wished He'd Never Got Married," mentioned in the introduction to this section.

My Wife's First Baby

The other night as I lay in my bed
    Along with my wife Mrs. Bunning,
She said, Tom, for the doctor pray run
    For I think our first baby is coming,
I dressed myself quick you'll suppose,
    The snow on the ground was fast falling,
Shut the door and was cutting away,
    When the policeman sent me a sprawling.

Hollo, my fine fellow, said he,
    You've been robbing the house of a neighbour,
In vain I implored to be free,
    And told him my wife was in labour,
Said he then, you'll soon follow suit,
    For confined you'll be I maintain,
To the station with me you must go,
    Your tale is all labour in vain.

The inspector on duty I knew,
    And got off very pleased with his manner,

For he said the policeman should go
  And find out the nurse Mrs. Tanner;
To the wrong house he went, and then
  Very loud at the door began knocking,
O they emptied the contents of the po
  On his head, and he looked very shocking.

The doctor he made matters right,
  And brought forth the precious young baby,
Which good reason I have to deplore,
  For the treatment I get is so shabby.
My bed is like one in a garden,
  Well watered each night, and I'm sure
You will pity my case when I say
  On my legs I oft find some manure.

Sometimes I'm awoke in the night
  By the child kicking up a great rout,
Out of bed I'm obliged for to get,
  And I trot the young fellow about;
But the weather is so very cold
  To pity me you'll be inclined,
For my shirt which is wet thro' and thro'
  Keeps flapping against my behind.

The folks tell me never to mind,
  My feelings I always should smother;
Tho' this may be all very well,
  But my wife she will soon have another,
She is such a rum 'un to go,
  I ought to have plenty of riches,
In the family way she will fall
  If I on the bed throw my breeches.

Of these to my wife I complain,
  And I tell her the game she should strike it,
But she says it's my fault and not hers,
  She'll have the whole lot 'cause she likes it!
So I try to bear up all I can,
  Though I own I'm a bit of a grumbler,
Yet it is better perhaps after all,
  Than to be called by the women a fumbler.

The printer of the ballad was C. Paul at 18 Great St. Andrew's Street. He is known to have been there between 1845 and 1848, and was possibly there later. I have added punctuation.

Poor Married Man

Oh, what sorrow a poor man's life is,
          Poor married man,
It full of trouble grief and strife is,
          Poor married man,
Soon as he's wed things sure to frown will,
Trades sure to go in country and town ill,
It's all up and down, down, down hill,
          Poor married man.

He goes to church brisk as a vulter,
          Poor married man,
With a "H" they ought to spell that Altar,
          Poor married man,
When wed the fair have fairly trick'd him,
Even the beadle grins to see how they nick'd him,
Cries there goes another Hymen's victim,
          Poor married man.

When single, he thought the parlour a slap room;
          Poor married man,
When married he smokes a short pipe in a tap room,
          Poor married man,
When he goes home, they're sure to bore him,
Tease and snarl, nag and jaw him,
And his eldest boy is good to floor him,
          Poor married man.

Visions of the workhouse landlord and broker,
          Poor married man,
Haunt his mind till he is nearly a croker,
          Poor married man,
Three children down with the scarlatina,
The measles seizes poor Georgina,
And a black man steps it with Angelina,
          Poor married man.

Soon after marriage he's sure to be hard up,
    Poor married man,
He begins to accumulate his uncle's cards up,
    Poor married man,
The feathers go pound by pound till the last one,
A brown sugar basin instead of a glass one,
The wedding ring gives place to a brass one,
    Poor married man.

Trousers wet and cradle rocking,
    Poor married man,
Buttonless shirt and feetless stockings,
    Poor married man,
He has no shirt, especially on one day,
When he lays at home without it on Sunday,
While the old gal rubs it out for Monday,
    Poor married man.

He lives on sodgers, rashers, faggots,
    Poor married man,
When in luck, block ornaments and chances the maggots,
    Poor married man,
Dreams of blow outs, kitchen clearings,
Fancies he's Lord Mayor, when eating tongue parings,
And longs for the time of cheap fresh herrings,
    Poor married man.

Last scene that ends the poor man's history,
    Poor married man,
He dies, how he liv'd had been a mystery,
    Poor married man,
Grim death comes kindly to relieve him,
Friends so poor, no time to grieve him,
And a parish egg chest perhaps may receive him,
    Poor married man.

Slap—excellent
Uncle's—pawnbroker's
Sodgers—red herrings
Block ornaments—inferior meat

The ballad is by J. A. Hardwick, who is the author of four slender comic songbooks published in the early 1850s. It comes from the first collection where it bears the title "The Poor Man's Life."[25] The broadside version, three stanzas shorter, is used here. In 1874 another songwriter picked up the broadside title and used it as a refrain in quite the same manner.[26] Another ballad in the same vein as "Poor Married Man" is "Matrimonial Miseries":

> In genteel apartments I used to reside,
>   Quite free from the world's troubled cares;
> But now in a garret I'm forc'd for to hide,
>   In an alley up five pair of stairs.

Hardwick is now identified as the author of "St. James's and St. Giles's," given in volume 1. It was published under his name as sheet music that dates about 1863. It does not seem to have appeared in any of his four collections of comic songs, published in about 1852–54, although known copies of the second, third, and fourth collections are missing some pages. Hardwick is also the author of a workhouse ballad quoted on page 193. Several of his songs appear in the second series of *Labern's Comic Minstrel* of 1865.

7

Poets

The three poets described in the ballads below are of three sorts. The first is a familiar doleful poet in a garret, except that he is on the road—a wandering bard. He is a man who "from scribbling can't refrain" and who must "either sing or cry." He is a humble version of Tennyson in *In Memoriam*, who sings because he must, pipes but as the linnet sings, sings with sorrow-drowning song. The second is a lighthearted poet—forthright, sensual, cynical. Billy Nutts is a minor Byron of *Don Juan*. He refers to Byron by name and perhaps alludes to an early stanza in *Don Juan* when he claims to possess attic wit. He might like to write his verses reeling with drink, but he lacks money; he celebrates an unsavory small world instead of a glittering large one; he is more wishful than successful with women. The third poet is more cadger than poet. He is preoccupied with poetic lies: catchpennies and cocks. He resembles no major poet's description of himself in the nineteenth century, and compares only with a few nameless scribes of Grub Street whom Isaac D'Israeli alludes to in *Calamities of Authors*—those who would not blush to admit that they write anything to earn a crust.[1]

What these three poets have most in common is their resemblance to ordinary or low human beings of the century. The first scribbles rather than warbles, the second is troubled with fleas, the third shows no shame. In the late twentieth century, when a perceived wide gap between poetic persona and petty poet causes distress and outrage, the three creators of these figures perhaps deserve admiration. Of the three, only the author of Billy Nutts is known in the slightest degree. He may have been less lowly and lively than Nutts.

It is the case, though, that ballads about poets are few in broadside literature. These three ballads themselves seem to have been popular in varying degree, but other examples of their sort are rare. Broadside balladry as a whole is not self-regarding, whether it was written for the street or came onto the street from elsewhere. Though the poets in the three ballads speak of themselves, they are concerned to describe their clothes, diet, and professional tricks rather more than their thoughts and feelings. In other broadside ballads a poet may declare that he will sing a song that will not detain you long, but that assertion is most likely to be the beginning and end of his self-regard. Once in a great while he speaks more self-consciously, as in "The New Times": "Ye working men where'er ye dwell, lend an attentive ear, / While I in humble verse relate the sufferings that you endure." But that poet too then forgets himself. In the main, poets in broadside verse are present chiefly in their voices. Insofar as the men and women behind them came from a wide range of class and culture, the emergent voices are various. Insofar as notions of poetic dignity were known to educated and uneducated alike, much of the verse aims for dignity in one way or another:

> When on these lands, which now are let so high,
> The ploughshare sped beneath our grandsire's eye . . .
> —"Lines on the Corn Bill," given here

> See the star breasted villain to yonder cot bound,
> Where the sweet honeysuckle entwines itself round . . .
> —"The Village Beauty," given here

> In a little blue garment all ragged and torn,
> With scarce any shoes to his feet . . .
> —"Poor Little Child of a Tar," written for stage
> or concert room and coming onto the street

> All you that fear the Lord who rules the sky,
> Praise his holy name that dwells on high . . .
> —"The Lamentation of Sarah Bursnell,
> by Herself, a Blind Woman"

Sometimes dressing up for a ballad meant dressing down. Cockney and canting ballads are of this sort. "Billy Nutts" and "Anything to Earn a Crust," both given below, owe something to these latter guises.

The most interesting poetic persona in nineteenth-century English broadside ballads is John Morgan's. As Morgan is depicted late in life by Charles Hindley, and as he appears in relation to Hindley in his late letters, he is humble and deferential, voluble and mirthful, made somewhat foolish by drink, and all the same possessed of certain confidence of knowledge. In the ballads of earlier years used here, he is quite different. In "Advice to Country Maidens on the Poor Law Bill" and in "Rigs and Flares-Up of the Fair" he is earthy, amused, knowing in the ways of young love and lust, male and female. In "The Drunken Husband" he is a detached but close observer of domestic violence, unsurprised by it, ready to offer a wry lesson from it. In "The Way to Live" he is newly wedded husband and wife who contemplate with good-humored equanimity a joint arduous life as shopkeepers—the husband perhaps expecting certain private pleasures on the side. In "Assessed Taxes" he is a man angry at and contemptuous of oppressors of the poor. In "Little Lord John Out of Service" he assumes the person of an anxious, demeaned, and absurd—instead of lordly—Lord John Russell. In "Camberwell & Reform!" (photographed on page 114 in the shape in which it was sold on London streets in June 1832) he shares popular exhilaration at a victory for social reform. The common presence in these several ballads—and in the quoted stanzas of a number of others—is that of an unpretentious man, a democrat, without pride or flourishes, detached from others and able to get outside himself; a man of humor and good sense, yet possessing passion and compassion, concerned mainly for the ordinary lives of those about him in the ordinary social and political world. It is a highly unusual poetic presence in nineteenth-century English poetry, and it perhaps bears a close resemblance to John Morgan on the street in younger, more vigorous, less vulnerable years. Two other ballads in the collection that are probably Morgan's—"The Queen & the Taxes" and "Agitation of Great Britain"—show the same character.

Wandering Bard

I'm the wandering bard of Exeter,
 from scribbling can't refrain,
It is poverty compels me
 to come out in the rain;
Hard is my fate, I have no estate,
 and must either sing or cry:
My lot is cast, I'm forc'd at last
 to ask of you to buy.

Cold winter's now approaching,
 but I have no clothes to pack,
None have I left behind me,
 for they are all on my back;
And I'll be bound that none around
 can tell me where these were made,
Nor can he be found in this town,
 to name that man of trade.

My coat cost ten-and-six-pence
 about six years ago,
I bought it of a clothesman,
 but his name I did not know.
This old hat I had of a soldier,
 but the lining's from it tore,

And an old oil skin has covered it
    for seven long years or more.

This old handkerchief about my neck,
    just to ornament the frame,
I bought of a w———e at a gin-shop door,
    the corner of Drury-lane.
My waistcoat cost me three-pence,
    you may think the price too high,
I found my old shirt among some dirt
    and hung it up to dry.

Now for to beg these breeches
    I had very much to do;
My stockings cost me four-pence
    in the year of ninety-two.
If these two shoes are fellows,
    I think it something rare,
For one I bought at St. Giles's,
    and the other in Rag-Fair.

O now that I am clothed, friends,
    you cannot say they're dear,
I come into this alehouse
    just to take a cup of beer,
It always makes me cheerful,
    tho' the times are very hard,
Now buy my song be it right or wrong
    it will help the wandering bard.

Rag Fair—market near Tower Bridge that sold cheap clothing; celebrated in an eighteenth-century ballad, "The Humours of Rag Fair"[2]

The wandering bard is often from Manchester instead of Exeter, and he is often mistaken for a bird—with "bird" being given in title, first line, and last line, as in the present copy, which I have corrected. The printer himself, or a printer before him, was aware that something was wrong, for he amended matters by removing "bird" from its rhyming position in the last line and creating a closing couplet. In so doing he ignored the general rhyme scheme:

> It always makes me cheerful,
>> tho' the times are very hard,
>> Now buy my song be it right or wrong,
>> it will help the wandering bird along.

I have made corrections from another printing.

Among minor variations in printings, one version gives "lass" instead of "w———e," and another, in which the bard is from Manchester, gives "Foundry Lane" instead of "Drury Lane."

A poet named Nathan Withy, active from about 1775 to 1810 or later, called himself the wandering bard. His territory extended between Wolverhampton and London, Wolverhampton and Worcester. He wrote in a rather formal style. If the ballad concerns him, it was written in his person by someone else. See the endnote for an account of some of his verses.[3]

The date that the bard buys his stockings suggests that the ballad was written at the turn of the century. The sum of ten and sixpence for his coat must mean sixteen pence (one shilling and fourpence), not ten shillings and sixpence. In "The Bailiffs Have Been," written in about 1830, the speaker of the ballad has bought a cheap coat in Monmouth Street for three shillings. He seems to be a person in slightly better circumstances than the wandering bard. It is the case, though, that all printings of the ballad that have been noticed date from the 1820s or later.

Billy Nutts, the Poet

Written by John Martin, Esq. and Sung by Mr. J. W. Sharp

> I'm Billy Nutts, wot always cuts
>> A swell throughout the town, sir;
> With clever men my learned pen
>> In grammar gains renown, sir.
> My clever verse I does rehearse,
>> In song, and catch, and ditty,
> And with each line in dying speech,
>> I does excite their pity.

>> CHORUS
> So all agree to welcome me,
>> With songs, with fifes, with viols,
> Because my name stands first with fame—
>> I'm the bard of Seven Dials!

My learned brains a fortin gains—
    A fact I'm never slighting—
For I can write on politics,
    And people's wrongs be righting.
I can prate about the State,
    Such subjects ne'er was writ on—
And oft I'm seen, all with the Queen,
    A dining like a Briton.

SPOKEN.

But talking about dining, 'tis not often us poets gets a dinner, but when we does—ah, there's the rub! What is there so delightful, so magnificent, so scrumptious as a sheep's head, alias—a mountain-pecker, or a Jemmy? But talking of a Jemmy—I've got a few lines on a sheep's head—I'll recite them to you.—"Lines on a *Sheep's Head*, after the style of Pope—improved by *Lamb*."

"Sheep's head, how hard thy *tale* to tell is!
How often have you filled the bellies
Of Marys, Sukeys, Janes, and Nellys?
Thy primest part each one knows well, is
The fat eye, from which luscious jellies
Flows. And then how sweet thy smell is!
The eager butcher tries to sell his
    Sanguinary Jemmies!" NUTTS.
    So all agree, &c.

The verse I write fills with delight
    The grave, the wise, and stupid,
And as I wend, a regular friend
    To me is Master Cupid.
Each buzzum swells at tales I tells—
    I'm versed in human natur—
Of flowery ware, in verses rare,
    I stands a common*tatur*.

SPOKEN.

Yes, I'm unfortunately a *common tatur*—in fact, I may say, a *diseased tatur*. I've got a few lines on a tatur. I'll recite them. "Lines on a Tatur, after the manner of Shakespeare—improved by *Murphy*."

"Oh, flowery ware, how well you suit
    The calls of human natur—

> None can compare, I do declare,
>   With thee, oh, flowery tatur.
> Kidney or round, you're always found
>   Amidst all noise and rackets,
> Sometimes in hash, sometimes in smash,
>   And sometimes in your jackets.
> How oft have I beheld young maids
>   Your flowery jackets peeling—
> With *pinted* knives dig out your eyes—
>   They've got no fellow feeling." NUTTS.

But, talking of a tatur, there is something else in my domestic economy that comes nearer home to me than a tatur—that's a red herring, alias a soger. I have got a few lines on a red herring. I'll recite them. "Lines on a Red Herring."

> "Oh herring! herring! herring red!
> Good with taturs, or with bread—
> How oft on you the poets fed—
> If it wasn't for you I should be dead.
> I eat you all except bones and head,
> And that the cat gnaws—'neath the bed,
>   I throw't her!
> You're never served up with kidney beans,
> Nor yet with turnips, carrots, and greens,
> A little vinegar doth embellish,
> And sends you down with a kind of relish,
> But worst of all—none can deny
> You make a poor man very dry,
> And if he hasn't got the stump,
> To quench his thirst, flies to the pump—
> For beer he cannot fork his mags out
> So at the pump he blows his bags out.
> Some like you *biled*, and some admire
> You done in front of a blazing fire.
> I like you best done on a grid—
> I always did, from a little kid.
>   Alas, poor bloater!"
>   NUTTS.
>   So all agree, &c.
>
> Although my wit is "attic wit,"
>   For attics well I loves 'em,

> Great men who snore in a first floor,
>   Must own that I'm above 'em.
> The pence amounts, while I recounts
>   In words sublime arrayed—
> Of murders done, and battles won,
>   And "Lines Upon a Barmaid."

SPOKEN.

Talking of a barmaid, I knew a barmaid once. Oh, she was a gal! She was a screamer! I've got a few lines I composed on her. I'll recite them to you. "Lines on a Barmaid, after the style of Byron. The music by Handel."

> "Oh, you scrumptious little dear,
> When I sees you draw the beer
> Out of the engine, it is clear,
> You at me casts a wicked leer—
> Oh, crikey! don't I then feel queer,
> With a tingling in each ear—
>   Sich ringins!
> But when your hand stretched out I sees,
> To take the money with such ease,
> The opportunity I seize
> To give your little hand a squeeze—
> And then together works my knees—
> With you I'd live on bread and cheese,
>   And inguns!"

NUTTS.

But talking of that barmaid, what with thinking of her, and the annoyance of the cursed tormentors, I could not get a wink of sleep. But talking of tormentors—I've got a few lines on tormentors—I'll recite them to you. "Lines on Tormentors, after the style of Leigh Hunt. Illustrated by Joe *Buggins*."

> "On summer nights—such nights as these—
> We're troubled very much with fleas.
> They nip so hard—they do so tease,
> We cannot get a moment's ease—
>   Sometimes, by gosh, they're racing.
> But when the nights is werry hot,
> The bugs they walk out like a shot,
> And with a toasting-fork you've got,
> You wake, and catch a tidy lot,

> And, with rage, you fling 'em in the ——
> Washhand basing!" NUTTS.
> So all agree, &c.

Billy Nutts—sometimes "Nuts"; Partridge gives nut as a noun to mean a delightful thing, practice or experience; as a verb to mean to curry favor with
Seven Dials—the place where Pitts, Catnach, the Birts, and other broadside printers had their businesses; see the General Introduction
Stump—money to pay out
Mags—halfpennies, pennies
Blow his bags out—breathe heavily after a long draught? (see the same phrase with a different meaning in "The Charity Boy" given elsewhere here)
Inguns—onions

"Billy Nutts, the Poet" was one of the most widely printed of later broadside ballads, and it appeared in a variety of forms. Most of the broadside material seems to have come from the concert hall. The version used here is taken from the second series of *Labern's Comic Minstrel,* 1865, where it is printed along with another ballad by John Martin called "The Dogs' Emancipation." The headings of both ballads say "sung by Mr. Sharp," with "Billy Nutts" adding "music sold by Duncombe & Moon, 17 Holborn."[4] Aside from negligible differences in punctuation and a few words, this version of "Billy Nutts" is the same as a broadside printing by Bebbington of Manchester in association with J. Beaumont as vendor. Victor Neuburg gives only the year 1855 for the Bebbington-Beaumont connection. Insofar as John Sharp died in 1856 and was not likely to be singing after 1853–54, and Duncombe & Moon seem to have gone out of business at the end of 1853, this version may date from two or three years earlier than 1855.

The first known version of "Billy Nutts" (under the title "The Bard of Seven Dials") appeared in *London Singer's Magazine* in issue number 66, which can be dated uncertainly to about 1843–44. This first version differs very considerably from the *Comic Minstrel* version, most notably in that it wholly lacks the prose asides and their verses addressed to sheep's head, taturs, herring, barmaid, and tormentors. It seems to be a work undergoing elaboration—though not in the direction of the *Comic Minstrel* version. It consists first of all of a ballad of five stanzas, the first stanza introducing Billy Nutts (spelling his name Nuts), the next three naming his literary talents, and the last contemplating the sad consequence of his death. To this ballad are appended four "encore" stanzas, the first three describing his talents further and last turning to his death again. Of the nine stanzas and chorus only three and a half stanzas and chorus survive in the *Comic Minstrel,* all with minor changes. The first stanza ("I'm Billy Nutts . . .") remains the first stanza; the third stanza ("My learned brains . . .") becomes the second stanza; the first encore stanza ("The songs I writes . . .") becomes—with conventional grammar in the first line—the stanza following the celebration of sheep's head; and the first four lines in the second encore stanza ("I knows my vit . . .") becomes—with conventional grammar and pronunciation in the first line—the first four lines following the celebration of herring.

The five stanzas and half-stanza that disappear are these. From the ballad:

> The flats I snares, all round the squares,
>   And sells 'em wot I chooses—
> All in the streets the gulls I meets,
>   I wisits all the Mewses,
> The pence amounts, vhile I recounts,
>   Wot I, a clever chap, penn'd,
> Of murders done, and battles won,
>   Ewents wot never happen'd.

———

Flats—dupes, gulls; line 3, which repeats the sense of line 1, is evidently defective

> And it's my plan, that some great man,
>   Dies with a broken head, sirs—
> Vith a bewail, I dost detail,
>   His death afore he's dead, sirs.
> And vhile his friends and foes contends,
>   They all my papers buy, sirs—
> Yes, vithout doubt, I sells 'em out,
>   'Cos there my talents lie, sirs.
>
> Some paltry scribes is taking bribes
>   To fix on me a quarrel—
> 'Cos vhy? It grieves, vithout their leaves,
>   I crowns myself vith laurel.
> And when I'm gone, all folks forlorn,
>   In tears the change vill find, sirs—
> No more to carve, they all must starve,
>   For food to fill the mind, sirs.

From encore stanzas:

> And vot is pat, I still gets fat,
>   While other bards gets thinner;
> To their dismay, I ev'ry day
>   From Grub Street gets my dinner.
>
> There's eddication's botherations,
>   All class of people rouses,

> 'Till it is sent in parleyment—
>   "A plague on both their houses!"
> But I can teach with pen and speech,
>   Vhile they my works is reading—
> Vithout concern all folks I'd learn,
>   And teach 'em real good breeding.
>
> Vhen life is spent, and I am dead,
>   And you are sorrow's mourner,
> Ah, I shall stand in Abbey grand,
>   Like Q. in Poet's Corner.
> And vhile my foes, as off I goes,
>   My mem'ry would be teasing,
> Let me but write—success tonight,
>   Shows I've the art of pleasing.

Q.—rogue, swindler: Nutts, successful swindler of his audience in life and death

The five-stanza ballad, without encore verses, found its way onto the street in a printing by Elizabeth Hodges of 31 Dudley Street. It retains "gulls" in the second stanza. This printing cannot date before 1845 when Monmouth Street became Dudley Street, with Hodges changing her address accordingly. As in *London Singer's Magazine,* the bard spells his name "Nuts." In about 1852 came a mingling of often garbled and misprinted parts of both *London Singer's Magazine* and *Comic Minstrel* versions. The printing bears no printer's name, but the sheet is reasonably datable by the presence of "Poor Married Man" (see page 477) as companion ballad. This version gives the first stanza and some parts of the second stanza of both ballad and encore verses of the *London Singer's Magazine* version along with celebratory verses on barmaid, taturs, sheep's head, and tormentors (in that order) of the *Comic Minstrel* version. The celebratory verses lack their prose introductions, and they are "spoken" rather than sung. Along with being garbled, some bits have evidently been revised ignorantly, and lose their humor. The first four lines of the second encore stanza go thus:

> I knows my vit is little vit,
>   For all things well I love them,
> Great men who snore in the first floor
>   Must own that I'm above them.

However, one stanza comes from an unknown true or truer text and provides correction to misprints in *London Singer's Magazine* and *Comic Minstrel*-Bebbington versions. The first correction is of "gulls." The stanza gives us, "Then in the streets the gals I meet, / And writes them all the newses." (The printing uses the spelling "galls.") The second correction will be dealt with below.

Quite as intriguing as the 1852 broadside is "Billy Nuts the Poet" as printed by H. Williamson of Newcastle. The reference to Monmouth Street in the ballad suggests that it dates from 1845 or earlier. Its material on Billy Nuts himself is different in substance from that of the other versions, and its prose and verse on barmaid, taturs, and sheep's head (in that order and with no mention of herring and tormentors) is markedly inferior to the *Comic Minstrel* material. Here are the verses on Nuts himself:

> Beat the drum and blow the fife,
> And let the world all know it—
> I must confess, I'm nothing less,
> Than Billy Nuts the poet;
> Tho' dress'd demure you'll own I'm sure.
> That I a clever start made—
> The first lines that I did pen,
> I penn'd upon a barmaid.
>
> I sometimes beat up Monmouth Street,
> Or pitch in Seven Dials;
> Misfortune's sting, I ofttimes sing,
> The worst of nature's trials.
> As I pass by the people cry,
> He's versed in human nature,
> The poor man's part he takes to heart,
> Like the Irish agitator.
>
> I soon expect, if I don't neglect,
> To start a penny paper,
> And then with pun, and wit, and fun,
> I'll scare away each vapour;
> I'll indite and write, by candle light,
> Each article so witty,
> And in time of course I'll dine,
> With the Mayor of our City.

Some of the celebratory lines are so clumsy that they look to be printed by mistake from draft rather than from completed work. Thus the last seven lines on the barmaid:

> Then you stretch forth your hand with ease,
> To take the monies;
> The opportunity I then seize,
> Your little hand I gently squeeze,
> And together knocks my knees—
> For I could live with thee on bread and cheese,
> And onions.

At all events, assuming the dating is right, the *Comic Minstrel* version of the ballad was underway in 1845 or earlier.

Four other lines in this version are perhaps improvisation by Williamson in dealing with corrupt text. Lines 5–8 of its second stanza (the first of the three stanzas printed above on Billy Nuts himself) are clumsy in sense, rhyme, and rhythm. The corrupt text they replaced was probably:

> The pence amounts, while I recounts,
> What I, a clever tar, made—
> Of murders done, and battles won,
> And "Lines upon a Barmaid."

This corrupt material appears in *Comic Minstrel* and Bebbington printings, with Bebbington giving "While I" instead of "What I." In reprinting the *Comic Minstrel* version I have taken the liberty of improvising from the 1852 version, which gives:

> The verse amounts, while I recounts,
> In words sublimely arrayed,
> Of murders done, and battles won,
> And lines upon a barmaid.

Taking *London Singer's Magazine* and *Comic Minstrel* versions as first and last versions, and regarding them in isolation from the others, Martin seems to have revised the ballad in notable ways. He has made it less insistently Cockney, eliminating the *v*'s for *w*'s, and diminishing the irregular grammar. He has reduced material on the boastful poet celebrating his skills, and has altogether eliminated the fraudulent aspect of those skills, making Nutts much less a caricature of a Cockney and of a bard of Seven Dials. In doing these things and in developing Nutts's celebration of sheep's head, taturs, herring, barmaid, and tormentors, he has made the ballad a comic and rueful celebration of poverty as endured by poets and other people of the time. The encore verses along with other stanzas in the other versions suggest uncertainties of direction in this transformation.

Of Martin the person little is known. The most interesting if perhaps most doubtful glimpse into his life is by way of a little book called *The Swell's Night Guide; or, a Peep Through the Great Metropolis,* published in about 1846.[5] Number three or four in a series of such guides, its chief business was to describe notable bowers of Venus in London. It was also interested in flash dialogue and verse. Such verse was exemplified by "The Fair Maid of Seven Dials," which is described as "a jingling infusion about love . . . , faked up by Billy Nuts." The maid is black, and she is in love with a thief, who steals a ring for their marriage. Her father manages to get him transported.

> But when she 'eard it didn't she come out?
> And when she saw all hope was up the spout,
> She spouted every thing a spout would take,
> And cleared the crib out, for her Billy's sake;
> She went ramp cranky—nor tasted bit nor sup,
> But every thing she got she put it up;
> Among Bill's pals she then blu'd every brown,
> And knocked off putting up for putting down;
> She lush'd a good 'un—all things went to wrack,
> She play'd the devil, and she turn'd up Jack.

In short, the maid went on a rampage, pawned everything in the house (crib), and got drunk on gin with her lover's friends. In the last two lines of the ballad, after poisoning her father's donkey and shooting the cat, "She fir'd the crib—she danced—she laughed and cri'd / Then cock'd her leg—she broke her wind—and died." If Martin was Billy Nuts in *The Swell's Night Guide,* perhaps in real life he was a London Bohemian, frequenter of dubious places and friend of libertines. His verse otherwise does not suggest so. In the main it is conventional middle-class fare, varying between the blandly comic and the sentimental, the latter mode exemplified by his ballad "Little Jessey, the Poor Flower Girl," given on page 322. Even "Billy Nutts," with its easy allusions to Pope, Lamb, Handel, and Leigh Hunt, and with its self-consciously clever puns and rhymes, suggests a conventional middle-class man and poet aiming to beguile a moderately sophisticated middle-class audience in concert hall and other like places. Only the display of flash language and the assumed or apparent acquaintance with poverty set the author of the ballad somewhat apart from that audience. It seems likely that some considerable part of the audience for "Billy Nutts" on the street was both conventional and Bohemian middle class.

Martin's ballads appeared frequently in *London Singer's Magazine* from 1838 until perhaps 1845 or later. In issue number 30 is "When I Became an Author," which may have personal reference and which suggests middle-class upbringing. It is quoted in the endnote.[6] Martin is presumably the John Martin who wrote a frivolous one-act farce called *Fairly Hit and Fairly Missed,* which is given in volumes 43–44 of *Duncombe's British Theatre.* John Martin there is identified as "the author of *My Man the Barber,* etc. etc.," and the play is printed "as performed at the London theatres." The date was about 1841.[7]

Three broadside ballads of the same sort as "Billy Nutts" in both subject and style, but showing little verve and variety, are "Jim Baggs the Musician," "Jimmy Jumps the Rhymer!," and "Brother to the Dustman." The first concerns a street musician, who in several stanzas says how excellent and unappreciated he is. It concludes:

> Then patronize old Jemmy Baggs—
> My toggery aren't very splendid,

> But talent's often found in rags—
>   (If they're coppers I shan't feel offended).
> Vhen I'm dead I know how it'll be,
>   You'll be sorry you sarv'd me so shabby;
> You'll all go in mourning for me,
>   Yes and lay me in Vestminster Habby!

"Jimmy Jumps" is less labored in its humor but little more successful. In "Brother to the Dustman" a ballad singer recounts his life. One of his stanzas mentions his long songs. He names four songs, making play with each one:

> Here's "Ellen, I'll Love Thee No More,"
>   I through the streets am hooting,
> Likewise "The Death of General Moore,"
>   Through "Goin' Out a Shooting!"
> I brings 'em round as quick as thought,
>   And sells a precious many;
> "Oh, Say Not Woman's Heart is Bought,"
>   At just three yards a penny!

A number of broadside ballads consist mainly of titles played off against one another, among them "Chanting Benny" and "A New Batch of Ballads."[8]

Anything to Earn a Crust

> I thought, when I entered into life,
>   By honesty to gain a name:
> But mortal selfishness and strife
>   Soon taught me a different game:
>
> Masters cheated, wack'd me, sack'd me,
>   Till at length a man I grew;
> Then in streets went yelling, selling—
>   Dying speeches, murders too.

(Spoken) Now, my customers, just printed and published, a full, true, and particular account of the life, trial, and execution of Jeremiah Slitwind, who was executed this morning—for the small charge of one half-penny. You have here every particular of that which he did, and that which he did not; with a pious and moral love letter which he wrote to his sweetheart the night after his execution, for the small charge of one half-penny. "Please sir, my mother wants her money back." "What for? my little dear?" "Cos the man isn't hung yet, and it's only a catch-penny."

"Can't help that my little dear; he ought to have been hung and that's just the same. And, if your mother thinks it a catch-penny, she may go to Jack Ketch for it, for she'll not catch me at it."

  So fakements such as these I try,
   Gain a living all men must,
  Honesty is all my eye—
   Anything to earn a crust.

  That 'ere business soon got queer,
   Hanging days so seldom came;
  Starvation I began to fear,
   So went to work at the swindling game.

  Tried all schemes so lary, wary,
   Nail'd the flats in every way;
  Worked at thimble rigging, prigging,
   Then started on the cadging lay.

(Spoken) Kind friends! I have come afore you, this morning, in spite of my native modesty—in which it's a great effort on my part—in order to make known my distresses; knowing that the hearts of the charitable are never deaf to a tale of misery, and are always ready to lend a helping hand to them as don't want it. Kind friends! I am an unfortunate tailor, and can't get work. I have, at home, a sick wife and starving family, of whom this little one is the youngest of seventeen, which I have got at home to support; and, to add to my distress, nineteen of 'em died last night, and was buried by the parish yesterday morning. Kind friends! consider my awful bereavement. I was obliged to sell all my goods to pay the undertaker, and now I haven't got no home to go to, and my hard-hearted landlord threatens to put in the bailiffs, and sell all my goods. Kind friends! I have been much afflicted with a severe illness, and have been in all the jails— hospitals I mean—and was turned out incorrigible, that is to say incurable. Kind friends, I have at home my dead wife, she died three days ago, in giving birth to this helpless orphan (showing a doll), and now she lies at home, without a bit of bread to put in her mouth, and expects to be confined again shortly.

  So fakements such as these, &c.

  The cadging dodge it wouldn't do—
   Folks they did me brown, d'ye see;
  Instead of browns they sent me to
   The Mendicity Society.

> Pea soup lacking, thickening, sickening,
>   A higher range my genius took;
> Round the town went touting, spouting,
>   *Punch's Riddles*, a penny a book.

(Spoken) Now my customers, just printed and published Pro Bono Publico, that is to say, for the benefit of publisher, an entirely novel and choice collection of "Punch's Favourite Conundrums," selected and arranged by Punch, in Propria Persona, that signifies to them that don't understand French, himself or somebody else; and the first conundrum in the little book is —Why can a cat see best in the dark? 'Cos it eats lights. —Now the next conundrum in the little book is—Why is Green's balloon like a policeman? 'Cos it takes people up.— Move on there, move on. Certainly Mr. Constable directly. Just allow me to ask you—Why are you like a man stripping to fight? 'Cos you are a Peeler.—Move on I say.—Just one more and I'm off.—Why am I like stinking meat? 'Cos the blue bottles are always after me.

> So fakements such as these, &c.

> Next teetotal spouter turned,
>   The water-drinking crew I cheats;
> Then the pious dodge I learned—
>   Sermonizing in the streets.

> Ranting, canting, teaching, preaching,
>   Till too stale the game did grow;
> Next behold me ramping, stamping,
>   Leading man at a travelling show.

(Spoken) Now, step forward, step forward. Be in time. "The Royal Victoria Pavillion, or Polling Refuge for the Destitute Drama." Patronized by the ghost of Billy Shakespeare, who has been bundled out of Covent Garden, where he found an asylum for many years; but in consequence of the March of Science and a refined taste, the old gentleman has become bed-ridden and is literally defunct; which has caused many of his brethren to be funct; and the functionaries what holds the reins of the Thespian vehicle is in a greater funk than all of 'em now. Astonishing performance. The real legitimate drama, and no gammon. None of the Drury Lane humbug in this shop. We are just a-goin' to commence with the spiflicating tragedy, in twenty-nine acts, entitled, "The Mysteries of the Member Mug, or the Smashed Bug, and the Bloody Bolster." Hi! hi! hi! And the admission is only one penny.

So fakements such as these, &c.

Low-liv'd games I cut at last—
    Better late than never:—Then
I reflect upon the past—
    Gain a living by my pen.

All day long rehearses verses,
    Courting, too, the muses nine;
Then at night, inditing, writing,
    Accidents a penny-a-line.

(Spoken) Yes, ladies and gentlemen! I am the genius of Grub Street, and the only genuine originator of the Greenacre style of novel-writing; poet, penny-a-liner, and political scribbler; lyric lays equally reasonable. Every facility for suicides. Made up murders on the shortest notice, and the most reasonable terms. I have here a most excellent murder dodge, which I wrote last night. I will rehearse it to you; and, if any gentleman thinks proper to purchase the copy, he can have it for two and sixpence, and commence business for himself tomorrow. It is as follows: just printed and published, an entire correct account of that fearful, dreadful, and horrible murder which was committed last night on the body of Betsy Jumps, alias Betsy Brown, by her murderer and seducer John Brown, alias Timothy Twisttail. You have here every particular of the manner in which he seduced her from her home, and led her up a dark street, by the side of a lamp-post, in a dark entry; and after accomplishing his wicked design, he drew his knife from his pocket, and severed off her jimmy. The little books are only a penny each, containing all the particulars of the murder, with his last dying speech and confession, which he made the night after he was hung, —Sings

    Come all you young men,
        And a warning take by me,
    I'm just in my prime,
        Condemned to be hang'd upon a gallows tree.

    My parents they did ruin me,
        By giving me my own way,
    I got into bad company,
        And went for to come for to go astray.

    I courted a fat young woman,
        Her name was Betsy Brown,

> Another young chap did court her,
> Which made her on me frown.
>
> I swore I'd have revenge,
> And my revenge it should be dimie,
> She refused to be my wife,
> So I took her life by cutting off her jimmy.

(Spoken) Now here's the history of Betsy Brown, who was murdered in this town, by a heartless clown, after which he threw her in a pit to drown, and now she is living tally with Dr. Brown.

> So fakements such as these I try;
> Gain a living all men must;
> Honesty is all my eye—
> Anything to earn a crust.

Fakements—tricks
Lary—artful
Flats—gulls
Thimble-rigging—trick with three thimbles and a pea
Prigging—thieving
Did me brown—worsted me completely
Browns—halfpennies, coppers
Mendicity Society—the Society for the Suppression of Mendicity
Punch's Riddles—possibly a pirated collection; the earliest collection of the sort in the British Library is *1000 Conundrums by Mr. Punch* (1863), eight pages, with paper covers
Green—Charles Green (1785–1870), famous aeronaut, who made his first ascent at the coronation of George IV in 1820 and made several hundred further ascents in the next decades
Peeler—policeman
Blue bottle—policeman
Covent Garden—until 1847 the "Theatre-Royal, Covent Garden," one of the two principal theatres in London; thereafter primarily concerned with opera
Spiflicating—to confound, overcome (humorous)
Gammon—humbug
Greenacre style of novel-writing—presumably an allusion to the conventional form of broadsides about murders and executions (parodied at the end of the ballad), with special reference to Catnach's supposedly having sold more than a million and a half copies of such a broadside about the murderer Greenacre, executed in 1837

Jimmy (jemmy)—head
Dimie—?
Tally—as mistress

Another printing of the ballad, "Anything to Yarn a Crust," is Cockneyfied, with "pertickler," "hexecution," "vhich," and so forth. In the printing used here, two such spellings appear, each once, "wot" and "sarmonizing." I have changed them. Their presence suggests that the Cockney version came first, and that presently spellings were normalized imperfectly. In the second set of verses I have preferred the Cockney rhyming pair "lary, wary" over "leary, weary" as given in the printing used here. "Lary" is the Cockney version of "leary," but "leary" has brought in "weary," which makes little sense. "Lary, wary" itself seems to be the earlier form. Also from the Cockney version I have used the double slip of jail and incorrigible. The printing used here gives only "ja—— hospitals, and was turned out incurable." The Cockney version has substantial differences in the prose passages; it does not have the final verses of the dying speech and confession.

The Cockney version was issued by M. A. Hodges, 31 Dudley Street. M. A. Hodges is the same as E. Hodges (Elizabeth Mary Ann). She published from 31 Dudley Street (Monmouth Street until 1845) from 1844 to 1855. At what point she used M. A. on her sheets instead of the more frequent E. is unknown, but the evidence of "Anything to Yarn a Crust" suggests a late date. Printings I have seen of "Anything to Earn a Crust" either give no printer or give a printer of later years.

In his comments on murders, trials, and executions in *Curiosities of Street Literature*, Hindley offers an example of the sort of patter of a balladmonger known as "Tragedy Bill." Some of the details of the patter are fairly much the same as part of the first prose passage and one later passage in "Anything to Earn A Crust." Given Hindley's plagiarisms noted elsewhere in these pages, he may have relied upon the broadside rather than upon a memory of Tragedy Bill.[9] Assuming that Tragedy Bill existed, one may doubt that he sold either cocks or actual accounts of murders and executions in such fashion unless he regarded himself as a comedian and was accepted as such by his audience.

The first four lines of verse on Betsy Brown parody the opening of "The Murder of Maria Marten," which Hindley says was reported to be by Catnach. See pages 57–58. Hindley gives the Corder-Marten ballad in *Curiosities*.

On the matter of cocks, see appendix 1.

8

Scenes of Mirth and Contentment

I

One of the facts of beggary offered by the House of Commons Select Committee on Mendicity in 1816 was that the clientele of the taverns the Rose and Crown and Robin Hood in Church Lane, St. Giles's, included two hundred to three hundred beggars, and that daily receipts from each of them ran between three and five shillings.[1] Such a sum from each beggar would have provided the essentials of life for a week in those days, and it may be imagined that scenes at the two taverns were very jolly. The members of the Select Committee were not amused. One suspects that insofar as they believed the figures they offered, they were outraged that beggars could so easily gull the middle and upper classes—and so shamelessly enjoy the profits of the gulling.

Five years later, Pierce Egan took a lighter view of beggary in *Life in London*. His book shows his three swells, Tom, Jerry, and Logic, participating in the jollities of the Rose and Crown. One of the several individual dramatizers of his book, W. T. Moncrieff, took a still lighter view, and elaborated upon the jollities there. "Song of the Cadgers in the Holy Land," probably by him and given below, asks no questions of how cadgers get their money, and it allows that cadgers may be happier than kings. Other ballads of the sort—in a long history of such ballads—are mentioned on pages 300–301. Beggars' feasts, and feasts among the poor, are exemplified by "The Coalheaver's Feast," given below, with other such ballads mentioned in the commentary. An unusual ballad of the sort (with accompanying prose) is "Beggar's Wedding," which is listed in Catnach's 1832 catalogue. It claims to describe a real wedding between George Williams, a former laboring man, and Mary Saunders, once a servant, both now beggars. Among the guests are a wooden-legged sailor who can dance a jig and a blind man who can recognize a pretty girl when he sees one. Food is plentiful: "bullocks heart stuffed with sawdust, cat-pie, and swipes [beer]." Bride and groom finish the evening drunk. One of the guests discovers that her master's cat went into the pie.

As a rule, ballads on jolly beggary, jolly poverty, imply simplemindedness, irresponsibility, immorality, or criminality among the participants. The authors generally take a light view of such frailties, and they presumably expect their readers to do likewise. Given the great popularity of Egan's book, the dramatizations of it, and the broadside ballads on it and on like scenes among the poor, it would appear that such jolly beggary and jolly poverty made a very considerable appeal to a broad audience of the general public. The inwardness of that appeal must have been manifold, and only a moralist would say that it too was simpleminded, irresponsible, immoral, or criminal.

II

Poverty and contentment was another matter, and here the ballad writers were very often moralists, and many in the audience apparently the same. On the outer fringe of such ballads were those that threatened unhappy effects of discontent. In "The Ploughman's Ditty: Being an Answer to That Foolish Question, What Have the Poor to Lose?" the sensible ploughman (speaking for Hannah More and her associates and other like-minded people) knows that he will lose everything if he rebels against his condition.

> My cot is my throne,
> What I have is my own,
>   And what is my own I will keep, sir;
> Should riot ensue,
> I may plough, it is true,
>   But I'm sure that I never shall reap, sir.

A later ballad of some apparent popularity, "Poverty and Contentment," cajoles "worthy people . . . that spent your time in rioting" to "be watchful of your latter end" and follow the example of Job, Lazarus, and the speaker of the ballad.

> Though poor, I am contented,
>   No riches do I crave,
> For they are but vanity
>   On this side of the grave.

Milder cajoling can be seen in ballads such as "There's Many Worse Off Than You" and "There's Better Times in Store."

Positive depictions of contented poverty are many and various. There is the thrasher in Charles Dibdin's ballad of that title. "No king be half so great," the thrasher avers, and "I merrily sing as I fling out the flail." Marginally less happy than he is the girl in "The Country Lass." Off she goes to her labors in the morning, treading the dew and listening to the larks, utterly carefree: "tho' poor I am contented and as happy as a queen." Other ballads celebrating humble labor in similar terms are "Working Men of England," "The Working Man," and two ballads entitled "The Honest Working Man." The first of these suggests that contentment may be abetted by "good masters and the founders of free trade." Among ballads of this sort, a few dwell upon ironies of class and condition. The best is "Chimney Sweep":

> For those who deal in smoke,
>   As I do every day,
> Sweeping never choaks,
>   We scrape and brush away.
> 'Twixt I and gentlefolks,
>   The difference between
> Is—they without the joke,
>   Do dirty work more clean.
>
> Some cry, how black my face is,
>   But Joe don't care a rush,
> I'm fairer than the graces,
>   Tho' never seen to blush.
> My heart in the right place
>   Is better further still,
> The black face ne'er disgraces,
>   The black heart ever will.

Others of the sort are "Dick the Dustman" and "The Dustman."

These ballads mainly show contentment in humble labor. Others show contentment more broadly in humble life. Settings are characteristically rural. In "Haymakers" the men work as merrily as the thrasher above, their children play about them, and they pause to invite "gentle ladies" and "noble masters" to join them on a carpet "as soft . . . as the pile of your carpeted floor."

> And more jolly are we, though in rags we may be,
> Than the pale faces over the loom.

"The Labourer's Return to His Family" and "The Labourer's Welcome Home" tell of cheerful labourers, clear consciences, and domestic bliss. In "The Wealth of a Cottage is Love" the speaker is "by poverty never distressed." "The Humble Roof" is likewise a setting for love: "what gold could never buy." In "Ground for the Floor" a man lives contentedly alone in a simple cottage, with ground for floor and fireplace and no seat but a three-legged stool. In "I'd Be a Gipsy" the speaker knows that "the bright halls of splendour and pleasure" are as nothing compared with a merry gipsy's life. All he requires is "coin just enough to be free as the air." These last two ballads seem to have been fairly popular.

Contentment in the city is usually less pure, less desirable, more believable. The scenes of "Owdham Streets at Dinner Time" and "Monmouth Street," both given below, are pictures of a moment rather than of an ideal. Each moment has its agreeable truth: the pleasure of breaking off work for dinner (with barely a glimpse of work itself), and the pleasure of replacing decayed clothing with better. Other ballads such as "The Last Farewell to Poor St. Giles's" and "The Brixton Lady and her Nice Beetle Pies," both given below, show more problematical contentment. They provide two of the most believable pictures in these pages of liveliness and good humor in the midst of poverty.

III

As the quotation from "Poverty and Contentment" suggests, Christian belief is often a key element in the notion of contented poverty. The temporal vanity of riches, the greater favor of Lazarus over Dives in the sight of God, and the leveling of rich and poor in death are themes of "The Rich Man's Dream" and its accompanying illustration. The ballad itself is given on page 139. Other ballads are more directly concerned with contentment while enduring the pains of poverty. At the extreme is the ballad by John Taylor given on page 387. Taylor has lost employment, home, friends; he and his wife and children are in distress. If he does not, like Job, say, "I loathe my life," he does complain, and like Job he questions God:

> O let thy ways of dealing, Lord,
> By me be understood.

He is not delivered at the end of his tale as Job is delivered, but he is certain that those who help him will themselves be helped by God. Other ballads take simpler views of "Job the patient man," which phrase itself is an alternative title for "Poverty and Contentment." "Distress of Trade" calls upon the poor to remember Job and trust in God. The poor tradesman in a ballad of that title has wife and five children, and he trusts in God to relieve him. "Patient Joe" tells a tale that is an example to patient Job himself, for Joe is firmly contented whether good or ill befalls him:

> In trouble he bow'd him to God's holy will,
> How contented was Joseph when matters went ill!

He is derided by fellow colliers, in particular by a man who drinks and gambles. He is mocked especially one day when a dog snatches his luncheon sandwich and runs off with it; but while he chases after the dog there is an explosion in the mine that kills the drinker and gambler.

Other ballads suggest that failure of religious practice invites poverty, and that return to it brings relief: "Dialogue on a Sunday Morning; or, the Sabbath

Breaker Reclaimed" and two ballads entitled "Prodigal Son." Others take contentment to mean a certain stoicism here on earth. "Heaven's My Home" says in two of its stanzas:

> Tho' poverty is my lot,
> Tho' the fig-tree blossoms not,
> I can sing the song of hope,
>   Heaven's my home.
>
> In the dark and cloudy day,
> On Jehovah I will stay,
> And pursue my happy way,
>   Heaven's my home.

Felicia Heman's "The Better Land" seems to have been popular as a broadside. It asks—implicitly rather than explicitly: where in the world might be a land without the sorrow and death of nineteenth-century England? One could emigrate there. The answer is nowhere. Heaven alone is such a place.

> Time does not breathe on its faultless bloom,
> Far beyond the clouds and beyond the tomb.

Among the most confident religious ballads on contented poverty are three that elaborate individual worldly metaphors to make their point. "The Gospel Beggar," quoted on page 303, shows a contented Christian beggar in his journey through life, begging of God the certain reward of heaven. "Lines Written on the Cover of an Old Bible," quoted on page 238, says that men can deal at all points of life with God the generous banker. "Trust in the Lord" relies upon the figure of trade over eight stanzas:

> Do not repine because you're poor,
> The Lord he will provide I'm sure
> For all who him depend upon
> And trade with Jesus Christ his son.
>
> If any here by man opprest,
> Trust in the Lord who knows what's best,
> Bear it with patience like poor Job,
> And still keep trading with your God.

In the face of such determined complacency, one needs to remember the religious anger expressed by others. The presumably poor man who wrote "The Labourer's Horizon at Sunrise," given on page 140, calls for destruction of his oppressors. So does the author (who describes himself as "a working man") of "The Christian's

Appeal Against the Poor Law Amendment Act," quoted on page 162. And Edward Lamborn, helpless in poverty, surrendered to prison of workhouse, says what many must have believed: "For those who made the poor laws, they are the spawn of hell."

See the endnote for mention of three obscure small volumes of the time that concern poverty, contentment, and religion.²

Hot Codlings

A little old woman a living she got,
By selling hot codlings, hot, hot, hot!
Now this little old woman, as I have been told,
Though her codlings were hot, she was monstrously cold,
So to keep herself warm, why she thought it no sin,
For to go and take a small drop of gin.
                    Tol de rol, &c.

Now this little old woman went off in a trot
To get a quartern of hot, hot, hot!
She swallow'd a glass, and it was so nice,
That she tipped off another in a trice;
She fill'd the glass till the bottle it shrunk,
And this little old woman I am told got drunk.
                      Tol de rol, &c.

Now this little old woman while muzzy she got,
Some boys stole her codlings hot, hot, hot,
Put powder in the pan, and 'neath. it round stones,
Cried this little old woman these apples are bones.
The powder and the pan up they did send
This little old woman on her latter end.
                      Tol de rol, &c.

Now this little old woman went off in a trot,
All in a fury hot, hot, hot!
Sure such boys as these never was known,
They never will let a poor woman alone,
There's a moral from this, so round let it buz,
If you want to sell hot codlings, you must never get muz.
                      Tol de rol, &c.

The ballad is by Charles Isaac Mungo Dibdin, usually known as Charles Dibdin Jr. He was a successful son of a more variously gifted father whose writing is represented by "The Beggar" on page 303. Dibdin Jr. was born in 1768 of his father's liaison with the actress Harriet Pitt. The father deserted Harriet Pitt when his son was five years old. She could not support the boy and his younger brother Thomas John Dibdin, and a maternal uncle assumed responsibility. Young Charles seems never to have seen his father thereafter, and he rarely saw his mother. He went off to boarding school, and reportedly for five years there he did not come away to any place that could be called home. At age fourteen he was apprenticed to a pawnbroker, and he remained with the broker for fourteen years. In his memoirs he says, "I had ever a greater predilection for poems than pawns." In 1792 he published by subscription his first volume of poetry. Presently he turned to writing for the stage, and achieved his first production in 1797. Over the next thirty years he wrote more than two hundred melodramas and pantomimes. He became proprietor and acting manager of the Sadler's Wells Theatre. "Hot Codlings" apparently dates from the first years of the century. It was popular for many years as broadside, stage, and parlor ballad. At least a dozen of Dibdin's lyrics came onto the street. They include "Betty Brill," "Giles Scroggin's Ghost," "Kitty of the Clyde," and "Tippetywitchet." Dibdin died in 1833.[3]

In *Modern Street Ballads* John Ashton remarks that for a number of years in London "no pantomime was complete" without a performance of "Hot Codlings." He ascribes the ballad to brother Thomas John in the pantomime *Harlequin and Mother Goose.* His opinion is echoed by Maurice Disher in *Victorian Song from Dive to Drawing Room.*[4] Thomas John Dibdin makes no mention of the ballad in his *Reminiscences,* and two early editions of his pantomime offer no evidence of its use.[5] He himself was a successful writer, actor, and manager. He wrote nearly two hundred theatrical entertainments and perhaps two thousand songs. Several of his songs came onto the street.

Another ballad entitled "Hot Codlins" dates from some centuries earlier. Its narrator has seen a girl on the street selling apples, and asks of reader or listener, "Have you observed the wench on the street- / She's scarce any hose, or shoes to her feet." He suggests that if she is merry (as he supposes she is), we should all be merry.[6]

(I am obliged to Alexandra Franklin for identifying Charles Dibdin Jr. as the author of "Hot Codlings.")

Beggars Opera—Tom, Jerry, & Logick, Among the Cadgers in the Holy Land

Now, to keep up the spree, Tom, Jerry, and Logick,
    Went disguis'd to the Slums in the Holy Land;

Through each crib and each court, they hunted for sport,
    Till they came to the *Beggars Opera* so nam'd;
But sure such a sight they had never set sight on,
    The quintessence of Tag, Rag, and Bob-Tail was there:
Outside of the door Black Molly was fighting,
    And pulling Mahogany Bet by the hair.
There was cobblers and tailors, sweeps, cadgers, and sailors,
    Enough to confound Old Nick with their din;
There was bunters, and ranters, and radical chaunters,
    Clubbing their halfpence for quarterns of gin.

Some were decrying the traps of Red Lion,
    Some were preparing their matches for sale;
A surly old duchess, with one of her crutches,
    Had floor'd a blindman for capsizing her ale.
A tinker was bawling, a dustman was hauling
    His drunk wife to bed, whom he'd given a black eye,
For the which Mother Drake, shook her fist in his face,
    And pray'd that his Last Dying Speech she might cry.
Our blades stood delighted, and view'd all around them,
    When in popp'd Black Billy as brisk as a bee,
He struck up his fiddle, they all gather'd round him,
    And chaunted this *classical* stave in high glee:—

    Song of the Cadgers in the Holy Land

    Come, let us dance and sing,
    While fam'd St. Giles's bells shall ring,
    Black Billy scrapes the fiddle string,
        Little Jemmy fills the Chair.
    Frisk away, let's be gay,
    This is Cadger's holiday,
    While knaves are thinking, we are drinking,
        Bring in more gin and beer.
        Come, let us dance and sing, &c.

    Here's Dough-boy Bet, and Silver Sall,
    Dusty Bob, and Yankee Moll,
    And Suke as black as any pall,
        The pinks of the Holy Land.
    Now, merry, merry, let us be,
    There's none more happier sure than we,

> For what we get we spend it free,
>   As all must understand!
>   Come, let us dance, &c.
>
> Now he that would merry be,
> Let him drink and sing as we,
> In palaces you shall not see,
>   Such happiness as here.
> Then booze about, our cash an't out,
> Here's sixpence in a dirty clout,
> Come, landlord bring us in more stout,
>   Our pension-time draws near.
>   Come, let us dance, &c.

For an account of the imaginary characters (Tom, Jerry, and Logick) and real people (the inhabitants of the Holy Land) mentioned in the ballad, see "The Merry Will & Testament of Master Black Billy" and its accompanying commentary, pages 307–11.

The overall title of the sheet on which these verses appear is "Life in London; or, the Sprees of Tom and Jerry; Attempted in Cuts and Verse." The sheet is very large; it is described as a third edition; and it sold for twopence. Ten small cuts of its thirteen cuts show Tom, Jerry, and Logick in a variety of scrapes. The first of two large cuts concerns their visit to the haunts of beggars —the so-called slums of the Holy Land—and shows the interior of the Beggars Opera. It is reproduced on page 310.

> *Slums*—Beggars Opera (the Rose and Crown tavern) and other such places
> *Holy Land*—the poorest section of St. Giles's; Partridge suggests that the term in part plays upon St. Giles
> *Crib*—house, apartment
> *Bunters*—loose women, whores
> *Red Lion*—the Society for the Suppression of Mendicity had its office in Red Lion Square; see the introduction to the section on Beggars
> *Pinks*—dashing fellows

Catnach, the publisher of the sheet, says beneath the title: "This is to give notice to those persons who are in the constant habit of pirating my copyrights that if they dare to print any part of this sheet, they shall be proceeded against according to law." He himself pirated some of the cuts, in rough imitation of the Cruikshank illustrations for *Life in London*. And he apparently pirated the verses printed here from William Thomas Moncrieff, pseudonym of William Thomas Thomas, died 1857, a prolific writer of theatrical entertainments. Moncrieff was one of several men who wrote individual dramatizations of Pierce Egan's book. All or most of them were Egan's friends—Douglas Jerrold, Charles Dibdin Jr., Thomas Dibdin, and men named Farrell and W. Barrymore. Egan himself dramatized the book. Moncrieff's version, with the title *Tom and Jerry*, seems to have been the most successful, and was performed upwards of three hundred times at the Adelphi Theatre. It gives proportionately much more space to Tom and Jerry in the Holy Land than does Egan's book. Black Billy, Dusty Bob, Black (Afric') Sal, and Little Jemmy appear in it.

An account of the dramatizations appears in Hindley's *The True History of Tom and Jerry*. Hindley prints a number of pages of what is apparently Moncrieff's published play, and they show the verses printed here along with some of the other verses that Catnach uses. But Hindley is such a scissors and paste author that one cannot be certain of what one is getting, and a search among several editions of Moncrieff's play—including one published in 1828 from an acting copy—did not turn up any of these verses. Catnach himself seems to have supplied at least the last four lines for the final cut, "Jerry Going Back to the Country." They are given on page 57 in the discussion of Catnach as author.[7]

Hindley comments at length on Catnach the pirate, but he himself pirated from Catnach. In *The True History* he offers what is supposedly his own account of the life of Black Billy, but some of it is fairly much word for word Catnach's account, written seventy years earlier, given here on page 310.[8]

The Coalheaver's Feast
An Original Broad-Humoured Song
Written by T. Prest

Oh! have you not heard of a party so gay,
That all met together so fine t'other day,
Men, women, and children, full fifty at least,
To kick up a row at the Coalheaver's feast.
    Laughing and joking,
    Chaffing and smoking,
Oh! what a spree at the Coalheaver's feast.

There were six drunken Chummies as black as could be,
Of scavengers too there was full two or three,
And half of St. Giles's came down in a troop,
To wolf up the gatter, the bacon and soup.
    Dancing and tearing,
    Prancing and swearing,
O, what a set-out at the Coalheaver's Feast.

Ten ragged Beggars all rushed to the scene,
Of Dustmen besides there was nearly fifteen,
And out of Duck Lane the girls made such a rout,
Determined to have a good jolly blow-out.
    Dancing and tearing,
    Prancng and swearing,
  Gorging away at the Coalheaver's Feast.

Of victuals besides, then they had such a lot,
Twenty sheeps-heads and six trotters they'd got,
Forty polonies and twelve saveloys,
A sack of potatoes and twenty savoys!
    Dancing and tearing, &c.

Twelve pounds of bacon—two inches in fat,
Two bullocks livers as black as your hat,
Thirty red herrngs—some bread that was brown,
And two buts o' swipes just to wash it all down.
    Dancing, &c.

Six gallons of gin for the kiddies to drink,
In case that their courage and spirits might sink,
Six pounds of backey, by way of a joke,
And twenty short pipes for the ladies to smoke.
    Dancing, &c.

Four pounds of tripe and three pounds of pigs-fry,
A dozen black-puddings all seasoned so high;
And as to be hungry, of course they were loath,
A copper they had full of pea-soup and broth.
    Dancing, &c.

It then would have done ev'ry person's eyes good,
To see how they all did pitch into the food;
They gulph'd down the pratees, tho' harder than stones,
They gorg'd up the meat and they swallow'd the bones!
    Dancing, &c.

Out of tea-kettles then they did guzzle the gin,
And the men and the women to smoke did begin,
The children the gatter did swallow like fun,
And they all fell to dancing as soon as 'twas done.

8 / SCENES OF MIRTH AND CONTENTMENT

>Dancing and tearing,
>Prancing and swearing,
>Jigging away at the Coalheaver's Feast.

At length a strange quarrel by chance did ensue,
And the tables and chairs at each other they threw;
They kick'd at their shins, and they trod on their toes,
And the women the men pull'd about by the nose!
>Pulling and tearing,
>Tugging and swearing,
>Milling away at the Coalheaver's Feast.

At last for to quiet the riot and din,
Policemen, by dozens, came tumbling in,
They took the whole party before the old Beak,
Who sent them off packing to quod for a week.
>Pulling and tearing,
>Cursing and swearing,
>Thus finish'd the spree at the Coalheaver's Feast.

Chummies—chimney sweeps
Gatter—beer
Duck Lane—a poor street in Westminster; the surviving part today is Matthew Street
Saveloys—sausage rolls of chopped beef, smoked
Savoys—cabbages
Swipes—beer
Kiddies—petty criminals
Pratees—potatoes

Thomas Peckett Prest is discussed briefly on pages 40–41, where he is mentioned as the author of three known broadside ballads. They are "Vive la Liberte," written to celebrate the insurrection in 1830 that brought Louis Philippe to the throne as king of the French, "Hercules Decapitating the Hydra of Corruption," written to celebrate the passage of the Reform Bill of 1832, and "Pretty Girls of London," quoted on page 41. "The Coalheaver's Feast" is one of three more to add to the list.

Prest seems likely to have earned a modest living from literary work, editing as well as writing. In 1834 he undertook the editing of the *Singer's Penny Magazine and Reciter's Album,* a quarto sheet of thin paper that accommodated fourteen to eighteen songs on its eight pages. The first number of apparently weekly issues, all undated, appeared in about June–July of that year. The first page of each number provided title, illustration, table of contents, and the first song or two. In early 1835 the first thirty-five numbers were gathered unaltered into a volume of the same title, the numbers preceded by proper title page, frontispiece, and index to all the songs. It was "a superior collection of all the most new and popular songs, duets, glees, trios, catches, and recitations"—some twenty-five of the last among six hundred of the others. The preface is dated 26 February 1835. It speaks of "monthly parts" of the magazine, presumably gatherings of four or five weekly numbers into slender booklets, but none of these booklets is known to have survived. The last page of the volume, which was the last page of the thirty-fifth number, promised that the first number of the second volume would follow "on Wednesday next." No part of a second volume seems to have survived.

The magazine published verse by Burns, Byron, Moore, Charles Dibdin, and Thomas Haynes Bayly, but it was more especially a vehicle for lesser known or obscure figures such as Prest himself, John Labern, Thomas Hudson, W. H. Freeman, and J. E. Carpenter. The songs are sometimes given with the name of author, performer, or place of performance, or with some bit of praise such as "the celebrated song" or "now singing with the most unbounded applause." "Mrs. Johnson" (given here on page 466) appears in the magazine as the work of T. Prest, and the verses of "The Vorkus Gal" (given here on page 169) are those that gained unbounded applause in the singing. The reader is informed that the author of "The Vorkus Gal" is "Aldridge Esq." and that Aldridge is also the "original author of 'The Vorkus Boy'" (presumably the first version of "The Workhouse Boy" quoted on page 168). "The Workhouse Boy" (given here on page 165) is also printed, and identified as the work of R. Flint. The magazine is thus a lesson in the intimate relationship between concert/theater and street. Perhaps one in forty of the songs in the magazine came onto the street. It is not immediately clear that any inference can be drawn about the sort of intimate relationship.

Sometime later, perhaps in the summer of 1836, Prest began editing a new magazine in the same format, *London Singer's Magazine and Reciter's Album*. The five known surviving numbers of volume 1 of either thirty or thirty-one numbers say, "edited by Mr. T. Prest." The more numerous known surviving numbers of volume 2, twenty of twenty-eight numbers from 32 (evidently the first number of the volume) to 59, say, "originally edited by Mr. T. Prest." They name no new editor. No later number is known than 59. The five numbers of volume 1 as held by the Bodleian Library, numbers 11–15, are bound together in a booklet that is lacking its cover. Presumably this is the third of a series of perhaps monthly parts. Issue number 11 contains "Monmouth Street," by Prest himself, which is printed below, page 514. A similar surviving booklet, Part VII, contains the first four numbers of volume 2:32–35. Songs and advertisements among all the known numbers of the magazine indicate that it was in existence for at least some part of 1836–37.

At the British Library surviving issues of the magazine are bound in together with many numbers from 1 to 67 of its successor, *London Singer's Magazine*. At the Bodleian Library numbers 1–30 of *London Singer's Magazine* are bound together, with a handwritten note therein saying that the first number was issued on 12 April 1838. Dating evidence in number 19 of the magazine indicates that the first nineteen numbers must have been issued on average about once every three weeks, with number 19 appearing in middle or late May 1839. The format of the magazine was the same as that of its predecessors. "After Serving Seven Years," given above on page 361, appeared in issue number 35.

London Singer's Magazine seems to have survived far longer than its predecessors and far longer than is indicated in volume 1 here, where its dates are given as 1838–40. Evidence is complicated by three main circumstances: firstly the absence of issue dates and volume numbers, secondly the reversion of numbering to 1 once or twice after the initial sequence to 61 or higher, and thirdly the presence of irregularities in page-numbering sequences. It seems likely too that publication was suspended once or twice. All that is clear is that certain numbers, presumably from the second or possibly third sequence, date from about 1842 to 1845. They do so first of all by advertising the third through sixth collections of John Labern's comic songbooks of the 1840s. Labern is the author of the parody of Charles Mackay's "Wait a Little Longer" given on page 267. The first of Labern's collections, the only one known to survive, dates uncertainly from 1842. Issue number 43 of *London Singer's Magazine* advertises his third collection; number 1 and number 51 advertise the fourth collection; number 66 advertises all five collections; and number 82 advertises the sixth collection. Such songbooks as these, often of no more than twenty-five or thirty pages, were sometimes issued in very quick succession, as seems to have happened with four later Labern collections that are all assigned by the British Library to about 1852. However, along with the advertisement for the sixth collection in number 82 is an advertisement for Labern's annual benefit concert to take place on 9 September 1845. Closer inspection of these and other numbers of the magazine might yield more clues to the magazine's life span. Labern is given as editor of the magazine on surviving numbers 61, 66, 82, and 110 of the second or possibly third sequence.

"The Coalheaver's Feast" does not appear in any known number of the three magazines. It was issued as a broadside by W. Taylor, who published during the middle 1830s and who often enough gave his address simply as "16 Waterloo Road"—and did so with the present printing. Another printing by him—the one originally found and selected for use here—lacks Prest's name. That printing, presumably a later one, gives Taylor's address as "16 Waterloo Road, near the Coburg." The Coburg Theatre became the Victoria Theatre in 1837. In the few remaining months of his publishing career after Victoria came to the throne, Taylor sometimes used "near the Victoria Theatre" on his sheets. The date, then, for "The Coalheaver's Feast" seems to be 1836 or before.

In the commentary on "Happy Land!! Comic Version" on page 132 four lines by Prest are quoted from one of his many ballads that are known only from his magazines. The lines have a harshness that might seem more attractive to street than to magazine.

Prest is the only ballad writer of the time who is known with reasonable certainty to have written one or another ballad expressly for the street and others expressly for concert hall and other like places. Most of his considerable output was apparently aimed at the latter market even though occasional ballads of the sort appeared on the street as well—perhaps pirated, perhaps not. The two political ballads mentioned above seem clearly to have been intended for the street, and neither has been seen elsewhere. The largish sheet for the second of them, "Hercules Decapitating the Hydra of Corruption; or a Broom for the Boroughmongers," has a carton above the ballad showing Lord Brougham performing the feat. Below the title are the words, "A New Patriotic, Satirical, & Quizzical Ditty, to be Sung by all Friends to Reform." Written in hand at the bottom of the sheet are the words, "Sung in the streets during the passing of the Reform Bill."

In an eighteenth-century broadside feast for the poor, "The Bunter's [whore's] Wedding," the coalheaver merely intends what he and others achieve at his own feast in Prest's ballad:

> Jack the coalheaver thought himself slighted,
>   They carried the rig on so quiet,
> And swore as he was not invited,
>   He'd go there and kick up a riot;
> Then hectoring, bouncing, and swearing,
>   So boldly he enter'd the house,
> But when he saw Joey the sandman,
>   The cull was as still as a mouse.[9]

Nineteenth-century broadside examples of this sort of ballad include "Burial Club," "Cadger's Ball" (by John Labern), "The Chummy's Wedding," "Most Humorous Description of Irish Paddy's Wedding," "Mrs. Lobsky's Rout," "Polly Cox's Party" (by Thomas Hudson), "Revolt of the Workhouse," and "Scavengers Ball."

Monmouth Street

> Oh there's a place in London Town,
> Romantic and of great renown,
> Where life of every sort you meet,
> The place I mean is Monmouth Street.

8 / SCENES OF MIRTH AND CONTENTMENT

When clothes decay and cash is low,
The only mart for you to go,
To rig your person out complete,
You'll find is famous Monmouth Street.

The beaux of ten may puff and boast,
That Regent Street they like the most,
But many who parade it there
Are oft compelled here to repair,
Fine togs they get at small expense,
A slap up coat for eighteen pence,
With dandy "canes" and "tile" so neat,
They return quite swells from Monmouth Street.

Oh, dear is this famed street to those,
With naked backs and shoeless toes,
So reasonable is every snob,
You may get new "buckets" for a bob,
For thrums you'll get a new bandana,
And a bran new shaker for a tanner,
Young ladies own the spot is sweet,
For they get renovated in Monmouth Street.

The lipeys that you meet with here,
Seem paragons of all that's fair,
With gammon they'll get you in a line,
"Py Got a Mightish dish ish fine."
With that a coat on you they fix,
Just big enough to cover six,
Then cry "Py Got, it fitsh von neat,
'Tis de greatesht pargain in Monmouth Street."

The old woman when she wants a drain,
And finds her purse can't ease her pain,
Looks o'er her wardrobe in a trice,
For something that will fetch the price,
Thus to her drunken pal she clacks,
"Ve'll quickly have a drain of max,
I'll raise the tin if you'll me meet,
Vhen I've sold this smock in Monmouth Street."

On Sunday when you're walking out,
You see some swells that strut about,

Bedizen'd out so fine and gay,
With a stick to keep the dogs away,
Upon their arm, they sport a fair
Who struts with consequential air,
While her and her man were togged so neat,
On Saturday night in Monmouth Street.

Some of the swell west end may talk,
And in the Regent's Park may walk,
But bless old togs, and rags, and phials,
And the classic air of Seven Dials.
For that's the spot indeed 'tis true,
To make your person "better ash new,"
So if you with fashion would compete,
Go and rig yourself in Monmouth Street.

Monmouth Street—famous for its shops and stalls selling cheap clothing new, secondhand, often unclean; see pages 34 and 36 and the map on page 35 for its location
Snob—cobbler
Buckets—boots
Shaker—shirt
Lipeys—hawkers
Gammon—plausible talk, humbug
Py Got a Mightish—By God Almighty
Drain—drink
Max—gin
Tin—money

"Monmouth Street" is by Thomas Peckett Prest, who is discussed on pages 40–41 and 511–14. It appears in issue number 11 of volume 1 of *London Singer's Magazine and Reciter's Album*. The magazine is discussed on pages 512–13. Issue number 11 probably appeared in late summer or autumn of 1836.

I have printed from a broadside source but restored the magazine text at several points. In both printings stanza 2, line 4 gives "there," which I have amended for the sake of clarity.

The ballad echoes the ballad "Regent Street," which begins:

> In London when the weather's fair,
> One grand attractive spot is there,
> A street to which e'er points the nose,
> Of pleasure seeking belles and beaux.

"Regent Street" goes on to tell of the fops and old gentlemen (trying to look young) who go there, and of the scavengers and dustmen who must not (unless in best clothes). In the next to last stanza it takes a turn:

> This morn I heard our milkman Chalk,
> Say in Regent Street he'd bought a walk,
> And a girl with matches did repeat,
> I sells them now in Regent Street,
> Our chimney sweeper is moving there,
> And I saw some writing I declare,
> On the barrow of one who sells dog's meat,
> "Going to remove to Regent Street."

"Monmouth Street" itself was imitated closely in "A New Comic Song of Dudley Street":

> There's a spot in Birmingham Town,
> Romantic and of great renown. . . .

An article in *Chamber's Edinburgh Journal* in 1845 gives a glimpse of Monmouth Street:

> It . . . is the grand entrepôt for old clothes for the west end, just as Petticoat Lane and Rag Fair are for the eastern quarter of the metropolis. The stranger, on passing through it, is struck with the unhealthiness depicted on the pallid faces of the children, with whom it absolutely teems; and with the strange disagreeable musty smell that arises from its overcrowded cellars. . . . In these cellars a family of eight or ten persons are cooped up, working, eating, and sleeping within the same dark, damp, unwholesome walls. If there is a father to the family, he is generally a cobbler, while the mother plies the mangle. . . .[10]

The Way to Live

> A man and his wife got married one day,
> And thus unto each other did say,
> As we the world must now begin,
> We will deal in all the following things.
> She. We will deal in apples, plums, and pears,
> He. We will mend old bellows, and bottom old chairs,
> She. We will buy old metal, rope, and bags,
> He. Yes, and I'll go out gathering rags.
>   A man and his wife, &c.

She. We will sell red herrings and ginger pop,
He. Hot baked sheep's heads and tatoes hot,
She. We will keep a school of high degree,
He. And learn the children A B C.
She. We'll sell fat bacon, butter, and lard,
He. And great long songs, a penny a yard,
She. I'll sell potash, starch, and blue,
He. And I'll go sweeping the ladies flues.

She. I'll make bustles and ladies frills,
He. And I'll sell mussels and pickled eels,
She. We will deal in razor straps and hones,
He. And I'll go out a picking up bones.
She. We will deal in paper, take in the news,
He. And I'll go cobbling ladies shoes,
Both. And we'll learn the ladies all complete,
  To dance the Polka at threepence a week.

She. We will deal in lollipops, sugar, and figs,
He. We will buy a donkey, duck, hens, and pigs,
She. We will have a mangle, and buy old clothes,
He. And I'll make salve for the ladies toes,
She. We will deal in pickled cabbage and eggs,
He. And make tin dishes and wooden legs,
She. We will deal in sausages, tripe, and lard,
He. And if we can't live, 'twill be devilish hard.

She. We will deal in oils, sperm, train, and neat,
He. I'll make stockings for children's feet,
She. We will sell hot muffins and homebaked bread,
He. Pins and needles, cotton and thread,
She. We will grind old razors, scissors, and knives,
He. And keep lodgings for single men and their wives,
She. We will deal in lobsters, shrimps, and sprats,
He. And I'll sell meat for the ladies cats.

She. We will deal in fish, fresh, boiled, and fried,
He. And let our donkeys a penny a ride,
She. I will the ladies fortunes tell,
He. And I'll cry old umbrellas to sell.
She. We will take in the blooming ladies bright,
He. To sleep in the garret at threepence a night,

She. I'll sing come buy my crockery ware,
He. And I'll go dressing the ladies hair.

She. We'll sell pea soup, ripe cherries, and milk,
He. Oranges, lemons, and pickled wilks,
She. Wooden rolling pins at the Royal Exchange,
He. And if we can't get on we may think it strange.

J. Morgan

Long songs—a number of songs printed on a sheet a yard long or longer; very popular in the 1830s; see the illustration on page 67
Polka—introduced to London in about 1842
Train—whale oil extracted from blubber by boiling
Wilks—whelks

This was one of John Morgan's more popular ballads. It presumably dates from the 1840s. A version of it without Morgan's name omits the quatrain at the end and puts the fourth stanza last. It also changes "sweeping the ladies flues" to "sweeping flues," "meat for ladies cats" (perhaps an allusion to "The Dogs-Meat Man," given elsewhere here) to "meat for dogs and cats," and "dressing the ladies hair" to "dressing hair." "Salve for the ladies toes" escapes attention.

In another ballad of the same sort, "Chandler's Shop" (He. Oh, Sally Sime, when we get wed), the man and woman give some lines to cheating:

> She. To give good weight, Sam, we'll not fail—
> He. Barring a penny under the scale.
> She. We'll sell the very best Bohea.
> He. And I'll chop some birch broom up, d' ye see.
> She. We'll sell the best sugar in the land,
> He. I'd improve it with a little sand.

The Last Farewell to Poor St. Giles's

Oh! here's a pretty go,
  Bawls out old mother Miles,
They are going to send us all to pot,
  And pull down all St. Giles's.
She begged they would not serve her so,
  But favour they denied her,

THE LAST FAREWELL TO POOR ST. GILES'S.

OH! here's a pretty go,
  Bawls out old mother Miles,
They are going to send us all to pot,
  And pull down all St. Giles's,
She begged they would not serve her so,
  But favour they denied her,
What a slaughter there will be among,
  The bugs, the fleas, and spiders.

CHORUS.

If stones and bricks & floors could speak,
  They would lay down before ye,
Concerning famed St. Giles's tricks,
  A very pretty story.

The Coach Yard says he will go to France,
  Across the briny ocean,
And Buckeridge Street will take a dance
  By steam to Nova Scotia;
George St., Maynard St., & Banbury St.
  Will kick up such a shindy,
And with Church Lane & Lawrence Lane
  Bolt off to the West Indies.

Old mother Flinn began to sing,
  Boys, I don't care a farden,
They are going to pull down Drury Lane
  Charles Street, and Short's Gardens;
Up and down and right around,
  And all the Seven Dials,
The bugs and fleas of all degrees,
  Are bawling poor St. Giles'.

St. Giles's, oh! this sad affair,
  Most horribly doth shake her,
Nine old women ran down Buckeridge St.
  Bawling, Paddy the baker.
The Hand & Crown, the Hare & Hounds,
  The little courts a parcel,
The Robin Hood, the Rose and Crown,
  Black Horse, and sweet Rat's Castle.

Since sweet Saint Giles's first was built,
  There's many years gone over,
Saint Giles's once was all alive,
  And people lived in clover,
But now she is condemned to die,
  As dead as any gander.
Cries Tommy Grout I'm up the spout,
  Wherever shall I wander.

In famed Saint Giles's I declare,
  Not more than thirty years since,
A man could buy a five pound note,
  And a bottle of wine for ninepence,
A good blow out of hot pea-soup,
  For seven-farthings lately,
A great big wife, a glass of gin,
  And a bed for two-pence halfpenny,

Oh dear! oh dear! I feel so queer,
  O! what can be the reason,
To kill Saint Giles's I declare,
  Is worse than petty treason,
The chimneys tremble do with fear,
  The very stones are quaking
And every alley, lane, and street,
  In agony is shaking.

Her glass is run, her time is come,
  Oh dear! says Mrs. Miles'
Bad luck to them who did invent,
  To murder poor Saint Giles's,
Oh sweet Saint Giles's I'm afraid,
  You will be hung drawn and quartered
Poor Tommy Grout is up the spout,
  And all his houses slaughtered.

BIRT, Printer, 39, Great St. Andrew Street, Seven Dials.

"The Last Farewell to Poor St. Giles's." By permission of the Bodleian Library, University of Oxford.

What a slaughter there will be among
    The bugs, the fleas, and spiders.

        CHORUS
If stones and bricks and floors could speak,
    They would lay down before ye,
Concerning famed St. Giles's tricks,
    A very pretty story.

The Coach Yard says he will go to France,
    Across the briny ocean,
And Buckeridge Street will take a dance
    By steam to Nova Scotia;
George St., Maynard St., and Banbury St.
    Will kick up such a shindy,
And with Church Lane and Lawrence Lane
    Bolt off to the West Indies.

Old mother Flinn began to sing,
    Boys, I don't care a farden,
They are going to pull down Drury Lane,
    Charles Street, and Short's Gardens;
Up and down and right around,
    And all the Seven Dials,
The bugs and fleas of all degrees,
    Are bawling poor St. Giles's.

St. Giles's, oh! this sad affair,
    Most horribly doth shake her,
Nine old women ran down Buckeridge Street
    Bawling, Paddy the baker,
The Hand & Crown, the Hare & Hounds,
    The little courts a parcel,
The Robin Hood, the Rose and Crown,
    Black Horse, and sweet Rat's Castle.

Since sweet St. Giles's first was built,
    There's many years gone over,
Saint Giles's once was all alive,
    And people lived in clover,
But now she is condemned to die,
    As dead as any gander,

   Cries Tommy Grout I'm up the spout,
    Wherever shall I wander.

  In famed Saint Giles's I declare,
    Not more than thirty years since,
  A man could buy a five pound note,
    And a bottle of wine for ninepence,
  A good blow out of hot pea-soup,
    For seven-farthings lately,
  A great big wife, a glass of gin,
    And a bed for two-pence halfpenny.

  Oh dear! oh dear! I feel so queer,
    Oh! what can be the reason,
  To kill Saint Giles's I declare,
    Is worse than petty treason,
  The chimneys tremble do with fear,
    The very stones are quaking,
  And every alley, lane, and street,
    In agony is shaking,

  Her glass is run, her time is come,
    Oh dear! says Mrs. Miles,
  Bad luck to them who did invent,
    To murder poor Saint Giles's,
  Oh sweet Saint Giles's I'm afraid,
    You will be hung, drawn and quartered,
  Poor Tommy Grout is up the spout,
    And all his houses slaughtered.

  Several of the streets of St. Giles's disappeared in the late 1840s to make way for New Oxford Street. Among the buildings destroyed were the pubs the Rose and Crown (Beggars Opera) and Robin Hood, both in Church Lane, and Rats Castle in George Street (formerly Diot or Dyot Street, latterly Dyott Street). Sweet Rats Castle was one of the most notorious of the rookeries—lodging houses—in the area. See the map of Seven Dials on page 35. Buckeridge Street appears on it as Buckbridge Street and on other maps of the time as Buckridge Street It is shown going west from Diot Street. As noted on page 36. Church Street on the map should be Church Lane, and Church Lane there should be Church Street.
  All the names familiar to the ballads of the early 1820s (as in "The Merry Will & Testament of Master Black Billy" and "Beggars Opera," pages 308 and 506, are

gone. Presumably the new names belong to real people, but none of them could be traced.

In another ballad, "The Cadger's Ball," some of the inhabitants celebrate the destruction of the streets with a party at another notorious rookery, Mother Swankey's. Their dancing is so vigorous that the place collapses beneath them.

Much more of the slum was destroyed in the 1880s with the construction of Charing Cross Road and Shaftesbury Avenue.

Owdham Streets at Dinner Time

In Owdham streets at dinner time
   The workfolk how they flock,
Just as you hear the church clock chime
   Each day at half-past twelve o'clock.
In such a hurry crowds you meet
At the turn of every street;
You'd think all t'world, as I'm a sinner,
Wur come to Owdham o' getting their dinner.

If you go to th' bottom o' th' moor,
   That's throngest place i' th' town,
When all those factories work give o'er,
   The crowds will nearly knock you down:
The spinner then can leave his wheel
To get a comfortable meal;
Just tell his piecer t' not off wander,
But look sharp back and get clean'd under.

There's Jones', Bell's, and Castle mill,
   Gleadhill's and Hilton's send out their ranks;
Till half-past one they're never still—
   It's like a fair at Lousey Banks.
The lasses then, who think they're fair,
Blackball their heels and curl their hair,
Saying, "Put up my hair nicely Nelly,
For today at noon I'st meet my felly."

There's Scholes' and the Union too,
   With Broadbent's make a decent stock;
From Seville's and Wright's there is a few
   Turn out at half-past twelve o'clock:

There's Barlow's and Cowper's German mill,
Ratcliffe's and Hague's a church would fill;
Fro' Collins' and Lancashire's out they rally,
And then make up fro' John's-o'-Sally's.

If you stop at th' Lackey Moor,
    Of foundry men you'll see a flock;
From Barns's and Hibbert's and Platt's some scores
    Turn out at half-past twelve o'clock:
The moulder then he leaves his sand—
Th' mechanic leads up rear o' th' band;
A man would think they're running races,
For they're every one gone black i' their faces.

On Monday at noon, when th' mills all stop,
    The lasses come up to th' town in flocks,
To see what's fresh in each fine shop,
    Just takes till half-past one o'clock:
Th're buying some smart thing at last,
When who but th' chap by chance comes past,
Then o'th bargain how they clack again,
But th're off like good uns when th' bells ring back again.

Bottom of the Moor—thoroughfare at the center of Oldham
Bell's and Castle's—cotton mills along Bottom of the Moor
Hilton's—possibly Croft Bank, cotton mill erected by Abraham Hilton in the first decade of the century
Lousey Bank—old name for Mount Pleasant; Oldham Workhouse stood here
Scholes' and Broadbent's—John Scholes and Daniel Broadbent, along with Benjamin Taylor, erected their cotton mill on Vineyard Street in 1818
Union—cotton mill near Scholes' and Broadbent's
Cowper's German Mill—cotton mill above the town
Collins' and Lancashire's—cotton mill of the firm Collinge and Lancashire on Glodwick Road
Hibbert's and Platt's—workshop built in 1829

(Maureen Burns of the Local Studies Library, Oldham, kindly provided the glosses above.)

In 1750 Oldham was a largely rural district. A hundred years later the area was dominated by cotton mills and coal pits. The ballad perhaps dates from the

1850s, when for a while times were better—before the blockades of the American Civil War brought crisis again.

A companion ballad, "Manchester at Twelve O'Clock," cruder in its versification, describes a similar scene in much the same language. The mill and street names are different, but the same lass asks Nelly to fix her hair. Unluckily her chap does not come along: the stanza mentioning him is not there.

The Brixton Lady and Her Nice Beetle Pies

Come all you fine ladies who in Brixton does dwell,
A curious story to you I will tell,
Such a nice little relish—it will you surprise,
The ladies are making black-beetle pies.

CHORUS
At Raglan-house, Brixton, you'll get a surprise,
You'll get a blow out of black-beetle pies.

All you that are hungry, do not despair,
To Raglan-house, Brixton, quickly repair;
You can wear ladies breeches, but its not very fly,
And have a nice tight'ner of black-beetle pies.

She is so benevolent to all who goes there,
They will get a nice supper, I vow and declare,
Your bellies to fill, before you depart,—
A mixture of yellow, and a nice beetle tart.

If a band of musicians pass by that way,
She will get them to stay all night and all day;
Their bellies to fill, before they depart,
She will give one and all a black-beetle tart.

The gard'ner next door, a very nice man,
She gave him a tart, such as nobody can,
It stunk like a pole-cat, he shut both his eyes,
It was stuff'd with black-beetles and blue-bottle flies.

A band of black niggers hearing the news,
Says, let us try it on, she will not refuse,

The Brixton Lady and her
NICE BEETLE PIES.

Come all you fine ladies who in Brixton does dwell,
A curious story to you I will tell,
Such a nice little relish—it will you surprise,
The ladies are making bleak-beetle pies.

CHORUS.

At Raglan-house, Brixton, you'll get a surprise,
You'll get a blow out of black-beetle pies.

All you that are hungry, do not despair,
To Raglan-house, Brixton, quickly repair;
You can wear ladies breeches, but its not very fly,
And have a nice tight'ner of black-beetle pies.

She is so benevolent to all who goes there,
They will get a nice supper, I vow and declare,
Your bellies to fill, before you depart,—
A mixture of yellow, and a nice beetle tart.

If a band of musicians pass by that way,
She will get them to stay all night and all day;
Their bellies to fill, before they depart,
They will give one and all a black-beetle tart.

The gard'ner next door, a very nice man,
She gave him a tart, such as nobody can,
It stunk like a pole-cat, he shut both his eyes,
It was stuff'd with black-beetles and blue-bottle flies.

A band of black niggers hearing the news,
Says, let us try it on, she will not refuse,
When up goes the window, the lady did cry.
Oh, will you accept of this nice little pie.

Straight to an alehouse they did repair,
Saying, we'll have a pot and a tight'ner here,
When they took off the crust, they found after a pause
The inside was stuff'd with this fine lady's drawers.

Look here, says Squash, just ripe for a lark,
Here's the fine lady's drawers, with a small water-mark
They are crack'd behind, don't send them to pawn,
For in them I'll dance in the front of the lawn.

The gard'ner to the station quickly did hie,
Saying, Gov'nor, just see the contents of this pie;
But when at the station the bobbies did shout,
Its black beetles and yellow will stink us all out.

The lady to the station follow'd straightway,
To see what everyone had for to say,
She laugh'd at them all—they opened their eyes—
Saying, I am longing to feed you on black-beetle pies

This is the treatment she gives to the poor,
That happen to call at her great lodge door;
If I had my will I would her surprise,
I would stuff her cram full of black-beetle pies.

Let us hope that the magistrate will see this out,
And this filthy fine lady be put to the rout ;
And her musty old drawers that do us surprise,
Her mixture of filth and her black-beetle pies.

LUCKSWAY,
Printer, York Street, Westminster.

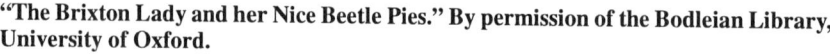

"The Brixton Lady and her Nice Beetle Pies." By permission of the Bodleian Library, University of Oxford.

When up goes the window, the lady did cry,
Oh, will you accept of this nice little pie.

Straight to an alehouse they did repair,
Saying, we'll have a pot and a tight'ner here,
When they took off the crust, they found after a pause,
The inside was stuff'd with this fine lady's drawers.

Look here, says Squash, just ripe for a lark,
Here's the fine lady's drawers, with a small water-mark,
They are crack'd behind, don't send them to pawn,
For in them I'll dance in the front of the lawn.

The gard'ner to the station quickly did hie,
Saying, Gov'nor, just see the contents of this pie;
But when at the station the bobbies did shout,
Its black beetles and yellow will stink us all out.

The lady to the station follow'd straightway,
To see what everyone had for to say,
She laugh'd at them all—they opened their eyes—
Saying, I am longing to feed you on black-beetle pies.

This is the treatment she gives to the poor,
That happen to call at her great lodge door;
If I had my will I would her surprise,
I would stuff her cram full of black-beetle pies.

Let us hope that the magistrate will see this out,
And this filthy fine lady be put to the rout;
And her musty old drawers that do us surprise,
Her mixture of filth and her black-beetle pies.

Raglan House—presumably named for Lord Raglan (1788–1855), who led British troops in the successful battle of Alma in 1854 and who led them in other failed attacks nine months later
Fly—knowing
Tightener—hearty meal
Yellow—egg yolk?

Brixton magistrate records do not survive from the time, and nothing could be learned of the Brixton lady in the *South London News* of 1856-57. The ballad has been seen in only one copy. The printer, Lucksway, York Street, Westminster, is known by just a few other ballads. Three of them are local and topical like "The Brixton Lady": "The Mad-Brained Earl of K.," "Weeping Parson in a Mess," and "The Naughty Poplar Man," the last one printed from Great Ormond Street.[11]

The unidentified author of the ballad seems to be the author of another ballad, "The Brixton Parson and His Double Fees," of very similar character.[12] This other ballad was issued by W. Dever of 18 Great St. Andrew's Street, who is known to have been in business in 1856–57.

APPENDIX 1

The Broadside Cock

I

Several of the ballads used or referred to in this book have been identified as possible or actual cocks.[1] Historically the term has been defined variously, and the material that has been exhibited as cock has never been examined in detail.

In *Curiosities of Street Literature* Charles Hindley begins with a definition from John Camden Hotten's *Dictionary of Modern Slang, Cant, and Vulgar Words* (1859): "fictitious narratives, in verse or prose, of murders, fires, and terrible accidents, sold in the streets as true accounts."[2] His comments on the type, though, slide quickly into confusion, and most of his apparent examples either do not meet Hotten's definition or meet it problematically. The problem is notably illustrated with "The Liverpool Tragedy," the most famous broadside among the fifty-one in the group supposedly illustrating "cocks . . . , street drolleries, squibs, histories, comic tales in prose and verse."[3] It tells of a sailor who returns to his humble home after many years. He is now wealthy, having married a wealthy woman, and he aims to provide well for his parents. They keep a lodging house, and to test their character he comes to them without identifying himself, takes a room for the night, and gives them a purse of gold. In the night they murder him to obtain the rest of his gold, the mother cutting his throat and severing his head, while the aged father holds the candle. The next morning the wealthy wife arrives, and when they tell her that the lodger has gone, she cries, "Impossible! . . . 'Tis your long lost son." She mentions a mole on his arm. The parents return to the corpse, see the mole, and take up a pair of pistols and blow each other's brains out.

The broadside adequately meets the first half of Hotten's definition, but it offers very little in the way of true account. Names, places, and time are no more precise than as given in these opening lines:

> A few days ago a sea-faring man, who had just returned to England after an absence of thirty years in the East Indies, called at a lodging house, in Liverpool, for sailors, and asked for supper and a bed; the landlord and landlady were elderly people, and apparently poor. The young man entered into conversation with them, invited them to partake of his cheer, asked many questions about themselves and their family, and particularly of a son who had gone to sea. . . .

Naive people may have been taken in, but the work aspires to nothing other than fictitious—or fictional—narrative of a sensational sort. Perhaps, then, Hotten's words "sold in the streets as true accounts" refer to the deceptive patter of broadside sellers. If so, the sellers of "The Liverpool Tragedy" must have been exceedingly skillful, or buyers exceedingly inattentive and gullible; for the broadside sold year after year for many years.

"The Liverpool Tragedy" was, in fact, a prose elaboration, with some differences, of the last sixty lines of a long, five-part ballad of the same title. The ballad dates from about 1760, and was still selling in London as late as about 1815. It gives considerable space to the son's disobedience to his father in going to sea, and also to his refusal to bargain with the devil while he is shipwrecked. Neither episode appears in the later prose broadside, and they are both given as much space as the murder. Although father and son have names, and the father a trade, the ballad is conventional poetic narrative of a sensational and moral sort, offered as "a warning to disobedient children and covetous parents."[4] The date that the prose broadside emerged is unknown. It was sold by Catnach probably well before 1836, and it is mentioned as a currently successful broadside at mid-century by one of Henry Mayhew's informants in *London Labour and the London Poor*. Compare this second life of fifteen or more years with the ephemeral life of a broadside on a real murder. "Why there was Rush," says Mayhew's informant, "I lived on him for a month or more."[5] For how long would a murder-cock survive that was fitted out with circumstantial detail comparable to true detail on Rush and others? One of the broadsides on Rush bears the following title: "The Execution of James Bloomfield Rush at Norwich Castle, April 23rd, 1849 for the Murder of Isaac Jermy, the Recorder of Norwich, and His Son, I. Jermy Jermy, Esq. at Stanfield Hall." It is succeeded by precise detail, the beginning of which goes thus:

> Between 11 and 12 o'clock the bell of St. Peter's, Mancroft, tolled the death knell of the criminal. When conducted to the turnkey's room to be pinioned he met Calcraft [the infamous executioner], whereupon he said to Mr. Pinson, "Is this the man that is to do the business?" The reply was "Yes." When he was pinioned he shrugged up his shoulders, saying, "This don't go easy; it's too tight". . .[6]

Though "The Liverpool Tragedy" does not seem to qualify as a cock under Hotten's definition, Hindley provides five other tales of murder that do.[7] Like "The Liverpool Tragedy" they are apparently fictitious and short on circumstantial detail. Unlike that broadside they have negligible intrinsic interest, and they are not known to have had anything but the briefest existence in the hands of individual printers or sellers—perhaps a few afternoons as true account in the speech of a patterer moving rapidly from place to place, telling himself he will not return until his face is forgotten. "The Life, Trial, Execution, Lamentation, and Letter Written by the Unfortunate Man James Ward" exhibits conventional aspects and language of gallows broadsides. It includes a stereotyped cut showing a multitude of people surrounding a gallows and a hanged man. Its descriptions make the baldest effort:

EXECUTION

The execution of the above prisoner took place early this morning at eight o'clock, the people flocking to the scene at an early hour. As the period of the wretched man's departure drew near, the chaplain became anxious to obtain from him a confession of the justice of the sentence. He acknowledged the justice of his sentence, and said he was not fit to live, and that he was afraid to die, but he prayed to the Lord for forgiveness, and hoped through the merits of his Saviour that his prayer would be heard. . . .

The most interesting of the others is "Cruel and Inhuman Murder Committed upon the Body of Captain Lawson." The author seems to have decided that as long as he was writing nonsense, he might as well enjoy himself. The opening sentence is slightly bizarre:

It is with surprise we have learned that this neighbourhood for a length of time, was amazingly alarmed this day by a crowd of people carrying the body of Mr. James Lawson to a doctor while streams of blood besmeared the way in such a manner that cries of murder re-echoed the sound of numerous voices.

The second sentence is more bizarre and five times as long. It includes a description of the murderess:

. . . Miss Lucy Gurd, a handsome young lady of refined feelings, with the intercourse of a superior enlightened mind, who lived with her aunt, who spared neither pain, nor cost, to improve the talents of Miss G these seven years past, since the death of her mother in Ludgate Hill. . . .

Sentence four, the same length as sentence two, describes the murder:

He demanded from her his letters at the peril of her life, which Miss G, like a distinguished young lady, refused, and prepared herself with unequal fortitude, and after stating to him the consequences of his unmanly conduct she cautiously ordered him to quit the premises, where to confirm his ambition (which crowned his reward) he readily attempted to get near her trunk, through which a sturdy scuffle ensued, and while she screamed for assistance, he attempted to commit an outrageous violation of her person, when to protect her virtue, she drew a large carving knife, and stabbed him under the left breast (which quickly brought him to subjection). . . .

The broadside is offered as a reprint of an account in the *Epping Telegraph*, a paper not known to the newspaper indexes of the British Library.

The five examples from Hindley, along with others, suggest that cocks as written were often clumsy and careless pieces of fictitiousness, uninteresting and unpersuasive in themselves, aiming to attract and deceive buyers only long enough for sellers to get away. They achieved negligible value as fictions. A noteworthy exception among them is one that is known in four versions: a presumed original and three variations, with the original perhaps plagiarizing two of its six sets of verses from an earlier broadside.[8] The prose tale common to all four broadsides concerns a boy aged twelve who is condemned to death for participating in a burglary. He is the only son of vicious parents with vicious friends, and from an early age he learns vicious ways. A humane parish binds him as apprentice to an honest master, but his evil ways bring dismissal. Later he is bound to a chimney sweep, and he robs places where he works. Eventually his parents bind him to a gang of thieves. With them he undertakes to rob a jewelry shop. He is apprehended as he passes goods out of the shop window. The others escape. After his trial and conviction he confesses to several murders. This prose account is accompanied by forty-eight lines of verse that dilate upon the horror and moral of the boy's situation.

In three of the broadsides the boy is named T. (or Thomas) King, in the other he is Thomas Mitchel. In all four accounts the parents move from somewhere in the country to East Smithfield in London. The place of burglary in two of the accounts is in Swallow Street in London, and the trial is at the Old Bailey. In one of the other two the victim of the burglary is "Widow Peany, a noted jeweller" in London, and the boy is tried in Chelmsford. In the other the victim is "an eminent jeweller" in Abingdon, and the boy lies under sentence of death there. Two of the broadsides were issued by the firms of Bonner and H. Shepherd in Bristol, each of whom printed other cocks. The others were issued by Horsen of London, who is not known otherwise, and by Carpue & Son of London, whose name has been seen on a few other broadsides.

The Bonner and Shepherd broadsides perhaps date from about 1821, and both of the others from perhaps 1829. Carpue's has "7 November 1829" written on it in hand. If the dating is accurate, the earliest among them took two of its stanzas from an earlier broadside, very likely from "The Trials of All the Prisoners at the Old Bailey, Commenced Wednesday, Feb. 17th. 1820."[9] This earlier broadside is not a cock. Four of the eight lines of one of its two plagiarized stanzas are modified to suit the fabricated circumstances of King / Mitchel. Insofar as sentence of death for a boy of twelve was not rare at the time, it might seem possible that all four broadsides were garbled versions of some true case; but London and provincial criminal records over the years 1819–31 show no appropriate young King or Mitchel. None of the four broadsides has been seen in more than one copy.

One example survives of a murder-cock that seems to have been ready-made for local occasions everywhere. The type is mentioned in an unpublished manuscript by Hotten now held at the Bodleian Library: "Popular Literature of the Olden Time, Merry and Serious." Hotten calls the type "standing forms."[10] It consists of a prepared text that can be fitted out from time to time with a new sensational title. The example Hotten mentions exists in two known copies.[11] In one the title is "Full Particulars of the Dreadful Murder"; in the other it is "Trial and Sentence of Dr. Barnard, This Day Guilty, Transported for Life." The identical texts begin thus:

> A scene of bloodshed of the deepest dye has been committed in this neighbourhood which has raised a painful and alarming sensation among all classes in this place, in consequence of its being committed by an individual that is well known to most of the inhabitants who are going in great numbers to the fatal spot where the unfortunate and illfated victim has met with this melancholy and dreadful end.

The rest of the text is preoccupied with the murder scene and with moral reflection. Only in the last line, "just as we are going to press," is mention made that one of the persons involved has been arrested. There is nothing about trial or sentence.

Hotten treats Barnard as a real person, and says that both sheets were printed before Barnard's trial was completed and Barnard acquitted. If Hotten is right, the text perhaps bears some relation to fact. However, Barnard is unnamed except in the one title, and no suitable Barnard could be found in the index to the *Times* or in the *Criminal Register*, 1858–60. Hotten apparently wrote his manuscript in 1858 or soon thereafter. The printer of the two broadsides names himself as "Barnett of Highgate."

II

Hotten's chief contemporary competitor as definer of cocks is Henry Mayhew. Mayhew is no match for Hotten as definer of words. His definition is a shambles. However, his discussion identifies cocks of sorts not covered by Hotten's definition. Charles Hindley, whose introduction to *Curiosities of Street Literature* progresses from Hotten's definition to Mayhew's in blithe ignorance of their incongruity, supplies a number of cocks of these sorts. A small aspect of the matter is that "The Liverpool Tragedy," presumably exhibited as a cock by Hindley, is explicitly named as one by Mayhew.

Mayhew defines cock as "a fictitious statement or even a pretended fictitious statement."[12] The two halves of the definition need to be considered separately. "Fictitious statement" gives only the first of Hotten's three prime requirements of the fictitious, the sensational, and the selling as true account. To discover whether Hotten's second requirement is meant to be involved, one has to ask whether Mayhew's examples are all sensational. The answer is yes. Among them are Queen Victoria's giving birth to triplets, the death of the Duke of Wellington in a fall from his horse, the Chartist Feargus O'Connor killing Louis Napoleon, "fabulous duels between ladies of fashion," and "The Liverpool Tragedy."[13] The question of the third requirement, however, yields varying answers. One may reasonably assume that broadsides on Victoria's giving birth to triplets and Wellington's dying in a fall from his horse were written to be sold briefly as true account. Fabulous duels are another matter. They suggest attractive marvel rather more than true account. No copies of such broadsides have been seen, but the one title Mayhew offers seems to suggest attractive marvel: "The Great and Important Battle Between the Two Young Ladies of Fortune."[14] "The Liverpool Tragedy" is a similar case. If it qualifies as a cock, it does so more readily for its fictional contrivances that lean towards the unbelievable than for its unlikely sale year by year as true account. One clear example of the marvellous mentioned by Mayhew is "The Remarkable Dream of a Young Man." The young man agrees with a friend to undertake a burglary, but then he dreams so powerfully of being in Hell that he refuses to do the deed. His friend goes alone, is caught, found guilty, and executed. Mayhew's informant says, "There is a very beautiful description of Hell in this paper that makes it sell very well among the old women and the apprentice lads, for the young man was an apprentice himself. It's all very pretty, and a regular cock."[15]

Hindley provides several examples of the sort in *Curiosities*: "Apparition of a Ghost to a Miller, to Discover a Hidden Murder," "Strange Warning to a Reprobate Publican," "Strange and Wonderful Account of the Rev. John Miller, Minister of the City of Bath, who Remained in a Trance for Four Days and Nights," and "Wonderful,

Just & Terrible Judgment on a Blasphemer."[16] The first of these is an echo of the reported true circumstance of William Corder's murder of Maria Marten in 1828, in which the stepmother of Maria Marten dreamed prophetically that the young woman's body lay buried in the red barn.[17] In "Apparition" the murdered young woman comes in ghostly form to tell the miller where she lies and who killed her. In "Strange Warning" a "good-looking female" appears before the publican to warn him to mend his ways lest his daughter die violently at the hands of the law. He does mend his ways, yet his daughter is burnt for counterfeiting. The Reverend John Miller seems to die, but recovers during his protracted laying out, and tells of his visits to Heaven and Hell. The blasphemer is struck rigid in his act of blasphemy, and becomes pious upon release.

In sum, Mayhew and Hindley exhibit a sort of cock that may be described as sensational invention sold on the street as wonder—broadsides concerned with apparitions, ghosts, miracles, or other circumstances beyond or at the edge of ordinary belief and not readily susceptible to ordinary tests of true account. Such broadsides are the second sort of Mayhew's "fictitious statement."

The other part of Mayhew's definition, "pretended fictitious statement," is equally inadequate as definition. However, surrounding discussion and illustration make clear that the phrase is meant to refer to an innocuous invention that is sold as sensational true account. The three prime elements of Hotten's definition are here, but the sensation rests explicitly in the patter of selling rather than in the written broadside. Mayhew's informant describes the sale of supposedly scandalous love letters:

> We give it out that they are from a tradesman in the neighbourhood, not a hundred yards from where we are standing. Sometimes we say it's a well-known sporting butcher; sometimes it's a highly respected publican. You have here, we say, the number of the house, the name of the place where she lives (there is nothing of the kind of course), and the initials of all the parties concerned. We dare not give the real names in full, we tell them. . . .[18]

Elsewhere an informant says that he and his fellow broadside sellers invent "every lie likely to go down."[19]

Mayhew provides two examples of pretended fictitious statements. They both appear, with some differences of detail, in *Curiosities*. As written, "Extraordinary & Funny Doings in This Neighbourhood" recommends itself only as a small piece of ingenuity.[20] It begins with thirty-two lines of verse that describe Mrs. Bubble-and-Squeak who puts more clothes on her back than she can afford, Mrs. Stradle who drinks like a fish, and Mrs. Carbuncle who assaults her husband. These portraits have almost no substance. The rest of the broadside is given to an exchange of love letters, the true meaning of which is only to be had by reading every other line. The opening lines of the first of two letters go thus:

> Madam,
> The love and tenderness I have hitherto expressed to
> You is false, and I now feel that my indifference towards
> You increases every day, and the more I see you the more
> You appear ridiculous in my eyes, and contemptible—

> I feel inclined and in every respect disposed and determined
> To hate you. Believe me I never had any inclination
> To offer you my hand. . . .

The letter continues in the same vein. No sensational details of relationship emerge, and no information is provided beyond the title phrase "this neighbourhood" to suggest local and identifiable scandal.

"The Love Letter, the Lady's Maid!! the Secret Found Out!!! or, the Husband Caught in a Trap" is equally bland in the writing.[21] It professes to give the husband's first name and initials, "Henry J. S. N.," and in a postscript the reader is invited to discover the undiscoverable:

> There are two ways of reading this to discover the parties. Henry ——— lives *in this street*, and Fanny ——— at the shop round the corner, and is said to be no better than she should be. The child's name we understand is to be called Anthony.

Hindley prints other broadsides of the sort, of which the best is "The Very Pretty Maid of This Town and the Amorous Squire Not One Hundred Miles from This Place."[22] It consists of thirty-two lines of verse in which the squire repeatedly asks the maid if she knows how to quench a raging fire. The third time round she pours a pail of water over him.

It appears, then, that there are at least three sorts of cocks: the sort defined by Hotten and the two other sorts exemplified by Mayhew and Hindley. An inclusive definition is called for. One minor unsatisfactory aspect of the two present definitions is that neither Hotten's "narratives" nor Mayhew's "statement" adequately covers the range of invention that broadsides of all three sorts illustrate.

A serious and sometimes indeterminate matter is uncertainty of label. Is, or is not, "The Liverpool Tragedy" a cock either of true account or of near marvel? Did the broadside seller of "Extraordinary & Funny Doings" invariably sell it as true account, or did he sometimes—on the basis of unusually skeptical or lighthearted audience—embroider it as amusing marvel? Uncertainty is especially a problem with broadsides that deal in the supernatural. "Comfort to the Afflicted; or, the Wonderous Works of God," a ballad dating from 1800 or earlier, described on pages 237–38, seems in both title and substance to have been written in all seriousness. Perhaps initially it was sold in all seriousness. If so, it was not a cock at the time—even if interested unbelievers bought it for a laugh. In the 1820s Catnach reprinted it on a large handsome sheet, with decorations and four cuts that show the rich man turning the widow from his door, her hungry children seizing a crust of bread from a dog, the heavenly figure appearing to the widow, and the heartless churchwarden lying dead and bloody. The sheet must have sold for twopence, perhaps more than the afflicted could afford. Catnach and his balladmongers may have seen it as a cock to catch unafflicted believers and curious half-believers. Today it is presumably no longer a cock either for believers or for nonbelievers.[23] Of a different sort is "A Full and Particular Account of the Sufferings and Melancholy Death of Three Atheists," described on page 343.[24] This broadside was issued in the 1820s by the firm of Shepherd in Bristol, printers of three known cocks of the Hotten sort. It seems altogether likely that they and their author (who may have been themselves) regarded "A Full and Particular Account..." as a cock to entertain believers and nonbelievers. It seems like a cock today.

III

Who were Hindley, Mayhew, and Hotten that they should be authorities on cocks? Comments elsewhere in this book suggest that Hindley was an unthinking commentator on a subject of great interest to him, and Mayhew a naive if vigorous investigator of a subject of no special interest to him.[25] Hotten apparently combined the more useful qualities of these two men. He made his living as bookseller and publisher, and also did some writing. His chief surviving work is his *Dictionary*, whose contents show knowledge of street life. He remarks in his preface that Seven Dials and Orchard Street, Westminster (where John Morgan lived for a time), were good places to pick up slang and cant. Canting ballads issued by the broadside presses must have been one of his sources. His other noteworthy work is the Bodleian manuscript. It is a three-hundred-page ragbag of information about the contents of chapbooks, garlands, broadsides, and other street literature of the eighteenth century, with just a couple of comments on nineteenth-century broadside ballads. He mentions conversation with a ballad singer named Jem Jones, who composes broadsides on dreadful fires and the like—with no suggestion by Hotten that the fires are invented.[26] All together the evidence suggests that his acquaintance with nineteenth-century broadsides was more thoughtful than Hindley's or Mayhew's, though not more substantial.

Despite their limitations, the three men have no serious competitors among contemporaries in their understanding of broadside cocks. No usage of the term is known prior to Mayhew's in 1851.[27] In years before, there was cock-and-bull story, a term used very generally to apply to tall stories or stories of a meandering, aimless sort. It seems likely enough that cock in the broadside sense derived from the phrase. Hotten is alone in suggesting instead that cock may be a corruption of cook in the sense of concoct or falsify.

It appears, then, that the active life of the word cock in the broadside sense was brief, from a decade or two or three before Mayhew stumbled upon the term until sometime not long after 1870 when the broadside press was fast disappearing. Given the scant attention that broadsides attracted in the middle-class literary world, it is not surprising that only four references to broadside cocks have been identified in the years to 1870 other than those by Hotten and Mayhew. Two of the references do not use the term itself. In 1852, in "The Literature of the Streets," an anonymous author remarks upon penny magazines and other street productions that are preoccupied with violent crime: "Is the public startled by the commission of any great crime? These writers seize on it, dress up all its details in their fictions, and represent them as newly drawn from life." In 1867, in "The Poetry of Seven Dials," B. Johns says that thirteen "dying speeches and confessions" lie before him and that several "are clearly by the same hand." He quotes a bard of the Seven Dials: "I gets a shilling a copy for the verses *written by the wretched culprit* the night previous to his execution."[28]

The word cock is used and defined in an article in 1856 by Charles Manby Smith:

A cock, then, is a pleasing fiction—a romance of a startling and exciting character—a tale of scandal concerning some celebrated personage or aristocratic family—an olio of sorrowful loves, heart-rending horrors, and desperate revenges—anything, in short, that is violently interesting and touching, and has not an atom of foundation in fact.

In common with Johns and the anonymous author, Smith expresses contempt for street literature, an attitude that leads to careless exaggeration in the final phrase of his definition.[29] Then in 1870, in the first edition of his *Dictionary of Phrase and Fable*, E. C. Brewer offers a curious etymology of cock-and-bull story, and remarks in passing that "the catch-pennies hawked about the streets are still called *cocks*."[30]

Subsequent to 1870, lexicographic definition of cock has relied upon the examples and definitions of Hotten and Mayhew, with interpretation of Mayhew tending in the direction of cock-and-bull story. Albert Barrère and Charles Leland's *Dictionary of Slang, Jargon, and Cant* (1889) contents itself with quoting Hotten and with suggesting derivation from cock-and-bull story. J. S. Farmer's *Slang and Its Analogues* (1890), paraphrases Hotten but omits the element of true account: "primarily fictitious narratives in verse or prose of murders, fires, etc. . . . , produced for sale in the streets." He notes possible derivation from cock-and-bull story, quotes Mayhew on "fabulous duels," and adds the rider: "Hence applied to any incredible story."[31] Eric Partridge's *Dictionary of Slang and Unconventional English* (1961) relies on Mayhew: "a fictitious narrative sold as a broadsheet [sic] in the streets. . . . From ca. 1860 it derivatively meant any incredible story." Lastly, the second edition of the *Oxford English Dictionary* (1989), leans towards Mayhew. It does not tie cock to broadsides:

> Short for *cock-and-bull story*: a fictitious narrative, a canard. Hence (esp. spoken) nonsense, an unfounded statement. . . . Mayhew. . . : "Getting rid of what are technically termed 'cocks,' which, in polite language, means accounts of fabulous duels, etc."

In relying upon Hotten and Mayhew, these several definitions are themselves defective. A more adequate definition might go thus: fictitious accounts or narratives, in verse or prose, of murders, fires, scandals, and other sensational happenings, sold in the streets either as true or wondrous; sometimes innocuous material sold as sensational happening either true or wondrous. This definition itself can hardly be known to apply to all sorts of broadsides that were characteristically called cocks. If broadside sellers so regarded "The Liverpool Tragedy," "The Scarborough Tragedy," and other like fictions, an ideal definition would need to find room for them. ("The Scarborough Tragedy" is an interesting case, lying betwixt and between true account, "The Liverpool Tragedy," and miraculous tale. It is discussed in the endnote.)[32] There is furthermore the issue of broadsides that seem to meet the definition but that no evidence suggests were regarded as cocks. "The Little Chimney Sweep" is an example. It tells of a hapless chimney sweep begging on a street on a cold snowy morning. Passersby ignore or laugh at him. Then a kindly damsel comes along, takes him into a friend's home, warms and washes him, and discovers beneath the soot her lost brother. One may suppose that the account is fiction, and that "founded on fact" which appears on one broadside copy (probably the copy of earliest date seen) is part of the fiction of true account. The discovery is sensational. Essential criteria for cock are met. However, the sensation, which comes in the twentieth of twenty-four lines, seems not a sensational end in itself but rather an instrument of sentimentality. Title and focus of the stanzas are sentimental. The ballad is not of a sort that, when new, would have been hawked about the streets by running patterers. It would instead have been sung. It appears to have come from concert room or stage early in the century. In the subsequent several decades during which it was printed, it would have been hung about the balladmonger's person or hung against a wall on Oxford Street for passersby to select. Perhaps once in a dozen years some desperate running patterer in desperate circumstance tried to hawk it as sensational news. Several broadsides in the present collection, both short and long, are of this sort: fictions whose sensations are incidental to sentimental, moral, or other like ends. The longer ones aspire to narrative interest in the manner of "The Liverpool Tragedy." Among them are "The Poor Widow and Her Praying Boy," "The Poor Lost Child Restored to its Mother," and "The White Slave." These three incline more towards true account than the wondrous.

IV

Information offered by Mayhew suggests that cocks were very important in the broadside trade. His assessment of various sorts of broadside-selling in London at mid-century adds up to nearly four hundred sellers.[33] Of that number, he says, eight sell only cocks—apparently of the funny doings and apparitions sorts—and ninety are running patterers, who hawk sensation. Thus one-quarter of all sellers are supposedly concerned to some degree with cocks. One running patterer tells Mayhew how he beat all the newspapers on the execution of Rush by having had his account prepared beforehand. He implies that such foresight is general practice. Mayhew twice makes the point elsewhere: "last dying speeches and executions are all printed the day before" and "patterers laugh at telegraphs and express trains for rapid communication, boasting that . . . the patterer has the full particulars . . . ready for his customers the moment the drop falls."[34] All running patterers would thus be selling a goodly proportion of cocks. Such estimates must then be considered in the light of the supposed dominance of broadsides on murders, trials, and executions in the broadside trade. As one informant tells Mayhew: "There's nothing beats a stunning good murder, after all." Mayhew's own figures on sales of gallows broadsides are startling: two and a half million copies each on the executions of Rush and the Mannings in 1849.[35] One might be forgiven for imagining that somewhere near a quarter of all broadside sales were of cocks.

An opposed view comes in part from Mayhew too. In the extended discussion of murders, trials, and executions, he says that broadside material is "usually . . . a condensation from the accounts in the newspapers." The contribution by the broadside author is likely to be a last letter or set of verses written by the condemned person in his cell. Mayhew's informant refers to such letters and verse as "established custom," the criminal's "being unable . . . to read or write being no obstacle to the composition." If this is so, the broadside author's contribution might properly be considered convention rather than cock, just as the cut that usually accompanies a gallows broadside is not fake representation of a particular scene but stereotyped primitive image of crowd, gallows, and hanged man. Elsewhere in his discussions, Mayhew remarks that "if the truth be saleable, a running patterer prefers selling the truth, for then—as one man told me—he can 'go the same round comfortably another day'."[36] This consideration itself might seem to cast doubt upon the importance of cocks of any sort in the broadside trade.

Charles Manby Smith adds some weight to these alternative views by Mayhew— though his article seems in part a mere echo of some of Mayhew's words. He says that gallows information "is generally collected from the newspapers, the only addition being the 'sorrowful lamentation'." He thinks that many other tales, which he identifies as "romances from real life," are likewise drawn from newspapers. "The cock," he says, ". . . sells . . . not so readily: partly because it is objectionable to the police, who will not allow it to remain long on its perch, and partly for want of faith on the side of the mob, whom, in these days of cheap newspapers, it is not so easy to delude in the article of news."[37] Nothing is known about such action by police except for the report of two incidents from nearly forty years earlier. In *The Life and Times of James Catnach* (1878), Hindley describes two cocks issued by the Catnach press.[38] One was printed by Catnach's mother while Catnach was in prison in 1818. It told a fabricated tale of a supposed local murder. The police recognized the fakery, took up two sellers of the broadside, and severely reprimanded them and Mrs. Catnach. Catnach was in prison because he himself had issued a cock of a special sort—malicious libel—that accused a local pork butcher of selling human remains as pork. Whether he quite intended buyers to take the accusation seriously is not known, but the pork butcher took it seriously, and then so did Catnach.

No modern assessment of the importance of cocks has been undertaken. Opinion and evidence that have emerged during the preparation of this book suggest relative unimportance. One perhaps substantial point is that Mayhew's sales figures on execution broadsides may be highly exaggerated. Mayhew's figures, and Hindley's additional figures, are examined on pages 72–75. It is certainly the case that murder, trial, and execution broadsides are very far from dominating major broadside collections in England. It is also the case that cocks of the funny-doings and apparitions sorts are rarely to be seen in such collections. Only the one example has been noticed (in two copies) of standing forms. It is in *Curiosities* alone that murders, trials, executions, and cocks may be said to dominate.

The King/Mitchel cocks considered above, and four broadsides on Charles Elliott considered on pages 339–43 and in the note on page x, help to make another point. Two of the King / Mitchel cocks were issued by the firms of Bonner and Shepherd in Bristol, the other two by altogether obscure printers in London. Two of the four Charles Elliott broadsides are cocks, and were issued by Bonner and Shepherd. The Bonners and Shepherds are indeed the only printers of a substantial body of broadsides whose productions seem to be seriously tainted with admixture of cocks. The British Library holds two volumes largely devoted to their broadsides, and a considerable proportion may be cocks.[39] No substantial gathering of the work of any other broadside printer has raised more than slight suspicion, if any suspicion at all. Comment on the Bonners and Shepherds appears on pages 340–43.

APPENDIX 1

The four Charles Elliott broadsides form a special mixture of true account and cock. Charles Elliott, aged nine, was sentenced to death in February 1820 for stealing six handkerchiefs. There was no recommendation of mercy, but presently the sentence was respited. The first broadside, "The Trials of All the Prisoners," issued shortly after his conviction, is the only known true account at the time to have much substance. Of four prominent newspapers examined, only one noticed the trial at all—in twenty-seven words. The broadside quotes from *Old Bailey Sessions Papers* that give Charles Elliott's testimony, and prefaces those words with the comment, "the prisoner set up the defence usually adopted by the most hackneyed thieves." The second broadside account is a filler for a sheet more largely devoted to the execution of the Cato Street conspirators on 1 May 1820. Its briefer true account says of Charles Elliott's testimony—without describing it—that "the boy made a most remarkable and altogether astonishing defence, hardly to be credited." This comment may have been sympathetic invention two and a half months after the fact, but neither it nor the hostile bias in the first broadside can be said to render either broadside a cock.

The third account (or fourth, depending on whether one is considering the chronology of Charles Elliott's life or the chronology of printing) is Mary Shepherd's undated broadside. Its title describes Charles Elliott as "now lying in Newgate, under sentence of death," a circumstance that was true for an unknown number of hours, days, or weeks after the trial. The account of the trial itself is very brief, and true. Only in the last line of the second of two sets of verses is there a presumed lie in the phrase about his impending death "on Monday morning next." It does not seem likely that he came so close to execution. Thus the broadside appears to be true account about Charles Elliott except in a single phrase, unobtrusively placed. However, the broadside was very probably produced six years after the trial instead of a few hours, days, or weeks, and thus would have been a thoroughgoing cock if it was sold as current crime, trial, and conviction—as seems altogether likely.

The fourth broadside is Bonner's, which is an unashamed cock in its subtitle, "the last awful moments of Charles Elliott," and in its comparatively long description of the execution, with "thousands of people assembled to witness so novel and mournful a scene." In between these two elements of cock is a true account of the trial, with comment repeating the words from the second broadside about Charles Elliott's remarkable defense. The broadside has no date except reference to the execution's having occurred on "Monday last, July 10." It seems possible that Bonner produced the broadside in July 1820 after having seen the second broadside in May or June. The discussion on page 343 suggests that he may have produced it in 1826 in conjunction with Mary Shepherd.

Six broadsides about four murders were also investigated in the course of preparing this book. The four murders proved to be real, and all the broadsides were reasonably true accounts. Material on the George Victor Townley and Samuel Wright murders appears on pages 152–58. The broadside that describes Wright's execution includes the "established custom" of the condemned man's last letter; but it is a real letter to Wright's foster-mother. The letter is alluded to but not given in the account of the execution in the *Times*. The overall reports in broadside and broadsheet are from independent witnesses. The two broadsides on the Walter Duggan murders and suicide, discussed on pages 362–73, are accounts independent of known newspaper reportage, with the second of the broadsides offering the only known social perspective on the tragedy. The murder of the policeman Robert Culley brought two true broadside accounts, one of them plagiarized. The first one, published by G. Smeeton in London, is an independent account that complements some but not all of the information in two separate reports in the *Times*. The second broadside, published by Bonner, is a piece of slightly garbled plagiarism. Somewhat less than half of his account consists of bits and pieces, almost word for word the same as in Smeeton's account. Much of the rest of it gives information that very likely came from the *Times*. The circumstance of the murder was a public meeting of tax protesters, broken up by the police. The two reports in the *Times* are at fundamental variance with each other, one saying that a peaceable gathering of two to three thousand people was set upon by the police, the other that a frenzied mob of three thousand people set upon the police. Smeeton's broadside is notable in that it expresses outrage at the murder but generally describes a frightened assemblage of a thousand people fleeing from thirteen hundred policemen. The coroner's inquest on the death provided supporting evidence for Smeeton's estimate of police numbers. The two broadsides are mentioned in the commentary on the ballad "Assessed Taxes" on pages 116–17. Appendix 2 reviews the reportage of the affray and its aftermath in the *Times*.

Overall, research for this book suggests that fewer cocks were sold in the streets than has commonly been supposed. Mayhew's informants may have gulled him. In "Anything to Earn a Crust," on page 494, a child catches out a seller who is selling an execution broadside of an execution that has not yet happened. One might guess from some of the evidence given above that cocks were often so inept, or so ineptly sold, that they would not fool a child. Nevertheless, a reasonably satisfactory opinion on the issue of cocks is unlikely to emerge until someone draws together extant copies of broadsides on several murders, trials, and executions over a span of years, and sets them against a number of newspaper accounts to see whether they appear to be independent true accounts, pieces of plagiarism, or pieces of invention. If invention proves to play a significant role, present evidence suggests that it will be careless rather than careful invention. The extraordinary fact about the King/Mitchel cocks is that there was no need for invention, only need for a bit of labor on real cases. *Old Bailey Sessions Papers* for 1819–21 show a boy aged fourteen sentenced to transportation for life for stealing a handkerchief valued at a shilling, two girls aged fourteen and fifteen sentenced to death (with recommendation of mercy) for stealing handkerchiefs valued at thirteen shillings, two boys aged sixteen sentenced to death for stealing blankets valued at thirty shillings, three boys aged twelve and thirteen sentenced to death (with recommendation of mercy) for stealing spoons valued at £1, a boy aged sixteen sentenced to death for stealing silver valued at £20.[40] Charles Elliott's case was the most extreme in those years. That Bonner and Shepherd were able to use him for cocks is evidence of a certain laziness in the rest of the broadside press and in the newspaper press in February 1820 in giving so little attention to him and his true plight.

APPENDIX 2

"Justifiable Homicide" of a Policeman: Jurors versus Coroner, the *Times,* and the Government, May 1833

With reference to the ballad "Assessed Taxes"
and its commentary, pages 113–17

The first reformed Parliament made only the slightest gesture to reform iniquitous taxes. On 30 April 1833, and again on 23 May, it successfully opposed motions to abolish the hated house and window tax. This tax was so designed that it fell heavily upon the shop-owning middle classes and lightly upon the rich. It also fell, indirectly, upon the poor, who often lived in airless dark tenements to enable their landlords to escape or minimize the tax. On the day of the first vote, the *Times* reported a number of public meetings and petitions against the tax (noted on page 117). On 23 May the *Times* spoke in the strongest terms against the two results. Was ever the country more united than against this tax? Was the vote not further evidence of the "arrogance and selfishness" imputed to the aristocracy? "Public murmurs at the indifference of Parliament, and of the upper ranks of Englishmen, to the feelings of their poor brethren, have recently grown to a frightful magnitude, and betoken some tragical result"— a result immediately named as "downright overwhelming revolution." The *Times* then alluded to the recent verdict of "justifiable homicide" passed by a coroner's jury upon the murder of a policeman at a recent public meeting. The details of the coroner's inquest as given below are all drawn from the *Times*.

A day or two after the first vote on house and window tax, placards began appearing in London to advertise a public meeting to be held in Coldbath Fields on 13 May. The meeting was arranged by order of the "Committee of the National Union of the Working Classes," and the aim was "to adopt preparatory measures for holding a national convention as the only means of obtaining and securing the rights of the people." Before the meeting the "Secretary of State" issued a proclamation (printed by the *Times* on 13 May itself) saying that such a meeting would be illegal, and that persons attending it would be breaking the law. Whether Viscount Melbourne, as Home Secretary, did indeed order the proclamation, and whether it was adequately—or even at all—

advertised on the streets before (rather than after) the event were matters subsequently in dispute, and perhaps never publicly resolved. The crowd that gathered was estimated variously to be from 1,000 up to 5,000 in number. Police opposing the crowd were similarly estimated to number from 1,300 to 1,700. During the melee the policeman (named Robert Culley) was stabbed to death with a dagger, and two other policemen were wounded.

The coroner's inquest took four days, 15 to 17 May, Wednesday to Friday, and 20 May, Monday. Among the witnesses who contributed to one version of events were a man who observed the meeting and affray from the balcony of his home, two strangers passing by, reporters from the *Courier, True Sun,* and *Morning Advertiser,* a surgeon who tended the policeman as he lay dying at the scene, several members of the crowd, and one police officer. Their accounts told of peaceable assembly and unprovoked and indiscriminately brutal assault by police: "crowds...running in every direction—the police pursuing and beating, and men and women falling"; "persons...prostrate upon the ground being beaten with great violence." At such descriptions, cries of "shame" came from one or another of the jurors.

Set against such testimony was that of several police officers, a reporter from the *Morning Post* (who acknowledged close connection with the dead policeman), and two or three other people in the crowd. The head of one large contingent of police said that he had told his men beforehand that they should show all forbearance, realizing that the crowd were their fellow countrymen. Individual constables spoke of police discipline and moderation in confronting a mob armed with stones, staves, and other weapons. "I never saw such a set of ruffians," said one officer. The first two days of the inquest dwelt upon such contradictory testimony.

The *Times* took a stand on the meeting and the affray before the inquest began. The law of the land must be obeyed as long as it was law. The very conditions of the meeting threatened usurpation of the rule of Parliament: the meeting had been declared illegal; people came to it in defiance of the law; the police were there to uphold the law; and a policeman had been killed. On the morning following the first two days of the inquest, the *Times* observed that in spite of much assertion about men, women, and children being severely injured by the police, no "undeniable evidence" had been forthcoming: "no such person is produced." That issue was faced at the inquest on the same day. The jurors wished to bring in witnesses who supposedly had been injured. The coroner, though, said that the jurors' proper concern was solely the cause of death of the policeman. The jurors replied that the inquest had wider scope, and read from the summons to them to suggest so. The coroner resisted the wider implication. The jurors were adamant. Furthermore, they wanted the coroner to provide assurance that any injured persons who did come forward would be safe in doing so. The coroner would not and could not offer anything more than guarantee of safe passage to and from the inquest. Eventually several people presented themselves, offering apparently visible evidence of injury: a stranger in London who had been beaten on the neck and back and had his arm broken; a man who had been beaten about the head; a man (employed by the Society for Suppressing Cruelty to Animals) who had been struck on the head and rendered senseless, and recollected nothing further until he regained consciousness in a doctor's surgery, and who now exhibited his blood-soaked clothing; a solicitor standing aside from the crowd who had been knocked down by the police, had remonstrated with them, and had been told, "Damn you, I'll knock you to the devil if you say another word"; and a surgical instrument-maker who had been "beaten without mercy by several policemen."

Such evidence caused the *Times* to modify its stand the next morning. That the police "should after the slaughter of one of their colleagues conduct themselves with indiscriminate fury is a matter of deep regret, but just and honest men will appreciate the cause." The editors did not go on to say that just and honest men would equally understand possible illegal assembly and perhaps even rioting by oppressed people; but they did acknowledge that if it were proven that the indiscriminate fury of the police had begun before the murder, "language is too weak to express at once our abhorrence of their violence and our contempt for their cowardice." They wanted a full investigation of this last point. They then reflected that the meeting itself "as regarded its real authors and abettors, was insignificant and contemptible." They thought that "a handful of police" could have handled it easily. Fourteen hundred or more police was "a sad blunder; a mob should never be made to feel that it is thought formidable."

That day was Saturday. No hearing took place that day. On Monday morning, despite the fact that nothing more had been disclosed at the inquest, the *Times* added an observation that seemed to suggest that they now knew—or were acknowledging for the first time—something further. In a brief leader they mentioned that "it is possible that the policeman, Culley, may have attempted some unlawful means of punishing . . . [the crowd]." The only relevant evidence hitherto reported by them was that one witness thought it possible that Culley had been among those officers who first rushed forward to seize banners from the crowd. Insofar as one or another officer testified that the police were under instruction to seize banners, such action hardly qualified as unlawful means. Monday was the final day of the inquest. As reported in the *Times* on Tuesday, it was an extraordinary occasion, both before and after the verdict. The central testimony on the day was by a woman who was servant at a tavern in Fetter Lane. She said she had gone to the meeting and had been stopped by the policeman Culley. He had said to her that she ought to be at home rather than at a disturbance. As they stood talking, a man rushed out of the crowd and stabbed Culley. She herself had then run away. Upon cross-examination she said that she did not see Culley strike the man first, and she did not see that the man carried a banner.

For the coroner, the woman's testimony marked the proper end of the inquest: "at all events, there is one fact established which cannot be disputed, namely, that the poor man was stabbed in cold blood." But one juror said, "I don't believe one iota of what she has stated." There then ensued a wrangle. The jurors still wanted to know whether Melbourne had ordered the proclamation; they wanted to know why such a large body of police had been used, and what precise orders had been given to the police. The coroner would not meet their demands, and insisted that their task was done. He repeated the woman's testimony, and added:

> If you can find any justification for this act, it is more than I can. If you are of opinion that the deceased met his death from that weapon in the way described, I think you will feel it your duty to bring in a verdict of wilful murder. . . .

The jury then retired. The time was seven o'clock in the evening. Within half an hour it was reported that all but one were agreed on a verdict against the police. In another two hours they were all agreed, and returned with their verdict.

> We find a verdict of *Justifiable Homicide* on these grounds: — that no Riot Act was read, nor any proclamation advising the people to disperse; that the Government did not take the proper precautions to prevent the meeting from assembling; and that the conduct of the police was ferocious, brutal, and unprovoked by the people; and we, moreover, express our anxious hope that the Government will, in future, take better precautions to prevent the recurrence of such disgraceful transactions in this metropolis.

There was loud cheering in the room.

The coroner refused to accept the verdict. The jury were not there to try the government or the police. They must reconsider their verdict. It was no verdict. The policeman had been willfully murdered, and the jury perhaps knew the murderer or perhaps did not. The only proper issue for them was how the policeman died, and the only clear evidence on the point was that of the servant.

At the coroner's suggestion that they perhaps knew the murderer, the jury laughed. When he said that their verdict was no verdict, they cried, "Oh! oh! indeed is it not?" Not one of them believed the servant. She had been tutored by the police. She was known to have been with the police since the affray. She was reported to be drinking with them even now.

The coroner took issue with the verdict on the matter of precautions. There had been many precautions. Yes, replied the jurors: inadequate and wrong. "We are all of opinion that if 100 policemen had occupied the ground, this man would not have been slain." Given the circumstances, they wondered only that more people had not been slain.

The coroner yielded. If "justifiable homicide" was their verdict, he would record those words, and strike out the rest.

No, said the foreman:

> Before God and our country, on our solemn oaths, we have given the subject all the consideration in our power; and that paper which I have handed to you contains the judgment in which we are unanimously agreed. If you strike out any part of that, it is not our verdict.

"So," said the coroner, "you say it was justifiable homicide because some persons broke other persons' heads some half hour after the man was murdered?"

"No," said one of the Jurors: "we are not of opinion that the heads were not broken till after the man was killed. If you record any verdict without the whole of what we say, it will be a false and untrue verdict." Several of the jurors then said, "You had better dismiss us if you won't take our verdict."

There then followed three remarkable exchanges. The coroner asked how the jury

could consider their verdict adequate: "Why are you finding fault with everybody with a vengeance? What reason was there to stab the man?"
One juror replied:

> Mr. Coroner, do you not recollect that before there was any stabbing or throwing of stones, or any other violence, a man rushed out from the body of police and violently struck about him, having said to those behind him, "Now go it, boys"? We are of opinion from the evidence that this was the same man.

Presently the coroner said, "So you think that a meeting to overturn the Government was a justification of this homicide?"
The foreman replied:

> No, Sir, far from it. We are all of us men who have families, and some stake in the country. Indeed, I think there is none of us but have some little property. We all of us are of one opinion about the impropriety of that meeting, and we are far from liking such meetings. If the police had acted with propriety, we would all of us have turned out to assist and protect them at any risk.

The coroner tried once more:

> Surely you could give a justifying verdict, and say that you did so for reasons peculiar to the case; but it is not right to give this verdict, which is slandering people whom you have no right to try.

One juror replied:

> Our reasons we have given; they are on that paper. If we say that it is "Justifiable Homicide" without that rider, it would appear that we approved of any brutal fellow stabbing a policeman in the ordinary execution of his duty and that we would encourage illegal meetings. We will not consent to any such verdict.

The many exchanges after the verdict were interspersed with long silences between coroner and jury. One juror suggested that the atmosphere was that of a Quaker meeting. At eleven o'clock the coroner accepted the verdict as given, saying, "Gentlemen, I consider your verdict disgraceful to you; but I thank you for your great attention to the case." The foreman bowed and said, "We thank you, Sir."

So far as reportage in the *Times* was implicated, the most remarkable of the three remarkable exchanges was the first. Nowhere earlier had the *Times* reported the testimony that a police officer incited the affray with the words "Now go it, boys." There was only the whiff of such testimony in the leader on Monday after the third day of the hearing. Now, following the verdict, the *Times* on the next day agreed with the jury in rejecting the testimony of the servant, but said that the verdict took no account of the fact that a man had come armed to an illegal meeting with a dangerous weapon, and had used the weapon. The verdict, if lawful, suggested that it "would henceforth be lawful for the people to go to all their public meetings, as the murderer of Culley went, secretly armed with daggers." The *Times* noted the improper conduct of jurors in their cries of "shame": "some of them acted almost in one breath as jurymen, witnesses, coroners, and even bystanders." Lastly, most significantly, and with some indirection, the *Times* seemed to acknowledge that the police had begun the violence; but "nothing could sanction in point of law . . . the use of deadly weapons in repelling the aggression, if we must so describe it, of the police constable, in even *the abuse* of his power." Not to just and honest men!

One altogether curious aspect of the shifting stance of the *Times* was that their own report of the affray, given immediately after it, on the 14th, consisted of two opposed accounts. The first was "From a Correspondent." It described a crowd "furiously attacked" and "lying in every direction, weltering in their blood and calling for mercy." It then said, "A policeman, belonging to C Division, 95, named James [Robert] Culley was stabbed in the heart by a man who was carrying a banner, and which he attempted to take from him." The other account, immediately below the first, was described as "Another Account." It told of an orator first addressing the crowd with "a most revolutionary speech," telling them that the government wanted to incite them to violence and so provide "a pretext for their being led to slaughter." He hoped they would be peaceable; but "a most fearful shout burst from the lips of the crowd and showed the people had been roused almost to a pitch of madness." The police received "renewed orders to act calmly and with forbearance," but they were "instantly attacked by the mob." In one notable respect the author here agreed with the correspondent: Culley had tried to seize one of the banners, and had thereupon been stabbed by the man with the banner.

The verdict of justifiable homicide was overridden by the Court of the King's Bench. A man was subsequently tried for the murder and found not guilty.

Notes

Locations given in the Title List of broadsides on poverty, 1790–1870, are not repeated here.

ABBREVIATIONS

BL = British Library collections

BOD = Bodleian Library collections

GU = Guildhall Library collections

Madden = Madden Collection, Cambridge University Library; locations are those for the microfilm copy

St. Bride = St. Bride Printing Library collection; ballads are filed alphabetically by first title on sheet, under Large Series (LS) and Small Series (SS)

UL = Goldsmiths' Library collections, University of London

CHAPTER 1. BEGGARS AND PAUPERS

1. *Report from the Select Committee on the State of Mendicity in the Metropolis, Parliamentary Papers, Reports from Committees* (1816), 5:391–416, these pages being a summary of a report of some eighty-five pages. The preface says, "The report . . . was accompanied by such a body of evidence as to ascertain beyond all possibility of doubt the gross and monstrous frauds practised by mendicants in the capital."

2. Annual reports, 1819–[1959], and other material of the Society for the Suppression of Mendicity are held at the British Library: PP1107. At UL 6-489 is a broadside advertisement issued by the society, stating its double aim to rid the streets of beggars and to inculcate "industry and virtue" in the populace. Two early attacks on the society are Horace Smith's "Beggars Extraordinary!—Proposals for their Suppression," *New Monthly Magazine* 8 (July 1823): 61–65, and "Castigator's" *The Mendicity Society Unmasked* (London: W. C. Wright, 1825). Smith's piece is broadly satirical, the other aims to expose the society's actual indifference to and ill-treatment of beggars. A century earlier "A Method for Suppressing of Beggars . . . in the Parish of St. Giles's" (BL 816 m9-81) offered two

shillings per head to anyone who would seize and apprehend beggars and swear oaths as to their begging before a justice of the peace. The government's efforts to tackle the problem through several centuries of poor law legislation are discussed in the introduction to the section on Workhouses, vol. 1.

3. "The Beggars Chorus" (seventeenth- and nineteenth-century printings): BL C40 m10-6l and BOD Harding B5-4; "The Beggar" (Of all the trades): Madden 1789–806; "The Jolly Beggar": J. S. Farmer, *National Ballad and Song* (Privately printed, 1897), 1: 5; "The Dorsetshire Garland": BL 11621 c11-11; "Sandman's Wedding": J. S. Farmer, *Musa Pedestris* (New York: Cooper Square Publishers, 1964), 64; "The Bunter's Wedding": BL LR31 b19 1.1-216.

4. "The Beggar Wench of Hull": *A Collection of Old Ballads* (London: J. Roberts, 1725), 2:228; "The Stout Cripple of Cornwall": *The Roxburghe Ballads*, ed. William Chappell and J. W. Ebsworth (London, 1869–99), 2:531–35; hereafter cited as *Roxburghe*.

5. "Robin Hood and the Beggar" and "Bold Robin Hood" (also called "Robin Hood Rescuing the Widow's Three Sons") appear in Joseph Ritson, ed., *Robin Hood, A Collection of All the Ancient Poems, Songs, and Ballads* (1823; rpt., Wakefield: E. P. Publishing, 1972). A nineteenth-century printing of "Bold Robin Hood" is at Madden 1804-422.

6. "The Maunding Soldier": *Roxburghe* 3:110–15; "The Map of Mock-Beggar Hall": *Roxburghe* 2:131–36.

7. "All Round My Hat": John Ashton, *Modern Street Ballads* (London: Chatto & Windus, 1888), 173; hereafter cited as Ashton. Ashton says that "All Round My Hat" was very popular on the street. Sheet music for it dates from 1834.

8. Biographical information on Dibdin is drawn from *New Grove Dictionary of Music* (London: Macmillan, 1980). George Hogarth, ed., *The Songs of Charles Dibdin* (London: How & Parsons, 1842), 113.

9. "Adieu My Native Land": Madden 1801-305.

10. Douglas Jerrold, "The Ballad Singer," *Writings* (London, 1851–54), 5:225.

11. Charles Hindley, *The History of the Catnach Press* (London: Charles Hindley, 1887), xxviii.

12. Leslie Shepard, *John Pitts* (London: Private Libraries Association, 1969), 51.

13. Richard Monckton Milnes, *Poetical Works* (1876), 2:232–33.

14. "The Beating of My Own Heart": BL 11621 k4-284.

15. Sheet music identified for these and other ballads is held in the Music Library of the British Library.

16. Victor Neuburg, *Chapbooks, A Bibliography* (London: Vine Press, 1964), gives the date for Bebbington along with dates for other printers; hereafter cited as Neuburg. Bebbington: BL 1876 d41 1-127; Hodges (imprint "from J. Pitts . . . , 31 Dudley Street"): BOD Harding B11-1633. Dudley Street was Hodges' address from some time in 1845. How much later than 1850 she used "from J. Pitts" is unknown.

17. Milnes, *Poetical Works* 2:206–7.

18. James Pope Hennessy, *Monckton Milnes*, 2 vols. (London: Constable, 1945, 1955).

Chapter 2. Children on the Street

1. "Vulgar Little Boy": BL 11621 k4 1-48.
2. Date given by Neuburg.
3. Madden 1793-405.
4. Henry Mayhew, *London Labour and the London Poor* (London: Frank Cass, 1967), 2:155–58. Hereafter cited as Mayhew.

Chapter 3. Criminals

1. "The Nobleman's Generous Kindness": Madden 1797-73. This ballad is not to be confused with an earlier ballad, "The Nobleman's Generous Kindness; or, the Countryman's Unexpected Happiness" (A nobleman lived in a village of late), *Roxburghe* 7:328–30, which was widely printed in the nineteenth century under three titles, "Generous Gift," "The Happy Couple," and "Squire and Thrasher," copies at BOD Harding B11-1299, Madden 1804-461, BOD Johnson-1653.
2. "A Statement of the Number of Persons Male and Female Committed to Newgate ... 1802–1808": GU B'side-6.90.
3. Assize calendars: BL 1875 d13-27 and 35.
4. Old Bailey Records, London Metropolitan Archive: X71/39.
5. Quoted from Pauline Gregg, *A Social and Economic History of Britain,* 4th ed. (London: Harrap, 1964), 178.
6. Eric Hobsbawn and George Rudé, *Captain Swing* (London: Lawrence & Wishart, 1969), 308–9.
7. Proclamation: BL 1875 d13-18 from end (unnumbered).
8. *Newcastle Chronicle*, 23 November 1822.
9. "Royal Mercy": BL 1875 d13-28 from end (unnumbered).
10. Preston: Madden 1797-1301 to 1345.
11. Another Bamford broadside ballad on Peterloo: "Song of the Slaughter." Other broadside ballads: "The Meeting at Peterloo," "The White Hat."
12. Riots and other agitation. Items below without locations are in the Title List.

Luddism: "The Framework-Knitters Lamentation" and "The Framework Knitters Petition," given along with Byron's poem in V. de Sola Pinto and A. E. Rodway, *The Common Muse* (London: Chatto & Windus, 1957), 117–19; "Hunting a Loaf."

Riots in 1816: Guildhall Library broadsides at and around 27.53; BL N Tab 2021/28-2; BL CUP407 mm29-13, 34.

Riots in 1826: Blackburn and Carlyle: James Lindsay, *Catalogue of English Broadsides, 1505-1897* (Aberdeen: Aberdeen University Press, 1898), no. 1637, and UL 6-502 (1), 502 (2). The first of the University of London items reports a mob of ten thousand people destroying power looms, with several people killed by soldiery and others arrested. The informant for the printer of the broadside says of those arrested, "They were persons of the most wretched looking appearance, extremely dejected, and seemed to be actually starving."

Captain Swing: BL 1880 c20 (2 vols.), BL LR271 c3 (3 vols.), BL N Tab 2021/28. Also Lindsay, *Catalogue*, no. 1697; BL 1875 d16-64; "The Odds and Ends of the Year 1830"; "Something or Other New Starts Every Day"; "Men of Kent": BL 1875 d16-64. At UL 6-517 is a huge broadside, thirty by sixty inches, "Sentences of the Prisoners Tried Before the Special Commission at Winchester, December 1830," with a long address by the judge in sentencing well above a hundred men and women for riot, machine-breaking, robbery, and other offences. See also "Particulars of a Riot . . . at the West End of London": BOD Harding B8-36.

Chartism, 1839: "Frost, Williams, and Jones's Farewell to England"; "Lamentation of Mrs. Frost": BL 1876 d41 2.2-1368; "Welcome Frost to England": Madden 1795-39; items at BL 1880 c20 1-34, 35; "A New Song on the Great Demonstration on Kersal Moor, May 25, 1839": Madden 1799-493.

Other Chartist ballads and prose: "The Charter": Madden 1801-111; "The Chartist Song": BOD Harding B15-43a; "The Chartists are Coming": BOD Johnson-480; "The Chartist's Flare-Up on Whitsun Monday": BOD Firth C16-39; "How to Repeal the Corn Laws, or the Six Points Explained"; "Lines, by a Chartist": BOD Harding B11-2137; "A New Song on the Great Demonstration Which is to be Made on Kersal Moor, September

24th, 1838": BOD Firth C16-40. Martha Vicinus, *Broadsides of the Industrial North* (Newcastle upon Tyne: Frank Graham, 1975), has two items: 44-45; and see comments on James Elmslie Duncan, pp. 58–59.

Two ballads on enclosure, the second of them describing riot: "Bonny Moor Hen"; "A New Song on the Disagreeable Confusion Which Took Place on the Otmoor Inclosure." Other information on the Otmoor enclosure, along with two other ballads, appears at BOD G.A. Oxon b96-4, 5, 5a, 10. See as well "Fall, Tyrants, Fall!"

Newspaper, broadside, and other material on industrial struggle: UL collections "Oastler and the Factory Movement," "White Slavery." Other information: Martha Vicinus, *The Industrial Muse* (London: Croom Helm, 1974).

Chris Cook and John Stevenson, *British Historical Facts, 1760-1820* (London: Macmillan, 1980), list riots year by year.

13. "County Gaol": Madden 1792-694; "Bellevue Gaol": BOD Harding B11-233; "A New Song on Preston Gaol": Madden 1799-557; "Wakefield Gaol": Roy Palmer, *A Touch on the Times* (Harmondsworth: Penguin Education, 1974), 250-53; "The Devil": BL 1876 e3-62. Coleridge's title is "The Devil's Thoughts."

14. "Gallant Poachers": Madden 1797-570.

15. Public Record Office, Kew: *Old Bailey Sessions Papers*, 1820, PCOM 1/16.

16. London Metropolitan Archive: *Old Bailey Sessions Roll*, OB/SR 507-40.

17. *Morning Post*, 19 February 1820.

18. London Metropolitan Archive: *Prisoners on Orders*, X71/39.

19. Public Record Office, Kew: *Criminal Register*, 1820, HO 26/26.

20. *Times*, 13 April 1820.

21. Caroline: BL 1880 c20 1-121; Bird brothers: BL 1880 c20 2-351. An enterprising printer in Edinburgh issued "The Last Sorrowful Lamentation," omitting allusions to Bristol: BL 1875 d13-28.

22. Atheists: BL 1880 c20 1-320.

23. The Bonner items are in the same two volumes of BL 1880 c20, which volumes are devoted to material printed in Bristol: assize calendars and reports of riots, murders, executions, and other sensational events and non-events. Bonner items: 1-1 to 60 (Waterloo, riots, Hunt), 1-36 (National Convention), 1-282 (Dreadful and Awful Effects) 1-288 (Romilly), 2-468 to 470 (Cato Street).

24. Knife-sharpening wheels, showering sparks like Catherine-Wheel fireworks, were perhaps called caton-wheels. Torture remains the implication.

25. "Tread-Mill": BL 1875 d7-8.

26. "The Bishop's See": William Henderson, *Victorian Street Ballads* (London: Country Life, 1937), 120; "The Fight! the Fight!": Madden 1804-468; "The Gin": BL 11602 i12-22; "The Land": BL LR271 a2 4-360; "The Omnibus": Hindley, *The True History of Tom and Jerry* (London: Charles Hindley, [1892]), 194; "The Road": BL 1876 e2-94; "The Spree": Madden 1794-219; "The Tea": Madden 1794-221; "The Ugly Sea": Madden 1794-363.

27. Barry Cornwall, *English Songs* (London: Edward Moxon, 1832), prefatory note.

28. "Horae Catnachianae," *Fraser's Magazine* 19 (April 1839): 413.

29. *Autobiographical Fragment* (London: George Bell & Sons, 1877), 93.

30. "Brixton Tread Mill"; "The Newcastle Tread Mill": Madden 1797-798; "Tom, Jerry, and Logic at the Treadmill": Madden 1791-708; "The Tread Mill; or, Tom and Jerry at Brixton."

31. John Camden Hotten, *A Dictionary of Modern Slang, Cant, and Vulgar Words* (London: John Camden Hotten, 1859).

32. J. S. Farmer, ed., *Musa Pedestris* (New York: Cooper Square Publishers, 1964).

33. C. J. Hunt, *The Book Trade in Northumberland and Durham* (Newcastle upon Tyne: Thorne's Student's Bookshop, 1975); hereafter cited as Hunt.

34. Public Record Office, Kew: Assize records, 1842: ASSI 45/66-245.
35. J. Latimer, *Local Records; or, Historical Register of Remarkable Events* (Newcastle upon Tyne, 1857), 157.
36. Public Record Office, Kew: Assize records, 1842: ASSI 45/66-246 (Bradford and Halifax), 229-39 (Leeds).
37. *Report from the Select Committee on the Bill to Regulate the Labour of Children in the Mills and Factories, Parliamentary Papers, Reports from Committees* (1831–32), 15:5.
38. "Johnston's Escort into a Better Clime": Madden 1799-1192; "Lament of Charlotte Mills"; "Lamentation of the Smugglers"; "The Transport's Return"; fragment of Sarah Collins' ballad: "Horae Catnachianae": 414-15. See also chapter 4, note 7.
39. William Todd, *A Directory of Printers..., London and Vicinity, 1800–1840* (London: Printing Historical Society, 1972).
40. John Ashton, *A Century of Ballads* (London: Elliot Stock, 1887), 23.

Chapter 4. People In and Out of Work

1. My general view of agricultural and industrial revolutions is drawn from Howard Newby, *Country Life* (London: Weidenfeld and Nicolson, 1987); and Pauline Gregg, *Social and Economic History*. Statistics are from Llewellyn Woodward, *The Age of Reform, 1815–1870*, 2d ed. (Oxford: Oxford University Press, 1990), 5, and Gregg, *Social and Economic History*, 47.
2. *Report from the Select Committee on the Bill to Regulate the Labour of Children*, 1–37, and *Children's Employment, First Report of the Commissioners (Mines), Parliamentary Papers, Reports from Commissioners* (1842), 15:9, 20, 84ff., 173ff.
3. Public Record Office, Kew: mf48-323.
4. Mayhew 4:393–448, 447.
5. Anthony Wood, *Nineteenth Century Britain* (Harlow: Longman, 1982), 435.
6. William Cobbett, *Rural Rides* (London: Everyman, 1957), 2:244.
7. Not in Title List: "Select Hymns": BL 872 a1-63 (consisting of seven hymns); also "I've Been to Australia O!": Madden 1802-158. Hugh Anderson's *Farewell to Old England* (London: Angus & Robertson, 1964) has ballads about enforced emigration—transportation—to Australia. Most of his examples have no connection with poverty, though he does print "Farewell Address" and "The Transport's Lamentation."
8. Anna Barbauld, *Poems*, ed. William McCarthy and Elizabeth Kraft (Athens: University of Georgia Press, 1994), 129.
9. John Harland and T. T. Wilkinson, eds., *Ballads and Songs of Lancashire*, 2d ed. (London, 1875), 162–75.
10. Palmer, *A Touch on the Times*, 209.
11. Samuel Bamford, *Walks in South Lancashire* (Blackley: Samuel Bamford, 1844), 171.
12. Further information from Lichenmoss appears with a reprinting of the ballad in the 1880s or later: BL 1865 c8-56. Some detailed information on Lees's background is given in an article by Charles Higson, "'Jone o' Grinfilt' and 'Oldham Rushbearing'," *Oldham Standard*, 1 May 1926. Other information can be had from Martha Vicinus, *Broadsides of the Industrial North*, 18, 21, and *The Industrial Muse*, passim, and from Brian Hollingworth, *Songs of the People* (Manchester: Manchester University Press, 1977).
13. Joan o' Grinfilt's Visit to Lunnon...," "Joan o' Grinfilt's Visit to Mr. Fielden...," "A New Song Called, Jone o' Greenfield's Lamentation...," "A Laughable and Interesting Dialogue between Joan o' Greenfield...."

14. "Not a Trap was Heard": BOD Harding B16-174a; "Not a Drum was Heard": BOD Harding B16-172a.

15. *Children's Employment, First Report . . . (Mines)*, 9, 20, 71.

16. Mine explosions: BL 1875 d13-31 and 95 from end (unnumbered).

17. Richard Oastler (1789–1861) wrote his letter on "Yorkshire Slavery" on 29 September 1830. A further letter, "Slavery in Yorkshire," appeared in the *Leeds Intelligencer* on 20 October 1831. The collection of material at the University of London, "Oastler and the Factory Movement," was made by him. One of the broadsides in it, "Slavery in Yorkshire" (534-3, 17 April 1832), is signed by him, and announces a meeting in York on the subject "Our Children Shall Be Free."

18. Fortey printed "Farmer's Boy" in 1859 or later: Madden 1792-813.

19. S. B. Gould, *English Minstrelsie* (Edinburgh: T. C. and E. C. Jack, 1895), 1:xxx.

20. Robert Bell, *Ancient Poems, Ballads, and Songs of the Peasantry of England* (London: J. W. Parker & Son, 1857), 148.

21. Julian Treuherz, *Hard Times, Social Realism in Victorian Art* (London: Lund Humphries, 1987), 26.

22. The tale of Biddell and of Hood's poem is told by J. C. Reid, *Thomas Hood* (Routledge & Kegan Paul, 1963), 207ff.

23. Irish "Hungry Army": BOD 2806 b11-27.

24. "I'm Afloat": BL C116 il-101; "The Old Arm Chair": Madden 1802-160; "Mother Be Proud of Your Boy in Blue": BL 11621 k5-67; "Song of the Haymakers."

25. Eliza Cook, *Poetical Works* (London: Fredrick Warne, 1870), 541, 280, 538.

Chapter 5. Maidens and Lovers

1. "King Cophetua": Thomas Percy, *Reliques of Ancient English Poetry*, ed. Henry Wheatley (London: Bickers & Son, 1876–77), 1:189–94; "Patient Grissel": *A Collection of Old Ballads* (London: J. Roberts, 1723–25), 1:252; "The Beggar's Daughter of Bednall-Green": Percy-Wheatley 2:171; "The Virtuous Milk-Maid": see note 8 below.

2. For tales of Strephon and friends: Madden 1787-1439-60.

3. Ashton, *Modern Street Ballads*, 98.

4. Mayhew 4:213; the discussion includes comments by a variety of observers, domestic and foreign.

5. "Burning Them Out": Madden 1794-32; "The Story of Sinful Sally": BL 1875 d6-105.

6. "The Old Lady & the Page": BOD Harding B13-122.

7. Maud Karpeles, ed., *Cecil Sharp's Collection of English Folk Songs*, 2 vols. (London: Oxford University Press, 1974), 2:213; Eva Ashton, "Songs from Sussex," *Journal of the Folk Song Society* 6 (1906): 34–38; E. J. Moeran, *Six Suffolk Folksongs* (London, 1932), 8–11.

8. "The Virtuous Milk-Maid": BL 11621 c4-83.

9. Printings of "The Virtuous Milk-Maid": BL LR31 b19 2-34/182 (1760?); Cambridge Garlands 3 (1760?); BL 11621 c5-16 (1765?); BL 11621 c4-83 (1780?), printing used here, possibly the same as preceding printing); BL 11621 c11-32.

10. Henry Wheatley, *London Past and Present* (London: J. Murray, 1891), 1:192–93.

11. "The Milk Maid": BL 11621 a4-14; "The Bonny Milk-Maid": BL 11621 b3-4; "The Pretty Milk-Maid": BL 11621 c2-59; "The Pretty Maid Milking Her Cow": BL 11621 b10-28; "The Milk-Maid and Squire": BL 11606 aa24-89.

12. "The Milk Maid": Madden 1791-190; "Pretty Maid Milking Her Cow": Madden 1791-201; "Milk-Maid Coming from the Wakes": Madden 1791-202.

13. Pierce Egan, *Life in London* (London: Sherwood, Neely, & Jones, 1821), book 2, chapter 7.

14. "Green in France": BL 1875 d8-101.

15. Hindley, *History of the Catnach Press*, xxvii.

16. Thomas Hood, "The University Feud," *New Monthly Magazine and Humorist* 64 (January 1842): 142–46.

17. "The Dandy Cats-Meat Lass": Madden 1791-360; "Kitty the Cats Meat Woman": Madden 1793-123.

18. Thomas Hudson, *Comic Songs, Collection the Fourth*, was privately printed in London. The booklet bears no date but was presumably published in 1823. *Green in France* opened at the Adelphi on 11 January of that year, and finished at the end of March, and Hudson published his next two collections in 1824.

19. Harold Scott, *The Early Doors* (London: Nicholson & Watson, 1945), 48, 25.

20. Hindley, *The True History of Tom and Jerry* (London: Charles Hindley, [1892]), 182–84.

21. George Speaight, *Bawdy Songs of the Early Music Hall* (London: Pan Books, 1977), 1.

22. "Her Majesty's Monkey," *London Singer's Magazine*, no. 53 (n.d.): 178–79.

23. W. Macqueen Pope, *The Melody Lingers On* (London: W. H. Allen, 1950), 49–50, 416.

24. "The White Cockade": Madden 1787-1924.

25. Arthur Aspinall, *Lord Brougham and the Whig Party* (Manchester, 1927), 240.

26. "The Maiden's Bantam Cock": Madden 1799-1186; "The New Bury Loom": Madden 1799-746; "A New Song Called Nine Times a Night": Madden 1797-722.

27. John Holloway and Joan Black, *Later English Broadside Ballads* (London: Routledge & Kegan Paul, 1975, 1979), 2:234.

28. "Blow the Candle In": Madden 1794-309; "The Beautiful Muff": Madden 1795-364.

29. "Polly Brindle": BOD Harding B11-3051; "The Broken Hearted Gardener": Ashton, *Modern Street Ballads*, 394; "Mr. Walker, the Twopenny Postman": Madden 1801-21.

30. Information on Clifton comes mainly from W. Macqueen Pope, *The Melody Lingers On*, 417; *Era* (21 July 1872): 12; and Raymond Mander and Joe Mitchenson, *British Music Hall* (London: Studio Vista, 1965), 19 (caption).

Chapter 6. Husbands and Wives

1. "Nobody Coming to Woo": Madden 1799-124; and *Roxburghe* 3:52–56. Locations below are of broadsides not named in the Title List.

2. "Bachelor's Complaint": Madden 1794-137.

3. "Bachelor of Sixty-Two": Madden 1791-322.

4. "I am Going to be Married": Madden 1795-429; "I am Married": Madden 1795-430; "I was Married": Madden 1795-431.

5. "Moll in the Wood": Madden 1789-536.

6. "Batchelor's Lesson": Madden 1802-648.

7. "I'm Ninety-Five": Madden 1802-447.

8. "Single Life": Madden 1790-252; and "What Do People Marry For": Madden 1795-237.

9. "I'll Be No Submissive Wife": Madden 1802-253.

10. "I'd Be a Butterfly": Madden 1793-99; "Fly Away": Madden 1794-44; and "She Wore a Wreath": Madden 1802-547.

11. "The Henpecked Husband": Madden 1789-1011.
12. "Termagant Wife": Madden 1802-387.
13. "That's the Way": Madden 1799-1037.
14. "The Fire Shovel": Madden 1797-678.
15. "A Wife's Resolution": St, Bride SS.
16. "The Woman That Conquered a Man": Madden 1800-173.
17. "Pop Him into Limbo": Madden 1792-547.
18. "Petticoat Government": Madden 1794-321; "Petticoats Forever": Madden 1794-419; and Petticoats is Master": Madden 1803-502.
19. "My Mama Did So Before Me": Madden 1802-28.
20. "Prince Albert in England": Madden 1795-436.
21. "Railway to Heaven": Madden 1799-1171.
22. "The Streets of London, No. 2—The Seven Dials," *Chamber's Edinburgh Journal*, new ser., 3 (10 May 1845): 294–96.
23. "True Picture": Madden 1794-11.
24. "The Pleasing Wife and Satisfied Husband": Madden 1794-350; "There's Nothing Can Equal a Woman": Madden 1794-281; "A Woman, Dear Woman for Me": Madden 1794-37; "The Married Man's Complaint": St. Bride SS; "Good Looking Man": Madden 1802-518.
25. J. A. Hardwick, *Comic Songs, First Collection* (London: John Duncombe, 1852).
26. "Poor Married Man" (Come listen to my doleful ditty), by H. J. Whymark; not seen as a broadside.

Chapter 7. Poets

1. Isaac D'Israeli, *Calamities of Authors* (London: John Murray, 1812), 1:ix.
2. "Humours of Rag Fair": BL 1876 f1-200.
3. Some of Withy's verses, including "The Present Case of the Wandering Bard" (While bards more learned sing their hapless fate), can be found at BL 1872 a1-140, 141, 142; BL 11622 c22-2, 3, 4; BL 11632 aaa-52, 60; 11633 aaa-49; 12330 cc42-17. Other items are noted in Charles Welsh and W. H. Tillinghurst, *Catalogue of English and American Chapbooks and Broadside Ballads* (Cambridge, Mass., 1905), 183.
4. John Labern, *Labern's Comic Minstrel*, 2d ser. (London: T. L. Allman, 1865), 160–64.
5. *The Swell's Night Guide* (London, c. 1846), 61-64: BL CUP361 ee13.
6. *London Singer's Magazine* is described with some inaccuracy in vol. 1. See above, p. 513, for a better account. Most of Martin's songs in it are comic or sentimental, and of generalized, indeterminate setting; but one song of his in the first volume of the magazine concerns the paving of Oxford Street (no. 5), another is a memorial tribute to Thomas Haynes Bayly (no. 19), and a third perhaps makes some degree of allusion to Martin's own social background, and to his experience as author (no. 30). The speaker of "When I Became an Author" begins his career in boarding school with verses against his master, "railing at his flogging times." He gets whipped for his work. Later he has some public success, but squanders money that a proud father gives him. Presently he marries, and finds his wife to be a scold, and takes to drink.

> And now, without a crown to spend,
> I through the streets so ragged wend
> And strive to find an honest friend
> To cheer a wretched author.

> Say, may I plead my hapless cause,
> To honour's friends—to honour's laws,
> And crave at least your kind applause
> To bless the humble author.
> Oh, may the soul-discerning few
> Award to talent what is due,
> And patrons be, or firm and true,
> To each poor but clever author.

7. *Duncombe's British Theatre*, vols. 43–44 (London: Duncombe, [1841?]), no. 340. John Duncombe seems to have been the publishing friend of a host of now wholly forgotten songwriters, poets, and dramatists who once had modest fame and negligible financial reward. One might guess that the demise of Duncombe and Moon in the 1850s was the consequence of his patronage.

8. "Chanting Benny": BOD Harding B11-568; "A New Batch of Ballads": BL 11621 h11 8-109.

9. Hindley, *Curiosities of Street Literature*, 160.

Chapter 8. Scenes of Mirth and Contentment

1. *Report from the Select Committee on the State of Mendicity in the Metropolis*, 393.

2. In 1820 John Miller, fellow of Worcester College, Oxford, published there *A Christian Guide for Plain People, and Especially for the Poor*. In his preface he says to the poor that he knows their condition wants mending, and that he knows the way and the people to do the mending: "the way is by keeping God's commandments; the persons are yourselves." In 1832 the Reverend James White of Bonchurch published anonymously a long poem called *The Village Poor House* (London: Smith Elder). In his introduction he writes:

> Five years' experience as a country curate has taught me many painful lessons and many bitter truths. It has shown me degraded and benighted peasantry, and convinced me that all the descriptions of country life which we admire in the poets are only poetical. "God made the country, and man made the town." Alas! God made both, and man defaces both.

The poem describes the blighting of lives of village poor. It concludes with an image of Britain and the poor man:

> Untaught—she asks him wise to be—
> In chains—she asks him to be free—
> She scorns his prayer, and mocks his moan,
> He asks for bread, and he receives a stone!

In 1849 Charles Sabine published in London *A Little Book for Our Poor Little People*. Most of the verses in it are addressed to "the poor little children in the Oswestry House of Industry." The first stanza of "Joyful Content" goes thus:

> And was my Lord, when here on earth,
> Of poor, despised, and lowly birth,
> And shall it be a grief to me
> That I by birth am poor as He?

3. *Memoirs of Charles Dibdin the Younger,* edited by George Speaight (London: Society for Theatre Research, 1956).

4. Ashton, *Modern Street Ballads,* 146. Maurice Disher, *Victorian Song from Dive to Drawing Room* (London: Phoenix House, 1955), 41.

5. Thomas Dibdin, *Reminiscences,* 2 vols. (London: Henry Colburn, 1827). The song is absent as well from Dibdin's *Last Lays* (London: Harding & King, 1833), a collection put together by Dibdin that includes a selection of 150 earlier songs. Details on Dibdin's life are drawn from the *Dictionary of National Biography.*

6. "Hot Codlins," no. 43 in Charles Mackay, *A Collection of Songs and Ballads Relative to the London Prentices . . . During the Fourteenth, Fifteenth and Sixteenth Centuries* (London, 1841).

7. Hindley, *True History,* 50–51. Along with Moncrieff's dramatizations, those by Egan himself and three unidentified authors were reviewed without finding the verses given here. In a forthcoming article, "James Catnach, Bard of Seven Dials," *Book Trade History Group Newsletter* (University of Birmingham), I extend my account of Catnach as author and suggest that in the present book I may have underestimated his poetic talents.

8. Hindley, *True History,* 105–6.

9. "The Bunter's Wedding": BL LR31 b19 1.1-216.

10. Bodleian Library booklet: Johnson 4767*. "The Streets of London, No. 1—Monmouth Street," *Chamber's Edinburgh Journal,* new ser., 3 (15 March 1845): 167–69.

11. Lucksway: "Mad-Brained Earl" and "Weeping Parson": Madden 1794-311; "Naughty Poplar Man": BOD Firth C17-286.

12. Dever: "Brixton Parson": BL C116 i1-50.

Appendix 1. The Broadside Cock

1. Among possible or actual cocks used or referred to in the book but not mentioned in this appendix are the following: "Ladies, Don't Go Thieving," p. 149; several broadsides on starvation, pp. 247–48, p. 343, and p. 373 ; lost children, p. 328; "Poverty No Crime" and others, pp. 332, 399.

2. Unnumbered first page of Division 1, Hindley, *Curiosities.*

3. "The Liverpool Tragedy": Hindley, *Curiosities,* 5. The printing is by Catnach, probably in the 1820s.

4. As a ballad, "The Liverpool Tragedy" is known in a number of printings, with some differences among them. *ESTC* gives printings from about 1760 to 1800. The British Library holds a London printing from about 1815 and a Liverpool printing from some years later. In *Ballads and Songs of Lancashire,* 2d ed. (London, 1875), 99, Harland and Wilkinson say that the ballad still "finds a ready sale in 1874." A short ballad strikingly similar to the prose "Liverpool Tragedy" and probably plagiarized from it is "Young William," printed in Ashton, *Modern Street Ballads,* 392.

5. Rush: Mayhew 1: 223.

6. Rush: Hindley, *Curiosities,* 196.

7. Murders: Hindley, *Curiosities,* a, b, c, d, 2.

8. Ballads on King / Mitchel: BL 1880 c20 2-421, 422; BL 1881 d8-12; BL 1888 c3-62.

9. A comparison of verses among the broadsides is on pp. 342.

10. John Camden Hotten, "Popular Literature of the Olden Time, Merry and Serious," 54–55: BOD MS Harding 1.

11. Standard forms: BL 1888 c3-8, 112.

12. Mayhew 1:222. On p. 234 Mayhew puts the first part of the definition into the mouth of one of his informants. On p. 214 he gives the definition entirely by example.

13. Mayhew 1:228 (Victoria and Wellington); 229 (O'Connor); 214 (fabulous duels); 223 ("The Liverpool Tragedy").

14. "Great and Important Battle": Mayhew 1: 223.

15. "Remarkable Dream": Mayhew 1: 235.

16. Four marvels: Hindley, *Curiosities*, 26, 25, 29, 24.

17. The stepmother's prophetic dream is not questioned in two twentieth-century accounts, Dorothy Gibbs and H. Maltby, *The True Story of Maria Marten* (Ipswich: East Anglian Magazine, 1949) and George MacCormick, *The Red Barn Mystery* (London: Long, 1967), though neither book aims to do much more than retell a famous grisly tale. There was reason for the stepmother to dream such a dream. She was present when plans were made for Corder to meet Maria in the red barn, and she knew that later in the day of the tryst Corder was observed leaving the barn with an axe in his hand. Maria was never seen or heard from again, and Corder's reports about her to the stepmother over a period of months came under increasing suspicion. The dreams then began.

18. Scandal: Mayhew 1:234.

19. Lies: Mayhew 1:234.

20. "Extraordinary & Funny Doings": Mayhew 1:238; Hindley, *Curiosities*, 13.

21. "Love Letter": Mayhew 1:238; Hindley, *Curiosities*, 14.

22. "Very Pretty Maid": Hindley, *Curiosities*, 35. Other examples of pretended fictitious statements may be seen among the final thirty or so broadsides in the volume BOD Firth C20.

23. *Eighteenth Century Short Title Catalogue* gives 1800? for a copy of "Comfort to the Afflicted" at the University of Edinburgh. Catnach's printing: BL 11621 k4-39.

24. Atheists: BL 1880 c20 1-320.

25. Hindley, chiefly pp. 50 and 509; Mayhew, p. 274 n. 24 and in Appendix 1.

26. Hotten, "Popular Literature," 49.

27. In 1851 came Mayhew's first version of *London Labour and the London Poor*, published privately in London in three volumes. No relevant definition of cock appears in Francis Grose, *Lexicon Balatronicum* (London, 1811), Grose, *Dictionary of the Vulgar Tongue* (London, 1823), John Bee, *Slang* (London: T. Hughes, 1823). None of seven small canting (flash) dictionaries, 1820s to1840s, has it.

28. "The Literature of the Streets," *British Journal* 2 (February 1852): 51; B. Johns, "The Poetry of Seven Dials," *Quarterly Review* 122 (1867): 398.

29. Charles Manby Smith, "The Press of the Seven Dials," *Chamber's Journal of Popular Literature*, no. 130 (28 June 1856): 403.

30. E. C. Brewer, *Dictionary of Phrase and Fable* (London: Cassell, 1870).

31. Albert Barrère and Charles Leland, *Dictionary of Slang, Jargon, and Cant* (London: Whittaker, 1889), and J. S. Farmer, *Slang and its Analogues* (London, 1890).

32. Like "The Liverpool Tragedy," "The Scarborough Tragedy" is a narrative of some intrinsic interest, the first problem of which is that the tale described in Mayhew—prose, with attached verses, about a seduced clergyman's daughter who destroys the infant she bears and who is executed—is not the tale that is known otherwise. The 206-line ballad that appears in *Curiosities*, 10–11, and in an earlier printing as "The Scarboro' Tragedy" (BOD Johnson-fol.402), concerns a young woman who is seduced, abandoned, and then killed by her lover. On her grave, as predicted by her, a damask rose blooms, unwilting. After a year, her lover, who has been undetected in his crime, touches the rose, and it dies. He confesses. In the ballad the young woman is named only Susannah. She is a farmer's daughter in Yorkshire, and lives near the sea. Scarborough is unmentioned except in the title. Her lover is a sea-captain. The narrative proceeds in tragical-pastoral manner, in unidentified past time:

> Into a mournful valley she crossed,
> Would often wander all alone,
> And for the jewel she had lost
> In the bower would often mourn.
> Oh! that I were some pretty bird,
> That I might fly to hide my shame;
> O silly maid, for to believe
> The fair delusions of a man.

As true account, "The Scarborough Tragedy" has little to persuade the reader. Like "The Liverpool Tragedy," it suffers from a long history. *ESTC* lists several copies of dates 1750–1800. They do, though, bear a different title: "The Oxfordshire Tragedy." I have seen two printings: BL LR31 b19 1.1-82 and *Roxburghe* 8:68–69, 175–76. These two distinct printings show minor differences from the Hindley and Bodleian texts, notably in that Susannah is Rosanna, and she is daughter of a knight and lady from near Woodstock in Oxfordshire. The chief reason for thinking that "The Scarborough Tragedy," if not "The Oxfordshire Tragedy," was offered for sale at some point or other as true account lies with the subtitle. The Bodleian printing, possibly the original transformation from "The Oxfordshire Tragedy," is on a large sheet of about 16 by 22 inches. It has one large cut showing Susannah and her lover beside the sea, and two small cuts showing murder and confession. The small cuts flank "Tragic Verses" in fifty-two lines that summarize the ballad. Title and subtitle go thus:

THE SCARBORO' TRAGEDY
Detailing
The Seduction of Susan Forster, a Farmer's Only Daughter,
Near Scarborough, Under Promise of Marriage
By R. Sanders, a Naval Officer, to Whom She Became Pregnant,
After Which the Wretch Appointed a Meeting With Her at a Retired Place,
Where He Basely Murdered Her, and Buried Her under a Tree

Unluckily the sheet is torn across the bottom where a printer's name might have been. However, the sheet is very much like the large sheets that James Catnach specialized in during the 1820s, and calls to mind that other tale of miracle, "Comfort to the Afflicted," that Catnach refurbished. If the printing is by Catnach, it is possible that the "Tragic Verses" are by him. Hindley's printing gives the subtitle with some differences, notably in mention of "the wonderful manner in which this base murder was brought to light, and he was committed to gaol." Hindley apparently reset the ballad, and he names no printer. In *The History of the Catnach Press*, 265–66, he gives the first three stanzas and concluding quatrain of the ballad, and names Catnach as printer. Catnach lists the ballad in his 1832 catalogue.

Claude Simpson, *The British Broadside Ballad* (New Brunswick, N.J.: Rutgers University Press, 1966), 563, says that the late-seventeenth-century ballad "The Constant Lady and False Hearted Squire" was known in the eighteenth century as "The Oxfordshire Tragedy: or, the Death of Four Lovers." The lady in that ballad is also a knight's daughter from near Woodstock. She is coldly abandoned by her lover and dies. Some while afterwards he is seized with guilt and with realization that she was his true love. He commits suicide, and is buried beside her.

33. Sellers: Mayhew 1:222, 306–8.
34. Beating newspapers: Mayhew 1:223–24, 234, 229. Mayhew's opinion is echoed in "Literature of the Streets," *J. & R. M. Wood's Typographic Advertiser* 1 (March 1863): 73. The author speaks of accompanying Mayhew on one of his inquiries. In *Random Recollections of*

an Old Publisher (London: Simpkin, Marshall, 1900), 1:11, William Tinsley says, "News of last dying speeches and confessions of murderers reached our village [in Hampshire] very early as a rule; in fact, now and then, before the execution had taken place."

35. Sales: Mayhew 1:223, 284.
36. Selling the truth: Mayhew 1:281–83, 228.
37. Charles Manby Smith, "The Press of the Seven Dials," 403.
38. Charles Hindley, *The Life and Times of James Catnach* (London, 1878), 84–88.
39. Bonner and Shepherd: BL 1880 c20.
40. *Old Bailey Sessions Papers*, Public Record Office, Kew: PCOM 1/15: 489, 347; 1/16: 355; 1/17: 169, 26.

Bibliography

The list is of works used in preparing this book. Several of the works contain bibliographies of street literature. The most substantial bibliography is that by Steve Roud, *Street Literature Bibliography*, an ongoing compilation.

Anderson, Hugh. *Farewell to Old England*. London: Angus & Robertson, 1964.

Annual Register, or a View of the History, Politics, and Literature for the Year 1833. London: J. G. & F. Rivington, 1834. (Other years from 1790 forward also consulted.)

Armstrong, Isobel. *Victorian Poetry: Poetry, Poetics, and Politics*. London: Routledge, 1993.

Ashton, Eva. "Songs from Sussex." *Journal of the Folk Song Society* 6 (1906): 34–38.

Ashton, John. *A Century of Ballads*. London: Elliot Stock, 1887.

———. *Modern Street Ballads*. London: Chatto & Windus, 1888.

Aspinall, Arthur. *Lord Brougham and the Whig Party*. Manchester, 1927.

Bamford, Samuel. *Walks in South Lancashire*. Blackley: Samuel Bamford, 1844.

Barbauld, Anna. *Eighteen Hundred and Eleven*. 1812. Reprint, Poole: Woodstock Books, 1995.

———. *Poems*. Edited by William McCarthy and Elizabeth Kraft. Athens: University of Georgia Press, 1994.

"Bards of the Seven Dials and Their Effusions." *The Town*, 27 July 1839, 899.

Barrère, Albert, and Charles Leland. *Dictionary of Slang, Jargon, and Cant*. London: Whittaker, 1889.

Bee, John. *Slang*. London: T. Hughes, 1823.

Bell, Robert. *Ancient Poems, Ballads, and Songs of the Peasantry of England*. London: J. W. Parker & Son, 1857.

Black Book. London: John Fairborn, 1820.

Boardman, Henry, and Roy Palmer. *Manchester Ballads*. Manchester: City of Manchester Education Committee, 1983.

Bratton, J. S. *The Victorian Popular Ballad*. London: Macmillan, 1975.

Brewer, E. C. *Dictionary of Phrase and Fable*. London: Cassell, 1870.

British Book Trade Index. Newcastle upon Tyne: University of Newcastle upon Tyne, Robinson Library. (An ongoing compilation.)

Brown, Phillip. *London Publishers and Printers, C. 1800–1870*. London: British Library, 1982.

"Bunn the Bird-Catcher." *Punch* 15 (July–December 1848): 150.

Burnett, John. *A History of the Cost of Living.* Harmondsworth: Penguin, 1969.

Castigator. *The Mendicity Society Unmasked.* London: W. C. Wright, 1825.

Clapham, Sir John. *An Economic History of Modern Britain.* 3 vols. Cambridge: Cambridge University Press, 1950–52.

Clinch, G. *Bloomsbury and St. Giles.* London: Truslove & Shirley, 1890.

Cobbett, William. *Rural Rides.* 2 vols. London: Everyman, 1957.

Cole, G. D. H., and Raymond Postgate. *The British People, 1746–1946.* New York: Knopf, 1947.

Collection of Old Ballads. London: J. Roberts, 1725.

Cook, Chris, and Brendan Keith. *British Historical Facts, 1830–1900.* London: Macmillan, 1975.

———, and John Stevenson. *British Historical Facts, 1760–1830.* London: Macmillan, 1980.

Cook, Eliza. *Poetical Works.* London: Fredrick Warne, 1870.

Corinthian. 6th ed. London: Duncombe, [1833?].

Cornwall, Barry. *Autobiographical Fragment.* London: George Bell & Sons, 1877.

———. *English Songs.* London: Edward Moxon, 1832.

Cunningham, Peter. *Handbook of London.* London: John Murray, 1850.

"Decease of a Norwich Poet." *Norwich Mercury* (27 October 1855).

Dibdin, Charles. *Songs.* Edited by George Hogarth. London: How & Parsons, 1842.

Dibdin, Charles Isaac Mungo. *Memoirs.* Edited by George Speaight. London: Society for Theatre Research, 1956.

Dibdin, Thomas John. *Reminiscences.* 2 vols. London: Henry Colburn, 1827.

———. *The Last Lays of the Last of the Three Dibdins: Containing Fifty New Songs . . . and One Hundred and Fifty Selections.* London: Harding & King, 1833.

Disher, Maurice. *Victorian Song from Dive to Drawing Room.* London: Phoenix House, 1955.

D'Israeli, Isaac. *Calamities of Authors.* 2 vols. London: John Murray, 1812.

Duncombe's British Theatre. Vols. 43–44. London: Duncombe, [1841?].

Egan, Pierce. *Life in London.* London: Sherwood, Neeley, & Jones, 1821.

Elkins, Charles. "The Voice of the Poor." *Journal of Popular Culture* 14 (Fall 1980): 262–74.

Elmes, James. *A Topographical Dictionary of London.* London: Whittaker, Teacher & Arnot, 1831.

Encyclopaedia Britannica. 15th ed. Chicago: Encyclopaedia Britannica, Inc., 1992.

"Extracts from the Private Diary of the Master of a London Ragged School. No. 7, The Literature of our Alley." *English Journal of Education*, n.s., 5 (January 1851): 33–38.

"Extracts from the Reports of the English Society for Bettering the Conditions of the Poor and Four other Papers on the Same Subject." 1799. British Library: 1507/1728.

Extraordinary Black Book. London: Effingham Wilson, 1831.

Farmer, J. S. *Musa Pedestris.* 1896. Reprint, New York: Cooper Square Publishers, 1964.

———. *National Ballad and Song, Merry Songs and Ballads Prior to the Year A.D. 1800.* 5 vols. Privately printed, 1897.

———. *Slang and its Analogues*. London, 1890.
Firth, Sir C. Harding. "Flogging in the Army." *Journal of the Society of Army Historical Research* 1 (1921): 255–59.
Fitch, J. G. "Charity Schools." *Westminster Review*, n.s., 43 (April 1873): 450–72.
Fox, William Johnson. "Poetry of the Poor." *London Review* 1 (April–July 1835): 187–201.
———. "The Poor and Their Poetry." *Monthly Repository*, n.s., 6 (March 1832): 189–201.
Friedman, Adele. "The Broadside Ballad Virago." *Journal of Popular Culture* 13 (1979–80): 469–75.
Friedman, Albert. *The Ballad Revival*. Chicago: University of Chicago Press, 1961.
Gatrell, V. A. C. *The Hanging Tree*. Oxford: Oxford University Press, 1995.
Gavin, Hector. *Sanitary Ramblings*. London, 1848.
Gibbs, Dorothy, and H. Maltby. *The True Story of Maria Marten*. Ipswich: East Anglian Magazine, 1949.
Gould, S. B. *English Minstrelsie*. 8 vols. Edinburgh: T. C. and E. C. Jack, 1895.
———. *Strange Survivals*. London: Methuen, 1892.
Gould, S. B., and H. F. Fleetwood Sheppard. *A Garland of Country Songs*. London: Methuen, 1895.
Gregg, Pauline. *A Social and Economic History of Britain*. 4th ed. London: Harrap, 1964.
Grose, Francis. *Dictionary of the Vulgar Tongue*. London, 1823.
———. *Lexicon Balatronicum*. London, 1811.
Hanchant, W. L. *Songs of the Affections*. London: Desmond Harmsworth, 1932.
Hardwick, J. A. *Comic Songs, First Collection*. London: John Duncombe, 1852.
Harland, John, and T. T. Wilkinson. *Ballads and Songs of Lancashire*. 2d ed. London, 1875.
Henderson, William. *Victorian Street Ballads*. London: Country Life, 1937.
Hennessy, James Pope. *Monckton Milnes*. 2 vols. London: Constable, 1945, 1955.
Higson, Charles. "'Jone O' Grinfilt' and 'Oldham Rushbearing'." *Oldham Standard,* 1 May 1926.
Hindley, Charles. *Curiosities of Street Literature*. London: Reeves & Turner, 1871.
———. *A History of the Catnach Press*. London: Charles Hindley, 1886.
———. *The Life and Times of James Catnach*. London, 1878.
———. *The True History of Tom and Jerry*. London: Charles Hindley, [1892].
Historical and Descriptive View of the County of Northumberland. Newcastle upon Tyne: MacKensie & Dent, 1811.
Hobsbawn, Eric, and George Rudé. *Captain Swing*. London: Lawrence & Wishart, 1969.
Hollingworth, Brian. *Songs of the People*. Manchester: Manchester University Press, 1977.
Holloway, John, and Joan Black. *Later English Broadside Ballads*. 2 vols. London: Routledge & Kegan Paul, 1975, 1979.
Hone, William. *The Political House That Jack Built*. London: William Hone, 1819.
Hood, Thomas. "University Feud." *New Monthly Magazine and Humorist* 64 (January 1842): 142–46.
Hopkins, Mary. *Hannah More and Her Circle*. New York: Longmans, Green, 1947.
"Horae Catnachianae." *Fraser's Magazine* 19 (April 1839): 407–24.
Hotten, John Camden. *A Dictionary of Modern Slang, Cant, and Vulgar Words*. London: John Camden Hotten, 1859.

———. "Popular Literature of the Olden Time, Merry and Serious": Bodleian Library: MS Harding 1.
Howkins, Alun, and C. Ian Dyck. "'The Time's Alteration': Popular Ballads, Rural Radicalism . . . ." *History Workshop Journal* 23 (1987): 20–38.
Hudson, Thomas. *Comic Songs, Collection the Fourth*. London, [1823?].
———. *Comic Songs, the Ninth Collection*. London, 1828.
Hughes, Michael. Introduction to *Curiosities of Street Literature*, by Charles Hindley. 1871. Reprint. London: Seven Dials Press, 1969.
Hunt, C. J. *The Book Trade in Northumberland and Durham*. Newcastle upon Tyne: Thorne's Student's Bookshop, 1975.
Jerrold, Douglas. "Ballad Singers." In *The Writings of Douglas Jerrold,* vol. 5. London, 1851–54.
Johns, B. G. "The Literature of Seven Dials." *National Review* 2 (1883–84): 478–92.
———. "The Poetry of Seven Dials." *Quarterly Review* 122 (1867): 382–406.
Jones, Trevor. *Street Literature in Birmingham*. Oxford: Oxford Polytechnic Book Publishing and Production Course, 1970.
Justice to the Poor. Northampton, 1820.
Karpeles, Maud, ed. *Cecil Sharp's Collection of English Folk Songs*. 2 vols. London: Oxford University Press, 1974.
Kidson, Frank. "The Ballad Sheet and Garland." *Journal of the Folk Dance Society* 7 (1905): 70–78.
Klingberg, Frank J., and Sigurd B. Hustvedt. *The Warning Drum*. Berkeley: University of California Press, 1944.
Labern, John. *Labern's Comic Minstrel*. 2d ser. London: T. L. Allman, 1865.
———. *Labern's Original Comic Songs*. London, 1842. This collection is the first of six such collections issued by Labern from 1842 to perhaps 1845. None of the other collections is known to survive. They were advertised in issues of *London Singer's Magazine*.
———. *Labern's Popular Comic Song Book*. London: J. Duncombe, [1852].
Latimer, J. *Local Records; or, Historical Register of Remarkable Events*. Newcastle upon Tyne, 1857.
Lindsay, James. *Catalogue of English Broadsides, 1505–1897*. Aberdeen: Aberdeen University Press, 1898.
"The Literature of the Streets." *British Journal* 2 (February 1852): 49–52.
"Literature of the Streets." *J. & R. M. Wood's Typographic Advertiser* 1 (1 February 1863): 65; (1 March): 73.
"The Literature of the Working Classes." *Englishwoman's Magazine and Christian Mother's Miscellany*, n.s., 5 (October 1850): 619–22.
Lloyd, A. L. *Come All Ye Bold Miners*. London: Lawrence & Wishart, 1952.
———. *Folk Song in England*. London: Lawrence & Wishart, 1967.
Londina Illustrata. 2 vols. London: Robert Wilkinson, 1819.
London Melodist. London: Diprose [c. 1831].
"London Minstrelsy." *New Monthly Magazine* 13 (June 1825): 542–47.
London Oddities. London: Hodgson, 1824.
London Singer's Magazine. London: John Duncombe, [1838–1845?]. Various numbers held by British Library and Bodleian Library.

London Singer's Magazine and Reciter's Album. London: John Duncombe, [1836–37?]. Various numbers held by British Library and Bodleian Library.

Longmate, Norman. *King Cholera.* London: H. Hamilton, 1966.

Lowe, Norman. *Mastering Modern British History.* 2d ed. Basingstoke: Macmillan, 1989.

MacCormick, George. *The Red Barn Mystery.* London: Long, 1967.

Mackay, Charles. *Poems and Songs.* London: Whittaker, 1888.

———, ed. *A Collection of Songs and Ballads Relative to the London Prentices . . . During the Fourteenth, Fifteenth and Sixteenth Centuries.* London, 1841.

Maidment, Brian. *The Poorhouse Fugitives.* Manchester: Carcanet, 1987.

Mander, Raymond, and Joe Mitchenson. *British Music Hall.* London: Studio Vista, 1965.

Mayhew, Henry. *London Labour and the London Poor.* 3 vols. London, 1851. 4 vols. London: Griffin, Bond, 1861–62. Reprint, 4 vols. London: Frank Cass, 1967.

"A Method for Suppressing of Beggars . . . in the Parish of St. Giles's." [1726?]. British Library: 816 m9-81.

Miller, John. *A Christian Guide for Plain People, and Especially for the Poor.* Oxford, 1820.

Milnes, Richard Monckton. *Poetical Works.* 2 vols. London, 1876.

Mitchell, B. R. *British Historical Statistics.* Cambridge: Cambridge University Press, 1988.

Model Song Book. 2 vols. London: T Goode, [c. 1848].

Moeran, E. J. *Six Suffolk Folksongs.* London, 1932.

National Melodist. London: William Strange, [c. 1845].

Neate, Alan. *The St. Marylebone Workhouse and Institution, 1730–1965.* London: St. Marylebone Society Publications, No. 9, 1967.

Neuburg, Victor. *Chapbooks, A Bibliography.* London: Vine Press, 1964.

———. "The Literature of the Streets." In *The Victorian City,* edited by H. J. Dyos and Michael Wolff. Vol. 1. London: Routledge & Kegan Paul, 1973.

Newby, Howard. *Country Life.* London: Weidenfeld & Nicholson, 1987.

Nicholson, Renton. *The Lord Chief Baron Nicholson.* London, 1860.

"Old Jemmy Catnach." *London, Provincial, and Colonial Press News,* 17 January 1867, 22–23.

Paine, Tom. *The Rights of Man, Part the Second.* 3rd ed. Dublin: P. Byrne, 1792.

Palmer, Roy. *A Ballad History of England.* London: Batsford, 1979.

———. *Everyman's Book of Ballads.* London: Dent, 1980.

———. *Poverty Knock.* London: Cambridge University Press, 1974.

———. *A Touch on the Times, Songs of Social Change, 1770–1914.* Harmondsworth: Penguin Education, 1974.

Parker, John. "On the Literature of the Working Classes." *Meliora,* 2d ser. London, 1853.

Parliamentary Debates. Ser. 3. Vol. 191. (March–May 1868), 1039.

Parliamentary Papers, Reports from Commissioners. Children's Employment, First Report of the Commissioners (Mines). Vol. 15 (1842).

Parliamentary Papers, Reports from Commissioners. Report from His Majesty's Commissioners for Inquiring into the Administration and *Practical Operation of the Poor Laws.* Vol. 27 (1834).

Parliamentary Papers, Reports from Committees. Report from the Select Committee on the Bill to Regulate the Labour of Children in the Mills and Factories. Vol. 15. (1831–32).

Parliamentary Papers, Reports from Committees. Report from the Select Committee on the State of Mendicity in the Metropolis. Vol. 5 (1816).

Partridge, Eric. *The Dictionary of Slang and Unconventional English.* London: Routledge & Kegan Paul, 1961.

———. *A Dictionary of the Underworld.* London: Routledge & Kegan Paul, 1971.

Pigot's Metropolitan . . . Directory for 1828. London: J. Pigot, [1829].

Pinto, V. de Sola, and A. E. Rodway. *The Common Muse.* London: Chatto & Windus, 1957.

"The Poet Bunn to Jenny Lind." *Punch* 12 (January–June 1847): 71.

Pope, W. Macqueen. *The Melody Lingers On.* London: W. H. Allen, 1950.

"The Present Taste for Cheap Literature." *The Bee,* no. 2 (16 March 1833): 9–10.

"The Press of the Seven Dials." *Chamber's Journal of Popular Literature,* no. 130 (28 June 1856): 401–5.

Le Prince d'Amour. London, 1660.

Radzinowicz, Leon. *History of English Criminal Law.* 5 vols. London: Stephens & Sons, 1948–86.

Raven, Jon. *The Urban and Industrial Songs of the Black Country and Birmingham.* Wolverhampton: Wolverhampton Broadside, 1977.

———. *Victoria's Inferno.* Wolverhampton: Wolverhampton Broadside, 1978.

Reid, J. C. *Thomas Hood.* London: Routledge & Kegan Paul, 1963.

Ritson, Joseph, ed. *Robin Hood, A Collection of All the Ancient Poems, Songs, and Ballads,* 1823. Reprint. Wakefield: E. P. Publishing, 1972.

Rose, Michael. *The English Poor Law, 1780–1930.* Newton Abbott: David & Charles, 1971.

Ross, John Wilson. "The Influence of Cheap Literature." *London Journal* 1 (10 April 1845): 115.

Roud, Steve, comp. *The Broadside Index.* (Updatable computer database: index of songs on broadsides, chapbooks, and popular songsters. Inquiries to compiler, c/o Vaughan Williams Library, Cecil Sharp House, 2 Regents Park Road, London.)

———. *Street Literature Bibliography.* Enfield Lock, Middlesex (No. 4 Catisfield Road): Hisarlik Press, 1994. (Computer database.)

Roud, Steve, and Paul Smith. *A Catalogue of Songs and Song Books Printed and Published by James Catnach 1832.* West Stockwith, Doncaster: January Books, 1985.

Roxburghe Ballads. Edited by William Chappell and J. W. Ebsworth. 9 vols. London, 1869–99.

Ryan, Kiernan, ed. *New Historicism and Cultural Materialism.* London: Arnold, 1996.

Sabine, Charles. *A Little Book for Our Poor Little People.* London, 1849.

Scott, Harold. *The Early Doors.* London: Nicholson & Watson, 1946.

Scott, J. W. Robertson. *The Story of the Pall Mall Gazette.* London: Oxford University Press, 1950.

Sharp, John W. *The Vauxhall Comic Song Book.* Ser. 1 and ser. 2. London, 1847.

Shepard, Leslie. *The Broadside Ballad.* London: Herbert Jenkins, 1962.

———. *The History of Street Literature.* Newton Abbott: David & Charles, 1973.

———. *John Pitts.* London: Private Libraries Association, 1969.

———. Introduction to *Curiosities of Street Literature,* by Charles Hindley. 1871. Reprint. London: Broadsheet King, 1966.

Silverman, James, ed. *Cheap Repository Tracts,* by Hannah More. New York: Garland, 1977.

Simpson, Claude. *The British Broadside Ballad*. New Brunswick, N.J.: Rutgers University Press, 1966.

Sims, George. *How the Poor Live*. London: Chatto & Windus, 1883.

Singer's Penny Magazine. 35 nos. London: G. Drake, 1834–35.

The Slang Dictionary, Etymological, Historical and Anecdotal. London: Chatto & Windus, [1874?].

Smith, Charles Manby. *The Little World of London*. London, 1857.

———. "The Press of the Seven Dials." *Chamber's Journal of Popular Literature*, no. 130 (28 June 1856): 401–5.

Smith, Horace. "Beggars Extraordinary!—Proposals for their Suppression." *New Monthly Magazine* 8 (July 1823): 61–65.

Society for the Suppression of Mendicity. London, 1819–[1959]. Annual Reports: British Library: PP1107.

Speaight, George. *Bawdy Songs of the Early Music Hall*. London: Pan Books, 1977.

Spinney, G. H. "Cheap Repository Tracts." *The Library*, 4th ser., 20 (1939): 295–340.

"Street Ballads." *National Review* 25 (July 1861): 397–419.

"Street Ballads by Poets and Educated Men." *Notes and Queries*, 4th ser., 6 (July–December 1870): 416.

"Street Songs and Their Singers." *St. James's Magazine* 13 (April–July 1865): 190–201.

"Streets of London, No. 1—Monmouth Street." *Chamber's Edinburgh Journal*, n.s., 3 (15 March 1845): 167–69.

"Streets of London, No. 2—The Seven Dials." *Chamber's Edinburgh Journal*, n.s., 3 (10 May 1845): 294–96.

Stuart, Charles, and J. Park. *The Variety Stage: A History of the Music Hall*. London: T. Fisher Unwin, 1895.

Swell's Night Guide. London, c. 1846.

Taylor, Gordon. "St. Giles in the Fields." London: Church of St. Giles in the Fields, 1989.

Thompson, E. P. *The Making of the English Working Class*. London: Gollancz, 1963.

Thomson, David. *England in the Nineteenth Century*. Harmondsworth: Penguin Books, 1971.

Thomson, Robert S. "The Development of the Broadside Ballad." Ph.D. diss., Cambridge University, 1972.

Tinsley, William. *Random Recollections of an Old Publisher*. 2 vols. London: Simpkin, Marshall, 1900.

Todd, William. *A Directory of Printers . . . , London and Vicinity, 1800–1840*. London: Printing Historical Society, 1972.

Treuherz, Julian. *Hard Times, Social Realism in Victorian Art*. London: Lund Humphries, 1987.

Vicinus, Martha. *Broadsides of the Industrial North*. Newcastle upon Tyne: Frank Graham, 1975.

———. *The Industrial Muse*. London: Croom Helm, 1974.

Vincent, David. *Literacy and Popular Culture*. Cambridge: Cambridge University Press, 1989.

"Visit to a Private Asylum." *Chamber's Edinburgh Journal*, new ser., 4 (20 September 1845): 183–85.

Watson, J. Steven. *The Reign of George III, 1760–1815*. Oxford: Oxford University Press, 1960.

Weinreb, Ben, and Christopher Hibbert. *The London Encyclopaedia*. London: Macmillan, 1992.

Wellesley Index to Victorian Periodicals. 5 vols. London: Routledge & Kegan Paul, 1966–90.

Welsh, Charles, and W. H. Tillinghurst. *Catalogue of English and American Chapbooks and Broadside Ballads*. Cambridge, Mass., 1905.

Wheatley, Henry. *London Past and Present*. 3 vols. London: J. Murray, 1891.

———, ed. *Reliques of Ancient English Poetry*. 3 vols. London: Bickers & Son, 1876–77.

White, James. *The Village Poor House*. London: Smith Elder, 1832.

Wood, Anthony. *Nineteenth Century Britain*. Harlow: Longman, 1982.

Woodward, Sir Llewellyn. *The Age of Reform, 1815–1870*. 2d ed. Oxford: Oxford University Press, 1962.

Title List of English Broadsides on Poverty, 1790–1870

The following list includes all broadsides on poverty, 1790–1870, used or referred to, along with some others. The list is mainly of ballads. Broadsides chiefly or wholly in prose are marked PR. Generally though not wholly excluded are ballads in dialect and ballads about trade unions and strikes, riot and rebellion, Peterloo and Chartism, and political matters other than corn laws, poor laws, taxation, and the Reform Act of 1832. Also excluded are numerous ballads on poverty by Samuel Lane that are held in the collection of Lane ballads at Norwich Central Library. For partial listings of ballads on trade unions and strikes, Luddism, Peterloo, Captain Swing, Chartism, and riot and rebellion generally, consult the index under those terms.

Alternative titles are listed if they vary significantly for alphabetical ordering. Minor variations of title are indicated by enclosing variant word or phrase in parentheses or by separating forms of title with diagonals. Significant variation in wording of first lines is indicated with diagonals. A few very long titles are not given in full, ellipses showing omissions. Variant forms of ballads are not otherwise noted, except those that are discussed in the body of the book. Locations of variants are given in the order used or referred to. Locations are in the main exact by page or ballad number—the last number given on any location number. With some ballads such numbers may be inexact by one or two places; those numbers preceded by "c" may be somewhat more in error. Page references to the body of the book are to quotations from the ballad (boldface if the whole ballad is given, italic if quoted in part) and to discussion and incidental reference.

Deciding whether or not a ballad concerns poverty is sometimes guesswork. I mention the matter on pages 24, 33–38, and 454–57.

For a general listing of broadside ballads, and also songs from garlands and songsters, see the entry on Steve Roud in the bibliography.

ABBREVIATIONS

Ashton	John Ashton, *Modern Street Ballads*
AT	Alternative titles for ballads wholly or mainly the same
BL	British Library collections
BOD	Bodleian Library collections
CUR	Charles Hindley, *Curiosities of Street Literature*

GU	Guildhall Library collections
Harland	John Harland and T. T. Wilkinson, *Ballads and Songs of Lancashire*
Henderson	William Henderson, *Victorian Street Ballads*
Lloyd C	A. L. Lloyd, *Come All Ye Bold Miners*
Lloyd F	A. L. Lloyd, *Folk Song in England*
Madden	Madden Collection, Cambridge University Library; locations are those for microfilm copy
ML	Music Library of the British Library
NOR	Bolingbroke Collection, Norwich Central Library
Palmer PK	Roy Palmer, *Poverty Knock*
Palmer TT	Roy Palmer, *A Touch on the Times*
Pinto	Vivian de Sola Pinto and Allan Edwin Rodway, *The Common Muse*
PR	Prose, wholly or mainly
Raven U	Jon Raven, *The Urban and Industrial Songs of the Black Country and Birmingham*
Raven V	Jon Raven, *Victoria's Inferno*
St. Bride	St. Bride Printing Library collection; ballads are filed alphabetically by first title on sheet, under Large Series (LS) and Small Series (SS)
SF	Charles Harding Firth Collection, Sheffield University Library
SH	Hewins Collection, Sheffield University Library
Shepard	Leslie Shepard, *The Broadside Ballad*
UL	Goldsmiths' Library collections, University of London
Vicinus	Martha Vicinus, *Broadsides of the Industrial North*
Woods	Frederick Woods, *The Oxford Book of Traditional English Ballads*

Abolition of the Corn Laws (Attend awhile and you shall hear) BOD Harding B14-275 • 129

An Address to the Meeting at Spa-Fields (What follies, what falsehoods were uttered in vain) SF D-17

Advice to Country Maidens on the Poor Law Bill (Come all you bucksome men and maids) Madden 1795-479 • **433–35**, 436, 481, 519

Advice to Drunkards (Come all you poor drunkards, you now may be free) Madden 1799-1120

Advice to Farmers (Come brother farmers all attend) Madden 1804-554 • 257

The Affectionate Mother; or, the Orphan Boy (Ye children, whom no absent joy) Madden 1797-562

TITLE LIST

The Affectionate Mother; or, the Orphan Girl (Ye children, whom no care or peril) Madden 1799-1217

After Serving Seven Years (After serving seven years) Madden 1795-448 • **361**, 362, 513

Agitation of Great Britain (Now there has been a pretty bother) BL C116 il-250 • **262–63**, 117, 263, 482

Alteration of the Times (Good people give attention unto a merry ditty) BOD 2806 c17-2; and see next item • 257

The Alteration of Times (Come listen my neighbours and hear a merry ditty) St. Bride SS; substantial differences from preceding item

Annie Gray (All young females I pray draw near) Madden 1799-783

Answer to Why Did She Leave Him (Oh! yes, I remember the days of our childhood) BOD Harding B15-4 • 433

Anti-Starvation Song (Rejoice ye half-starv'd poor, for now the war is o'er) BL 1875 d9-120 • 99

Anything to Earn (Yarn) a Crust (I thought when I entered / first entered into life) BOD Harding B20-5; Madden 1792-10 • **494–98**, 75, 57–58, 69, 333, 480, 481, 541

An Appeal by Unemployed Ex-Service Men (Some thousands in England are starving) BOD Johnson-1158

> AT: Copy of Verses on the Unemployed and the great Distress . . .

The Appeal of a Body of Unemployed Operatives to a Humane and Sympathizing Public (When nature in the voice of pain) BOD Johnson-1979

> AT: A Copy of Verses by a Poor Tradesman; To the Friends of Industry; The Tradesman's New Hymn

The Appeal of the Unemployed (Oh, list you feeling Christians) BOD Johnson-1159

Artichokes & Cauliflowers (An old woman there lived at Rumford) Madden 1802-647 • **436–37**, 68, 414, 437–38

> AT: Old Woman of Rumford

As I Wandered by the Cook Shop (As I wandered by the cook shop) Madden 1802-83; BOD Harding B11-1633 • **317**, 76, 317–18

Assessed Taxes (Awake, awake! without delay) Madden 1794-21 • **113–16**, 116–17, 481, 542–47

The Australia Mania (Oh, have you heard the news so grand) BOD Firth C16-392

Ax My Eye (I deals in costermongery) St. Bride SS • **349–51**, 72, 136, 351–52

The Back and the Belly (A story I'm going to tell ye) Madden 1804-413 • 431

> AT: Belly and Back; Flashy Back and Hungry Belly

The Bailiffs Are Coming (The bailiffs are coming, oh dear, oh dear) Thomas Hudson, *Comic Songs, Ninth Collection*; Madden 1804-342 • **202–3**, 43, 69, 77, 168, 203–4, 431

The Bailiffs Have Been (The bailiffs have been here, oh la! oh la!) Madden 1791-321 • *203–4*, 77, 203, 484

The Baker Roasted (Ye poor men of Leicester come listen to me) Madden 1801-157

The Ballad Singer (Gentle people as ye throng) BL 1875 d16-2

The Ballad Singer's List (You know I'm always singing songs) BOD Harding B11-133

The Balls in Mourning; or, the Downfall of Mr. Gripe, the Pawnbroker (Well met neighbour gossip, what news do you hear) Madden 1791-708 • 216

The Bard of Seven Dials (I'm Billy Nutts, wot always cuts) BL 11621 h5-189 • *488–90*, 488–90, 492

> AT: Billy Nutts, the Poet

572   TITLE LIST

The Barrow Girl (My name's saucy Kate, I all others excel) BOD Harding B12-4

Bavarian Girl's Song (From Teutschland I came with my light wares all laden) Madden 1803-273
    AT: Buy a Broom

Beadle of the Parish (I'm a very knowing prig) Madden 1803-8 • 201

Bear It Like a Man (I gaily sing from day to day) BOD Harding B15-17

The Beggar (A beggar I am, and of low degree) St. Bride SS

The Beggar (Why good people all, at what do you pry) Madden 1789-806 • **303–5**, 42, 305, 408

The Beggar Boy (Long I've been an orphan poor) BOD Harding B28-264 • 303

The Beggar Boy (What ills my infant days await) BOD Harding B11-3088 • 303

The Beggar Girl (Over the mountain and over the moor) BOD Harding B22-15; Madden 1799-893 • **305–6**, 42, 61, 63, 68, 69, 75, 277, 302–3, 306

Beggars and Ballad Singers BOD Firth C21-2 with verses drawn in part from next item PR

Beggars and Ballad Singers (There's a difference to be seen 'twixt a beggar and a queen) BOD Harding B11-223

The Beggar's Lament (The beggars are ruined oh dear—oh dear) BOD Harding B11-224 • **313–14**, 204, 314–16, 324

Beggars Opera—Tom, Jerry, & Logick, Among the Cadgers in the Holy Land (Now to keep up the spree, Tom, Jerry, and Logick) St. Bride LS (Life in London) • **506–8**, 508–9, 522

The Beggar's Petition (Pity the sorrows of a poor old man) Madden 1790-379

The Beggar's Ramble (Mark ye well my neighbours all, and pray now can you tell) BOD Harding B11-225

. . . A Beggar's Wedding . . . (I'll sing of a wedding, a wedding of fame) Madden 1791-14 • *500*, 500

The Begging Box (Come ye Britons all listen with serious attention) BOD Harding B22-16 • 303

The Begging Imposter's Petition (Pity the sorrows of a poor old man) St. Bride SS (£100 Reward!)

Behold the Man That is Unlucky (Behold the man that is unlucky) BOD Firth C19-51

Belly and Back (A story I'm going to tell ye) Palmer TT-190
    AT: The Back and the Belly; Flashy Back and Hungry Belly

Ben Low (Kind friends excuse me asking) BOD Harding B11-3623
    AT: Old Ben Lowe; Poor Ben Low

Bessy Bloom the Flower Girl (I am Bessy Bloom the flower girl) BOD Harding B11-246 • 323

The Betrayed Maiden (Of a brazier's daughter who lived near) Woods-43

The Better Land (I hear thee speak of a better land) BL 11621 k5-157 • *504*, 504

Betty of Billingsgate (A boat unmoor'd from off Bankside) BL 11602g28 1-36 (unnumbered)

The Big Bomb. In the Park (Ye merry men trotting along) BOD Firth B34-26

Bill Bobstay (Tight lads I have failed with but none e'er so slightly) BOD Firth C13-126

Bill Bounce the Swell Cove Now in Luck (Have you heard of the news concerning Bill Bounce) BL LR27 a2 1.1-27 • *391*, 391

Bill Bounce, the Swell Cove Out o' Luck (In London town there once did dwell) BOD Harding B11-275 • **389–91**, 391

Billy Nutts, the Poet (I'm Billy Nutts, wot always cuts) John Labern, *Labern's Comic Minstrel*, Second Series: 160-64; BOD Harding B11-289; *London Singer's Magazine,* no. 66; BL 11621 h5-189; BL 1876 d41 1-104; BL LR271 a2 3-26 • **484–88**, 42, 43–44, 269–70, 480, 481, 488–93

  AT: The Bard of Seven Dials

Birds of a Feather (Life is like a day's journey, we truly may say) Madden 1798-223; Madden 1799-174

The Birmingham Investigation (The dreadful deeds of Birmingham) Madden 1802-80 • 337

Birmingham Jack of All Trades (I am a jovial roving blade) Palmer TT-210

The Bishop's See (The see, the see, the bishop's see) Henderson-120 • *209*, 209, 346

The Biter & the Bitten ('Tis a wonderful thing amongst all human creatures) BOD Johnson-3055

Blessings Below (As I was a walking for pleasure) BOD 2806 c18-33 • 138

The Blessings of a Good Little Wife (Some people 'gainst women are railing) Madden 1798-2 • **461–63**, 454, 463

  AT: The Charms of a Good Little Wife

The Blessings of Peace (Good people all listen to what I now say) BOD Harding B15-14a

The Blind Man's Lamentation (Good Christians give attention / You tender Christians, pray give attention) St. Bride SS; Madden 1804-397 • *302*, 302

Blind Man's Petition (Good people all pray pity me) BOD Harding B25-216

The Blooming Lady Worth £500,000 and Her Footman (It is of a blooming lady) Madden 1800-118 • *444–45*, 411, 444–45

Blue Ey'd Mary (In a cottage embosom'd within a deep shade) Pinto-122 • 448

Bob the Groom (Come all you swells and pray take pity on the life of poor old Bob) Madden 1799-1174

  AT: Poor Old Bob the Groom

The Boggart "Oastler and the Factory Movement" UL-530 PR • *255*, 255

Bonny England (Down by a chrystal fountain as I alone one morn did stray) Madden 1801-115 • 257

The Bonny Labouring Boy (As I rov'd out one morning, being in the blooming spring) Madden 1795-81

  AT: My Bonny Labouring Boy

Bonny Moor Hen (You brave lads of Wardhill I pray lend an ear) Madden 1799-846 • 551

The Boroughmongers' Defeat or, the Book of King William the Fourth St. Bride SS PR

Bread, Cheese and Ale (When I was young and healthy I rambled up and down) BOD Harding B11-3126

The Brick Dust Boy (I'm rolling Sam the brick dust boy) St. Bride SS

Britannia's Lamentation for Old England (As Britannia sat viewing the shores of old Albion) Madden 1794-29

British Ragged Schools (Now once I was a helpless child) BOD Firth C16-325

  AT: God Bless the Earl of Shaftesbury

The British Tars (Come all you thoughtless young men) BOD Firth C12-397 • 303

British Working-Man (Our city's in a fearful state at present, all will own) BOD Firth C16-232
Britons, Awake (Come all you Britons list awhile) Madden 1794-30 • 46, 274 n. 28
Britons Glory (Come listen awhile and make no delay) Madden 1795-14 • *122*, 122
Britons Rights (You Britons all draw near) Madden 1795-594 • *54*, 117
Britons United; or, the Downfall of Tyranny (Come all you truebred Englishmen wherever you may be) Madden 1802-742 • *257*, 257
The Brixton Lady and Her Nice Beetle Pies (Come all you fine ladies who in Brixton does dwell) BOD Harding B13-145 • **525–27**, 28, 78, 503, 527–28
Brixton Tread Mill (Have you seen the new prison, no more you'll desire) BOD Harding B11-471 • 347
Brixton Treading-Mill (The mill, the mill, the Brixton mill) Madden 1799-184
    AT: The Mill; The Treading Mill
Broken Down (Once I'd money plenty) BOD Harding B11-472
Broken Down Swell (I'm remembered well—a slap-up swell) BOD Harding B11-474
    AT: A Tidy Suit for all That
Broker Spare That Bed (O, broker spare that bed) Madden 1802-436 • 77, 204
    AT: O Broker Spare That Bed
Brother to the Dustman (My moralizing muse attunes) BOD Harding B11-478 • *494*, 494
    AT: The Dustman's Brother
A Bundle of Truths (You tradesmen all I pray attend) BOD Harding B28-173
Burial Club (My old 'oman one day says to me) Madden 1799-35 • 514
Buy a Broom (Buy a broom, buy a broom, buy a broom) Madden 1795-9 • 108
    AT: The New Song of Buy a Broom
Buy a Broom (From Teutchland I come with my light wares all laden) Madden 1798-99 • 108
    AT: Bavarian Girl's Song
Cadger's Ball (Oh, what a spicey flare up, tear up) BOD Harding B11-517 • 269, 514, 523
The Cadger's Tear (The cadger vonce in the rookery stood) BL C116 il-43
California Gold (To high and low of each degree) Madden 1799-1184 • *380*, 380
California or, Who Wants Gold! (Oh! have you heard the news of late) Madden 1795-331 • *380*, 380
Camberwell & Reform! (Arouse! Arouse! this glorious day) Madden 1795-487 • **114**, 113, 289, 482
Can You Wonder at Crime (I've been thinking, of late I've been thinking) BOD Harding B11-1220 • **134–35**, *64*, 64, 135–36, 256, 333
    AT: The Increase of Crime; John Bull, Can You Wonder at Crime
Captain Grant (My name is Captain Grant) Madden 1799-800
Careless Billy (You frolicksome sparks of game, ye being both wretched and old) BOD Harding B21-26
Carlisle Gaol (Good people all give ear, I do pray) Madden 1799-1145
The Carpet Weaver's True Tale (The day was dark and sad and drear) Palmer PK-10
Catch 'em Alive (Here's your catch 'em alives, and to sell 'em I strives) BOD Harding B16-45a

TITLE LIST 575

Catch 'em All Alive O! (My name is Tommy Tadpole, I does things with eclat) BOD Johnson-1575

Chandler's Shop (He. —Oh, Sally Sime, when we get wed) BOD Harding B11-567 • *519*, 269, 519

The Chandler's Shop (They call me smirking Bobby) BOD Harding B17-45b

The Chandler's Shop (When I married Miss Wiggins says she my dear Spriggins) BOD Harding B16-45b

Chanting Benny or the Batch of Ballads (When quite a babe my parents said) BOD Harding B11-569 • 494

Chapter of Cheats (Come all you honest tradesmen, and listen unto me) BOD Harding B11-571 • 198

The Charity Boy (I am a charity boy, dressed blue) Madden 1794-327 • 245
    AT: I Am a Charity Boy

The Charity Boy (No doubt you wonders who I is) Madden 1790-393 • **243–44**, 245, 354, 488

The Charity Girl (I'm a charity girl as you may see) Madden 1792-179 • 245
    AT: Factory Girl; The Flare-Up Factory Girl

The Charlie's Holiday; or, the Tears of London at the Funeral of Tom and Jerry; also the Death and Last Will of Poor "Black Billy Waters" (Round let us bound, this is Charlie's holiday) BL 1875 d8-99 • 56

The Charms of a Good Little Wife (Some people 'gainst women are railing) Madden 1794-53 • 463
    AT: The Blessings of a Good Little Wife

The Charter (Scroll of Britain's Just Demands) Madden 1801-111 • 550

The Chartist Song (Art thou poor but honest man) BOD Harding B15-43a • 550

The Chartists are Coming (What a row and a rumpus) BOD Johnson-480 • 550

The Chartist's Flare-Up (The Chartists are all going mad) BOD Firth c16-39 • 550

The Chaunt Seller or, a New Batch of Ballads (Come all you chanting vocalists) BOD Harding B11-583

Cheap Food Laws (Come, old and young, and rich and poor) BOD Harding B17-48a

Cheap Times! or, the Blessings of 1850 (O what an age this is for puff) Madden 1793-45

Cheer Boys! Cheer! (Cheer—boys—cheer! no more of idle sorrow) Madden 1799-1255 • *410*, 43, 62, 172, 258, 266, 408, 409–10

Cheer Up Again! Good News for the Poor (As Victoria was walking and lovingly talking) BOD Harding B13-274 • 129

Cherry Cheek Patty (Down in yon valley I live so snug) BOD Firth C18-41

Child of a Tar (In a little blue garment all ragged and torn) Madden 1791-503
    AT: Poor Little Child of a Tar

A Child's Faith (I knew a widow very poor) BOD Harding B11-598 • 247
    AT: The Poor Widow and Her Praying Boy

The Child's Inquiry (You oft have told me, mother dear) Madden 1797-402 • **323–24**, *64*, 64, 324–25

Chimney Sweep (They call me little Joe, sir) BOD Harding B17-50b • *502*, 502
    AT: Little Joe, the Chimney Sweeper

The Chimney Sweep (Tho' late and early I do pad) Madden 1797-51

A Chinese Puzzle (In China, that region of wisdom celestial) BOD Johnson-1543

Cholera Humbug (All you that does in England dwell) BL C116 i2-33

The Christian's Appeal Against the Poor Law Amendment Act (Priests of the living God! awake, arise) St. Bride SS • *162*, 162, 504–5

The Chummy's Wedding (If you'll listen to me, I'll sing of a spree) St. Bride SS • 514
    AT: The Sweep's Wedding

Church and State; or, the Rector's Creed (A rector am I, do you mind what I say) BL N Tab 2021 / 28-7 • *208*

The Civil Authorities Regret to Find the Deluded Keelmen Still Continue to Insult His Majesty's Boats BL 1875 d13-19 from end (unnumbered) PR • *335*, 335

Claughton Wood Poachers (Come all you men of courage bold and listen unto me) Madden 1799-738 • *337*, 337

Close the Ale-House Door (We may be happy yet, I think) BOD Firth C22-120

The Clothiers' Lamentation on the Badness of Trade (All you that have got ears to hear) Raven V-132 • 109
    AT: The Mechanic's Lamentation; The Mechanic's Lamentation on the Stagnation of Trade

The Coalheaver's Feast (Oh! have you not heard of a party so gay) BOD Harding B11-627; Madden 1794-110 • **509–11**, 500, 513, 514

The Coal-Owner and the Pitman's Wife (A dialogue I'll tell you as true as my life) Pinto-54

The Cobbler and Poet (William and Jonathan came to town together) BOD Harding B10-71

The Cold Winter Night (O now the cold winter comes on) BL 11606 aa22-58

The Cold Winter's Day (I was brought up in Lincolnshire, but not of high degree) BOD Harding B15-48a

The Collier Lad's Lament (In taking of my lonely walk on a cold and wintry day) Lloyd C-266

The Collier Lads, Who Labour Under Ground (Come attend you working men wherever you may be) Madden 1802-98

The Collier Lass (My name is Polly Parker, I'm come o'er from Worsley) Madden 1799-664

The Collier's Appeal (Many sad and weary years they have toiled in the mine) BOD Harding B11-2484

The Colliers' Defence (Oh! dear o' me what fearful cries, from left to right we hear) BOD Harding B20-28

The Collier's Hymn (Come all you humble and Christian colliers) Madden 1792-689

The Collier's (New) Hymn (Each feeling heart pray lend an ear) Madden 1792-1129; BOD Harding B11-646

Collier's Song (In the depths of a coal-pit a young lad grew) Lloyd C-40

Come Hark! to the Strains of a Plaintive Band (Come hark! to the strains of a plaintive band) BL 1876 d41 2.2-1343

Comfort to the Afflicted; or, the Wonderous Works of God (In Strutton Parish did a widow dwell) St. Bride SS • *238*, 237–38, 535, 558, 559
    AT: The Wonderous Works of God

Comic Version of a Good Time Coming (There's a good time coming, boys) Madden 1795-334 • *267–69*, 42, 269–70

Commerce in Tears (Our ports are now shut to exclude foreign grain) UL 5- 482 (2)

The Complaint of the Poor (Poor people of England) BL 1876 e20-13

The Contented Peasant (Happy is the peasant's lot) Madden 1801-486

The Contented Wife, and Her Satisfied Husband; or One Pound One (You married people, high and low, come listen to my song) Madden 1798-66
    AT: One Pound One; The Pleasing Wife and Satisfied Husband

Conversation Between a Farmer and His Wife (I am a poor farmer sore oppress'd, free trade has ruin'd me) BOD Harding B16-239a

Conversations on the Present Times (Good folks of every station, come listen to my rhymes) BOD Johnson-1287

The Cook Shop (I knew by the smoke that so gracefully curl'd) BL 1876 e3-271

A Copy of Verses by a Poor Tradesman (When Nature in the voice of pain) BOD Harding B13-268
    AT: The Appeal of a Body of Unemployed Operatives; To the Friends of Industry; The Tradesman's New Hymn

A Copy of Verses Composed by a Distressed Pudler (At an ironmaster's meeting a short time ago) BL L23 c4-13

Copy of Verses on the Dreadful Murder at Finsbury (You tender Christians pay attention) BOD Harding B14-211 • *414*, 414

Copy of Verses on the Lamentable Death of Mr. and Mrs. Jessup (You feeling Christians lend an ear) BOD Firth C17-270 • 333, 373

A Copy of Verses on the Life and Death of a Most Cruel and Hard-Hearted Overseer of the Poor (In this county as we've been told) Madden 1801-13; Madden 1801-75 • **209–12**, 162, 212–13
    AT: Lines on the Death . . .

A Copy of Verses, on the Life and Death of Miss Sophia Wright (Ye young and blooming females all) BOD Harding B13-149 • 448

A Copy of Verses on the Unemployed and the Great Distress in England (Some thousands in England are starving) BOD Harding B13-276
    AT: An Appeal by Unemployed Ex-Service Men

A Copy of Verses Written by a Lady on Two Orphans (My chaise the village inn did gain) Madden 1790-1
    AT: The Orphans; The Two Orphans; Two Orphans at Their Mother's Grave

A Copy of Verses Written on the Present State of Old England (Old England's in a dreadful state) BOD Harding B13-277 • *260*, 260

The Corn Bill (To the standard rally quick) UL 6-601
    AT: They Must Repeal the Corn Bill

The Corn Laws (As I mused on the wrongs that my country bears) UL 6-671

The Corn Laws (Ye millions that so keenly feel) BOD Firth C16-49

The Costermonger (I'm pretty well known here in town) BOD Harding B16-60a

The Cottage Boy (When morning streaks the east with gold) BOD Harding B11-704

Cottage on the Moor (My mam is no more, and my dad in the grave) Madden 1789-176

Cottage That Stands by the Sea (O talk not of fortune or jewels or splendour) BOD Harding B25-429

Cottager's Daughter (Down in a valley my father did dwell) Madden 1800-119

The Cottager's Saturday Eve (How I envy the cottager's Saturday eve) Madden 1804-360

The Cottager's Widow ('Tis down in yon valley my mother does dwell) Madden 1803-463
Cotton Spinners from Manchester, for the Master or Mistress (We are cotton spinners by our trade) BOD Johnson-646 • *377*, 377
    AT: Redditch in Worcestershire
The Counterfeit Halfpence (What racket, disturbance, what strife and delusion) BOD Harding B14-19
Country Hirings (Come all you blooming country lads and listen unto me) BOD 2806 c14-14
A Country Lad Am I (Come farming lads and lasses all) BOD Firth C16-303 • 378
The Country Lass (I am a brisk and bonny lass that's free from care and strife) Madden 1789-828 • *501–2*, 501
Country Statute (Come all you lads of high renown) Madden 1803-312
The Cove Vot Has Seen Better Days (I once could sport the blunt about) Madden 1794-156 • **352–53**, 353–54
The Cove Wot Sings! (No doubt a song you've heard) BL 1876 e2-24
    AT: The Luck of a Cove Wot Sings
Cries of the Nation (Gentlemen give attention unto my song) Madden 1802-18
The Cries of the Poor (All you distressed tradesmen in country and town) Madden 1797-37
Crikey! What Will Master Say (From a country village t'other day) BOD Harding B11-2689
The Crisis, 1846 (When fell corruption's bands conspire) Ashton-331
The Crossing Sweeper (Though a sweeper by trade, and though queer my estate) Madden 1802-785 • 415
The Cruel Sea Captain, and Nancy of Yarmouth (It's of a sea captain in Yarmouth did dwell) Madden 1794-158 • *46–47*
A Cry from Lancashire (No more the merry spindles go whistling hour by hour) BL 1876 d41 2.2-1346
Cupid the Pretty Ploughboy (As I walked out one May morning) BL 11621 k4-257 • *443*, 443, 444
A Curious Account of the Distressed Labourers Near Brighton BOD Harding B13-271; PR
Curious Dialogue Between Four Selfish Landlords . . . (Well Mr. Skinflint, how do you do, sir) Madden 1802-306
The Dairy Maid (I was d'ye see a dairy maid) BOD Harding B21-66 • *415*, 415
The Dark Gipsey Girl (One May morning bright I pass'd thro' the valley) BOD Harding B15-84b
The Day Poor Benny Died (One day as through the street I rambled) BOD Harding B11-1175
The Dead, Alive (A man at an alehouse was sitting one night) BOD Harding B11-813 • **392**, 392–93
Dear Woman is the Joy of an Englishmans Life (Come all you young men and young maidens around) Madden 1789-236 • *454*, 454
The Death, Last Will, and Funeral of "Black Billy": overall title for sheet containing "The Merry Will & Testament of Master Black Billy" and "Life of Billy Waters": BL 1875 d7-15 • 56, 309–11
Death of the Corn Bill (Says old John Bull, here is a job) UL 6-612 • 129
    AT: John Bull & the Corn Bill

Death of the Corn Bill (There's lots of fun, the Corn Bill's done) BOD Harding B14-280

Death of the Poor Orphan Sweep (Behold my Saviour is come to save) Madden 1799-1237

Depression of Trade (I wish there wou'd be an alteration) BOD Harding B11-866

Despised for Being Poor (Farewell, false girl, I leave you) BOD 2806 c16-305
    AT: I was Despis'd Because I was Poor

The Devil and the Grinder (Come all friends and neighbours I pray you draw near) BL 11606 aa24-97 • 91

A Dialogue and Song on the Starvation Poor Law Bill, Between Tom and Ben (I would take them into Cheshire, and there they should sow) Madden 1802-578

A Dialogue Between Dives and Lazarus (Behold these lines crave thy most solid view) BOD Johnson-1766 • 140

A Dialogue Between Ned and His Wife on the Hard Times (Now wife whatever shall we do the times they are so bad) Madden 1799-510 • 41

A Dialogue Between the Farmers and Landlords (You gentlemen all give ear to my song) BL 1875 d16-10

Dialogue on a Sunday Morning; or, the Sabbath Breaker Reclaimed (On a fine Sabbath morn, in the sweet month of May) Madden 1799-11 • 503–4

Dick the Dustman (I'm dashing Dick the dustman) Madden 1789-202 • 502

Dick's Courtship (Last new year's day, as I've heard say) Madden 1802-10

Dicky Numbscull's Ramble in Town (When I was young and in my prime) BOD Harding B11-896

Did You All Fast (I hope you all both great and small) Madden 1793-60

The Disabled Tar (Ye friends of compassion, and friends of the brave) BOD Firth C13-93

The Disobedient Daughter (If you want a good hymn pray buy one of me) BOD Firth B34-86

Distress of Trade (Good people now I pray attend) BOD 2806 c17-100 • 503
    AT: Friend of the Distressed; The Friend to the Distressed

The Distressed Citizen (A wealthy citizen, who long) BOD Harding B5-48

The Distressed Farmer ('Tis all my cry by night and day) BOD Harding B14-281 • **224–25**, 226–28, 257

The Distressed Seaman (O listen to a tale of woe) BOD Firth C12-410

The Distressed Sempstress (You gentles of England) BL 11621 k5-194 • 406

Distressed Wanderer (If you want a good song, will you buy it of me) BL LR271 a2 3-60

Do a Good Turn When You Can (How little we think as we travel) Madden 1795-151 • 237

The Dodger (Fare-ye-vell, my Vitechapel boys, fare-ye-vell for a-vhile) BOD Harding B16-322b

The Dogs-Meat Man (In Grays Inn Lane not long ago) St. Bride SS; BL LR271 a2 8-44 (3rd Catnach printing) • **425–29**, 43, 63, 168, 424, 429–32, 519

Domestic Economy (If there's anything that I detest) BOD Harding B11-929

Don't Despise a Man Because He Wears a Ragged Coat (O what a world of flummery, there's nothing but deceit in it) BL LR271 a2 2-51
    AT: The Ragged Coat; Song of the Ragged Coat

Don't Leave Your Father, Boy (Ah! well do I remember now my little cottage home) SH-561

Don't Put My Father's Picture Up for Sale (I've been thinking of the day that has long since passed away) BL LR 271 a2 2-62

Don't Speak of a Man as You Find Him (It's a fashion to make a great bother) BOD Harding B11-2332 • 237

Don't Tell the Society (Oh, dear! these are shocking hard times) BL LR271 a2 1.1-176

Dot and Carry One (Pounds, shillings, pence, and farthings I) Madden 1804-77

The Double Dealer (Strange times are come when stones must bleed) BL 1876 e3-277 • **109–11**, 111–13, 196, 335

Down in a Coal Mine (In me you see a collier, a simple honest man) BOD Harding B11-4304

Downfall of Monopoly (Good folks I pray attend to me) BOD Harding B14-282

Dreadful and Awful Effects of Acute Distress, an Account of Edward Price, Shoemaker of Cheltenham, Who . . . Took the Desperate Resolution of Destroying His Family . . . BL 1880 c20 1-282 PR • *343*, 343

Dreadful Cruelty to a Servant (A gentleman farmer has got in a mess) BL LR271 a2 1.1-126

The Dreadful Murder of a Wife and Six Children (Draw near all you fathers, and mothers as well) BOD Harding B14-203 • **362–64**, 73, 74, 78, 260, 333, 364–73, 540–41

Driven from Home (Out in this cold world, out in the street) BOD Firth C13-232

The Drunkard's Child (Oh! my clothes are all ragged, and tatter'd, and torn) Madden 1799-996 • 306

The Drunkard's Child (Taking my walks on a cold winter's day) Madden 1793-152
    AT: The Poor Drunkard's Child

The Drunkard's Confession (I've drunk away my precious time) BOD Harding B11-1523

The Drunkard's Looking Glass (What will a drunkard do for ale) Madden 1799-1120 • 465

The Drunkard's Ragged Child (A little ragged laddie goes wand'ring thro' the streets) Madden 1792-720

The Drunken Husband (You married women draw near awhile) St. Bride SS (Old Towler) • **471–72**, 473, 481

The Drunken Wife (Young men of each degree in life) Madden 1799-909 • 473

Duck-Leg Dick (Duck-Leg Dick had a donkey) BOD Harding B11-1017

The Dustman (I'm dashing Dick the dustman) Madden 1789-201 • 502

The Dustman's Brother (My moralizing muse attunes) BOD Harding B11-1264
    AT: Brother to the Dustman

The Dustman's Cousin (Oh, modesty's a moral thing) BL 1876 d41 2.1-672

The Dyer's Lamentation (All you that have a feeling heart) BL 1876 d41 2.2-1336

Dyot Street, or Parlour Next to the Sky (My lodging is in Leather Lane) BL C116 il-118

Eat, Ye Paupers, Eat (Times are getting worse and worse) BOD Firth C16-315

Eighteen Shillings a Week (A man and his wife in ——— Street) Madden 1792-724 • **248–51**, 236, 251

The Emigrant (Come all you gallant Englishmen and listen to my song) Madden 1803-342

The Emigrant (Come all you gallant Englishmen wherever you may be) Madden 1804-599 • *379*, 379

Emigrant's Adieu (O! father dear, the time is come) BL 1876 d41 1-406 • 379

The Emigrant's Farewell (The shamrock, rose, and thistle I overheard conversing) BOD Harding B11-1061 • *381*, 381

Emigrants' Farewell to Old England (As walking near the docks at Liverpool, I heard some emigrants to say) Madden 1799-655 • *381*, 381

Emigration (All you whose minds are bent on straying) BOD Harding B11-1878 • 381

Encore Verses or the Answer to Parson Brown's Sheep (My thanks accept kind friends) BOD 2806 c16-241
    AT: Second Edition of Parson Brown's Sheep

England Demands Reform: and Reform She'll Have (Cheer up! cheer up, Britannia cries) BOD Firth C16-193

England's Decline (The trade of old England's decaying) BOD Harding B11-4013
    AT: If there's a Will There's a Way

England's Glory (Industrious men, give ear awhile) BOD Harding B25-582

England's Glory, or, a Large Loaf for Sixpence (Come all you sighing brothers, give ear to my song) Madden 1804-319

England's Maiden Queen (Britons all of each degree) Madden 1804-164 • *122*, 122, 263

England's Stagnation (The oldest person in the world on land or on the water) Madden 1799-1085 • *259*, 259

The English Butcher's Lament (The butchers of England are growing quite cranky) BOD Harding B12-235 • *234*

English Emigrant (I'm standing at the stall Sarey with Pincher by my side) BOD Harding B11-1076

The English Exile (I've oft seen you smiling, dear mother) BOD Harding B11-548 • *379*, 379

The Englishman, Irishman, and Scotchman; or, Dearly You Must Pay for Your Mutton (As an Englishman, an Irishman, and a Scotchman, too, one day) Madden 1792-726 • *357*, 356–57

The Exile of Erin (There came to the beach a poor exile of Erin) Madden 1804-444

The Factory Bell (Oh happy man, O happy thou) Madden 1799-1298

Factory Bells of England (Oh, the bell of that 'ere factory) BOD Harding B16-83b • *231*, 232

The Factory Child / The Factory Child's Complaint (I hear the blythe voices of children at play) Madden 1799-1305; Central Library, Bradford • **403–4**, 404

The Factory Girl (All you that love a merry jest, give ear to what I say) BOD Harding B20-216

Factory Girl (I'm a factory girl as you may see) Madden 1795-743
    AT: The Charity Girl; The Flare-up Factory Girl

The Factory Girl (The sun was just rising one fine May-Day morning) Madden 1804-379

The Factory Girl's Last Day ('Twas on a winter's morning) BOD Harding B11-1111 • 398
    AT: The White Slave

Fair Play for Working Men (Come all you jolly tradesmen of this famous little town) BOD Johnson-2073

Fall, Tyrants, Fall! (The trumpet of liberty sounds through the world) Madden 1798-290 • 551

The Famine Fast Day (Ye working men both far and near) Madden 1799-1047 • 209

The Fancy Lad (When first I came to town) Madden 1802-24 • **422–24**, 414, 424

Farewell Address to Their Countrymen and Friends . . . (The assizes they are over now, the Judge is gone away) Madden 1797-29 • **357–59**, 333, 359–61

    AT: The Transport's Lamentation

The Farmer (Gentlemen farmers, I pray now attend) BOD Harding B2-31

The Farmer Boy (Indeed my simple tale is true) BL LR271 a2 4-273

The Farmer Relieved by His Landlord (Come listen to my ditty, both young and old I pray) BOD Harding B25-624

The Farmer's Boy (The sun had set behind the hill) Madden 1799-551 • **403**, 403, 553

    AT: The Lucky Farmer's Boy

The Farmer's Complaint (A farmer on a market day was coming from this town, sir) Madden 1799-33

The Farmer's Daughter and the Gay Ploughboy (You constant lovers give attention) SF-C34 • *412*, 412

    AT: Mary and the Handsome Factory Boy; Rosetta and Her Gay Plough Boy

The Farmers Done Over (Come all you swaggering farmers, of courage stout and bold) Madden 1802-752

Farmers Don't You Cry! (You Britons bold of each degree) BOD Harding B11-1157 • 226

The Farmer's Downfall (You broken down farmers, give ear to my song) BOD Harding B17-91b • 226

The Farmers Downfall and the Poor Man's Distress (Come all you English poor folk) Madden 1800-130 • 226

The Farmers' Keep Sake (Can you save us from starving by promoting a bill) BOD Harding B25-628

The Farmers Lament (Come all you good people that live in this shire) BOD Johnson-2490 • 226

Farmers Lamentation (Come cheer up your hearts there's good news come to town) BOD Harding B28-60

The Farmers Lamentation (Draw near my good people and a story I'll tell) Madden 1802-628

The Farmer's Lamentation (Sad dreadful cries and moans we hear) Madden 1802-627

The Farmer's Lamentation, But the Poor's Rejoicing (Good people all I pray attend) BOD Firth C16-277

The Farmers, Millers, and Bakers (A good time is coming, now mind what I say) BOD Firth C16-291

The Farmer's Prayer (Thou great creator of this earth) Madden 1804-152

Farmer's Rent Day (A farmer's employment's the best I e'er saw) Madden 1797-428 • 226

The Farmer's Son (Good people give attention while I sing in praise) Madden 1802-497 • 226

Farmers Warning (Come gentlemen farmers, I pray now attend) Madden 1789-253

The Fast Day (Young ladies and young gentlemen come listen to my song) Madden 1799-1048

The Fasting Man Turned Hungry (There is a man, you all must know) Madden 1793-237

The Fat Old Parish Vestryman (I sing a modern ballad, made by a modern pate) Madden 1798-7 • **222–23**, 162, 196, 223–24

TITLE LIST 583

The Fatal English Poor Law Bill or, the Ways of the World (Come all you gallant Englishmen) Madden 1803-142 • 162

Father, Dear Father, the Brokers Are In (Oh father, dear father, come home with me now) BOD Harding B11-1703 • *204*

The Felting Machines (Mechanics and artisans now pray give ear) BL 1876 d41 2.2-1333

Fifteen Shillings a Week (A man and his wife in ——— street) Madden 1793-72 • 251
> AT: A Week's Reckoning (with one less stanza)

The Fine Old English Gentleman (I'll sing you a good old song, made by a good old Pate) ML H1623 • **216–18**, 41, 42, 60, 61, 63, 66, 76–77, 218–22, 237, 257, 258, 345
> AT: The Old English Gentleman

The Fine Old English Labourer (Come lads and listen to my song) BOD Harding B11-1201 • 218

Fine Old English Pawnbroker (I'll sing you a good old song) Madden 1799-1262 • **214–15**, 76, 216–18

The Fine Young English Gentleman (I'll sing you a prime new song, that was made by a young chap's pate) Madden 1801-182 • 257

The Firm Bank (I have a never-failing bank) BOD Firth B34-110

The Fisherman's Boy (It was down in the lowlands a poor boy did wander) Madden 1804-728
> AT: The Poor Fisherman's Boy; The Poor Little Fisherman's Boy

The Fisherman's Girl (It was down in the country a poor girl was weeping) Madden 1797-128 • 306, 320
> AT: The Poor Fisherman's Girl; The Poor Little Fisherman's Girl

Five and Twenty Shillings (Are) Expended in a Week (Its of a tradesman and his wife) BOD Harding B20-55
> AT: How Five and Twenty Shillings Was/Were/Are Expended in a Week; some difference from A Song Called My £1 5s.

Five O'Clock in the Morning (At five in the morning, the miner doth rise) BOD Harding B11-1220

A Flare Up Amongst the Lambeth Guardians (Oh Lambeth is a funny place) BOD Harding B11-1221 • 163

The Flare-Up Factory Girl (I'm a factory gal as you may see) Madden 1799-671 • 245
> AT: The Charity Girl; Factory Girl

Flashy Back and Hungry Belly (A story I am going to tell ye) Madden 1803-384 • *236*, 236, 431
> AT: The Back and the Belly; Belly and Back

Flashy Bet (I'm saucy leering rolling Bet) BOD Harding B22-88

Forced to be Contented (You Britons all where e'er you be) Madden 1804-537
> AT: We Are Forced to be Contented

The Forestallers in the Dumps (Come neighbours attend now and listen awhile) Madden 1799-80

Forestalling Done Over (Come all you poor people, I pray lend an ear) BOD Harding B11-1242 • 95

The Forester's Daughter (The father of Nancy a forester was) BL 11606 aa24-17

584 TITLE LIST

Fortunate Factory Girl (The sun had just risen/was just rising one fine summer's morning) Madden 1799-1052 • *422*, 422

The Fortunate Lovers (Come all you young people and listen awhile) Madden 1794-169

Forty Years Ago ('Tis now some forty years ago) Madden 1792-742

Found Dying in Our Streets (See yonder stands a trembling form) BOD Harding B11-1247 • *414*, 414

Frame Work Knitters' Petition (Good people all attend awhile) BOD Johnson-2509; much the same as next two items • 378

Frame Work Weavers Petition (Good people all attend awhile) BOD Johnson-2510; same as next item

The Framework-Knitters Appeal (Good people all attend awhile) BOD Johnson-1850; same as preceding item

The Framework-Knitters Lamentation (Come now each gen'rous feeling heart) Pinto-49 • 550

The Framework-Knitters Petition (Could we obtain our food by work) Pinto-50 • 550

Frauds and Pickpockets, or Rogues All (Come come my good masters, what's all this about) BOD Harding B11-3533

Free and Easy (I'm the lad that's free and easy) Madden 1800-132

Free Trade (Since free trade's the cry both in country and town) Madden 1797-546

Free Trade in Beer! (Come all good people far and near) Madden 1793-65

Free Trade or Downfall of the Farmers (Good people all I pray attend) BOD Harding B11-1262 • 129, 257

Free Trade; or the Coalition (Free trade has been carried) Madden 1792-607

Free Trade or, the Farmers' Downfall (Come all English poor folks, and listen to my song) Madden 1793-77

Free Trade, or the Farmers' Downfall (Good people all give ear awhile) BOD Firth C16-288

A Friend in the Pocket (A friend in the pocket is a friend indeed) BOD Harding B11-2529 • *235–36*, 235–36

Friend of (to) the Distressed (Good people all I pray attend) BOD 2806 c18-121; Madden 1804-229

    AT: Distress of Trade

Friendless Boy (On a dark lonesome night, when nature's at rest) BOD 2806 c17-139

The Friendless Boy (Pity a poor and friendless boy) Madden 1789-962 • 303

Friends Are Few When Foak (Folk) Are Poor (When aw had wark an brass to spend) BOD Harding B11-198; BOD Harding B11-3051 • **251–53**, 24, 60, 236, 237, 253–55

Frost, Williams, and Jones's Farewell to England (As I walked through the town of Portsmouth) BOD Johnson-1480 • 550

The Gambler's Wife (Dark is the night! how dárk! no light! no fire!) BOD Harding B11-1291

General Distress (You surely have heard of great General Distress) Madden 1789-271 • *104*, 104–5

General Distress of the Nation; or, the Downfall of Banks (Why, neighbours, what ails you? what makes you look sad?) Madden 1804-329 • 104

The Generous Farmer and (or) Poor Soldier (A jolly old farmer once soaking his clay) Madden 1793-518 • 226
    AT: The Jolly Old Farmer
The Gin Shop; or, a Peep Into Prison (Look through the land from north to south) BL 1870 dl 1-85 • 58, 465
The Gipsey Wanderer ('Twas night, and the farmer his fireside near) Madden 1803-513
The Gipsey's Tent (Our fire on the turf and tent 'neath the hill) BOD Harding B11-1321
Give Me the Man of Honest Heart (Give me the man of honest heart) BOD Harding B11-2002
Glorious News for the Wives (All you that do in London dwell) BOD Firth B34-125
Glorious Reformation (What wond'rous changes every day) BOD Harding B14-284 • 113
The Glorious Times That We Now Have (O dear, what schemes and alterations) Madden 1795-26 • 209
Go Along Bob (As Joe, the dustman, drove his noble team) BOD Harding B17-114a
Go It My Kiddies and Fake Away (I once was a peeler and played the deuce) BOD Harding B11-1324
Go It Neddy (My toggery I took out of pawn) Madden 1798-293 • *458,* 459
    AT: Love and Liver
God Bless Our King (God bless our king, and long may he reign) Madden 1798-15
God Bless the Earl of Shaftesbury (Now once I was a helpless child) BOD Harding B11-2871
    AT: British Ragged Schools
God Bless These Poor Folk! (God bless these poor folk that are strivin') BL 1876 d41 1-466
God Save the Poor (God save the starving poor) BOD Harding B16-103c • **92–93**, 28, 87, 93, 256, 260, 262
God Speed the Good Ship; or, the English Emigrant! (God speed the keel of the trusty ship) BOD Harding B11-3470 • **408–9**, 43, 409–10
    AT: English Emigrant
Going Out to Market (Once I was never satisfied with how the cash was laid out) BOD Harding B11-1351 • 236
The Golden Act (What confusion this act has made) BOD Firth B33-34
The Golden Days of Good King George (Since very few are well disposed to praise the present times, Sirs) Madden 1796-113
The Good Husband (Come all you frolicsome fellows) Madden 1797-277 • *454–55,* 454
Good News for the Poor BOD Harding B30-11 PR
A Good Time Coming, Boys! (There's a good time coming, boys—) Madden 1799-1105 • 266
    AT: There's a Good Time Coming, Boys!; Wait a Little Longer
Good Times are Coming (Come listen to my ditty) BL 1875 b19-46 • 270
The Good Times Are Coming (The good times are coming, O dear, O dear) BOD Harding B11-899 • 204, 270
The Good Times Are Gone (The good times, they say, are coming, boys) BOD Firth C16-55 • 270
Gospel Beggar (A beggar I am at the end of my days) BOD Johnson-1816 • *303,* 303, 504

Grand Conversation Under the Rose (As Mars and Minerva was viewing of some implements) BOD Johnson-848

The Grand Dissolving Views (While thinking of some past events at home the other night) BOD Harding B11-1394 • 139

The Great Battle for Freedom and Reform (You working men of England) Madden 1792-762

The Great Meetings in England, or the Free Trades and Protectionists (Come all you gallant Englishmen and listen to my song) BL 11621 k4-176

The Great Reform Bill (You noble patriots of reform) BOD Harding B14-287

Gregory, the Wealthy Old Squire (When some people die) Madden 1803-201; *London Oddities*, no. 4 (1824): 5: BL 12314 c13 • **199–200**, 200–201, 235

The Grinders; or, More Grist to the Mill (Search all the world high and low) Madden 1799-82

Ground for the Floor (I lived in the woods for a number of years) Madden 1801-439 • 502
    AT: The Neat Little Cottage

The Grumbling Farmers (Farmers Marco and Pedro were jogging along) Madden 1788-108

Happy Land!! Comic Version (I sing the pleasures of these glorious days) Madden 1793-90 • **130–31**, 132

Happy Man (Come all you merry buxom blades) BOD Harding B11-1465

Happy Man, or, It Can't Last (I'm the happiest man 'neath the sun) BOD Harding B11-1468

Hard Struggle for the Breeches (Husband. About my wife I mean to sing a very funny song) Madden 1797-571 • 461
    AT: Struggle for the Breeches

Hard Times (Hard, hard is the times, and the cry it's no wonder) BL 1871 f13-37

Hard Times (We say the times are grievous hard) Madden 1804-462 • 465

Hard Times Among the Farmers (Times never were so bad before) BL 1875 d13: one-third through (unnumbered)

Hard Times and Fair Trade (O what hard and trying times most people now do see) BL 1874 e4-21

Hard Times and No Beer (You Englishmen, and Irishmen, Scotchmen and Welshmen too) Madden 1792-486

Hard Times Come Again No More (Let us pause in life's pleasures and count its many tears) BOD Harding B11-866

Hard Times; or, How to Get a Dinner (Hard times so badly stings us) Madden 1795-310 • **105–7**, 107–8

Haughty Lords Have Us Degraded (Come my fellow slaves of Britain) Madden 1798-223 • **206–7**, 28, 61, 207–8, 235

Haymakers (The noontide is hot and our foreheads are brown) BOD Harding B15-127b • *502*, 502
    AT: Song of the Haymakers

The Hearth Stone Man (As through the streets I take my way) BOD Harding B11-3606

Heaven Bless Lovely Women and Succour the Poor (I'll be proud just to say I'm a plain honest farmer) Madden 1788-279
    AT: The Honest Farmer

Heaven's My Home (The Christian pilgrim sings) Madden 1799-1172 • *504*, 504

He'll Be Back Bye-&-Bye (The wife of a soldier was starving with hunger) BOD Harding B11-1506

Help for Lancashire (Abroad as I was walking one bitter winter's day) BOD Firth C16-256

Hercules Decapitating the Hydra of Corruption or, a Broom for the Boroughmongers ('Tis known old England long has been) Madden 1796-157 • 41, 113, 279, 511

Here's a Health to the Hard Working Man (Who is the prop and support of the land) BOD Harding B11-1683

Hertford Approaching Election (All you that dwell in Hertford Town) Madden 1794-56 • *6, 53*, 116, 197, 275 n. 39

He's Only a Poor Orphan Boy (A poor little lad all forsaken) NOR-59

High Price of Meat (Oh! here's a pretty go, said a tradesman to his wife) Madden 1792-868 • 234

The Hiring Day (Was you at ———, or did you see) Madden 1804-585

The Honest Farmer (I'ze proud just to say, I'ze a plain honest farmer) Madden 1799-84
    AT: Heaven Bless Lovely Woman and Succour the Poor

The Honest Grocer (The grocers, poor creatures, long time have complained) BOD Firth B34-136

Honest John Bull (Here's a health to old honest John Bull) BOD Harding B11-1569 • *137–38*, 137
    AT: John Bull and His Mother

The Honest Ploughman, or Ninety Years Ago (Come all you jolly husbandmen and listen to my song) Madden 1793-94 • 257
    AT: The Life of an Honest Ploughman

The Honest Soldier and Generous Farmer (One evening 'twas late, and the hamlet was still) St. Bride SS

Honest Working Man (The country's in a dreadful state) BOD Harding B11-547 • 138–39

The Honest Working Man (Oh, the great men of the day, they) BOD Harding B11-2193 • 502

The Honest Working Man (We've sung of heroes brave and good) BOD Harding B11-1573 • 502

Honesty in Tatters (This here's what I does, I, d'ye see, forms a notion) BOD Harding B22-113

Hope for the Best (The good times in England are gone to decay) BOD Harding B16-113c • *258*, 258

Horrible Disclosures of Starvation and Death BL 12330 i42-2 PR • 247

Horrible Discovery! BL 12330 i42-9 PR • 247, 248

A Horrid and Dreadful Account of John Marlew, Who with His Three Starving Children Went for Assistance . . . BL 1888 c3-72 PR

The Horrid Murder Committed by Mary Wilson (Oh, list awhile, good people all) BOD Firth C17-94

Horrid Murder of Four Children (Come all good people and pay attention) BOD Firth C17-95 • 333, 373

Hot Codlings (A little old woman a living she got) BOD Harding B11-3897 • **505**, 38, 42, 506

House and Window Taxes (I pray draw near with one accord, and listen to my ditty) Madden 1795-494 • *117*, 117, 279 n. 24

House Keeping or, Two Pounds Two (A man and his wife got into strife) BOD Harding B11-1577 • 251

How Five and Twenty Shillings Was/Were/Are Expended in a Week (It is of a tradesman and his wife) Madden 1792-162 • 251

> AT: Five and Twenty Shillings Expended in a Week; some difference from A Song Called My £1 5s.

How the Poor Live (You'll own this is true, if you just pay attention) BL LR271 a2 2-178 • **117–19**, *77, 78*, 28, 69, 77, 119–20, 230

How to Get a Living in This Town (I'll please you all both great and small, if you will give attention) BOD Harding B11-600 • *198*, 198

How to Repeal the Corn Law, or the Six Points Explained (You workingmen where'er you be) Madden 1799-513 • 41, 550

Howls of the Farmers (What a dust the poor devils of farmers are making) BOD Harding B25-865

Humanity is Calling (We have come to ask your assistance) BOD Harding B11-1594

The Humble Roof (When first this humble roof I knew) Madden 1798-434 • *502*, 502

A Hundred Years to Come (You've heard about Macaulay, and the great New Zealander too) BOD Firth C16-414

The Hungry Army (When I was young and in my prime) BL 11621 h11 1-167 • **407–8**, 408

Hunting a Loaf (Good people I pray give ear unto what I say) BOD Firth C16-9 • 550

I am a Charity Boy (I am a charity boy, dressed blue) Madden 1801-191

> AT: The Charity Boy

I Never Takes No Notice (I'm no busy body, no, not I) BOD Harding B11-1650

I Was Despis'd Because I Was Poor (Farewell, false girl) Madden 1792-798

> AT: Despised for Being Poor

I Wish I'd a Thousand a Year (I wish I'd a thousand a year) BOD Harding B11-2389

I Wonder Where the Money Goes (Of money's worth I'm going to sing) Madden 1804-586; Madden 1794-74; Madden 1803-187; Madden 1797-698 • **240–42**, 236, 242

I'd Be a Gipsy (I'd be a gipsy merry and free) Madden 1800-15 • *502*, 502

If I Had a Thousand a Year (Oh! If I had a thousand a year, Gaffer Green) BOD Harding B11-1692

If there's a will there's a way (The trade of old England's decaying) BOD Firth C16-254

> AT: England's Decline

I'm a Poor Shepherd Maid (I'm a poor shepherd maid) Madden 1799-568

I'm Going to See the Exhibition for a Shilling (Let all the world say what they will) BOD Harding B13-39

I'm His Only Daughter (Down in the valley my father did dwell) Madden 1803-387

I'm Like to be There (Eh, my father he not a shilling will give) BOD Harding B15-137a

I'm Not Such a Swell as I Us'd to be (At the time when the clothes I have on were quite new) BL 1876 d41 1-209

An Imaginary Conversation Between Gladstone and a Working Man (You working men are discontented) BOD Harding B14-288

In England there is One Law for the Rich and Another for the Poor (Come all you buxom females) BOD Harding B11-1741 • 149

In Tatter'd Weed from Town to Town (In tatter'd weed, from town to town) BOD 2806 c18-226

In the Days When I Was Hard Up (In the days when I was hard up) Madden 1802-156 • *376*, 376

The Increase of Crime (I've been thinking, of late I've been thinking) BOD Firth C17-83 • 136
    AT: Can You Wonder at Crime; John Bull, Can You Wonder at Crime

An Interesting Dialogue Between the Poor Law Commissioners and the Poor People that Apply for Relief BOD Harding B20-135 PR

An Interesting Dialogue Concerning Emigration (Good people give attention and you shall understand) Madden 1804-467; with substantial prose

Irish Stranger (O pity the fate of a poor Irish stranger) Madden 1802-677
    AT: The Poor Irish Stranger

The Irishman's Picture of England/London ('Tis myself dat was born now in Dublin / It is myself that was born now in Dublin) Madden 1794-176; BOD Harding B11-1783 • 209

The Iron Times (That mankind were always grumblers) BOD Johnson-1303

Is There Anything Low about Me? (I'm a genteel respectable youth) BOD Harding B11-1804

It is only the Way it was Played on the Stage (To a fashionable theatre one evening I went) BOD Harding B11-3098

Jack Rag (Although my name's Jack Rag and I wears a ragged tile) BL 1875 b19-131

Jack's as Good as His Master (Jack is as good as his master we are told) NOR-63 • 149

Jane of Spitalfields (It's of a weaver's daughter as I to you declare) BL LR271 a2 6-201

Jenny Jenkins (My name's Jenny Jenkins, I'm a wandering old lady) BL LR271 a2 9-67

Jig, Jig, to the Hirings (You farmers' servants far and near) BL 1876 d41 2.1-663

Jim Baggs the Musician (I'm a musical genius in rags) BOD Harding B11-1873 • *493–94*, 493

Jimmy Jumps the Rhymer! (Oh, you've heard talk of Billy Nuts) BL 11621 h11 4-58 • 494

Joan o' Grinfield! (I'm a poor cotton weaver as many a one knows) Madden 1799-689; BOD Harding B20-80; Harland-169 • **384–85**, 385–87, 552 n. 12
    AT: Jone o' Grinfield; The Poor Cotton Weaver

Joan o' Grinfilt's Visit to Lunnun, to See What the State Doctor Intends to Do for the Nation (Sed Joan eawt o' Grinfilt I've news for to tell) BOD Harding B16-118b • 552

Joan o' Grinfilt's Visit to Mr. Fielden, with a Petition to the Queen to Fill Every Hungry Belly (Ses Joan eawt o' Grinfilt I'll tell yo what Nan) BOD Harding B16-118c • 552

Job, the Patient Man (Come all you worthy Christians that dwell within this land) Madden 1799-984 • 503
    AT: One God Has Made Us All; Poverty and Contentment

Joe Bradley, the Runaway Workhouse Boy (Kind folks all list my ditty) BOD Harding B11-1887

John Bull and His Mother (Here's an health to old honest John Bull) Madden 1802-339 • *137–38*, 137, 279 n. 2
    AT: Honest John Bull

John Bull & the Corn Bill (Says old John Bull, here's a job) Madden 1792-500
> AT: Death of the Corn Bill

John Bull and the (New) Taxes (Here is some lines about the times) BL 11621 k4-63; Madden 1801-98 • *125*, 52, 63, 125, 279 n. 27

John Bull, Can You Wonder at Crime (I've been thinking, of late I've been thinking) BOD Harding B11-1902 • 136
> AT: Can You Wonder at Crime; The Increase of Crime

John Bull in a Rage at the Corn Laws (Little Boney done over, hostilities o'er) Madden 1788-423

John Bull's Alphabet (A stands for Aristocracy, on luxuries they fare) BOD Harding B20-252 • 274

John Bull's Nothing More (One night my thoughts they wander'd, and then to mend the scene) BOD Harding B11-1906

John Groves, a Poor Labourer, of Ferrybridge in Yorkshire, Who Destroyed Himself and His Three Starving Children BL 1880 c20 1-272 PR • 373

... John Taylor, Cotton Spinner ... , Being out of Employ ... (O friend of sinners hear my cry) BOD Johnson-2994 • **387–89**, *503*, 40, 377, 389, 503

Johnny Raw and Polly Clark (One night quite bang up to the mark) Madden 1789-421 471

Jolly Old Farmer (A jolly old farmer once soaking his clay) Madden 1802-533 • *237*, 226, 237, 257
> AT: The Generous Farmer and Poor Soldier

Jolly Thrasherman (A jolly old thrasherman lived by the seaside) BL 11621 k4-56

Jone o' Grinfield (I'm a poor cotton weaver as many one knows) Vicinus-34
> AT: Joan o' Grinfield!; The Poor Cotton Weaver

Jone o' Grinfilt (Says Jone to his wife on a wet summer's day) BOD Harding B16-118a • 386–87

Jordan (I look'd in the east, I look'd in the west) BOD Harding B15-153b

Joyful News for the Poor, or, the Wonders of the New Year (Ye grumblers and growlers attend and give ear) NOR Samuel Lane Collection • *59–60,* 59–60

The Joys of an Englishman's Life (Many assert, but I ne'er heed 'em) BOD Harding B11-1942

Judge Not a Man by the Coat that He Wears (Judge not a man by the cost of his clothing) BOD Harding B15-154b • 237

The Judicious Poet (A poet there was, and he lived in a garret) BL 1163 a19-9

Justice in England (This is a free and happy land) BOD Harding B20-84

Just-Starve-Us (Hear, oh, hear us, our parish king) Madden 1801-199 • *213–14*, 213

The Keelman's Complaint (Come all you brave fellows that belong to the coal trade) BOD Harding B25-1019 • 140

The Keelmen's Lament for the Frost (Come all ye brave tradesmen) BOD Harding B25-1020

Kind Old Daddy O! (If you want a cheap lodging) Madden 1792-816 • **189–90**, 28, 39, 78, 190–94, 260

Kind Relations (We have all our shares of ups and downs) Madden 1799-1062 • 236–37

King & People (Each Briton awhile come listen to me) St. Bride SS (The Boroughmongers' Defeat)

The King of the British People, or the Boroughmongers Purge (O have you heard the doleful fate) BOD Firth C16-426

The King of the Factory Children (Friends, stop and listen unto me) BL 1876 d41 1-97 • 399

King William IV and His Ministers Forever (You heroes of England) BOD Firth C16-32

The Kingdoms Complaint (Has there not been a sad to do) Madden 1792-196 • 209

The Knife Grinder (There's grinders enough, Sir, in every degree) Madden 1788-529

The Labourer (A poor, unprotected, and fatherless boy) Madden 1788-142

The Labourer's Horizon at Sunrise (How pure the air, how sweet the breeze) BOD Harding B11-2016 • **140–42**, 61, 139, 142, 335, 504

The Labourer's Return to His Family (Now, wife and children, let's be gay) Madden 1803-50 • *138*, 138, 502

The Labourer's Welcome Home (The ploughman whistles o'er the furrow) Madden 1791-429 • 305, 502

The Labouring Man (You Englishmen of each degree) Madden 1792-959

The Labouring Man and His Wife (Good people of England wherever you be) Madden 1795-168

Ladies, Don't Go Thieving (O don't we live in curious times) Henderson-46 • 149

Ladies Don't Go Thieving! (What funny times we see) BOD Firth B25-557 • 149
    AT: Rich & Poor Law!

The Lady and the Welsh Ploughboy (All in the month of May) BOD Harding B20-86; BOD Harding B11-2036 • **440–42**, 414–15, 442–45

The Lady and Weaver (It's of a rich merchant near London did dwell) BOD Harding B11-3981 • 411

The Lady Lov'd Her Father's Groom (Come all you buxom men and maids) Madden 1795-128 • 411, 444

Lady Who Fell in Love with a Prentice Boy (Down in Cupid's garden for pleasure I did walk) BOD Harding B16-124a • 411, 444

A Lady's Love and Loyalty for her Sweetheart (Come all you loyal lovers, I hope you will draw near) Madden 1799-666 • 444

The Lady's Loyalty to her Bonny Labouring Boy (As I roved out one evening being in the blooming spring) BL LR271 a2 3-131 • 411

Lament of Charlotte Mills (Ye British maids pray lend an ear) BOD Firth C17-44

Lament of Two Stocking Makers from Nottingham (Pardon our visit to this place) BOD Harding B20-89

Lamentation of Poor Mechanics (Ye British sons of freedom) Madden 1790-396

The Lamentation of Sarah Bursnell . . . (All you that fear the Lord, who rules the skies) BOD Harding B1-26 • *302*, 40, 302, 481

Lamentation of the Smugglers (Forced from home and all its pleasures) Madden 1803-339

Lancashire Dick (It's now for a new song, gentlemen all) BL LR271 a2 7-251
    AT: Yorkshire Dick

The Lancashire Emigrant's Farewell (Farewell, parents, we must leave you) BOD Harding B11-2050 • *379*, 379

Lancashire Tragedy (All you that have feeling hearts wherever that you be) BOD 2806 c17-214 • 332
    AT: Poverty No Crime (with some differences)

The Landowners Thrown Overboard (Well done Robert Peel! You may say what you will) UL 6-613

A Large Loaf for Sixpence (You poor of old England) BL 11602 gg30-2

Larry O'Broom (I am a poor weaver that's out of employ) BOD Harding B28-45

The Lary Man (Of ups and downs I've felt the shock) BOD Harding B11-2065

The Lass with her Jet-Braided Hair (As I roamed out one morning quite early) Madden 1794~54

The Last Farewell to Poor St. Giles's (Oh! here's a pretty go) BOD Harding B13-283 • **519–22**, 33, 503, 522–23

The Last New Act of Parliament (Now is there not a piece of work throughout the British nation) Madden 1802-178

The Last Shilling (As pensive one night in my garret I sat) BOD Harding B16-127c • 305
    AT: The Poet's Last Shilling

The Last Sorrowful Lamentation of a Boy under Twelve Years of Age (All tender mothers lend an ear); extracted from next item • **338**, 334, 336, 339–43, 539–40, 541, 551 n. 21

The Last Sorrowful Lamentation of 15 Young Men Now Lying in Newgate Under Sentence of Death . . . (All tender mothers lend an ear) BL 1880 c20 2-395

A Laughable & Interesting Dialogue Between Joan o' Greenfield, Nosey and Earl Grey (Come Britons all rejoice and sing) Vicinus-35 • 552

A Laughable and Interesting Picture of Drunkenness (What a cry in this country about the free trade) Madden 1799-1103 • 465

Lay of the Lash (Why should the soldier or sailor—back stripped) BOD Harding B11-2093 • **149–50**, 150–52

Lazy Society (Oh, this world is so hard to get through) BOD Harding B11-1544

Leicester Stocking Weaver's Complaint (No wail of woe, or deep distress) BOD Harding B25-1092

Let Us All Be Unhappy Together (Poor people, deficient of food) Madden 1796-86 • **101–2**, 102
    AT: A New Song Called a Touch of the Times

Let Us Go Cadging Together (Come let us go cadging together) Madden 1802-62 • 301

The Life and Awful Death of a Rich Miser (This farmer had ten thousand pounds in store) BL 1875 d13-123 • 201

Life and Confessions of the Poor Orphan Sweep (O, when a boy just four years old) Madden 1797-402

Life in London: or, the Sprees of Tom and Jerry; Attempted in Cuts and Verse: overall title for sheet on which appear "Beggars Opera—Tom, Jerry & Logick Among the Cadgers in the Holy Land" and "Song of the Cadgers in the Holy Land": St. Bride LS • **506–8**, *56–57*, 63, 72, 310, 508–9

Life of a Cadger (I am a known cadger as ever tramp'd the town) BOD Harding B11-2122
    AT: The Manchester Cadger • *302*, 269, 301–2

Life of a Vagabond (How gaily and how merrily my life has pass'd along) Madden 1792-219 • 301

The Life of a Working Man (Come one and all and list to these lines) Madden 1792-825

The Life of an Honest Ploughman (Come all you jolly husbandmen, and listen to my song

TITLE LIST 593

/ Good people give attention and listen to my song) Madden 1794-343; Madden 1797-539 • 52
    AT: The Honest Ploughman
Lines by a Chartist (In one thousand and eight hundred and thirty and nine) BOD Harding B11-2137 • 550
Lines on the Corn Bill (When on these lands, which now are let so high) BOD Harding B25-420; UL 5-482 (4) • **97–99**, *22, 64*, 39, 40, 64, 88, 99–101, 140, 481
Lines on the Death of a Most Cruel, Hard-Hearted Overseer of the Poor (In this county, as I've been told) BOD Firth C16-309
    AT: A Copy of Verses on the Life and Death . . .
Lines on the Death of an Old Pauper (Oh! Englishmen, come drop a tear or two) CUR-89
Lines on the Factory System (Come all you master-spinners dear) "Oastler and the Factory Movement" UL-557 (3) • 276
Lines on the Unemployed and the Terrible Distress (Thousands in England are starving) BOD Johnson-1178
Lines Written on the Cover of an Old Bible (This is my never failing bank) BOD Harding B11-2146 • *238*, 238, 504
The Literary Dustman (Some folks may boast of sense, egad) Madden 1794-467
Little Anne and Her Mother (Little Anne and her mother were walking one day) BOD Johnson-1548 • *238*, 237
Little Bess the Ballad Singer (When first a babe upon the knee) St. Bride SS
The Little Chimney-Sweep ('Twas a keen frosty morn, and the snow heavy falling) BOD Harding B10-70; Madden 1796-228 • *320*, 319, 320, 323
    AT: Poor Little Sweep
Little Jessey, the Poor Flower Maid (I am poor little Jessey, I'm come here to shew) Madden 1791-181 • **322**, 319, 322–23, 493
    AT: Poor Little Jessy
Little Jim, the Collier Boy (The cottage was a thatched one) Madden 1792-828
    AT: Poor Jim the Collier Lad
Little Joe, the Chimney Sweeper (They call me little Joe, sir) St. Bride SS
    AT: Chimney Sweep
The Little Sailor Boy (The bitter wind blew keen and cold) Madden 1797-860
    AT: The Poor Little Sailor Boy; The Sailor Boy
The Little Shoeblack (As I walk'd slowly down the street a few days ago) BOD Firth B28-18
The Little Sweep (The morn was dark, the hour was four and heavy fell the snow) BOD Harding B11-598
The Little Town's Boy (One cold winter's evening the stormy winds did blow) Madden 1791-43
    AT: Old England Is Going Down the Hill
Live and Let Live (Live and let live is the first law of nature) Madden 1802-169 • 237
London Kate (In the city of London there lived of late) BL 11606 aa24-83
The London Newsboy (The night air is chill, the snow is fast falling) BOD Harding B11-2189 • *319*, 319

Look at Home Boys (Mankind is censorious and apt to condemn) BOD Harding B15-174a

The Loom and the Lathe (Like most other men who've been knocking about) BOD Harding B11-3578

Love and Liver (My toggery I took out of pawn) Madden 1791-374 • **458–59**, 459
> AT: Go It Neddy

Love & Poverty (I've seen life in pleasure, I've seen life in sorrow) BOD Harding B11-3255 • 236

The Lovers Discussion (One pleasant evening when pinks and daisies) BOD Firth C18-202

The Luck of a Cove Wot Sings (No doubt a song you've heard) BOD Firth C21-6
> AT: The Cove Wot Sings

The Lucky Factory Boy (The sun had set beyond yon hill) BOD Harding B11-2414 • **402–3**, 403

The Lucky Farmer's Boy (The sun had set behind the hill) Madden 1803-435 • *403*, 403
> AT: The Farmer's Boy

The Lucky Footman! (Come all you ladies list to me) Madden 1795-140

The Man That Has Seen Better Days (No doubt you all wonder what this object is) BOD Johnson-1624 • 354

The Man Who Wished He'd Never Got Married (Once I was a bachelor bold) Madden 1792-621 • 456, 475

The Managers Last Kick, or, the Distruction of the Boroughmongers (Come Britons, here's a huzza) BL N Tab 2021/28-14

Manchester at Twelve O'Clock (In Manchester at dinner time) Madden 1799-486 • 525

The Manchester Cadger (I am a cunning cadger as ever tramped the town) BOD Harding B11-2304 • *302*, 301–2
> AT: Life of a Cadger

The Manchester Cotton Spinner's Petition (We cotton spinners of Manchester) Madden 1799-516 • 377–78, 377

The Market Basket ('Twas Saturday night—the busy streets) BL 11621 h11 4-37

Marriage of the Blooming Lady and the Groom (There was a beauty bright) CUR-132 • 444

Marsh-Gate Costermonger (Joe was a Marsh-Gate costermonger) BOD Harding B15-185a • 362

Mary and the Handsome Factory Boy (You constant lovers give attention) BL 1876 d41 2.1-711 • 403
> AT: The Farmer's Daughter and the Gay Plough Boy; Rosetta and Her Gay Ploughboy

Mary Ann and Her Servant Man (It's of a damsel both fair and handsome) BOD Harding B11-2339

Mary of the Lowly Cot (The lark melodious sung above) BOD Harding B16-144b • 433

The Match Boy (Would you think that I who's now so grand) Madden 1797-84 • *321*, 321

The Match Boy (Ye wealthy and proud, while in splendour you roll) BOD Harding B15-193a • *321*, 321

The Match Song (Come buy my deal matches, come buy of me) Madden 1789-1112 • **320–21**, 320, 321

Matrimonial Miseries (Some married men boast of their true happy state) Madden 1794-477 • *479*, 479

The Mechanic's Appeal to the Public (Give attention awhile to my rhyme) BL 1876 d41 2.2-1334

The Mechanic's Boy ('Twas in the autumn of the year, the evening it was fine) BOD Johnson-3111

The Mechanic's Lamentation (All you that have a feeling heart, come listen unto me) Madden 1803-377 • 109

    AT: The Clothiers' Lamentation on the Badness of Trade; The Mechanic's Lamentation on the Stagnation of Trade

Mechanics' Lamentation (Come listen, dear neighbours, to these lines which I've made) BOD Johnson-2671 • *109, 377,* 109, 377

    AT: Spinner's Lamentation

The Mechanic's Lamentation on the Stagnation of Trade (All you who have got ears to hear, come listen unto me) BOD 2806 c17-267 • **108–9**, *377,* 109, 377

    AT: The Clothiers' Lamentation on the Badness of Trade; The Mechanic's Lamentation

The Medley Song (If you'll lend me your attention, I will return to you) Madden 1802-183

The Meeting at Peterloo (Come lend an ear of pity while I my tale do tell) BOD Johnson-2673 • 550

Meeting of Parliament or Future Prospects in 1847 (Now Parliament again has met) BOD Harding B14-310

Melancholy Death of Five Poor Distressed Hay Makers (O listen to a tale of woe) St. Bride SS • 247–48

The Merry Haymakers (In the merry month of June) Madden 1789-1114

Merry Little Grey Fat Man (There's a little man dressed all in grey) BOD 2806 d31-29

The Merry Will & Testament of Master Black Billy (I Master William Waters, O) BL 1875 d7-15 • **308–9**, 33, 309–11, 508, 522

The Middleton Overseer (There was a noble overseer, as crafty as a mouse sir) Harland-196 • 281

    AT: The Overseer; The Overseer and the Madman; The Overseer Outwitted

Milkmaid of Blackberry Fold (It's of a rich squire in Bristol doth dwell) Madden 1803-300 • 46, 420

    AT: Squire and Milkmaid; Young Squire

The Mill (The Mill—the Mill—the Brixton treading-mill) Madden 1794-208 • **343–44**, 77, 344–46

    AT: Brixton Treading-Mill; The Treading Mill

The Miners' Binding (It happen'd on March the twenty-third day) BOD Harding B25-1255

The Miners' Complaint (You miners all attend to these lines that I have penn'd) BOD Harding B11-2427

Minstrel Girl ('Twas in the month of last December) BL LR271 a2 2-26

The Miseries of Living up Five Pairs of Stairs (Such a thing as true bliss in this life is a bubble) Madden 1795-638

Miseries of the Framework-Knitters (Ye kind-hearted souls pray attend to our song) Madden 1801-72

The Miser's Man (Oh, dear, these are shocking hard times) BOD Harding B11-2436

The Model (My friend is the man I would copy thro' life) Madden 1804-60

The Model Workhouse Master! (Come all you females pay attention) BOD Harding B13-111 • **181–82**, 72, 182–89, 260

Money is Your Friend (Of friendship I have heard much talk) Madden 1791-265 • *235*, 235

Monmouth Street (Oh there's a place in London town) BOD Harding B11-3003 • **514–16**, 36, 236, 503, 512, 516–17

A Monstrous Good Song (Good people attend here awhile to my song) BL 11606 aa23-85

Most Humorous Description of Irish Paddy's Wedding (There was a wedding held of late) St. Bride SS • 514

Mrs. Jenkins, of Billingsgate ('Twas on Good Friday eve, the neighbours all state) BOD Harding B15-208b

Mrs. Johnson (Oh, I have got a charming bride) Madden 1804-493; Madden 1791-206 • **466–67**, 467–68, 512

Mrs. Lobsky's Rout (Mrs. Lobsky sold sprats and shrimps they say) BL 11602 g28 1-56 (unnumbered) • 514

Mrs. Money's Departure (O what a strange oration in every place we hear) BOD Harding B12-152 • *91*, 91

Murder at Cambridge (In the quiet town of Cambridge a deed has been done) BOD Firth C17-185 • 414

Murder of a Child Near Measham (Attend you feeling Christians all) BOD Firth C17-93 • 163

My Bonny Labouring Boy (As I roved out one morning, being in the blooming spring) Madden 1790-262
    AT: Bonny Labouring Boy

My Grandfather's Days (Give attention to my ditty and I will not keep you long) Palmer TT-83 • *257*, 52, 257

My Grandmother's Days (Attention pay to what I say, I'll not detain you long) Madden 1797-28

My Husband was a Good for Nothing Man (When I was gay and keen, and aged seventeen) Madden 1793-860 • 457

My Master and I (Says master to me, is it true? I am told) BOD Harding B11-2566

My Old Hat (I am a poor old man, in years, come listen to my song) Madden 1801-453
    AT: Old Hat; When My Old Hat Was New; When This Old Hat Was New

My Uncle is a Most Kind-Hearted Man (You have heard of my grandfather— wonderful man!) BL 1876 d41 2.1-748 • 216

My Uncle's Card (Oh dear! what a crime it's thought) BOD Harding B11-2588 • 216

My Wife's First Baby (The other night as I lay on my bed) Madden 1795-375 • **475–76**, 477

Naked Truth (Tax-gatherers now how thick they swarm) BL 1876 d41 2.2-1377 • **399–401**, *64*, 40, 64, 226, 401–2
    AT: The Times

Natty Sam (A tinker I am) St. Bride SS

Navvy on the Line (I am a navvy bold, that has tramp'd the country round sir) Madden 1799-1107

The Neat Little Cottage with Ground for its Floor (I've lived in the woods for many a year) Madden 1803-241
    AT: Ground for the Floor

The Needle Makers Lamentation of Redditch, Worcestershire (Good people all attend awhile) BOD Harding B13-290 • 377

Never Dull Care (Why should we at our lot repine) Madden 1799-327

Never Mind What You Do for a Living (I've lived a few years in this valley of tears) BOD Firth C16-251

A New Alphabetical Song on the Corn Law Bill (Good people draw near as you pass along) Ashton-322

A New Batch of Ballads (Childhood's days now pass before me) BL 11621 h11 8-109 • 494

New Building Act (Oh dear! oh lacks it is a fact) Madden 1792-267

The New Coal Act (See how the people thro' the streets) BOD Harding B14-311

A New Comic Song of Dudley Street (There's a spot in Birmingham town) Madden 1802-526 • *517*, 517

New Dialogue and Song on the Times (You working men of England one moment now attend) Madden 1799-1042

The New Fashioned Farmer (Good people all attend awhile) Madden 1801-454 • 226

The New Gipsy Laddy (Of a rich young lady I'm going to tell) BOD Harding B11-2646

The New Gruel Shops (Good people all I pray draw near that in this country dwell) Madden 1798-406

A New Hunting Song (Now those that are low spirited I hope won't think it wrong) BL C116 il-146

A New Hymn Composed on a Factory Boy & Girl Who were Found Drowned in the River Aire (With purest love Joe Bolland's heart) BL 1876 d41 1-444

A New Litany on the People's Rights BOD Firth C16-221 PR

A New National Song, for the Wise, the Bold, and the Brave, Dedicated to the Oppressed and Starving People of this Country (Ye slaves who are treated like beasts) BL N Tab 2021 / 28-7 • 208

The New Overseer (Some people are always contending) Madden 1803-161
    AT: The Overseer; The Union Overseer

The New Parliament: or, the House Turned Upside Down! (Englishmen give ear to me) Madden 1794-188

A New Political & Reform Alphabet (A stands for Aristocrat, who nothing will do) BOD Harding B14-351 • 274

A New Political Form of Matrimony BOD Harding B13-121 PR

The New Poor Law and the Farmer's Glory (I was forced as a stranger to wander from home) BL LR271 a2 1.2-52 • **163–64**, *22–23, 370, 505*, 24, 28, 40, 77, 88, 139, 164–65, 370, 505

The New Poor Law Bill (There is a sighing o'er the land, a voice upon the wind) BOD Johnson-1529

The New Poor Law Bill in Force (All round the country there is a pretty piece of work) BOD Johnson-1148

New Rigs of the Races! (See the ladies how they strut along) Madden 1794-97 • 440

The New Social & Political Alphabet (I am going to sing a ditty upon the present time) BOD Harding B14-352

A New Song (Come all you canny pitmen here come listen to my song) Madden 1797-777

A New Song (Come all you jolly labourers) St. Bride SS

New Song (Come Britons, strike boldly, weather the storm) Madden 1795-312

A New Song (Come, friends and voters, let's consent) Madden 1795-313

A New Song (Come listen awhile I will tell you the rigs) BL 1876 e3-255

A New Song (What a pother in this land about our French neighbours) BL 835 M10-13 • 138

A New Song and Dialogue on the Opening of the Ports (Come listen awhile to my song) BOD Harding B14-313; some difference from next item • 129

A New Song & Dialogue on the Times (Come listen awhile to my song) BL 1876 d41 1-604; some differences from preceding item • **126–28**, 128–30

A New Song Called a Touch of the Times (Poor people, deficient of food) Madden 1802-355 • 102

    AT: Let us All Be Unhappy Together

A New Song, Called Jone o' Greenfield's Lamentation, or the Unfortunate Poverty Knockers (Ses Jone eawt o' Grinfilt au tell thee wot Nan) BOD 2806 c17-199 • 552

A New Song Called Little England (You poor of old England give ear and attend) BOD Harding B25-1119 • 105

A New Song Called Pills of Parliament (Ye sons of Briton lend an ear) BOD 2806 c13-279

A New Song, Called the Golden Act (What confusion this act has made) St. Bride SS

A New Song Called the Hiring Day (Come all you young men and maidens so gay) Madden 1803-470

A New Song, Call'd the Red Whig (You good folks of Nottingham I would have you draw near) Pinto-45

A New Song Called the "Turncoat" (What news today? Why, one maintains) Madden 1803-332

A New Song, Called Times as They Are (Ye tradesmen of the nation, I am sorry it is true) BOD Harding B11-1192

A New Song in Favour / Praise of Her Majesty, Queen Victoria (Welcome now Victoria!) Madden 1802-594; Madden 1804-498

    AT: Queen Victoria

The New Song of Buy a Broom (Buy a broom! buy a broom! buy a broom!) Madden 1803-474

    AT: Buy a Broom

A New Song of Songs (I'm going to sing a song, as well as I can do) BOD Harding B11-2672

A New Song on Reform (Oh! Reform now it is the rage) BOD 2806 c14-58

A New Song on Stanley's Corn Bill (Lord Derby's got a new corn bill) Madden 1799-1236

A New Song on the Alteration of the Times (His faithful subject Martha Bird) St. Bride SS • 257

A New Song on the Bread Act (Attention awhile to my song) St. Bride SS (The New Baker's Act)

A New Song on the Corn Bill (Hurrah, my boys, a bumper fill) Ashton-327

A New Song on the Coronation (Come women all of Britain's isle) BOD Firth C16-429

A New Song on the Disagreeable Confusion Which Took Place on the Otmoor Inclosure ('Twas on the 6th of September, that glorious day) Madden 1800-204 • 551

A New Song on the Emancipation Bill for Debtors (To the bum crushers truck you must tumble) BOD Firth C16-31

A New Song on the Glorious Victory Over the Boroughmongers (Rejoice, rejoice, Britannia's sons, while I do sing a song) Madden 1803-478 • 41, 113

A New Song on the Hard Times (Come all bad husbands, I'd have you be wise) Madden 1787-1382
A New Song on the Hard Times (Come all you bold Britons give ear to my song) Madden 1789-20 • *99*, 99
A New Song on the Hiring of the Servants (You young men and maidens draw near for a while) BOD Johnson-3065
A New Song on the Hirings (You servant lads and lasses, come listen for a while) Madden 1798-390
A New Song on the Jubilee (Come all ye Britons, bold and free) BOD Harding B16-169b • *95*
A New Song on the Present Times (Now Britons rejoice at the tidings you hear) BOD Harding B22-119
A New Song on the Preston Tyranny (We are going to sing a song) Madden 1799-1304 • *196*, 196
A New Song on the Reduction of the Colliers' Wages (Come all ye jolly colliers, and colliers' wives as well) BL 11621 h11 3-162
A New Song on the Repeal of the Corn Laws (Come every heart rejoice with me) Madden 1799-973 • 130
A New Song on the Times (As strikes have become the order of the day) Madden 1799-1289
A New Song on the Times (Come old and young and rich and poor) Madden 1795-717 • 234
A New Song on the Times (Good people all I pray draw near) Madden 1799-1061
A New Song on the Times (The Mounseers, they say, have the world in a string) BL 835 m10-11 • 138
A New Song on the Times (You British subjects now attend) Madden 1790-28 • *105*, 105
    AT: The Times; A True Statement of the Present Times
A New Song on the Times (You gentleman all I understand) Madden 1789-21 • *105*, 105
A New Song on the Times (Ye gentlemen of England I pray you lend an ear) BOD Harding B25-1360 • *97*, 97, 140
A New Song on the Times or the Mystery of the Large Loaf Reduced Small, Explained (Come, come brother freeman let's hasten away) BL 11602 gg30-2
A New Song on the Whig Poor Laws (Come listen a while and I'll sing you a song) Madden 1797-659
A New Song, or a Word of Advice to Servants (You servant lads and lasses come listen to my ditty) Madden 1798-41
A New Song Written on the State of the Times (As old trade and commerce were conversing on the present times) Madden 1791-6
The New Spinning Wheel (One summer's morning as Nancy fair) Madden 1788-555
    AT: The Spinning-Wheel
The New Starvation Law Examined (Come you men and women unto me attend) Vicinus-49 • 276
A New Statutes Song (And now the ——— Statutes is come again) Madden 1795-35
The New Times (Ye working men where e'er ye dwell) BOD Harding B11-2690 • 481
The New Times (You Britons all attention give, and listen to my rhymes) Madden 1794-190

The New Times (You lads and lasses give ear to my song) Madden 1800-158 • 257

New Touch on the Times (You gentlemen and ladies, I pray lend an ear) Madden 1797-428 • 140

A New Touch on the Times; or, the Comforts of the Labouring Poor (Come you hardworking people attend to my rhymes) BL 1875 d6-16

A New Way for Paying the Taxes . . . (Draw near awhile and listen to me) Madden 1798-361

The New Way of the Blind Boy (I'm now depriv'd of the light) BL 11606 aa23-90

New Way to Make a Good Husband (Attend ye married women while I tell you a plan) Madden 1795-495 • 457

The Newcastle Swineherds Proclamation (O yes! Ye swinish multitude) BL 1875 d13-102 • *111,* 111–12, 140

A Night in a London Workhouse (All you that dwell in Lambeth, listen for a while) BOD Harding B13-154 • 193

A Night's Repose in Lambeth Workhouse (Come listen to me one and all) BOD Harding B13-155 • 193

Nix My Dolly, Pals, Fake Away (In a box of the stone jug I was born) BOD Harding B11-430 • 43

No More Shall the Chummies (No more shall the chummies bawl out sweep) Madden 1802-547

The North Briton, or, Economy (These, these, are the rigs of the times) Madden 1787-1433

The Nosegay Girl (Sweet nosegays come buy my sweet nosegays / Thro' the town or village gay) BL 1875 b19-42; Madden 1803-167 • *320,* 320

Not a Trap was Heard (Not a trap was heard, or a Charley's not) BOD Harding B16-174a • 393

O Broker Spare That Bed! (O, broker spare that bed, touch not a single screw) BOD Harding B11-716

    AT: Broker Spare That Bed

O Gracious God! (Oh! Gracious God, extend thy helping hand) BOD Harding B20-89

Oastler is Free (Exalt your voices high) UL 6-609 (2)

Oastler is Welcome (You sons of Labour pay attention) UL 6-609 (1)

The Odd Fellows Benefit (In all combined societies in England all around) BOD Harding B11-2770

The Odd Fellow's Home (The night of affliction had darken'd my cot) Madden 1801-220

Odd Matters (Oh I will get wed in a trice) BOD Harding B16-179b

Odds and Ends of the Year 1830 (Come hither a while, I'll sing you a song) Madden 1804-276 • 550

Oh, Ain't I Nuts on Sarah (One evening, going thro' the market place) BOD Harding B11-2736 • **448–49,** 449

Oh Dear, How I Long to Get Married! (I am a damsel so blooming and gay) Madden 1798-287 • *452–53,* 452

Oh, What a Stagnation in Trade (First listen and I'll be bound) Madden 1798-380

Old Adam Was a Gentleman (Old Adam was the first man, that everybody knows) Madden 1799-551 • *258,* 257–58

Old Ben Lowe (Kind friends excuse my asking) BOD Firth C18-266

    AT: Ben Low; Poor Ben Low

TITLE LIST 601

Old England For Ever Shall Weather the Storm (Old England, thy stamina never has yielded) Madden 1799-775
    AT: Old England Shall Weather the Storm

Old England is Going Down the Hill (We talk of England's greatness) BOD Johnson-1228 • *258–59*, 258

Old England is Going Down the Hill (One cold winter's evening the stormy winds did blow) Madden 1792-287
    AT: The Little Town's Boy

Old England Shall Weather the Storm (Old England, thy stamina never has yielded) Madden 1793-453 • *258*, 258
    AT: Old England Forever Shall Weather the Storm

Old England What Have You Come To (One cold winters morning as the day was dawning) Madden 1792-278

Old England's Brightest Ornament is the Honest Working Man! (One night at sea while perusing) BOD Firth C16-237

The Old English Gentleman (I'll sing you a good old song, made by a good old pate) Madden 1803-492 • 216
    AT: The Fine Old English Gentleman

The Old English Lady (I'll sing you a good old chant, since now 'tis so much the rage) BL 1876 d41 2.1-713 • 218

Old Hat (I am a poor old man in years, come listen to my song) BOD Harding B22-228
    AT: My Old Hat; When My Old Hat Was New; When This Old Hat Was New

Old John Bull Kicking Up Behind and Before (Old John Bull went to Britannia's gate) BOD Harding B14-317

Old Weaver's Daughter (As I walk'd out one sweet May morn) Madden 1799-726
    AT: The Weaver's Daughter

Old Woman of Rumford (There was an old woman of Rumford) BOD Harding B16-186c
    AT: Artichokes & Cauliflowers • 437

The Old Woman's Wish (As I walked by an hospital gate) Madden 1802-206 • *453*, 453

Oldham Workshops (When I'd finished off my work last Saturday at neet) BOD Firth C16-255

On the Times, Corn Bill, Paper Money, and Trade (In war time when banks left off paying in cash) UL 5-482 (5)

Once All Things Went Glad and Joyful (Once all things went glad and joyful) BL 1876 d41 2.2-1346

One God Has Made Us All (Come all you worthy Christians) Madden 1799-1128
    AT: Job, the Patient Man; Poverty and Contentment

One Pound One (You married people high and low) Madden 1797-492 • 251
    AT: The Contented Wife and Her Satisfied Husband; The Pleasing Wife and Satisfied Husband

One Pound Two (Now Maggie dear, I do hear, you have been upon the spree) Madden 1797-521 • 251

One Suit Between Two (All you who are reduced and wish to cut a shine) BOD Harding B11-2858 • 236

Open the Ports (To list a while you can't refuse) Madden 1800-151

Opening of the Ports (Men, women and children come listen to my story) Madden 1799-1045 • 41

The Opinions of an Honest Working Man (I stood beside a factory where) BOD Firth C16-412

The Oppressed Englishman's Catechism, or the Poor Man's Dialogue BOD Firth C16-188 PR

The Orphan Boy (Stay lady—stay, for mercy's sake) Madden 1789-1163
    AT: The Orphan Boy's Tale

The Orphan Boy (Tell me little wanderer, why) BOD Harding B25-1425

Orphan Boy's Prayer / Tale (One fine summer's eve, as I careless was straying) BOD Harding B11-1944; BOD Harding B11-872

The Orphan Child (The night was dark as I did ramble) Madden 1794-106; Madden 1795-680 • 47, 49

The Orphan Drummer Boy (It was in a country village, by a neat little cottage) Madden 1803-492

The Orphan Factory Boy (My parents dear I miss them) BOD Harding B11-2874

The Orphan Girl (An hapless orphan girl am I) BOD 2806 c18-226

The Orphan Girl (An orphan once in doleful plaint) BL 1875 bl9-42

The Orphan Girl (I am a poor maiden, distressed and forlorn) Madden 1788-666

The Orphan Girl (If pity, sweet maid, ever dwelt in thy breast) Madden 1788-189
    AT: The Orphan, Wet with Rain

The Orphan in Distress (The thunder roars loudly, the wind howls around me) BOD Harding B16-192b

The Orphan Shepherd Boy (Poor Lubin was an orphan boy) BOD Johnson-1744

The Orphan, Wet with Rain (If pity sweet maid ever dwelt in thy breast) Madden 1789-1167
    AT: The Orphan Girl

The Orphans (My chaise the village inn did gain) Madden 1801-62
    AT: A Copy of Verses Written by a Lady; The Two Orphans; Two Orphans at Their Mother's Grave

The Orphan's Lament (Child, is thy father dead?) Madden 1791-484

The Orphan's Prayer (The frozen streets in moonshine glitter) BOD Harding B25-1430

Our New Queen, the Flower of England (Come all you bold Britons and list to my rhymes) Madden 1794-316 • *123*, 122

Out in the Cold (Gazing on noblemen's mansions) BOD Harding B11-2884

Out in the Cold (With blue cold hands and stockingless feet) BOD Harding B11-2882

Out in the Streets! (Out in the streets, forsaken, alone) BOD Harding B11-2885

The Overseer (Some people are always contending) Madden 1803-638
    AT: The New Overseer; The Union Overseer

The Overseer / The Overseer and the Madman / The Overseer Outwitted (There was a noble overseer, as crafty as a mouse sir) Madden 1803-496; BOD Harding B11-1440; Madden 1791-488 • 214
    AT: The Middleton Overseer

Owdham Streets at Dinner Time (In Owdham streets at dinner time) BOD Harding B16-194b • **523–24**, 503, 524–25

Paddy Magee's Dream (John Bull he was an Englishman, he went on the tramp one day) BOD Harding B11-2917

The Parish Pays the Piper (Good morning Mr. Grasp) BOD Harding B11-3339
    AT: The Rose-Water Select

Parson Brown's Sheep / Parson, Molly and Sheep (Not long ago, in our town) BOD Harding B11-2952; BL 1875 b19-100; BOD Firth C16-359 • **354–56**, 356–57

Past, Present and Future (Good people give attention, who now around do stand) Madden 1794-417 • *47*, 47, 48, 49

Patent Bread, or a New Plan for Lowering the Price of Grain (This well may be called a wonderful age) BOD Harding B16-200a • **260–62**, 93, 262

Patient Joe; or the Newcastle Collier (Have you heard of a collier of honest renown) BOD Harding B11-2963 • *503*, 503

Pauper and the Minister (I'm living on the parish now as happy as a king) BOD Firth C16-316

The Pauper's Child (A poor child in grief was weeping) Madden 1792-821 • *320*, 306, 320

The Pauper's Drive (There's a grim one-horse hearse in a jolly round trot) Thomas Noel, *Rymes and Roundelayes*; BL 11621 h11 2-26 • **311–12**, 43, 69, 312–13

The Pawn Shop (A song I'm going to sing you, & presently will bring you) BOD 2806 c17-328
    AT: Pawnbroker's Shop; A Pawnbroker's Shop on a Saturday Night

The Pawnbroker ('Twas on Saint Monday morning cross Mother Bung was snarling) BOD Harding B11-2977

Pawnbroker's Shop / A Pawnbroker's Shop on a Saturday Night (A song I am going to sing you and presently I shall bring you) Madden 1801-457; Madden 1793-11 • *216*, 216, 431
    AT: The Pawn Shop

The Pawnbroker's Shop (A song I will recite to you, I hope it will delight you) Madden 1804-736 • *216*, 216

Peace and Plenty, Love and Liberty (Arise, ye sons of freedom, and burst your galling chain) BOD Harding B11-2980

Peel's Income Tax, or a Miss at Popularity (Ye political critics who pore o'er the news) UL 6-602 (1)

Peggy Bann (One dark rainy night as I walk'd thro' the street) BL 1876 e3-191

The Penny and the Bob (No matter what your means may be) BOD Harding B11-2332

A Pen'orth of Irish Stew (Old John Bull was a farmer and well known among his neighbours) BOD Johnson-1528

Pensioner's Complaint / The Pensioner's Complaint Against His Wife (You neighbours all listen, a story I'll tell) Madden 1792-715 • 456

The People's Anthem (Lord, from thy blessed throne) BOD Johnson-1472

The People's Comic Alphabet (A stands for alphabet, I've turned it into rhyme) Palmer TT-270

People's Litany on Land and Labour BOD Firth C16-220 PR

Peterloo (See see where freedom's noblest champion stands) Madden 1799-738 • 336

Petition from the Working People to the King BL 1875 b19-108 PR • 247–48

The Picture of England ('Tis myself dat was born now in Dublin) BOD Harding B11-3008
    AT: The Irishman's Picture of England

The Pitman's Complaint (O Lord hear the poor pitman's cry) Lloyd C-221

The Pitman's Widow's Lament (In the dark gloomy mine) BOD Harding B8-24 • **393–95**, 395–96

Pity (the) Poor Labourers (You sons of old England come list to my rhymes) BL 1875 b19-62 • *376*, 69, 376
    AT: The Poor Labourers

Pity the Farmers, the Broken Down Farmers (In our sweet little villages all through the land) BOD Harding B13-296 • *228*, 228

Pity the Orphan (O winter is set in) Madden 1791-352

Pity the Poor Costermongers (We are in a mess. Oh, Dear! Oh, Dear!) BL 1875 b19-23 • *376–77*, 204, 376

A Plaintive Pastoral (Ye ancient sons of ancient days) Madden 1799-636

A Plan for Alleviating the Price of Coals to the Poor in the Winter Season GU B'side-6.127; others similar: 3.35; 5.43; 6.103; 16.144; 32.43 PR

Please, Give Me a Penny, Sir (Please give me a penny, sir) BOD Harding B11-3774 • 303

The Pleasing Wife and Satisfied Husband (You married people high and low) Madden 1802-372 • 52
    AT: The Contented Wife and Her Satisfied Husband; One Pound One

The Pleasures of a Country Life (How melancholy crows the cock) St. Bride SS

The Plough (Martinmas holidays are short I must say) BOD Johnson-1385

The Ploughman's / Plowman's Ditty (Because I'm but poor) SF D-21; BOD Johnson-2751 • *501*, 501

The Poet's Last Shilling (As pensive one night in my garret I sat) Madden 1799-64
    AT: The Last Shilling

The Poet's Petition (Your friendship I court) BL 1163 a19-96

The Policeman's Pet (That boy? No, he's not mine exactly) BOD Harding B11-3044 • **328–30**, 237, 330–31

A Political Litany and General Supplication BL 1875 b19-63 PR

Political Litany on the Present Times BL 1875 b19-63 PR

A Political Parody on Tubal Cain (Sir Robert Peel was a man of might) Madden 1792-550

Polly Cox's Party (Soon after Polly Cox got wed, to Mr. Wick, lamplighter) BOD Harding B11-3052 • 431, 514

Polly Perkins' Answer (I'm the Polly Perkins that once used to be) BOD Harding B11-3054 • 451

Polly Perkins, of Paddington Green (I'm a brokenhearted milkman, in grief I am arrayed) BOD Harding B11-3384 • **449–50**, 451

Poor Ben Low (Kind friends, excuse me asking) BOD Harding B20-88
    AT: Ben Low; Old Ben Lowe

Poor Blind Boy (A maid with a heart that could feel) BL 11621 k5-279

The Poor Blind Boy (O say! what is that thing called light) St. Bride SS

Poor But Honest Soldier (When th' wars were o'er and peace proclaimed / When wild war's deadly blast was blown, and gentle peace returning) Madden 1793-474; Madden 1789-648

The Poor Charlies Lamentation (O hear the act of Mr. Peel) BOD Harding B13-297

The Poor Cotton Weaver (I'm a poor cotton weaver as many one knows) Woods-256
    AT: Joan o' Grinfield; Jone o' Grinfield
The Poor Discharged Soldier (Gather round me, one an' all, great and small, short and tall) BOD 2806 c13-267 • 303
The Poor Drunkard's Child (In taking my walks on one cold winter's day) Madden 1799-657
    AT: The Drunkard's Child
Poor England in the Year 1811 (Good people what will you of all be bereft) Madden 1803-76 • **95–96**, 96–97
... A Poor Faraway Stranger ... (Behold a stranger as you pass along) Madden 1802-798
The Poor Fisherman's Boy (It was down in the lowlands, a poor boy did wander) Madden 1802-712
    AT: The Fisherman's Boy; The Poor Little Fisherman's Boy
Poor Fisherman's Girl (It was down in the country a poor girl was weeping) Madden 1801-28
    AT: The Fisherman's Girl; Poor Little Fisherman's Girl
Poor Frozen-Out Gardeners (We're brokenhearted gardeners, scarce got a bit of shoe) Palmer TT-230
The Poor Irish Stranger (Pity the fate of a poor Irish Stranger) Madden 1797-234 • 303
    AT: Irish Stranger
Poor Jim the Collier Lad (The cottage was a thatched one) BOD Harding B11-3082
    AT: Little Jim, the Collier Boy
Poor Joe (Weary and worn with a face full of woe) BOD Harding B11-3145
The Poor Labourers (You sons of old England, now list to my rhymes) BOD Firth C16-300
    AT: Pity Poor Labourers
The Poor Law Bastile (Is this that happy England) Madden 1795-27 • *162*, 161
Poor Law Bill! (Let high and low, let old and young give ear unto my ditty) UL 6-579 (1)
The Poor Law Bill in Force (Good people all attend, and listen to my ditty) Madden 1791-632
The Poor Law Catechism CUR-89 PR • *162, 370*, 162, 274, 370
The Poor Law Starvation Act (Pray grant, good sir, some small relief) Madden 1795-640 PR • *223–24*, 223–24
Poor Law Starvation Bill BL 1876 d41 2.2-1374 PR • *162*, 162
Poor Little Child of a Tar (In a little blue garment all ragged and torn) Madden 1788-197
    AT: Child of a Tar • *319, 481*, 42, 69, 235, 319, 323
The Poor Little Fisherman's Boat (One day for recreation, as I left my habitation) Madden 1804-608
The Poor Little Fisherman's Boy (It was down in the lowlands a poor boy did wander) Madden 1793-508
    AT: The Fisherman's Boy; The Poor Fisherman's Boy
The Poor Little Fisherman's Girl (It was down in the country a poor girl was weeping) Madden 1800-78
    AT: The Fisherman's Girl; Poor Fisherman's Girl
The Poor Little Gipsey (A poor little gipsey I wander forlorn) Madden 1789-1177

Poor Little Jessy (I'm poor little Jessy, I'm come here to shew) Madden 1795-413
> AT: Little Jessey, the Poor Flower Maid

Poor Little Joe (Cold, cold was the night, the snow had been falling) BOD Harding B11-54

Poor Little Joe (While strolling one night thro' London's gay throng) BOD Harding B13-226 • *320*, 320

Poor Little Mary Ann, or the Smuggler's Bride (As I was walking one cold frosty morning) Madden 1803-561

The Poor Little Sailor Boy (The bitter wind blew keen and cold) Madden 1799-941 • 319
> AT: The Little Sailor Boy; The Sailor Boy

Poor Little Sweep (On a cold winter's morn as the snow was a falling / 'Twas a keen frosty morn and the snow heavy falling) Madden 1789-656; Madden 1804-282 • *319*
> AT: The Little Chimney-Sweep

The Poor Lost Child Restored to His Mother (The mother mourned her infant lost) BOD Harding B11-3090; BL 1888 c3-112; BL 1870 dl 1-109 • **325–27**, 328, 538

The Poor Man's Companion (You tradesmen of England give attention to my song) Madden 1799-368

Poor Man's Complaint (Good people all I pray attend and listen to my ditty) Madden 1789-650

Poor Man's Complaint for Want of Labour (Poor people of England I pray you all draw near) Madden 1789-657

The Poor Man's Dream (T'other night as I slumbering lay on my bed) Madden 1789-1182 • *199*, 199

The Poor Man's Health; or, Advice to All True Hearts and Sound Bottoms (Come listen awhile my friends to my ditty) Madden 1787-1566; slight differences from next item

The Poor Man's Health, or Decay in Trade (Come listen awhile my friends to my ditty) Madden 1787-1565; slight differences from preceding item

Poor Man's Lamentation for the Bach-Bag (Good people all I pray attend) BOD 2806 c17-344

The Poor Man's Litany (From four pounds of bread, at sixteen-pence price) BOD Harding B11-3091 • **93–94**, 94–95

The Poor Man's Wish for a Wife (For now the cold winter comes on) Madden 1789-1178

Poor Married Man (Oh, what a sorrow a poor man's life is) BOD Harding B11-170 • **477–78**, 42, 193, 269–70, 478–79, 490

Poor Mechanic's Boy ('Twas in the autumn of the year) Madden 1791-219 • 303

Poor Nan of Wapping (Attend, ye thoughtless, young, and gay) St. Bride SS

Poor Old Bob the Groom (Come all you swells and pray take pity on the life of poor old Bob) Madden 1798-260
> AT: Bob the Groom

Poor Old Mike (I was reared in Doncaster some forty years ago) BL 1876 d41 2.1-777

Poor Old (Worn Out) Sailor ('Twas one summer's eve all labours o'er) Madden 1803-514; Madden 1794-204
> AT: Poor Worn-Out Sailor!

The Poor Peasant Boy (Thrown on the wide world, doomed to wander and roam) Madden 1791-51

The Poor Poet (Ah! dreadful state of my half-famish'd maw) BL 1163 al9-82

Poor Robin (Welcome, pretty little stranger) Madden 1797-525
Poor Savoyard Boy (I came from a land far away, far away) Madden 1791-254
> AT: Savoyard Boy

The Poor Smuggler's Boy (One cloudy cold morning, as abroad I did steer) Madden 1791-506
The Poor Soldier's Daughter (Some pity afford to a poor soldier's daughter) BOD Harding B25-1541
The Poor Spinners (You friends of the poor, both high and low) BL 1876 d41 2.2-1343
The Poor Threadmaker's Lamentation (Neighbours, countrymen and friends) Madden 1799-984
The Poor Tradesman ('Twas in Yorkshire I were born and bred) BOD 2806 c18-254
The Poor Tradesman's Lamentation (You working men where e'er you be) BL 1876 d41 2.2-1335
The Poor Voter's Song (They knew that I was poor) Madden 1803-229 • **197–98**, 197–98
The Poor Whores Complaint (Come listen awhile and you shall hear) Madden 1787-1573 • *447*, 447
The Poor Widow and Her Praying Boy (I knew a widow, very poor) BOD Johnson-2044 • **245–47**, 237, 247–48, 538
> AT: A Child's Faith

Poor Will's Wish (I wish in my song I may not offend) St. Bride SS
The Poor Workhouse Boy (The cloth vos laid in the Vorkhouse hall) Madden 1801-351
> AT: The Vorkhouse Boy; The Workhouse Boy

The Poor Working Man (Old England my country, my own native land) BOD Firth C16-324
Poor Worn-Out Sailor! (One summer's eve, all labour o'er) Madden 1802-217
> AT: Poor Old (Worn Out) Sailor

A Pound or a Penny (Some very good sayings I've heard in my time) BOD Johnson-430
Poverty and Contentment (Come all you worthy people) Madden 1791-312 • *501*, 335, 501, 503
> AT: Job, the Patient Man; One God Has Made Us All

Poverty No Crime (It was in the town of Manchester) BL 1876 d41 1-82 • 332, 333, 334
> AT: Lancashire Tragedy; some differences

Poverty Ruins Confidence (A few remarks I beg to make, touching both rich and poor) BOD 2806 c17-349 • 139
Poverty's Appeal (O'erwhelming griefs my soul oppress) Madden 1789-659
Poverty's No Sin (Poor Kate with nosegay basket trim) Madden 1790-318; *Lovers' Jubilee:* BL 1077 g46-7 • **421–22**, 332, 333, 415, 422
The Power of Hot Water or Plain Hints to the Millions (I'll sing, I'll sing, awhile, attend sir) BOD Firth C16-234
Pray Remember the Poor (Now winter is come with its ice and its snow) Madden 1790-643 • 237, 240
The Present Condition of British Workmen (Now Poor Laws thus breaks God's command) BOD Harding B13-299
Present Fashions or the Pride of the Times (Good people give attention and listen to my rhymes) Madden 1792-320

The Present Times (Attend you gallant heroes, of high and low degree) BOD Johnson-1333

The Present Times, or a Row about the Boroughmongers (Come attention give you Britons, and listen to my rhymes) Madden 1795-532

Present Times, or Eight Shillings a Week (Come all you bold Britons, where'er you be) Madden 1792-546 • *251*, 251, 406

The Preston Steam-Loom Weavers (You power-loom weavers far and near, come listen to my song) BL 1876 d41 2.2-1332

Pretty Betty Brill (I'm very fond of fish) St. Bride SS

Pretty Little Sarah on 18s. a Week (My heart is like a pumpkin, swollen big with love) BOD Harding B11-3157 • 236

The Pretty Primrose Girl (Come buy of poor Mary, primroses I sell) BL 1875 d16-22
    AT: The Primrose Girl

Price of Flour Keeps Falling (Good people give ear to my song) BOD 2806 c17-350

The Pride of Old England, or, the Folly of Man (As in sweet slumber I was laid) Madden 1803-519

The Pride of the Nation, or Old England Turned New (Now Britons attend, while I give you a song) St. Bride SS • 105

The Primrose Girl (Come buy of poor Kate, primroses I sell) BOD Johnson-568 • 319, 322–23
    AT: The Pretty Primrose Girl

The Prodigal Son (Afflictions though they seem severe) Madden 1795-534 • 504

Prodigal Son (My father gave me a portion in hand) Madden 1799-1030 • 504

Prosperity's Smile (Prosperity's smile, we are taught to believe) Madden 1788-200

Protect the Soldiers Wives and Children (You fair sex we pray give attention) Madden 1792-548

P——'s Farewell to Chelsea (Oh knock me silly, here's a go) BOD Harding B11-2904

Pull Devil, Pull Baker!!! (Ye bakers of London beware) Madden 1796-139 • 91

The Quarter Day ('Twas on a quarter's day, my money was nearly spent) Madden 1804-78 • **204–6**, 206, 391

Quarter Day, Being a Curious and Laughable Dialogue Which Occurred Between the Landlord and His Tenants (The landlords now lately so nice they are grown) BOD Johnson-962 • *206*, 206

The Queen and John Bull (Parliament again has met) Madden 1799-1052

The Queen & the Taxes (O in the house, the other night) BOD Johnson-2779 • **123–25**, 117, 125, 482

Queen Victoria (Welcome now Victoria) Madden 1801-375
    AT: A New Song in Favour / Praise of Her Majesty, Queen Victoria

Queer, Boys, Queer (Queer, boys, queer, is the house we live in) Madden 1798-347 • **171–72**, 172–73

Rag Bag! (The landlord too long hath sat at his ease) BL 1876 d41 2.2-1300 • 465

The Ragged Coat (O what a world of flummery, there's nothing but deceit in it) Madden 1792-553 • 236
    AT: Don't Despise a Man Because He Wears a Ragged Coat; Song of the Ragged Coat

The Ragged Riot (A lot of snobs set out one day) BOD Harding B13-302

Railroad to Hell (If you are determined and wishful to go) Madden 1799-1115 • *465*, 465

The Railway Calls (Oh have you felt distress of trade) Madden 1795-723

The Rambling Factory Girl's Return (Come, all you pretty factory girls) BOD Harding B11-3223

A Rare Row about the Income Tax; or, the Cat Let out of the Bag (You may talk about taxes and say what you will) UL 6-602 (2)

The Ratcatcher's Daughter (Not long ago in Vestminster) BOD Harding B11-3234 • 38, 273 n. 14

The Reason Why (There once was a time but it's happily past) BL 1870 d1 1-120 • 266

Red Sage Sal (If you'll listen to me, a tale I'll relate) BOD Harding B11-2844

Redditch in Worcestershire, for the Master or Mistress (We needle-makers are in great distress) Madden 1794-328 • *377*, 377

    AT: Cotton Spinners from Manchester

Reform, and King William For Ever! (Who said that King William was not the Main Mast) Madden 1803-485 • 113

Reform & Victory, the Grey Horse & the Union Coach (Come all you sporting heroes of high and low degree) Madden 1795-560

The Reform Demonstration in Hyde Park, May 6th 1867 (Good people come listen, I'll tell you of a lark) Madden 1795-212

Reform Meeting at Blackheath (For Reform, meet again, boys, on Monday, I say) BOD Harding B14-322

Reform Song (Now, my friends, we've gained our will) Madden 1801-413

Reform! "The Bill, the Whole Bill, and Nothing but the Bill" (Come listen, come listen, I'm going to sing) St. Bride SS • *112*, 112

Reformed Drunkard (All you that have money, and you that have none) BL LR271 a2 7-226

The Reformed Drunkard's Children's Song (As I rambled about on a fine summer's night) Madden 1799-1214 • *465*, 465

The Reformers Attack on the Old Rotten Tree (The Reformists are coming, oh! dear; oh! dear) BL 1875 d8-107

Regent Street (In London when the weather's fair) Madden 1794-336 • *516–17*, 516–17

Remarks on the Times (Good people of England I pray lend an ear) BOD Harding B25-1607

Remember the Poor (Cold winter is come with its cold chilling breath) Madden 1802-40 • 237, 239

    AT: Time to Remember the Poor; Winter Piece

Remember You Have Children of Your Own (As we travel through the street we very often meet) BOD Harding B11-3255 • 237

The Rent Day; or, Black Monday Morning (Oh! black Monday morning I dread, I'm sure) Madden 1798-345

    AT: The Way to Live Rent Free

The Request of the Poor (You gentlemen of England, wherever you be) Madden 1790-540 • 69, 75, 237, 240

Resignation of His Majesty's Minister (Oh dear, what a row there's all over the nation) BOD Harding B14-323

A Respectable Farmer's Farewell to Northumberland (In Northumberland I've a farmer been) BOD Harding B25-627

Retaliation; or, Upstart Pride (A solicitor vile, in a high-flying way) Madden 1787-450 • 140

Revolt of the Workhouse (Revolts the men do now engage) Madden 1803-299 • 163, 514

Rich and Poor (I pray give attention and listen to me) BOD Harding B11-3270 • 138

Rich and Poor (This world may be a paradise quite) BOD Firth C17-85

Rich & Poor Law! (What funny times we see) Madden 1795-321; BOD Johnson-1352 • **146–47**, 148–49

    AT: Ladies Don't Go Thieving!

The Rich and the Poor, or the Gentleman and the Bricklayer (George Victor Townley, step this way) BOD Harding B13-222 • **152–54**, 154–58, 260, 540

    AT: Townley and Wright

The Rich Man's Dream (I dreamt that, buried in my fellow-clay) BOD Johnson-1954 • **139–40**, 140, 503

Rigs and Flares-Up of Greenwich Fair (You blooming lads and lasses gay, come listen to my song) Madden 1794-122 • 440

Rigs and Flares-Up of the Fair (——— Fair is come without delay) Madden 1794-123 • **438–39**, 440, 481

The Rigs and Sprees of Leeds Town (You lads and lasses blythe and gay) Palmer TT-98

Rigs of Carlisle Hiring (You country lads and lasses all) Madden 1798-180

    AT: Rigs of the Mops

The Rigs of London (I'll sing a song and the truth be giving) BOD Harding B11-3280

The Rigs of the Mops! (You country lads and lasses all) BOD Harding B16-227c

    AT: Rigs of Carlisle Hiring

The Rigs of the Times (Ye men of high and low degree, come listen to my song) BOD Harding B15-261a • *198–99*, 198

Riley the Fisherman / Riley's Farewell (As I roved out one morning down by the river side) BOD Firth C13-225; Ashton-390

The Riot; or, Half a Loaf is Better Than No Bread (Come neighbours, no longer be patient and quiet) Madden 1796-69 • *383*, 58, 335, 383

Robin Rough-Head (Come listen awhile to a story of fate) BOD Harding B11-3296

The Robin's Petition (When the leaves had deserted the trees) Madden 1801-20 • *237*, 237

Rogues of All Sorts / Rogues of All Sorts Found Out (Poor people of England I pray now attend) Madden1787-1627; Madden 1804-132 • *199*, 198–99

Rose of Lucerne; or, the Swiss Toy Girl (I've come across the sea) Madden 1799-583 • 322

    AT: The Swiss Toy Girl

Rosetta (the Farmer's Daughter) and Her (the) Gay Ploughboy (You constant lovers give attention) BL 1876 e2-96; BL 1876 e3-25 • 403

    AT: The Farmer's Daughter and the Gay Plough-Boy; Mary and the Handsome Factory Boy

The Rose-Water Select, the Parish Pays the Piper, O the Parish Pays for All (Good morning, Mr. Grasp) BOD Harding B11-3339

    AT: The Parish Pays the Piper

Royal Mercy: A Petition for Mercy for Several People Who Have Been Convicted or are about to be for Incendiarism BL 1875 d13-28 from end (unnumbered) PR • *336*, 336

A Rummy Old Cadger Am I (Oh, a rummy old cadger am I) BOD Harding B11-3366 • 301

'S for Money (Why is the world so busy is what I want to know) BOD Harding B11-1506 • *235*, 235

Sailor Boy (The bitter wind blew keen and cold) Madden 1791-395
    AT: The Little Sailor Boy; The Poor Little Sailor Boy

The Sailor Boy's Good Bye (Sweet mother dear, I go) Madden 1802-546

Sailor's Return (Young William to his wife did say, my dear, I must away) BOD Firth C13-111

St. James and St. Giles BOD Firth C16-359 PR • *137*, 137, 279 n. 1

St. James's and St. Giles's (To the tourist of London, who's curious in fact) Ashton-399; BOD Harding B11-3394; ML H1773i(37) • **142–44**, 138, 144–45, 479

The St. James's Looking Glass GU B'side-3.31 PR • 279 n. 1

The St. Pancras Prigging Overseers (There was a naughty man) BOD Firth C16-312 • 163

St. Paul's and the Monument (Late one night, when the moon shone bright) BOD Harding B11-3396

Sal Sly, and Billy Snivel (At siven in the morning avaking) BOD Harding B11-2765

Sally Carter (I'ze a simple honest country clown) BL 1876 e3-101

Sally Sly (At six in the morning awaking) Vicinus-34

Sammy Slap the Bill Sticker (I'm Sammy Slap the bill sticker) BOD Harding B11-3418 • 269

Sandman Joe the St. Giles's Pet (The other day as Sandman Joe) BOD Harding B11-3400

Satire on All Trades (There's ne'er a thriving trader who daily cheats the town) BL 1876 e3-258

Saucy Sailor Boy (Oh, come my own one, come my fond one) BOD Firth C13-252

Save a Penny for a Rainy Day (Now the times are altered amongst us many ways) Madden 1789-699

The Savoyard (From the cold snowy mountains of Savoy) BOD Harding B21-41

The Savoyard (A little boy a Savoyard) Madden 1789-1232

Savoyard Boy (I came from a land far away, far away) Madden 1794-464 • 306
    AT: Poor Savoyard Boy

Scavenger's Ball (Oh sure such a party, so gay and so hearty) Madden 1799-911 • 514

The Scullion Sprite ('Twas at the hour, when sober cits) BOD Harding B11-3439

Second Edition of Parson Brown's Sheep (My thanks except of me kind friends) BOD Harding B11-2956 • *356*, 356
    AT: Encore Verses or the Answer to Parson Brown's Sheep

Seizure of Goods for Assessed Taxes . . . (If you'll listen to me, I'll tell you a spree) Madden 1793-193 • 117

A Serious Caution to the Poor UL 5-442 PR • 138, 279 n. 3

The Servant Boy (You lovers all, both great and small, attend unto my theme) Madden 1794-467

Seven Shillings a Week (Come all you gallant husbandmen) BOD Firth C16-302 • 251

The Seven-Shilling Piece (The king's picture and Abraham Newland are sung) St. Bride SS
Shabby Genteel (We have heard it asserted a dozen times o'er) BOD Harding B11-3459 • 236
The Shabby Swell (About this town I'm told there dwells) BOD Harding B11-3460
The Shady Green Tree (As I was walking one midsummer morning) St. Bride SS
The Sheffield Grinders (The Sheffield grinder's a terrible blade) Lloyd F-374
Shelter Your Mother and Me (The home was so bright and so happy within) BOD Harding B13-347
She's Honest (She is honest, she is good and she is wise) BOD Harding B17-282b
The Shipwrecked Sailor Boy (Over the ocean and over the land) BOD Firth C12-406
Shocking Hard Times (The banners of cheap bread you know has lately been unfurl'd) Madden 1797-503
Shocking Murder of a Wife and Six Children (Attend you feeling parents dear) BL 11621 h11 8-47; BOD Harding B14-202 • *372–73*, 372
The Shoddy Chap (Oh! aw wur once very poor) BOD Harding B11-3022
A Short Sketch of the Times (Farewell and adieu to the year ninety three) Madden 1787-1704 • *91*, 91–92
The Shortness of Work, and Present State of the Times (Both young and old, come list to me) BL 12330 i42-3
Shovel & Broom (Tho' I'm but a chimney-sweep I took a ticket) Madden 1794-134
Signs of the Times (All you that wish your fortune for to know) St. Bride SS
Since Johnny's Been Out of Work (Excuse these salt and briny tears) BOD Firth C16-266 • 216
Singing for the Million (Oh! England is a curious nation) BOD Harding B11-3525
Singular Scene Under the New Poor Law Act (Good people all attend) Madden 1794-128
Sir Robert Peel and His New Taxes (Oh, is not there a piece of work) BOD Harding B14-325
Sketch of Roguery (Come all you people in this place) BOD Johnson-2848
Skilly Night and Morning (Come all you roving bachelors, listen to me awhile) Madden 1799-403 • 337
The Small Farmer's and Labourer's Complaint (All you that have a father's heart) Madden 1804-526 • 226
The Snob and the Bottle (Good people attend to my song) BOD Harding B11-3556 • 465
The Snob's Confession (Now I am a jolly cobbler) BOD Harding B11-3557 • 465
Society Instituted for the Purpose of Supplying the Poor with Meat Soup, at One Penny per Quart BL L23 c6-76 PR
The Soldier's Boy (The snow was fast descending) Madden 1803-456 • 306
The Soldier's Orphan (O dark is the night and the wintry wind whistles) BOD Johnson-1009
The Soldier's Orphan's Prayer (It was the son of a soldier, who in battle was slain) Madden 1789-1256 • 306
The Soldier's Wife ('Twas night, the loving mother sat) BOD Firth C14-347
Soliloquy on the Last Shilling (In the dry desert of a leathern jacket) BOD Harding B11-3588

The Somers Town Sausage Maker (To ——— Street in Somers town) BOD Harding B11-3591

Something or Other Starts New Every Day (You gentle and simple come listen awhile) BOD Firth C16-34 • 550

Song and Dialogue on the Times, or Jacob and Jonathan (Come listen to my ditty) BOD Harding B20-158

A Song Called My £1 5s. (It's of a tradesman and his wife I hear the other day) BOD Harding B19-120; some differences from Five and Twenty Shillings . . . / How Five and Twenty Shillings . . . • 251

A Song for the Times (Once England was acknowledged the mistress of the seas) BL 1876 d41 2.2-1344

Song of the Cadgers in the Holy Land (Come, let us dance and sing) St. Bride LS (Life in London) • **507–8**, 500, 508–9

Song of the Cotton Factory Operatives (We have come to ask for assistance) BL 1876 d41 2.2-1347

Song of the Haymakers (The noontide is hot and our foreheads are brown) Madden 1802-236 • 409

    AT: Haymakers

The Song of the Lower Classes (We plough and sow—we're so very, very low) Ashton-338

Song of the Ragged Coat (O, what a world of flummery, there is nothing but deceit in it) Madden 1800-36

    AT: Don't Despise a Man Because He Wears a Ragged Coat; The Ragged Coat

The Song of the Shirt (With fingers weary and worn) Madden 1802-189 • 43, 406

Song of the Slaughter (Parent of the wide creation) BOD 2806 c16-299 • 550

Song of the Times, Frightful Rises and High Prices (Oh! hear the astounding doleful news) BOD Harding B14-326 • **120–22**, 122

The Song of the Truck (With fingers jewell'd and gemm'd) BOD Johnson-1997 • 406

The Song of Work (Work! work! work!) BOD Johnson-1325

A Song on the Times, We Are All Wrong Up to Now (I have indited these few verses to try to show to you) BOD Johnson-1197

A Song Sung at a Meeting in Philadelphia (In what a sad state is the true British nation) Madden 1798-12

Sons of John Bull (Oh England my country, how blest is thy nation) BL 11621 k4-64 • **133**, 134

The South Australian Emigrant (Farewell, adieu to England) Madden 1802-238 • *379*, 41, 379

Speak Not of a Man as You Find Him: *see* Don't Speak of . . .

The Spinners Lamentation (Come listen dear neighbours to these lines we have made) BL 1876 d41 2.2-1335

    AT: Mechanics' Lamentation

The Spinning-Wheel (One summer's eve, as Nancy fair) Madden 1802-472

    AT: The New Spinning Wheel

The Sporting Farmer (You farmers all, both great and small) Madden 1803-547

Spring Water Cresses (When hoary frost hung on each thorn) BOD Harding B17-300b

The Squire and Gipsy Girl (One spring morning early, a squire was straying) BOD Harding B11-2431

Squire and Milkmaid; or, Blackberry Fold (It's of a rich squire in Bristol does dwell) BL 11621 h11 8-380; Madden 1802-39; BOD Harding B25-2146 (Young Squire); Madden 1799-410; Madden 1803-300; BL 1875 d5-86; Maud Karpeles, *Cecil Sharp's Collection of English Folk Songs*, 1974, 2: 213; Eva Ashton, "Songs from Sussex," *Journal of the Folk Song Society* 6 (1906): 34–38; E. J. Moeran, *Six Suffolk Folksongs* (1932), 8–11; Madden 1803-300 (Milkmaid of Blackberry Fold) • **415–16**, *24*, 39, 46, 91, 416–20

    AT: Milkmaid of Blackberry Fold; Young Squire

The Staffordshire Nail-Makers' Humble Petition (We nail makers are in great distress) Madden 1801-272 • *378*, 377, 378

The Stage of Life (All the world is one great stage, this Shakespeare said of old) BOD Firth C16-408

Stanza (Friends of humanity think of the strangers) BOD Harding B13-268

Starve Away and No Beer (I wish you all a happy new year) BOD Harding B11-3650

Starve Us All (Oh! is it not a gallows shame) BOD Harding B13-306

The Starving Times of England (You ladies of old England) BOD Firth C16-274

The State Beggar (Of all the sturdy beggars) Madden 1787-1758

The State of Great Britain, or a Touch at the Times (As old John Bull was walking) Madden 1792-373; same as next item

The State of Great Britain, or, a Touch at the Times for 1841 / for 1843 (As old John Bull was walking) BOD Harding B14-327; Madden 1795-729; same as preceding item

The State of Old England or, John Bull in Uniform (They call me poor old Farmer Bull, it's true I'm getting old) BOD Johnson-1405

The State of Poor Old England (You British subjects high and low) BOD Harding B14-328

The State of the Nation, or, a New Touch of the Times (Now we have bid adieu to the year ninety-four) Madden 1787-1757; same as next item • 92

State of the Nation; or, New Touch of the Times (Now we have bid adieu to the year 95) Madden 1787-1756; same as preceding item • 92

State of the Times (Come all you working people what shall we do now / Victoria she's got a daughter, and what shall we do now) Madden 1797-24; Madden 1795-706

The State of the Times and Their Causes (Come all you philanthropists attend awhile to me) Madden 1797-39 • 209

Stitch Goes the Needle! (Females work too hard I'm told) BOD Harding B11-1166 • **405–6**, 406

Stones a-Breaking (In the year eighteen hundred, I think, in sixteen) BL 1871 f13-78

The Stowaway or Little Hero (From Liverpool, 'cross the Atlantic) BOD Harding B20-160

Struggle for the Breeches (Husband. —About my wife I mean to sing a very funny song) Madden 1802-243; Madden 1797-571 (Hard Struggle for the Breeches); Madden 1791-97 • **460–61**, 456, 461

Study Economy / Studying Economy (I'm a gent reduced by railway speculation) Madden 1792-959; BL 1875 b19-33 • 349

The Subjects of the Times; or, Scenes of 1848 (You shall hear a funny ditty) Madden 1793-313

The Suicide Club (You've none of you heard, I suppose) BOD Harding B11-3690 • 269

TITLE LIST 615

Sunshine After Rain (I left my love in England) BOD Firth C16-388
Th' Surat Weyver (We're werkin lads frae Lankisheer) BL 1876 d41 2.2-1345 • 255
Swaggering Farmers (Come all you swaggering farmers wherever you may be) BL LR271 a2 3-39
    AT: Times Are Altered
The Sweeps Lament (Oh, no I mustn't think of it) BOD Harding B11-1348
The Sweep's Wedding (If you'll listen to me I'll sing of a spree) Madden 1797-826
    AT: The Chummy's Wedding
The Swiss Toy Girl (I've come across the sea) Madden 1803-257 • *322*, 322
    AT: Rose of Lucerne
The Tables Turned; or the Tories Reduced to the Workhouse) Madden 1794-224
The Tater Can (I keeps a slap up tater can) BOD Harding B11-3741
The Tax on Gin! (There's something new starts every day) BOD Firth C22-62
The Tears of Pity (Oh pity dear friends the poor framework-knitters) Madden 1801-72 • 377
A Terror to the Rent Day (Working hard is my delight. Industry I crave) BOD 2806 c17-421
There's a Good Time Coming, Boys! (There's a good time coming, boys) Madden 1793-335 • **264–66**, 43, 61, 62, 68, 251, 256, 258, 266, 267–69, 270, 513
    AT: A Good Time Coming, Boys! Wait a Little Longer
There's Brighter Days in Store (Don't talk of life's troubles with sad rueful face) BOD Harding B13-336 • 258, 501
There's Many Worse Off Than You (Now I'm a chap that never grumbles) BOD Harding B11-3779 • 237, 501
There's None Like a Mother, If Ever So Poor (You tell me you love me, I fain would believe) Madden 1792-690
There's Room Enough for All (What need of all this fuss and strife) Madden 1799-1285 • *380*, 380
They Are All Sliding (The Tories are a sliding) BL LR271 a2 1.1-46
They Must Repeal the Corn Bill (To the standard rally quick) Madden 1795-708
    AT: The Corn Bill
They Say 'Tis a Crime to be Poor (So quietly one evening reclining) BOD Firth C16-467
They're All Boxing (You tradesmen all, both high and low, come listen unto me) Madden 1794-234
Things I Should Like to See (Come all you true Britons, of every degree) BOD Harding B11-1147
Things I'd Like to See (Come all you good people) BOD 2806 c16-229
Things I'd Like to See (Draw near, with attention, both young and old) BOD 2806 c13-151
Think on the Poor (As you sit in warm circles secure from the tempest) Madden 1791-612 • **239**, 69, 237, 239–40
Though Poor, I'm a Gentleman Still (Don't think by my dress that I come here to beg) BOD Johnson-2272 • 236
The Thrasher (Can any king be half so great) BOD Harding B11-4379 • *501*, 305, 501
Three Acres and a Cow (You have heard a deal of talk about) BOD Firth C16-305 • 129
A Tidy Suit for All That (I'm remembered well—a slap-up swell) BL LR271 a2 1.2-117
    AT: Broken Down Swell

Tim Snooken, the Cadger (I never had money, I ne'er larnt a trade) Madden 1798-346 • 302

Time to Remember the Poor (Now winter is come with her cold chilling breath) Madden 1802-726 • 69, 239

    AT: Remember the Poor; Winter Piece

The Times (Oh, England oh England thy glory is fled) BOD Harding B28-242 • 105

The Times (Tax-gatherers now how thick they swarm) Madden 1804-677 • *401,* 401

    AT: Naked Truth

The Times (You British subjects now attend) Madden 1791-592

    AT: A New Song on the Times; A True Statement of the Present Times

The Times (You gentlemen who keep horses) Madden 1804-136

Times Altered or, the Grumbling Farmers/Times Are (Come all you swaggering farmers wherever you may be) Madden 1792-390; Madden 1801-466; Pinto-51 • *226–27,* 226–27

    AT: Swaggering Farmers

The Times in Hertfordshire (Come all you gallant heroes and listen to my rhymes) Madden 1794-223

The Times or 50 Years Ago (Good times they say are coming boy) BOD 2806 c13-16

The Times Will Mend (Good people now I pray attend) BOD 2806-c17-431

'Tis Hard to Leave This Land (Tho' to work your will is strong, glad to labour all the day) BL 1876 d41 1-124 • 379

To Hereford Old Town (To Hereford Old Town a new hero is come down) Palmer TT-268

To the Friends of Industry (When nature in the voice of pain) BOD Johnson-2922

    AT: The Appeal of a Body of Unemployed Operatives; A Copy of Verses by a Poor Tradesman; The Tradesman's New Hymn

To the Poor Inhabitants of Manchester BL L23 c4-14 PR

To Young Women (The times are much worse, our grandmothers declare) Madden 1795-298

Tom Blunt, or the Poor Sailor (Oh! my name is Tom Blunt) Madden 1804-147

Tom Tackle (Tom Tackle was noble, was true to his word) BOD Johnson-1030 • 305

Tom Topsail (Tom Topsail he died and the folks piped their eyes) BOD Firth C13-87

The Tommy Note (You boatmen and colliers all) Raven U-53

Tommy Trank, the Glove Cutter (A glove cutter is Tommy Trank) Raven V-134

The Tooting Tragedy (You tender mothers, parents dear) BL 1888 c3-102 • 163

The Tories They Govern the Nation (Come listen awhile to a song that is new) BOD Harding B14-333

Touch at the Times for the Year 1807 (Come neighbours and friends I beg you'll attend) Madden 1787-1836

A Touch on the Times (Come people all I pray attend) BOD Firth C16-294

A Touch on the Times (You jovial sons of Britain come listen unto me) BOD Harding B25-1940 • 99

Townley and Wright (George Victor Townley step this way) BOD 2806 c16-228

    AT: The Rich and the Poor

The Trade Man's Lamentation (Ye liberal I pray) BOD 2806 c17-437

The Trades Unions of England, Huzza! (Come all you bold Britons attend to my rhymes) Madden 1794-226 • 54, 275 n. 39

The Tradesman's Complaint (Come, all you poor tradesmen, I pray lend an ear) BOD Johnson-1955 • *376*, 140, 376

The Tradesman's Complaint (Draw near brother tradesmen, listen to my song) Madden 1790-22 • 105

The Tradesman's Complaint (You Englishmen wherever you be, come listen to what I say) Madden 1801-84

The Tradesman's Complaint in Time of Distress (Come all you brave tradesmen that dwell round this land) Madden 1803-389

The Tradesman's Lamentation (Farewell dear wife and children for now I'm bound to sea) Madden 1804-137

The Tradesman's Lamentation for the Loss of Trade (Now the times altered among us many ways) BOD Harding B12-159 • 93

The Tradesman's New Hymn (When nature in the voice of pain) Madden 1797-585 • *377*, 377

    AT: The Appeal of a Body of Unemployed Operatives; A Copy of Verses by a Poor Tradesman; To the Friends of Industry

The Tradesman's Wish for a Better New Year (Come all ye brave tradesmen I pray you) BOD Harding B25-1942

The Tradesmen's Lamentation (Neighbours, countrymen, and friends) Madden 1799-1128

The Tramp (I'm a broken-down man, without money or credit) BOD 2806 c16-147

The Transport's Lamentation (All you distressed tradesmen wherever you may be) Madden 1799-759 • 360–61

    AT: Farewell Address to Their Countrymen and Friends

The Transport's Return (Ye true sons of freedom I pray you attend) BOD Firth C17-304

The Travelling Tinker (I am a travelling tinker with my workshop on my back) BOD Firth B34-301

The Tread Mill (Though I'm a simple country lad) Madden 1803-379

The Tread Mill; or, Tom and Jerry at Brixton (No doubt you know as well as I) Madden 1803-601 • *345*, 345

The Treading Mill (The Mill! the Mill! the Brixton Treading Mill) Madden 1799-698

    AT: Brixton Treading-Mill; The Mill

The Treading Mill; or the Ups and Downs of Life (Let sages talk on as they will) Madden 1796-146

Trials and Executions of the Rick Burners St. Bride LS PR • *336*, 335, 336

The Trials of All the Prisoners at the Old Bailey, Commenced Wednesday, Feb. 17th, 1820 BL 1888 c3-87 PR • *340*, 339–40, 342, 532, 539–40

A True and Correct Account of the Melancholy Death of Mrs. Rogers BL 1880 c20 1-286 PR • 247

A True, Full, and Particular Account of the Melancholy Death of Mary Sawyers . . . BL 1880 c20 1-219 PR • 373

A True, Full, and Particular Account of Two Poor Children That Were Found Starved to Death BL 1880 c20 1-301 PR • 247, 373

The True Joke, or the Poor Man's Complaint (Come listen a while and give ear to my song) Madden 1797-49 • 199

A True Picture of the Present Times (Come all you who have got a few minutes to spare) Madden 1802-611 • 199

A True Picture of the Times, or, the Poor Man's Consolation from Reform (Come you that can tell us, we should just like to know) Madden 1794-383 • *266*, 209, 266

The True Rights of Men; or, the Contented Spitalfields Weaver (I've been searching the sorrows that trouble my mind) GU B'side-28.7 • 58

The True Sons of Freedom (You true sons of freedom, who join hand in hand) Madden 1794-228

True State of the Nation (As there's but little news and lack of conversation) Madden 1802-c612

The True State of Trade (You tradesmen all pray attend) Madden 1804-656

A True Statement of the Present Times (You British subjects now attend) BL LR271 a2 4-249: 1830s refurbishment of ATs

    AT: A New Song on the Times; The Times

The True-Hearted Sailor (I'm one of those sailors who think 'tis no lie) Madden 1803-651

Trust in the Lord (Though some complain that trade is bad) Madden 1799-1140 • *504*, 504

The Truth, the Whole Truth, and Nothing But the Truth (You hard working people attend to my rhymes) Madden 1803-574 • 199

Turn the Carpet; or, the Two Weavers (As at their work two weavers sat) BOD Harding B7-8 • **381–83**, 58, 383

Two Bob a Week and My Board (What a poor fellow I am sir) Madden 1802-554

Two Orphan Girls (Two orphan girls the tother day) BOD Harding B11-2809

The Two Orphans / Two Orphans at Their Mother's Grave (My chaise the village inn did gain) Madden 1792-984; Madden 1799-656

    AT: A Copy of Verses Written by a Lady; The Orphans

Two Orphans in the Snow (One bitter night in winter when the wind was fierce and cold) NOR-112

Two Shilling Suit (Come all you young fellows and list unto me) BL 11621 h11 1-48

The Unfortunate Author of the Following Verses . . . (In Bellona's red field I have oft been contending) BOD Johnson-2992

Unfortunate Factory Girl (Will you list the true but simple lay) BL LR271 a2 6-69

The Unfortunate Lad (I am a poor lad, my fortune is bad) Madden 1797-514

The Unfortunate Wife (A maid I was, and a maid was I) BL 1876 e3-191

The Union Houses Must Come Down and Railroads Go to Pot (Come all you English poor folks) Madden 1792-270

The Union of Freedom (You friends of the Union I pray give attention) Madden 1790-641 • *256*, 256

The Union Overseer (Some people are always contending) BOD Harding B11-2895 • 214

    AT: The New Overseer; The Overseer

Up the Monument (Some like to spend their leisure time) BOD Harding B11-3953

An Uproar in St. Pancras (As through St. Pancras I was walking) BL 1875 b19-99 • 163

Vengeance to Come: reference lost.

Verses Composed on the Distress of the Times (Supposing the rich to the poor man will give) Madden 1795-24

Very Respectable (One day going out for a walk, sir) Madden 1799-439; BL LR271 a2 8-95 • **347–49**, 349

The Vestry Dinner (Churchwarden I've been—let me see) St. Bride SS • 224

TITLE LIST 619

Victoria Bridge on a Saturday Night (Whoever may travel o'er Manchester gravel) BOD Harding B16-296b

Victory (I am a youthful lady, my troubles they are great) Ashton 223

Vilikins and His Dinah (Oh! 'tis of a rich merchant, in London did dwell) BOD Harding B11-3981 • *412–13*, 38, 43, 61, 270, 412–13

The Village (Village-Born) Beauty (See the star breasted villain to yonder cot bound) Madden 1792-737 • **445–47**, 414, 447–48, 481

The Village Maid ('Twas morn when the lark's cheerful note) BL 1876 e2-116A • 433

The Villager (The villager born humbly, and bred hard) BL 11622 c7-145

Vive la Liberte (Hail to ye brave sons of Gall) BOD Harding B15-350a • 40–41, 511, 514

A Voice from the Factory! (Come, all working men here assembled) BOD B11-3993

The Voice of the People; or, the King and Reform (Britons, be firm, and stick close to your king) Madden 1803-582 • 113

The Vorkhouse Boy (The cloth vos laid in the vorkhouse hall) Madden 1802-784

    AT: The Poor Workhouse Boy; The Workhouse Boy

The Vorkus Gal (You ax me to sing, of course I shall) BOD Harding B11-3995 • **169–71**, 171, 289, 512

    AT: The Workhouse Girl

The Vulgar Little Girl (Had Mr. Ward sung of the boy he met on Margate Pier) BOD Harding B11-3999 • *324*, 324

Wait a Little Longer (There's a good time coming, boys) *Daily News*, 22 January 1846 • **264–66**, 43, 61, 62, 68, 251, 256, 258, 266, 267–69, 270, 513

    AT: A Good Time Coming, Boys!/There's a Good Time Coming Boys!

The Waiter (I met the waiter in his prime) BOD Harding B11-4003 • *270*, 271

Wandering Ann (Chill winter had mantled the mountains in white) Madden 1799-885

Wandering Bard (I'm the wandering bard of Exeter/Manchester) Madden 1804-307; Madden 1799-443 (Manchester); BOD Harding B11-4024; BOD Harding B11-3049 • **482–83**, *480*, 480, 483–84

The Wandering Boy (I was born in the country far over the mountains) BOD Johnson-1465

The Wandering Boy (When the winter wind whistles along the wild moor) Madden 1801-420 • *319*, 43, 319

The Wandering Girl (Once I loved a young man as dear as my life) Madden 1803-587

The Wandering Savoyard (Ah, hear the wandering Savoyard's tale) Madden 1791-240

War Cry Come Again No More! (Let us pause in life's pleasures, and count its many tears) BL 1876 d41 2.2-1345

The War, or What Do They Say in England (Come all you poor of London town, and listen unto me) BOD Harding B13-214

A Warning to Young Men, the Last Awful Moments of Charles Elliott BL 1880 c20 2-396 PR • *341–42*, 341–42, 343, 373, 539–40, 541

A Warning to Youth (Each tender mother lend an ear) St. Bride SS (The Sorrowful and Weeping Lamentation of the Wives and Orphans of the Late Sufferers . . .) • *340*, 340, 342, 539–40

The Wars Are Not Over (As I was travelling the country up and down) Shepard-143; Madden 1787-1898; BOD Harding B22-329 • **89–90**, 90–91

    AT: When the Wars Are All O'er

The Water-Cress Girl (While strolling out one evening by a running stream) BOD Harding B11-4047

The Way of the Landlords (Labouring people wherever you be) Madden 1802-55

The Way of the World (As you travel through life, if you're wealthy you'll find) Madden 1795-232 • 236

The Way of the World (The ways of the world I am going to review) BOD Harding B15-353a

    AT: The Ways of the World; see also the next title here

Way of the World; or an Alteration to the Short Sketch of the Times ('Tis the way of the world I'm a going to review) Madden 1787-1902 • 92

The Way to Live (A man and his wife got married one day) BOD Johnson-124; BOD Harding B11-945 • **517–19**, 519

The Way to Live Rent Free (Oh black Monday morning, I dread, I am sure) BOD Harding B11-4058 • 206

    AT: The Rent Day; or, Black Monday Morning

The Ways of the World (The ways of the world I am going to review/show) Madden 1802-558 • *138, 236,* 92

    AT: The Way of the World

We Are All Beggars (Attention give to one and all unto a begging song / Great Britain is a curious place, a place of high renown / We are all beggars, beg, beg, beggars) BOD Harding B11-4065; BOD Harding B11-4063; BOD Harding B11-4064; some differences of material • 303

We Are Forced to be Contented (You Britons all where'er you be) Madden 1795-735

    AT: Forced to be Contented

We Will Not Stop Again (The servant lads and lasses gay, now Martinmas draws near) BOD Harding B11-4096

The Wealth of a Cottage is Love (A blessing unknown to ambition and pride) Madden 1789-1327 • *502,* 502

Wealthy Farmer (It's of a wealthy farmer) Madden 1799-113

Weaver's Crime (Come all ye cotton hand weavers) BL 1876 d41 2.2-1332

The Weaver's Cry (When will America's cruel war cease?) BL 1876 d41 2.2-1348

The Weaver's Daughter (Across the fields one sweet May morn) Madden 1791-429; Madden 1791-430 • **432–33**, 433

    AT: Old Weaver's Daughter

The Weaver's Garland or the Downfall of Trade (You weavers of England I pray now attend) BOD Harding B25-2016

The Weaver's Lamentation (O listen to our mournful tale) Madden 1797-35

The Weaver's Lamentation (O Lord look down with pitying eye) BOD Harding B11-4073

The Weaver's Petition (Pity kind friends in our great distress) Madden 1798-412

The Weavers Triumph (Come all you friends to liberty, and listen to my song) Madden 1788-662 • 274 n. 28

A Week's Matrimony (On Sunday morning I went out for a spree) Madden 1791-10; Madden 1794-14 • **468–70**, 470–71

A Week's Reckoning (A man and his wife in ―――― Street) Madden 1802-266

    AT: Fifteen Shillings a Week (with additional stanza)

TITLE LIST

The Welsh Boy's Answer (The Welsh boy overhearing) Madden 1799-834 • *444*, 444

What is the Matter with the Farmers (What is the matter with the farmers, they all look so dull) Madden 1790-626

What Shall We Do for Meat! (Old England, once upon a time) Madden 1795-239 • 234

What Shocking Hard Times (Good people all, both great and small, come listen to my rhymes) Palmer TT-223

What Will Old England Come To? (Come all you jolly young fellows, and listen awhile to my song) Madden 1791-50 • 259

What Won't Money Do? (Oh this money, money, money) Madden 1801-470
    AT: The Wonderful Effects of Money

What's Old England Come To! (One cold winter's morning as the day was dawning) Madden 1795-23 • 259

When My Old Hat Was New (I am a poor old man in years, come listen to my song) Madden 1799-533
    AT: My Old Hat; Old Hat; When This Old Hat Was New

When the Wars Are All Over/O'er (As I was travelling the country up and down) BL 11606 aa24-102; BL 11621 b7 1-17 • 90
    AT: The Wars Are Not Over

When These Old Clothes Were New (Eight years ago I was a swell, sir) BOD Harding B11-4134

When This Old Hat Was New (I am a poor old man in years, come listen to my song) Madden 1791-214 • 257
    AT: My Old Hat; Old Hat; When My Old Hat Was New

When This Old Hat Was New (This old hat was new once, but I cannot tell you when) BOD Harding B11-4138

The White Hat (In sixteen hundred and forty-one) BOD Harding B11-4162 • 550

The White Slave; or the Factory Girl's Last Day ('Twas on a winter's morning) Madden 1801-38 • **396–98**, 398–99, 538
    AT: The Factory Girl's Last Day

White Slaves of England (O England that boasts of her riches so rare) BOD Harding B15-373b • 406

Who Prigged the Mutton (You Pimlico ladies of every degree) BOD Harding B11-4170 • 149

Who's Your Butcher? Or, What's the Price of Meat? (Oh! crikey, what a piece of work) Madden 1795-241 • **232–34**, 234

Why Did She Leave Him Because He Was Poor (Why did she leave him, they grew up together) Madden 1792-786 • *433*, 433

Why is Man Denied by Man His Daily Bread? (Nature! thy matchless power) Madden 1798-243 • 208

The Wicked Life and Alarming Death of Jane Wilson BL 1875 d13-11 PR • 448

The Widow Waddle (Mrs. Waddle was a widow, and she got no little gain) Madden 1799-521

Will You Go to California (To high and low of all degrees) BL 11621 k4-72
    AT: California Gold

William and Dinah (It's of a liquor merchant in London did dwell) Madden 1794-338 • *412*, 412

Willie, Drunk Again (Oh, Willie, you've come home, lad) BL LR271 a2 2-16

Winter Piece (Now winter is come with his cold chilly breath) Madden 1789-37 • *239–40*, 239–40

>AT: Remember the Poor; Time to Remember the Poor

The Winter's Evening / Night ('Twas on one winter's evening when fast fell the snow) BOD Harding B25-2087; BOD Harding B25-2085

With Lowly Suit (With lowly suit and plaintive ditty) BOD Harding B17-342b

The Wives Lamentation (Ten years ago I married a man who's such a drunken sot) Madden 1804-72; Madden 1791-609 • **463–64**, 464–65

Woeful Marriage (On Monday night I married a wife) Madden 1799-721 • 471

The Woman That Wished She'd Never Got Married (Young ladies have pity on me) Madden 1792-647 • **473–75**, 475

The Women Flogger's Lament of Marylebone Workhouse! (Oh dear here's a shocking disaster) BOD Harding B13-160 • **173–75**, 175–79, 256

The Wonderful Effects of Money (Oh this money, this glittering money, what won't money do) Madden 1798-207 • *235*, 235

>AT: What Won't Money Do?

Wonderful Times (Come listen unto my wonderful song) Madden 1799-1059 • 199

Wonderful World This Would Be (I have seen life in its changes, in towns low and big) BOD Harding B11-256

The Wonderous Works of God (Come all you poor distressed souls) BOD Douce adds. 137-82

>AT: Comfort to the Afflicted

Won't You Buy My Pretty Flowers (Underneath the gas light's glitter) BL LR271 a2 2-78

Won't You Tell Us Why, England? (You are not what you were, England) BOD Firth C16-248

Woodland Mary (With sloe-black eyes and jet-black hair) Madden 1804-417

A Word from Wm Rider to Edward Baines (Why, Noddy, didst thou really say) UL 6-564

A Word of Advice to Servants (You servant lads and lasses all come listen to my ditty) Madden 1799-1094

Work, Boys, Work! (I'm not a wealthy man, but I've hit upon a plan) BOD Harding B11-4147

The Workhouse Boy (The cloth vos laid in the Vorkhouse hall) Madden 1792-34; ML H1252-23; Madden 1794-145; Madden 1795-648 • **165–66**, 38, 61, 68, 76, 163, 166–69, 171, 289, 430, 512

>AT: The Poor Workhouse Boy; The Vorkhouse Boy

Workhouse Door (One day as I was walking through streets) BOD Firth C16-308

The Workhouse Door (One day while out walking not knowing where to go) SH-561

The Workhouse Girl (You ax me to sing, so of course I shall) Madden 1794-61 • 76

>AT: The Vorkus Gal

Workhouse Wooing (Oh! have you heard the news abroad) BL 1872 a1-180 • 163

The Working Man (There's a class that bears the stamp of the great) BOD Harding B15-392b • 502

The Working Man's A.B.C. (A Alphabet, that we used to learn at school) BOD Firth C16-204

Working Men of England (Oh! the working men of England, we labour for the great) BOD Harding B11-3483 • *502*, 502

Working Poor of Old England (Let them brag, until in the face they are black) BL LR271 a2 5-240 • **228–30**, 230

The World on Credit (Come all you brisk and jovial blades) BOD Firth C16-243 • **103–4**, 104–5

The World Turn'd Upside Down (I am a poor unhappy man) BOD Harding B22-351 • 199

The World Was Not Made for One Man Alone (The world was not made for one man alone) BOD Harding B13-241

The World's in a Terrible State (Good people I pray give attention / You landsmen and seamen attention) Madden 1799-962; St. Bride SS • *47*, 47–48, 49

The Wounded Seamens Lamentation (All good worthy people that's able to draw near) BOD Firth C12-396

Wrekington Hiring (Oh, lads and lasses hither come) Madden 1797-396

W——'s Thirteen (That monster oppression behold how he stalks) Vicinus-28

Yellow and Blue (Good people of England come listen to me) St. Bride SS

Yorkshire Dick (It is now for a new song gentlemen all) BOD 2806-cl8-343

    AT: Lancashire Dick

You Must All Fast (The people say the times are hard) Madden 1795-410

Young Mat Hyland (There was a lord lived in this town) BOD Firth C18-206

Young Squire (It's of a rich squire in Bristol doth dwell) BOD Harding B25-2146 • 416

    AT: Milkmaid of Blackberry Fold; Squire and Milkmaid

First-Line List of English Broadside Ballads on Poverty, 1790–1870

Locations are given in the Title List.
Slight variants in first lines are given in the Title List.

A Alphabet that we used to learn at school (The Working Man's A.B.C.)
A stands for alphabet, I've turned it into rhyme (The People's Comic Alphabet)
A stands for Aristocracy, on Luxuries they fare (John Bull's Alphabet)
A stands for Aristocrat, who nothing will do (A New Political & Reform Alphabet)
About my wife I mean to sing a very funny song (Hard Struggle for the Breeches / Struggle for the Breeches)
About this town I'm told there dwells (The Shabby Swell)
Abroad as I was walking one bitter winter's day (Help for Lancashire)
Across the fields one sweet May morn (The Weaver's / Old Weaver's Daughter)
Afflictions though they seem severe (The Prodigal Son)
After serving seven years (After Serving Seven Years)
Ah! dreadful state of my half-famish'd maw (The Poor Poet)
Ah, hear the wandering Savoyard's tale (The Wandering Savoyard)
Ah! well do I remember now my little cottage home (Don't Leave Your Father, Boy)
All good worthy people that's able to draw near (The Wounded Seamens Lamentation)
All in the month of May (The Lady and the Welsh Ploughboy)
All round the country there is a pretty piece of work (The New Poor Law Bill in Force)
All tender mothers lend an ear (The Last Sorrowful Lamentation of 15 Young Men Now Lying in Newgate Under Sentence of Death . . .)
All the world is one great stage, this Shakespeare said of old (The Stage of Life)
All you distressed tradesmen in country and town (The Cries of the Poor)
All you distressed tradesmen wherever you may be (The Transport's Lamentation / Farewell Address . . .)
All you that do in London dwell (Glorious News for the Wives)
All you that does in England dwell (Cholera Humbug)
All you that dwell in Hertford town (Hertford Approaching Election)

All you that dwell in Lambeth, listen for a while (A Night in a London Workhouse)
All you that fear the Lord, who rules the skies (The Lamentation of Sarah Bursnell . . .)
All you that have a father's heart (The Small Farmer's and Labourer's Complaint)
All you that have a feeling heart (The Dyer's Lamentation)
All you that have a feeling heart, come listen unto me (The Mechanic's Lamentation / The Mechanic's Lamentation on the Stagnation of Trade / The Clothier's Lamentation on the Badness of Trade)
All you that have feeling hearts wherever that you be (Lancashire Tragedy / Poverty No Crime)
All you that/who have got ears to hear (The Clothiers' Lamentation on the Badness of Trade / The Mechanic's Lamentation on the Stagnation of Trade / The Mechanic's Lamentation)
All you that/who have money, and you that have none (Reformed Drunkard)
All you that love a merry jest, give ear to what I say (The Factory Girl)
All you that wish your fortune for to know (Signs of the Times)
All you who are reduced and wish to cut a shine (One Suit Between Two)
All you whose minds are bent on straying (Emigration)
All young females I pray draw near (Annie Gray)
Although my name's Jack Rag and I wears a ragged tile (Jack Rag)
And now the ——— Statutes is come again (A New Statutes Song)
Arise, ye sons of freedom, and burst your galling chain (Peace and Plenty, Love and Liberty)
Arouse! arouse! this glorious day (Camberwell & Reform!)
Art thou poor but honest man (The Chartist)
As an Englishman, an Irishman, and a Scotchman, too, one day (The Englishman, Irishman, and Scotchman; or, Dearly You Must Pay for Your Mutton)
As at their work two weavers sat (Turn the Carpet; or, the Two Weavers)
As Britannia sat viewing the shores of old Albion (Britannia's Lamentation for Old England)
As I mused on the wrongs that my country bears (The Corn Laws)
As I rambled about on a fine summer's night (The Reformed Drunkard's Children's Song)
As I roamed out one morning quite early (The Lass with her Jet-Braided Hair)
As I rov'd out one morning, being in the blooming spring (The Bonny / My Bonny Labouring Boy)
As I roved out one evening being in the blooming spring (The Lady's Loyalty to her Bonny Labouring Boy)
As I roved out one morning down by the river side (Riley the Fisherman / Riley's Farewell)
As I walk'd out one sweet May morn (Old Weaver's Daughter / The Weaver's Daughter)
As I walk'd slowly down the street a few days ago (The Little Shoeblack)
As I walked by an hospital gate (The Old Woman's Wish)
As I walked out one May morning (Cupid the Pretty Ploughboy)
As I walked through the town of Portsmouth (Frost, Williams, and Jones's Farewell to England)
As I wandered by the cook shop (As I Wandered by the Cook Shop)

As I was a walking for pleasure (Blessings Below)
As I was travelling the country up and down (The Wars Are Not Over / When the Wars Are all O'er)
As I was walking one cold frosty morning (Poor Little Mary Ann, or the Smuggler's Bride)
As I was walking one midsummer morning (The Shady Green Tree)
As in sweet slumber I was laid (The Pride of Old England, or, the Folly of Man)
As Joe, the dustman, drove his noble team (Go Along Bob)
As Mars and Minerva was viewing of some implements (Grand Conversation Under the Rose)
As old John Bull was walking (The State of Great Britain, or, a Touch at the Times / Times for 1841 / for 1843)
As old trade and commerce were conversing on the present times (A New Song Written on the State of the Times)
As pensive one night in my garret I sat (The Last / Poet's Last Shilling)
As strikes have become the order of the day (A New Song on the Times)
As there's but little news and lack of conversation (True State of the Nation)
As through St. Pancras I was walking (An Uproar in St. Pancras)
As through the streets I take my way (The Hearth Stone Man)
As Victoria was walking and lovingly talking (Cheer Up Again! Good News for the Poor)
As walking near the docks at Liverpool, I heard some emigrants to say (Emigrants' Farewell to Old England)
As we travel through the street we very often meet (Remember You Have Children of Your Own)
As you sit in warm circles secure from the tempest (Think on the Poor)
As you travel through life, if you're wealthy you'll find (The Way of the World)
The assizes they are over now, the Judge is gone away (Farewell Address to Their Countrymen and Friends . . . / The Transport's Lamentation)
At an ironmaster's meeting a short time ago (A Copy of Verses Composed by a Distressed Pudler)
At five in the morning, the miner doth rise (Five O'Clock in the Morning)
At siven in the morning avaking (Sal Sly, and Billy Snivel)
At six in the morning awaking (Sally Sly)
At the time when the clothes I have on were quite new (I'm Not Such a Swell as I Us'd to be)
Attend awhile and you shall hear (Abolition of the Corn Laws)
Attend ye married women while I tell you a plan (New Way to Make a Good Husband)
Attend you feeling Christians all (Murder of a Child Near Measham)
Attend you feeling parents dear (Shocking Murder of a Wife and Six Children)
Attend you gallant heroes, of high and low degree (The Present Times)
Attend, ye thoughtless, young, and gay (Poor Nan of Wapping)
Attention awhile to my song (A New Song on the Bread Act)
Attention give to one and all unto a begging song (We Are All Beggars)
Attention pay to what I say, I'll not detain you long (My Grandmother's Days)
Awake, awake! without delay (Assessed Taxes)

The bailiffs are coming, oh dear, oh dear (The Bailiffs Are Coming)
The bailiffs have been here, oh la! oh la! (The Bailiffs Have Been)
The banners of cheap bread you know has lately been unfurl'd (Shocking Hard Times)
Because I'm but poor (The Ploughman's / Plowman's Ditty)
A beggar I am, and of low degree (The Beggar)
A beggar I am at the end of my days (Gospel Beggar)
The beggars are ruined oh dear—oh dear (The Beggar's Lament)
Behold a stranger as you pass along (. . . A Poor Faraway Stranger . . .)
Behold my Saviour is come to save (Death of the Poor Orphan Sweep)
Behold the man that is unlucky (Behold the Man That is Unlucky)
Behold these lines crave thy most solid view (A Dialogue Between Dives and Lazarus)
The bitter wind blew keen and cold (The Little / The Poor Little / Sailor Boy)
A blessing unknown to ambition and pride (The Wealth of a Cottage is Love)
A boat unmoor'd from off Bankside (Betty of Billingsgate)
Both young and old, come list to me (The Shortness of Work, and Present State of the Times)
Britons all of each degree (England's Maiden Queen)
Britons, be firm, and stick close to your king (The Voice of the People; or, the King and Reform)
The butchers of England are growing quite cranky (The English Butcher's Lament)
Buy a broom, buy a broom, buy a broom (Buy a Broom / The New Song of Buy a Broom)
By my friends turn'd adrift (A Song on Myself)
The cadger vonce in the rookery stood (The Cadger's Tear)
Can any king be half so great (The Thrasher)
Can you save us from starving by promoting a bill (The Farmers' Keep Sake)
The Chartists all are going mad (The Chartist's Flare-Up)
Cheer—boys—cheer! no more of idle sorrow (Cheer Boys! Cheer!)
Cheer up! cheer up, Britannia cries (England Demands Reform: and Reform She'll Have)
Child, is thy father dead? (The Orphan's Lament)
Childhood's days now pass before me (A New Batch of Ballads)
Chill winter had mantled the mountains in white (Wandering Ann)
The Christian pilgrim sings (Heaven's My Home)
Churchwarden I've been—let me see (The Vestry Dinner)
The cloth vos laid in the vorkhouse hall (The Vorkhouse / Workhouse / Poor Workhouse Boy)
Cold, cold was the night, the snow had been falling (Poor Little Joe)
Cold winter is come with its cold chilling breath (Remember the Poor / Time to Remember the Poor / Winter Piece)
Come all bad husbands, I'd have you be wise (A New Song on the Hard Times)
Come all English poor folks, and listen to my song (Free Trade or, the Farmers' Downfall)
Come all friends and neighbours I pray you draw near (The Devil and the Grinder)
Come all good people and pay attention (Horrid Murder of Four Children)
Come all good people far and near (Free Trade in Beer!)

Come, all working men here assembled (A Voice from the Factory!)
Come all ye brave tradesmen (The Keelmen's Lament for the Frost)
Come all ye brave tradesmen I pray you (The Tradesman's Wish for a Better New Year)
Come all ye Britons, bold and free (A New Song on the Jubilee)
Come all ye cotton hand weavers (Weaver's Crime)
Come all ye jolly colliers, and colliers' wives as well (A New Song on the Reduction of the Colliers' Wages)
Come all you blooming country lads and listen unto me (Country Hirings)
Come all you bold Britons and list to my rhymes (Our New Queen, the Flower of England)
Come all you bold Britons attend to my rhymes (The Trades Unions of England, Huzza!)
Come all you bold Britons give ear to my song (A New Song on the Hard Times)
Come all you bold Britons, where'er you be (Present Times, or Eight Shillings a Week)
Come all you brave fellows that belong to the coal trade (The Keelman's Complaint)
Come all you brave tradesmen that dwell round this land (The Tradesman's Complaint in Time of Distress)
Come all you brisk and jovial blades (The World on Credit)
Come all you Britons list awhile (Britons, Awake)
Come all you bucksome men and maids (Advice to Country Maidens on the Poor Law Bill)
Come all you buxom females (In England there is One Law for the Rich and Another for the Poor)
Come all you buxom men and maids (The Lady Lov'd Her Father's Groom)
Come all you canny pitmen here come listen to my song (A New Song)
Come all you chanting vocalists (The Chaunt Seller or, a New Batch of Ballads)
Come all you English poor folk (The Farmers Downfall and the Poor Man's Distress)
Come all you English poor folks (The Union Houses Must Come Down and Railroads Go to Pot)
Come all you females pay attention (The Model Workhouse Master!)
Come all you fine ladies who in Brixton does dwell (The Brixton Lady and Her Nice Beetle Pies)
Come all you friends to liberty (The Weavers Triumph)
Come all you frolicsome fellows (The Good Husband)
Come all you gallant Englishmen (The Fatal English Poor Law Bill or, the Ways of the World)
Come all you gallant Englishmen and listen to my song (The Emigrant)
Come all you gallant Englishmen and listen to my song (The Great Meetings in England, or the Free Trades and Protectionists)
Come all you gallant Englishmen wherever you may be (The Emigrant)
Come all you gallant heroes and listen to my rhymes (The Times in Hertfordshire)
Come all you gallant husbandmen (Seven Shillings a Week)
Come all you good people (Things I'd Like to See)
Come all you good people that live in this shire (The Farmers Lament)
Come all you honest tradesmen, and listen unto me (Chapter of Cheats)
Come all you humble and Christian colliers (The Collier's Hymn)

Come all you jolly husbandmen and listen to my song (The Honest / The Life of an Honest Ploughman, or Ninety Years Ago)
Come all you jolly labourers (A New Song)
Come all you jolly tradesmen of this famous little town (Fair Play for Working Men)
Come all you jolly young fellows, and listen awhile to my song (What Will Old England Come To?)
Come all you ladies list to me (The Lucky Footman!)
Come all you lads of high renown (Country Statute)
Come all you loyal lovers, I hope you will draw near (A Lady's Love and Loyalty for her Sweetheart)
Come all you master-spinners dear (Lines on the Factory System)
Come all you men of courage bold and listen unto me (Claughton Wood Poachers)
Come all you merry buxom blades (Happy Man)
Come all you people in this place (Sketch of Roguery)
Come all you philanthropists attend awhile to me (The State of the Times and Their Causes)
Come all you poor distressed souls (The Wonderous Works of God)
Come all you poor drunkards, you now may be free (Advice to Drunkards)
Come all you poor of London town, and listen unto me (The War, or What Do They Say in England)
Come all you poor people, I pray lend an ear (Forestalling Done Over)
Come, all you poor tradesmen, I pray lend an ear (The Tradesman's Complaint)
Come, all you pretty factory girls (The Rambling Factory Girl's Return)
Come all you roving bachelors, listen to me awhile (Skilly Night and Morning)
Come all you sighing brothers, give ear to my song (England's Glory, or, a Large Loaf for Sixpence)
Come all you sporting heroes of high and low degree (Reform & Victory, the Grey Horse & the Union Coach)
Come all you swaggering farmers, of courage stout and bold (The Farmers Done Over)
Come all you swaggering farmers wherever you may be (Swaggering Farmers / Times Altered or the Grumbling Farmers)
Come all you swells and pray take pity on the life of poor old Bob (Bob / Poor Old Bob the Groom)
Come all you thoughtless young men (The British Tars)
Come all you true Britons, of every degree (Things I Should Like to See)
Come all you truebred Englishmen wherever you may be (Britons United; or, the Downfall of Tyranny)
Come all you who have got a few minutes to spare (A True Picture of the Present Times)
Come all you working people what shall we do now (State of the Times)
Come all you worthy Christians/people that dwell within this land (Job, the Patient Man / One God Has Made Us All / Poverty and Contentment)
Come all you young fellows and list unto me (Two Shilling Suit)
Come all you young men and maidens so gay (A New Song Called the Hiring Day)

Come all you young men and young maidens around (Dear Woman is the Joy of an Englishmans Life)

Come all you young people and listen awhile (The Fortunate Lovers)

Come attend you working men wherever you may be (The Collier Lads, Who Labour Under Ground)

Come attention give you Britons, and listen to my rhymes (The Present Times, or a Row about the Boroughmongers)

Come Britons all rejoice and sing (A Laughable & Interesting Dialogue Between Joan o' Greenfield, Nosey and Earl Grey)

Come Britons, here's a huzza (The Managers Last Kick, or, the Distruction of the Boroughmongers)

Come Britons, strike boldly, weather the storm (A New Song)

Come brother farmers all attend (Advice to Farmers)

Come buy my deal matches, come buy of me (The Match Song)

Come buy of poor Mary/Kate, primroses I sell (The Pretty Primrose Girl / The Primrose Girl)

Come cheer up your hearts there's good news come to town (Farmers Lamentation)

Come come brother freeman let's hasten away (A New Song on the Times or, the Mystery of the Large Loaf Reduced Small, Explained)

Come come my good masters, what's all this about (Frauds and Pickpockets, or Rogues All)

Come every heart rejoice with me (A New Song on the Repeal of the Corn Laws)

Come farming lads and lasses all (A Country Lad Am I)

Come, friends and voters, let's consent (A New Song)

Come gentlemen farmers, I pray now attend (Farmers Warning)

Come hark! to the strains of a plaintive band (Come Hark! to the Strains of a Plaintive Band)

Come hither a while, I'll sing you a song (Odds and Ends of the Year 1830)

Come lads and listen to my song (The Fine Old English Labourer)

Come lend an ear of pity while I my tale do tell (The Meeting at Peterloo)

Come, let us dance and sing (Song of the Cadgers in the Holy Land)

Come let us go cadging together (Let Us Go Cadging Together)

Come listen a while and give ear to my song (The True Joke, or the Poor Man's Complaint)

Come listen a while and I'll sing you a song (A New Song on the Whig Poor Laws)

Come listen awhile and make no delay (Britons Glory)

Come listen awhile and you shall hear (The Poor Whores Complaint)

Come listen awhile I will tell you the rigs (A New Song)

Come listen awhile my friends to my ditty (The Poor Man's Health)

Come listen awhile to a song that is new (The Tories They Govern the Nation)

Come listen awhile to a story of fate (Robin Rough-Head)

Come listen awhile to my song (A New Song & Dialogue on the Opening of the Ports)

Come listen awhile to my song (A New Song and Dialogue on the Times)

Come listen, come listen, I'm going to sing (Reform! "The Bill, the Whole Bill, and Nothing but the Bill")

Come listen dear neighbours to these lines I have made (Mechanics' Lamentation / Spinners Lamentation)
Come listen, dear neighbours, to these lines which I've made (Mechanics' Lamentation)
Come listen my neighbours and hear a merry ditty (The Alteration of Times)
Come listen to me one and all (A Night's Repose in Lambeth Workhouse)
Come listen to my ditty (Good Times are Coming)
Come listen to my ditty (Song and Dialogue on the Times, or Jacob and Jonathan)
Come listen to my ditty, both young and old I pray (The Farmer Relieved by His Landlord)
Come listen unto my wonderful song (Wonderful Times)
Come my fellow slaves of Britain (Haughty Lords Have Us Degraded)
Come neighbours and friends I beg you'll attend (Touch at the Times for the Year 1807)
Come neighbours attend now and listen awhile (The Forestallers in the Dumps)
Come neighbours, no longer be patient and quiet (The Riot; or, Half a Loaf is Better Than No Bread)
Come now each gen'rous feeling heart (The Framework-Knitters Lamentation)
Come, old and young, and rich and poor (Cheap Food Laws)
Come old and young, and rich and poor (A New Song on the Times)
Come one and all and list to these lines (The Life of a Working Man)
Come people all I pray attend (A Touch on the Times)
Come women all of Britain's isle (A New Song on the Coronation)
Come ye Britons all listen with serious attention (The Begging Box)
Come you hardworking people attend to my rhymes (A New Touch on the Times; or, the Comforts of the Labouring Poor)
Come you men and women unto me attend (The New Starvation Law Examined)
Come you that can tell us, we should just like to know (A True Picture of the Times, or, the Poor Man's Consolation from Reform)
The cottage was a thatched one (Little Jim / Poor Jim the Collier Boy / Lad)
Could we obtain our food by work (The Framework-Knitters Petition)
The country's in a dreadful state (Honest Working Man)
Dark is the night! how dark! no light! no fire! (The Gambler's Wife)
The day was dark and sad and drear (The Carpet Weaver's True Tale)
A dialogue I'll tell you as true as my life (The Coal-Owner and the Pitman's Wife)
Don't talk of life's troubles with sad rueful face (There's Brighter Days in Store)
Don't think by my dress that I come here to beg (Though Poor, I'm a Gentleman Still)
Down by a chrystal fountain as I alone one morn did stray (Bonny England)
Down in a valley my father did dwell (Cottager's Daughter)
Down in Cupid's garden for pleasure I did walk (Lady Who Fell in Love with a Prentice Boy)
Down in the valley my father did dwell (I'm His Only Daughter)
Down in yon valley I live so snug (Cherry Cheek Patty)
Draw near all you fathers, and mothers as well (The Dreadful Murder of a Wife and Six Children)
Draw near awhile and listen to me (A New Way for Paying the Taxes . . .)

Draw near brother tradesmen, listen to my song (The Tradesman's Complaint)
Draw near my good people and a story I'll tell (The Farmers Lamentation)
Draw near, with attention, both young and old (Things I'd Like to See)
The dreadful deeds of Birmingham (The Birmingham Investigation)
Duck-Leg Dick had a donkey (Duck-Leg Dick)
Each Briton awhile come listen to me (King & People)
Each feeling heart pray lend an ear (The Collier's Hymn / The Collier's New . . .)
Each tender mother lend an ear (A Warning to Youth)
Eh, my father he not a shilling will give (I'm Like to be There)
Eight years ago I was a swell, sir (When These Old Clothes Were New)
Englishmen give ear to me (The New Parliament: or, the House Turned Upside Down!)
Exalt your voices high (Oastler is Free)
Excuse these salt and briny tears (Since Johnny's Been Out of Work)
———— Fair is come without delay (Rigs and Flares-Up of the Fair)
Farewell, adieu to England (The South Australian Emigrant)
Farewell and adieu to the year ninety three (A Short Sketch of the Times)
Farewell dear wife and children for now I'm bound to sea (The Tradesman's Lamentation)
Farewell, false girl (Despised for Being / I Was Despis'd Because I Was Poor)
Farewell, parents, we must leave you (The Lancashire Emigrant's Farewell)
Fare-ye-vell, my Vitechapel boys, fare-ye-vell for a-vhile (The Dodger)
A farmer on a market day was coming from this town, sir (The Farmer's Complaint)
A farmer's employment's the best I e'er saw (Farmer's Rent Day)
Farmers Marco and Pedro were jogging along (The Grumbling Farmers)
The father of Nancy a forester was (The Forester's Daughter)
Females work too hard I'm told (Stitch Goes the Needle!)
A few remarks I beg to make, touching both rich and poor (Poverty Ruins Confidence)
First listen and I'll be bound (Oh, What a Stagnation in Trade)
For now the cold winter comes on (The Poor Man's Wish for a Wife)
For Reform, meet again, boys, on Monday, I say (Reform Meeting at Blackheath)
Forced from home and all its pleasures (Lamentation of the Smugglers)
Free trade has been carried (Free Trade; or the Coalition)
A friend in the pocket is a friend indeed (A Friend in the Pocket)
Friends of humanity think of the strangers (Stanza)
Friends, stop and listen unto me (The King of the Factory Children)
From a country village t'other day (Crikey! What Will Master Say)
From four pounds of bread, at sixteen-pence price (The Poor Man's Litany)
From Liverpool, 'cross the Atlantic (The Stowaway or Little Hero)
From Teutchland I came/come with my light wares all laden (Bavarian Girl's Song / Buy a Broom)
From the cold snowy mountains of Savoy (The Savoyard)
The frozen streets in moonshine glitter (The Orphan's Prayer)
Gather round me, one an' all, great and small, short and tall (The Poor Discharged Soldier)

FIRST-LINE LIST 633

Gazing on noblemen's mansions (Out in the Cold)
Gentle people as ye throng (The Ballad Singer)
A gentleman farmer has got in a mess (Dreadful Cruelty to a Servant)
Gentlemen farmers, I pray now attend (The Farmer)
Gentlemen give attention unto my song (Cries of the Nation)
George Victor Townley step this way (The Rich and the Poor / Townley and Wright)
Give attention awhile to my rhyme (The Mechanic's Appeal to the Public)
Give attention to my ditty (Grandfather's Days)
Give attention to my ditty and I will not keep you long (My Grandfather's Days)
Give me the man of honest heart (Give Me the Man of Honest Heart)
A glove cutter is Tommy Trank (Tommy Trank, the Glove Cutter)
God bless our king, and long may he reign (God Bless Our King)
God bless these poor folk that are strivin' (God Bless These Poor Folk!)
God save the starving poor (God Save the Poor)
God speed the keel of the trusty ship (God Speed the Good Ship; or, the English Emigrant! / English Emigrant)
Good Christians give attention / You tender Christians, pray give attention (The Blind Man's Lamentation)
Good folks I pray attend to me (Downfall of Monopoly)
Good folks of every station, come listen to my rhymes (Conversations on the Present Times)
Good morning, Mr. Grasp (The Parish Pays the Piper / The Rose-Water Select, the Parish Pays the Piper, O the Parish Pays for All)
Good people all attend (Singular Scene Under the New Poor Law Act)
Good people all attend, and listen to my ditty (The Poor Law Bill in Force)
Good people all attend awhile (Frame Work Knitters' Petition / Frame Work Weavers Petition / The Framework-Knitters Appeal)
Good people all attend awhile (The Needle Makers Lamentation of Redditch, Worcestershire)
Good people all attend awhile (The New Fashioned Farmer)
Good people all, both great and small, come listen to my rhymes (What Shocking Hard Times)
Good people all give ear awhile (Free Trade, or the Farmers' Downfall)
Good people all give ear, I do pray (Carlisle Gaol)
Good people all I pray attend (The Farmer's Lamentation, But the Poor's Rejoicing)
Good people all I pray attend (Free Trade or Downfall of the Farmers)
Good people all I pray attend (Friend of / Friend to the Distressed / Distress of Trade)
Good people all I pray attend (Poor Man's Lamentation for the Bach-Bag)
Good people all I pray attend and listen to my ditty (Poor Man's Complaint)
Good people all I pray draw near (A New Song on the Times)
Good people all I pray draw near that in this country dwell (The New Gruel Shops)
Good people all listen to what I now say (The Blessings of Peace)
Good people all pray pity me (Blind Man's Petition)
Good people attend here awhile to my song (A Monstrous Good Song)
Good people attend to my song (The Snob and the Bottle)

Good people come listen, I'll tell you of a lark (The Reform Demonstration in Hyde Park, May 6th 1867)
Good people draw near as you pass along (A New Alphabetical Song on the Corn Law Bill)
Good people give attention and listen to my rhymes (Present Fashions or the Pride of the Times)
Good people give attention and you shall understand (An Interesting Dialogue Concerning Emigration)
Good people give attention unto a merry ditty (Alteration of the Times)
Good people give attention while I sing in praise (The Farmer's Son)
Good people give attention, who now around do stand (Past, Present and Future)
Good people give ear to my song (Price of Flour Keeps Falling)
Good people I pray give attention / You landsmen and seamen attention (The World's in a Terrible State)
Good people I pray give ear unto what I say (Hunting a Loaf)
Good people now I pray attend (Distress of Trade / Friend of—to—the Distressed)
Good people now I pray attend (The Times Will Mend)
Good people of England come listen to me (Yellow and Blue)
Good people of England I pray lend an ear (Remarks on the Times)
Good people of England wherever you be (The Labouring Man and His Wife)
Good people what will you of all be bereft (Poor England in the Year 1811)
A good time is coming, now mind what I say (The Farmers, Millers, and Bakers)
The good times are coming, O dear, O dear (The Good Times Are Coming)
The good times in England are gone to decay (Hope for the Best)
Good times they say are coming boy (The Times or 50 Years Ago)
The good times, they say, are coming, boys (The Good Times Are Gone)
Great Britain is a curious place, a place of high renown (We Are All Beggars)
The grocers, poor creatures, long time have complained (The Honest Grocer)
Had Mr. Ward sung of the boy he met on Margate Pier (The Vulgar Little Girl)
Hail to ye brave sons of Gall (Vive la Liberte)
An hapless orphan girl am I (The Orphan Girl)
Happy is the peasant's lot (The Contented Peasant)
Hard, hard is the times, and the cry it's no wonder (Hard Times)
Hard times so badly stings us (Hard Times; or, How to Get a Dinner)
Has there not been a sad to do (The Kingdoms Complaint)
Have you heard of a collier of honest renown (Patient Joe; or the Newcastle Collier)
Have you heard of the news concerning Bill Bounce (Bill Bounce the Swell Cove Now in Luck)
Have you seen the new prison, no more you'll desire (Brixton Tread Mill)
He. —Oh, Sally Sime when we get wed (Chandler's Shop)
Hear, oh, hear us, our parish king (Just-Starve-Us)
Here's a health to old honest John Bull (Honest John Bull / John Bull and His Mother)
Here's your catch 'em alives, and to sell 'em I strives (Catch 'em Alive)
His faithful subject Martha Bird (A New Song on the Alteration of the Times)

The home was so bright and so happy within (Shelter Your Mother and Me)
How gaily and how merrily my life has pass'd along (Life of a Vagabond)
How I envy the cottager's Saturday eve (The Cottager's Saturday Eve)
How little we think as we travel (Do a Good Turn When You Can)
How melancholy crows the cock (The Pleasures of a Country Life)
How pure the air, how sweet the breeze (The Labourer's Horizon at Sunrise)
Hurrah, my boys, a bumper fill (A New Song on the Corn Bill)
Husband. About my wife I mean to sing a very funny song (Struggle / Hard Struggle for the Breeches)
I am a brisk and bonny lass that's free from care and strife (The Country Lass)
I am a charity boy, dressed blue (The Charity Boy / I am a Charity Boy)
I am a damsel so blooming and gay (Oh Dear, How I Long to Get Married!)
I am a jovial roving blade (Birmingham Jack of All Trades)
I am a known / cunning cadger as ever tramped the town (The Manchester Cadger / Life of a Cadger)
I am a navvy bold, that has tramp'd the country round sir (Navvy on the Line)
I am a poor farmer sore oppress'd, free trade has ruin'd me (Conversation Between a Farmer and His Wife)
I am a poor lad, my fortune is bad (The Unfortunate Lad)
I am a poor maiden, distressed and forlorn (The Orphan Girl)
I am a poor old man in years, come listen to my song (Old Hat / My Old Hat / When My—This—Old Hat Was New)
I am a poor unhappy man (The World Turn'd Upside Down)
I am a poor weaver that's out of employ (Larry O'Broom)
I am a travelling tinker with my workshop on my back (The Travelling Tinker)
I am a youthful lady, my troubles they are great (Victory)
I am Bessy Bloom the flower girl (Bessy Bloom the Flower Girl)
I am going to sing a ditty upon the present time (The New Social & Political Alphabet)
I am / I'm poor little Jessey / Jessy, I'm come here to shew (Little Jessey, the Poor Flower Maid / Poor Little Jessy)
I came from a land far away, far away (Savoyard Boy / Poor Savoyard Boy)
I deals in costermongery (Ax My Eye)
I dreamt that, buried in my fellow-clay (The Rich Man's Dream)
I gaily sing from day to day (Bear It Like a Man)
I have a never-failing bank (The Firm Bank)
I have indited these few verses to try to show to you (A Song on the Times, We Are All Wrong Up to Now)
I have seen life in its changes, in towns low and big (Wonderful World This Would Be)
I hear the blythe voices of children at play (The Factory Child / The Factory Child's Complaint)
I hear thee speak of a better land (The Better Land)
I hope you all both great and small (Did You All Fast)
I keeps a slap up tater can (The Tater Can)

I knew a widow, very poor (A Child's Faith / The Poor Widow and Her Praying Boy)
I knew by the smoke that so gracefully curl'd (The Cook Shop)
I left my love in England (Sunshine After Rain)
I / I've lived in the woods for a number of years / many a year (Ground for the Floor / The Neat Little Cottage with . . .)
I look'd in the east, I look'd in the west (Jordan)
I Master William Waters, O (The Merry Will & Testament of Master Black Billy)
I met the waiter in his prime (The Waiter)
I never had money, I ne'er larnt a trade (Tim Snooken, the Cadger)
I once could sport the blunt about (The Cove Vot Has Seen Better Days)
I once was a peeler and played the deuce (Go It My Kiddies and Fake Away)
I pray draw near with one accord, and listen to my ditty (House and Window Taxes)
I pray give attention and listen to me (Rich and Poor)
I sing a modern ballad, made by a modern pate (The Fat Old Parish Vestryman)
I sing the pleasures of these glorious days (Happy Land!!)
I stood beside a factory where (The Opinions of an Honest Working Man)
I thought when I entered / first entered into life (Anything to Earn / Yarn a Crust)
I was born in the country far over the mountains (The Wandering Boy)
I was brought up in Lincolnshire, but not of high degree (The Cold Winter's Day)
I was d'ye see a dairy maid (The Dairy Maid)
I was forced as a stranger to wander from home (The New Poor Law and the Farmer's Glory)
I was reared in Doncaster some forty years ago (Poor Old Mike)
I wish I'd a thousand a year (I Wish I'd a Thousand a Year)
I wish in my song I may not offend (Poor Will's Wish)
I wish there wou'd be an alteration (Depression of Trade)
I wish you all a happy new year (Starve Away and No Beer)
I would take them into Cheshire, and there they should sow (A Dialogue and Song on the Starvation Poor Law Bill, Between Tom and Ben)
I'd be a gipsy merry and free (I'd Be a Gipsy)
If pity sweet maid ever dwelt in thy breast (The Orphan Girl / The Orphan, Wet with Rain)
If there's anything that I detest (Domestic Economy)
If you are determined and wishful to go (Railroad to Hell)
If you want a cheap lodging (Kind Old Daddy O!)
If you want a good hymn pray buy one of me (The Disobedient Daughter)
If you want a good song, will you buy it of me (Distressed Wanderer)
If you'll lend me your attention, I will return to you (The Medley Song)
If you'll listen to me, a tale I'll relate (Red Sage Sal)
If you'll listen to me I'll sing of a spree (The Chummy's / Sweep's Wedding)
If you'll listen to me, I'll tell you a spree (Seizure of Goods for Assessed Taxes . . .)
I'll be/I'ze proud just to say I'm a plain honest farmer (Heaven Bless Lovely Women and Succour the Poor / The Honest Farmer)
I'll please you all both great and small, if you will give attention (How to Get a Living in This Town)

I'll sing a song and the truth be giving (The Rigs of London)
I'll sing, I'll sing, awhile, attend sir (The Power of Hot Water or Plain Hints to the Millions)
I'll sing of a wedding, a wedding of fame (. . . A Beggar's Wedding . . .)
I'll sing you a good old chaunt, since now 'tis much the rage (The Old English Lady)
I'll sing you a good old song (Fine Old English Pawnbroker)
I'll sing you a good old song, made by a good old pate (The Old / The Fine Old English Gentleman)
I'll sing you a prime new song, that was made by a young chap's pate (The Fine Young English Gentleman)
I'm a broken-down man, without money or credit (The Tramp)
I'm a brokenhearted milkman, in grief I am arrayed (Polly Perkins, of Paddington Green)
I'm a charity/factory girl as you may see (The Charity Girl / Factory Girl / The Flare-Up Factory Girl)
I'm a gent reduced by railway speculation (Study Economy / Studying Economy)
I'm a genteel respectable youth (Is There Anything Low about Me?)
I'm a musical genius in rags (Jim Baggs the Musician)
I'm a poor cotton weaver as many a one knows (Joan o' Grinfield! / Jone o' Grinfield / The Poor Cotton Weaver)
I'm a poor shepherd maid (I'm a Poor Shepherd Maid)
I'm a very knowing prig (Beadle of the Parish)
I'm Billy Nuts, wot always cuts (The Bard of Seven Dials / Billy Nutts, the Poet)
I'm dashing Dick the dustman (The Dustman / Dick the Dustman)
I'm going to sing a song, as well as I can do (A New Song of Songs)
I'm living on the parish now as happy as a king (Pauper and the Minister)
I'm no busy body, no, not I (I Never Takes No Notice)
I'm not a wealthy man, but I've hit upon a plan (Work, Boys, Work!)
I'm now depriv'd of the light (The New Way of the Blind Boy)
I'm one of those sailors who think 'tis no lie (The True-Hearted Sailor)
I'm pretty well known here in town (The Costermonger)
I'm remembered well—a slap-up swell (Broken Down Swell / A Tidy Suit for all That)
I'm rolling Sam the brick dust boy (The Brick Dust Boy)
I'm Sammy Slap the bill sticker (Sammy Slap the Bill Sticker)
I'm saucy leering rolling Bet (Flashy Bet)
I'm standing at the stall Sarey with Pincher by my side (English Emigrant)
I'm the happiest man 'neath the sun (Happy Man, or, It Can't Last)
I'm the lad that's free and easy (Free and Easy)
I'm the Polly Perkins that once used to be (Polly Perkins' Answer)
I'm the wandering bard of Exeter / Manchester (Wandering Bard)
I'm very fond of fish (Pretty Betty Brill)
In a box of the stone jug I was born (Nix My Dolly, Pals, Fake Away)
In a cottage embosom'd within a deep shade (Blue Ey'd Mary)
In a little blue garment all ragged and torn (Child / Poor Little Child of a Tar)
In all combined societies in England all around (The Odd Fellows Benefit)

In Bellona's red field I have oft been contending (The Unfortunate Author of the Following Verses . . .)
In China, that region of wisdom celestial (A Chinese Puzzle)
In Grays Inn Lane not long ago (The Dogs-Meat Man)
In London town there once did dwell (Bill Bounce, the Swell Cove Out o' Luck)
In London when the weather's fair (Regent Street)
In Manchester at dinner time (Manchester at Twelve O'Clock)
In me you see a collier, a simple honest man (Down in a Coal Mine)
In Northumberland I've a farmer been (A Respectable Farmer's Farewell to Northumberland)
In one thousand eight hundred and thirty and nine (Lines, by a Chartist)
In our sweet little villages all through the land (Pity the Farmers, the Broken Down Farmers)
In Owdham streets at dinner time (Owdham Streets at Dinner Time)
In sixteen hundred and forty-one (The White Hat)
In ――― Street in Somers town (The Somers Town Sausage Maker)
In Strutton Parish did a widow dwell (Comfort to the Afflicted, or, the Wonderous Works of God / The Wonderous Works of God)
In taking my walks on one cold winter's day (The Drunkard's / The Poor Drunkard's Child)
In taking of my lonely walk on a cold and wintry day (The Collier Lad's Lament)
In tatter'd weed, from town to town (In Tatter'd Weed from Town to Town)
In the city of London there lived of late (London Kate)
In the dark gloomy mine (The Pitman's Widow's Lament)
In the days when I was hard up (In the Days When I Was Hard Up)
In the depths of a coal-pit a young lad grew (Collier's Song)
In the dry desert of a leathern jacket (Soliloquy on the Last Shilling)
In the merry month of June (The Merry Haymakers)
In the quiet town of Cambridge a deed has been done (Murder at Cambridge)
In the year eighteen hundred, I think, in sixteen (Stones a-Breaking)
In this county, as I've/we've been told (A Copy of Verses on the Life and Death / Lines on the Death of a Most Cruel and Hard-Hearted Overseer of the Poor)
In war time when banks left off paying in cash (On the Times, Corn Bill, Paper Money, and Trade)
In what a sad state is the true British nation (A Song Sung at a Meeting in Philadelphia)
Indeed my simple tale is true (The Farmer Boy)
Industrious men, give ear awhile (England's Glory)
Is this that happy England (The Poor Law Bastile)
It happen'd on March the twenty-third day (The Miners' Binding)
It is / It's now for a new song, gentlemen all (Yorkshire Dick / Lancashire Dick)
It is of a blooming lady (The Blooming Lady Worth £500,000 and Her Footman)
It is / It's of a tradesman and his wife (How Five and Twenty Shillings Was / Five and Twenty Shillings Expended in a Week)
It was down in the country a poor girl was weeping (The Fisherman's / Poor Fisherman's / Poor Little Fisherman's Girl)

It was down in the lowlands a poor boy did wander (The Fisherman's / Poor Fisherman's / Poor Little Fisherman's Boy)
It was in a country village, by a neat little cottage (The Orphan Drummer Boy)
It was in the town of Manchester (Poverty No Crime / Lancashire Tragedy)
It was the son of a soldier, who in battle was slain (The Soldier's Orphan's Prayer)
It's a fashion to make a great bother (Don't Speak of a Man as You Find Him)
It's of a damsel both fair and handsome (Mary Ann and Her Servant Man)
It's of a liquor merchant in London did dwell (William and Dinah)
It's of a rich merchant near London did dwell (The Lady and Weaver)
It's of a rich squire in Bristol doth dwell (Milkmaid of Blackberry Fold / Squire and Milkmaid / Young Squire)
It's of a sea captain in Yarmouth did dwell (The Cruel Sea-Captain, and Nancy of Yarmouth)
It's of a tradesman and his wife I hear the other day (A Song Called My £1 5s.)
It's of a wealthy farmer (Wealthy Farmer)
It's of a weaver's daughter as I to you declare (Jane of Spitalfields)
I've been searching the sorrows that trouble my mind (The True Rights of Men; or, the Contented Spitalfields Weaver)
I've been thinking, of late I've been thinking (Can You Wonder at Crime / John Bull, Can You Wonder . . . / The Increase of Crime)
I've been thinking of the day that has long since passed away (Don't Put My Father's Picture Up for Sale)
I've come across the sea (The Swiss Toy Girl / Rose of Lucerne; or . . .)
I've drunk away my precious time (The Drunkard's Confession)
I've lived a few years in this valley of tears (Never Mind What You Do for a Living)
I've oft seen you smiling, dear mother (The English Exile)
I've seen life in pleasure, I've seen life in sorrow (Love & Poverty)
I'ze a simple honest country clown (Sally Carter)
I'ze proud just to say, I'ze a plain honest farmer (The Honest Farmer)
Jack is as good as his master we are told (Jack's as Good as His Master)
Joe was a Marsh-Gate costermonger (Marsh-Gate Costermonger)
John Bull he was an Englishman, he went on the tramp one day (Paddy Magee's Dream)
A jolly old farmer once soaking his clay (The Generous Farmer and /or Poor Soldier / Jolly Old Farmer)
A jolly old thrasherman lived by the seaside (Jolly Thrasherman)
Judge not a man by the cost of his clothing (Judge Not a Man by the Coat that He Wears)
Kind folks all list my ditty (Joe Bradley, the Runaway Workhouse Boy)
Kind friends excuse me asking (Ben / Old Ben / Poor Ben Low)
The king's picture and Abraham Newland are sung (The Seven-Shilling Piece)
Labouring people wherever you be (The Way of the Landlords)
The landlord too long hath sat at his ease (Rag Bag!)
The landlords now lately so nice they are grown (Quarter Day, Being a Curious and Laughable Dialogue Which Occurred Between the Landlord and His Tenants)
The lark melodious sung above (Mary of the Lowly Cot)

Last new year's day, as I've heard say (Dick's Courtship)
Late one night, when the moon shone bright (St. Paul's and the Monument)
Let all the world say what they will (I'm Going to See the Exhibition for a Shilling)
Let high and low, let old and young give ear unto my ditty (Poor Law Bill!)
Let sages talk on as they will (The Treading Mill; or the Ups and Downs of Life)
Let them brag, until in the face they are black (Working Poor of Old England)
Let us pause in life's pleasures and count its many tears (Hard Times Come Again No More)
Let us pause in life's pleasures, and count its many tears (War Cry Come Again No More!)
Life is like a day's journey, we truly may say (Birds of a Feather)
Like most other men who've been knocking about (The Loom and the Lathe)
Little Anne and her mother were walking one day (Little Anne and Her Mother)
Little Boney done over, hostilities o'er (John Bull in a Rage at the Corn Laws)
A little boy a Savoyard (The Savoyard)
A little old woman a living she got (Hot Codlings)
A little ragged laddie goes wand'ring thro' the streets (The Drunkard's Ragged Child)
Live and let live is the first law of nature (Live and Let Live)
Long I've been an orphan poor (The Beggar Boy)
Look through the land from north to south (The Gin Shop; or, a Peep Into Prison)
Lord Derby's got a new corn bill (A New Song on Stanley's Corn Bill)
Lord, from thy blessed throne (The People's Anthem)
A lot of snobs set out one day (The Ragged Riot)
A maid I was, and a maid was I (The Unfortunate Wife)
A maid with a heart that could feel (Poor Blind Boy)
A man and his wife got into strife (House Keeping or, Two Pounds Two)
A man and his wife got married one day (The Way to Live)
A man and his wife in ——— Street (Eighteen Shillings a Week)
A man and his wife in ——— Street (A Week's Reckoning / Fifteen Shillings a Week)
A man at an alehouse was sitting one night (The Dead, Alive)
Mankind is censorious and apt to condemn (Look at Home Boys)
Many assert, but I ne'er heed 'em (The Joys of an Englishman's Life)
Many sad and weary years they have toiled in the mine (The Collier's Appeal)
Mark ye well my neighbours all, and pray now can you tell (The Beggar's Ramble)
Martinmas holidays are short I must say (The Plough)
Mechanics and artisans now pray give ear (The Felting Machines)
Men, women and children come listen to my story (Opening the Ports)
The Mill—the Mill—the Brixton treading-mill (The Mill / The Treading Mill / Brixton Treading-Mill)
The morn was dark, the hour was four and heavy fell the snow (The Little Sweep)
The mother mourned her infant lost (The Poor Lost Child Restored to His Mother)
The Mounseers, they say, have the world in a string (A New Song on the Times)
Mrs. Lobsky sold sprats and shrimps they say (Mrs. Lobsky's Rout)

Mrs. Waddle was a widow, and she got no little gain (The Widow Waddle)
My chaise the village inn did gain (The Orphans / The Two Orphans / Two Orphans at their Mother's Grave / A Copy of Verses Written by a Lady on Two Orphans
My father gave me a portion in hand (Prodigal Son)
My friend is the man I would copy thro' life (The Model)
My heart is like a pumpkin, swollen big with love (Pretty Little Sarah on 18s. a Week)
My lodging is in Leather Lane (Dyot Street, or Parlour Next to the Sky)
My mam is no more, and my dad in the grave (Cottage on the Moor)
My moralizing muse attunes (Brother to the Dustman / The Dustman's Brother)
My name is Captain Grant (Captain Grant)
My name is Polly Parker, I'm come o'er from Worsley (The Collier Lass)
My name is Tommy Tadpole, I does things with eclat (Catch 'em All Alive O!)
My name's Jenny Jenkins, I'm a wandering old lady (Jenny Jenkins)
My name's saucy Kate, I all others excel (The Barrow Girl)
My old 'oman one day says to me (Burial Club)
My parents dear I miss them (The Orphan Factory Boy)
My thanks accept / except of me, kind friends (Encore Verses or the Answer to Parson Brown's Sheep / Second Edition of Parson Brown's Sheep)
My toggery I took out of pawn (Go It Neddy / Love and Liver)
Nature! thy matchless power (Why is Man Denied by Man His Daily Bread?)
Neighbours, countrymen and friends (The Poor Threadmaker's Lamentation)
Neighbours, countrymen, and friends (The Tradesmen's Lamentation)
The night air is chill, the snow is fast falling (The London Newsboy)
The night of affliction had darken'd my cot (The Odd Fellow's Home)
The night was dark as I did ramble (The Orphan Child)
No doubt a song you've heard (The Cove / The Luck of a Cove Wot Sings!)
No doubt you all wonder what this object is (The Man That Has Seen Better Days)
No doubt you know as well as I (The Tread Mill; or, Tom and Jerry at Brixton)
No doubt you wonders who I is (The Charity Boy)
No matter what your means may be (The Penny and the Bob)
No more shall the chummies bawl out sweep (No More Shall the Chummies)
No more the merry spindles go whistling hour by hour (A Cry from Lancashire)
No wail of woe, or deep distress (Leicester Stocking Weaver's Complaint)
The noontide is hot and our foreheads are brown (Haymakers / Song of the Haymakers)
Not a trap was heard, or a Charley's not (Not a Trap was Heard)
Not long ago, in our town (Parson Brown's Sheep / Parson, Molly and Sheep)
Not long ago in Vestminster (The Ratcatcher's Daughter)
Now Britons attend, while I give you a song (The Pride of the Nation, or Old England Turned New)
Now Britons rejoice at the tidings you hear (A New Song on the Present Times)
Now I am a jolly cobbler (The Snob's Confession)
Now I'm a chap that never grumbles (There's Many Worse Off Than You)

Now is there not a piece of work throughout the British nation (The Last New Act of Parliament)
Now Maggie dear, I do hear, you have been upon the spree (One Pound Two)
Now once I was a helpless child (British Ragged Schools / God Bless the Earl of Shaftesbury
Now Parliament again has met (Meeting of Parliament or Future Prospects in 1847)
Now Poor Laws thus breaks God's command (The Present Condition of British Workmen)
Now the times altered among us many ways (The Tradesman's Lamentation for the Loss of Trade)
Now the times are altered amongst us many ways (Save a Penny for a Rainy Day)
Now there has been a pretty bother (Agitation of Great Britain)
Now those that are low spirited I hope won't think it wrong (A New Hunting Song)
Now to keep up the spree, Tom, Jerry, and Logick (Beggars Opera—Tom, Jerry, & Logick, Among the Cadgers in the Holy Land)
Now we have bid adieu to the year 95 (State of the Nation; or, New Touch of the Times)
Now we have bid adieu to the year ninety-four (The State of the Nation, or, a New Touch of the Times)
Now wife whatever shall we do the times they are so bad (A Dialogue Between Ned and His Wife on the Hard Times)
Now winter is come with its / her / his cold chilling breath (Remember the Poor / Time to Remember the Poor / Winter Piece)
Now winter is come with its ice and its snow (Pray Remember the Poor)
Now, my friends, we've gained our will (Reform Song)
Now, wife and children, let's be gay (The Labourer's Return to His Family)
O broker, spare that bed, touch not a single screw (O, Broker / Broker Spare That Bed)
O dark is the night and the wintry wind whistles (The Soldier's Orphan)
O dear, what schemes and alterations (The Glorious Times That We Now Have)
O don't we live in curious times (Ladies, Don't Go Thieving)
O England that boasts of her riches so rare (White Slaves of England)
O! father dear, the time is come (Emigrant's Adieu)
O friend of sinners hear my cry (. . . John Taylor, Cotton Spinner . . . , Being out of Employ . . .)
O have you heard the doleful fate (The King of the British People, or the Boroughmongers Purge)
O hear the act of Mr. Peel (The Poor Charlies Lamentation)
O in the house, the other night (The Queen & the Taxes)
O listen to a tale of woe (The Distressed Seaman)
O listen to a tale of woe (Melancholy Death of Five Poor Distressed Hay-Makers)
O listen to our mournful tale (The Weaver's Lamentation)
O Lord hear the poor pitman's cry (The Pitman's Complaint)
O Lord look down with pitying eye (The Weaver's Lamentation)
O now the cold winter comes on (The Cold Winter Night)
O pity the fate of a poor Irish stranger (Irish Stranger / The Poor Irish Stranger)
O say! what is that thing called light (The Poor Blind Boy)

O talk not of fortune or jewels or splendour (Cottage That Stands by the Sea)
O what a strange oration in every place we hear (Mrs. Money's Departure)
O what a world of flummery, there's nothing but deceit in it (Don't Despise a Man Because He Wears a Ragged Coat / The Ragged Coat / Song of the Ragged Coat)
O what an age this is for puff (Cheap Times! or, the Blessings of 1850)
O what hard and trying times most people now do see (Hard Times and Fair Trade)
O, when a boy just four years old (Life and Confessions of the Poor Orphan Sweep)
O winter is set in (Pity the Orphan)
O yes! Ye swinish multitude (The Newcastle Swineherds Proclamation)
O'erwhelming griefs my soul oppress (Poverty's Appeal)
Of a brazier's daughter who lived near (The Betrayed Maiden)
Of a rich young lady I'm going to tell (The New Gipsy Laddy)
Of all the sturdy beggars (The State Beggar)
Of friendship I have heard much talk (Money is Your Friend)
Of money's worth I'm going to sing (I Wonder Where the Money Goes)
Of ups and downs I've felt the shock (The Lary Man)
Oh, a rummy old cadger am I (A Rummy Old Cadger Am I)
Oh! aw wur once very poor (The Shoddy Chap)
Oh! black Monday morning, I dread, I'm sure (The Rent Day; or, Black Monday Morning / The Way to Live Rent Free)
Oh, come my own one, come my fond one (Saucy Sailor Boy)
Oh! crikey, what a piece of work (Who's Your Butcher? Or, What's the Price of Meat?)
Oh dear here's a shocking disaster (The Women Flogger's Lament of Marylebone Workhouse)
Oh dear! oh lacks it is a fact (New Building Act)
Oh! dear oh me what fearful cries, from left to right we hear (The Colliers' Defence)
Oh, dear! these are shocking hard times (Don't Tell the Society)
Oh, dear, these are shocking hard times (The Miser's Man)
Oh dear! what a crime it's thought (My Uncle's Card)
Oh, dear, what a row there's all over the nation (Resignation of His Majesty's Minister)
Oh! England is a curious nation (Singing for the Million)
Oh England my country, how blest is thy nation (Sons of John Bull)
Oh, England oh England thy glory is fled (The Times)
Oh! Englishmen, come drop a tear or two (Lines on the Death of an Old Pauper)
Oh father, dear father, come home with me now (Father, Dear Father, the Brokers Are In)
Oh! Gracious God, extend thy helping hand (O Gracious God!)
Oh happy man, O happy thou (The Factory Bell)
Oh have you felt distress of trade (The Railway Calls)
Oh! have you heard the news abroad (Workhouse Wooing)
Oh! have you heard the news of late (California or, Who Wants Gold!)
Oh, have you heard the news so grand (The Australia Mania)
Oh! have you not heard of a party so gay (The Coalheaver's Feast)

Oh! hear the astounding doleful news (Song of the Times, Frightful Rises and High Prices)
Oh! here's a pretty go (The Last Farewell to Poor St. Giles's)
Oh! here's a pretty go, said a tradesman to his wife (High Price of Meat)
Oh, I have got a charming bride (Mrs. Johnson)
Oh I will get wed in a trice (Odd Matters)
Oh! If I had a thousand a year, Gaffer Green (If I Had a Thousand a Year)
Oh! is it not a gallows shame (Starve Us All)
Oh, is not there a piece of work (Sir Robert Peel and His New Taxes)
Oh knock me silly, here's a go (P——'s Farewell to Chelsea)
Oh, lads and lasses hither come (Wrekington Hiring)
Oh Lambeth is a funny place (A Flare-Up Amongst the Lambeth Guardians)
Oh, list awhile, good people all (The Horrid Murder Committed by Mary Wilson)
Oh, list you feeling Christians (The Appeal of the Unemployed)
Oh, modesty's a moral thing (The Dustman's Cousin)
Oh! my clothes are all ragged, and tatter'd, and torn (The Drunkard's Child)
Oh! my name is Tom Blunt (Tom Blunt, or the Poor Sailor)
Oh, no I mustn't think of it (The Sweeps Lament)
Oh pity dear friends the poor framework-knitters (The Tears of Pity)
Oh! Reform now it is the rage (A New Song on Reform)
Oh, Sally Sime, when we get wed (Chandler's Shop)
Oh sure such a party, so gay and so hearty (Scavenger's Ball)
Oh, the bell of that 'ere factory (Factory Bells of England)
Oh, the great men of the day, they (The Honest Working Man)
Oh! the working men of England, we labour for the great (Working Men of England)
Oh there's a place in London town (Monmouth Street)
Oh this money, money, money / this glittering money (What Won't Money Do? / The Wonderful Effects of Money)
Oh, this world is so hard to get through (Lazy Society)
Oh! 'tis of a rich merchant, in London did dwell (Vilikins and His Dinah)
Oh, what a sorrow a poor man's life is (Poor Married Man)
Oh, what a spicey flare up, tear up (Cadger's Ball)
Oh, Willie, you've come home, lad (Willie, Drunk Again)
Oh! yes, I remember the days of our childhood (Answer to Why Did She Leave Him)
Oh, you've heard talk of Billy Nuts (Jimmy Jumps the Rhymer!)
Old Adam was the first man, that everybody knows (Old Adam Was a Gentleman)
Old England my country, my own native land (The Poor Working Man)
Old England, once upon a time (What Shall We Do for Meat!)
Old England, thy stamina never has yielded (Old England Shall / For Ever Shall Weather the Storm)
Old England's in a dreadful state (A Copy of Verses Written on the Present State of Old England)
Old John Bull was a farmer and well known among his neighbours (A Pen'orth of Irish Stew)

Old John Bull went to Britannia's gate (Old John Bull Kicking Up Behind and Before)
An old woman there lived at Rumford (Artichokes & Cauliflowers / Old Woman of Rumford)
The oldest person in the world on land or on the water (England's Stagnation)
On a cold winter's morn as the snow was a falling (Poor Little Sweep / The Little Chimney Sweep)
On a dark lonesome night, when nature's at rest (Friendless Boy)
On a fine Sabbath morn, in the sweet month of May (Dialogue on a Sunday Morning; or, the Sabbath Breaker Reclaimed)
On Monday night I married a wife (Woeful Marriage)
On Sunday morning I went out for a spree (A Week's Matrimony)
Once all things were glad and joyful (Once All Things Were Glad and Joyful)
Once England was acknowledged the mistress of the seas (A Song for the Times)
Once I loved a young man as dear as my life (The Wandering Girl)
Once I was a bachelor bold (The Man Who Wished He'd Never Got Married)
Once I was never satisfied with how the cash was laid out (Going Out to Market)
Once I'd money plenty (Broken Down)
One bitter night in winter when the wind was fierce and cold (Two Orphans in the Snow)
One cloudy cold morning, as abroad I did steer (The Poor Smuggler's Boy)
One cold winter's evening the stormy winds did blow (The Little Town's Boy / Old England is Going Down the Hill)
One cold winter's morning as the day was dawning (Old England What Have You Come To / What's Old England Come To!)
One dark rainy night as I walk'd thro' the street (Peggy Bann)
One day as I was walking through streets (Workhouse Door)
One day as through the street I rambled (The Day Poor Benny Died)
One day for recreation, as I left my habitation (The Poor Little Fisherman's Boat)
One day going out for a walk, sir (Very Respectable)
One day while out walking not knowing where to go (The Workhouse Door)
One evening, going thro' the market place (Oh, Ain't I Nuts on Sarah)
One evening, 'twas late, and the hamlet was still (The Honest Soldier and Generous Farmer)
One fine summer's eve, as I careless was straying (Orphan Boy's Prayer / Tale)
One May morning bright I pass'd thro' the valley (The Dark Gipsey Girl)
One night at sea while perusing (Old England's Brightest Ornament is the Honest Working Man!)
One night my thoughts they wander'd, and then to amend the scene (John Bull's Nothing More)
One night quite bang up to the mark (Johnny Raw and Polly Clark)
One pleasant evening when pinks and daisies (The Lovers Discussion)
One spring morning early, a squire was straying (The Squire and Gipsy Girl)
One summer's eve, all labour o'er (Poor Worn-Out Sailor!)
One summer's morning/eve as Nancy fair (The New Spinning Wheel / The Spinning-Wheel)
An orphan once in doleful plaint (The Orphan Girl)
The other day as Sandman Joe (Sandman Joe the St. Giles's Pet)

The other night as I lay on my bed (My Wife's First Baby)
Our city's in a fearful state at present, all will own (British Working-Man)
Our fire on the turf and tent 'neath the hill (The Gipsey's Tent)
Our ports are now shut to exclude foreign grain (Commerce in Tears)
Out in the streets, forsaken, alone (Out in the Streets!)
Out in this cold world, out in the street (Driven from Home)
Over the mountain and over the moor (The Beggar Girl)
Over the ocean and over the land (The Shipwrecked Sailor Boy)
Pardon our visit to this place (Lament of Two Stocking Makers from Nottingham)
Parent of the wide creation (Song of the Slaughter)
Parliament again has met (The Queen and John Bull)
The people say the times are hard (You Must All Fast)
Pity a poor and friendless boy (The Friendless Boy)
Pity kind friends in our great distress (The Weaver's Petition)
Pity the fate of a poor Irish Stranger (The Poor Irish Stranger)
Pity the sorrows of a poor old man (The Beggar's Petition)
Pity the sorrows of a poor old man (The Begging Imposter's Petition)
Please give me a penny, sir (Please, Give Me a Penny, Sir)
The ploughman whistles o'er the furrow (The Labourer's Welcome Home)
A poet there was, and he lived in a garret (The Judicious Poet)
A poor child in grief was weeping (The Pauper's Child)
Poor Kate with nosegay basket trim (Poverty's No Sin)
A poor little gipsey I wander forlorn (The Poor Little Gipsey)
A poor little lad all forsaken (He's Only a Poor Orphan Boy)
Poor Lubin was an orphan boy (The Orphan Shepherd Boy)
Poor people, deficient of food (Let Us All Be Unhappy Together / A New Song Called a Touch of the Times)
Poor people of England (The Complaint of the Poor)
Poor people of England I pray now attend (Rogues of All Sorts / Rogues of All Sorts Found Out)
Poor people of England I pray you all draw near (Poor Man's Complaint for Want of Labour)
A poor, unprotected, and fatherless boy (The Labourer)
Pounds, shillings, pence, and farthings I (Dot and Carry One)
Pray grant, good sir, some small relief (The Poor Law Starvation Act)
Priests of the living God! awake, arise (The Christian's Appeal Against the Poor Law Amendment Act)
Prosperity's smile, we are taught to believe (Prosperity's Smile)
Queer, boys, queer, is the house we live in (Queer, Boys, Queer)
A rector am I, do you mind what I say (Creed)
The Reformists are coming, oh! dear; oh! dear (The Reformers Attack on the Old Rotten Tree)
Rejoice, rejoice, Britannia's sons, while I do sing a song (A New Song on the Glorious Victory Over the Boroughmongers)

FIRST-LINE LIST 647

Rejoice ye half-starv'd poor, for now the war is o'er (Anti-Starvation Song)
Revolts the men do now engage (Revolt of the Workhouse)
Round let us bound, this is Charlie's holiday (The Charlie's Holiday)
Sad dreadful cries and moans we hear (The Farmer's Lamentation)
Says Jone to his wife on a wet summer's day (Jone o'Grinfilt)
Says master to me, is it true? I am told (My Master and I)
Says old John Bull, here is a job (Death of the Corn Bill / John Bull & the Corn Bill)
Scroll of Britain's Just Demands (The Charter)
ScrobSearch all the world high and low (The Grinders; or, More Grist to the Mill)
Sed Joan eawt o' Grinfilt I've news for to tell (Joan o'Grinfilt's Visit to Lunnun, to See What the State Doctor Intends to Do for the Nation)
See how the people thro' the streets (The New Coal Act)
See see where freedom's noblest champion stands (Peterloo)
See the ladies how they strut along (New Rigs of the Races)
The see, the see, the bishop's see (The Bishop's See)
See the star breasted villain to yonder cot bound (The Village / Village-Born Beauty
See yonder stands a trembling form (Found Dying in Our Streets)
The servant lads and lasses gay, now Martinmas draws near (We Will Not Stop Again)
Ses Jone eawt o' Grinfilt au tell thee wot Nan (A New Song, Called Jone o' Greenfield's Lamentation, or the Unfortunate Poverty Knockers)
Ses Joan eawt o' Grinfilt I'll tell yo what Nan (Joan o'Grinfilt's Visit to Mr. Fielden, with a Petition to the Queen to Fill Every Hungry Belly)
The shamrock, rose, and thistle I overheard conversing (The Emigrant's Farewell)
She is honest, she is good and she is wise (She's Honest)
The Sheffield grinder's a terrible blade (The Sheffield Grinders)
Since free trade's the cry both in country and town (Free Trade)
Since very few are well disposed to praise the present times, Sirs (The Golden Days of Good King George)
Sir Robert Peel was a man of might (A Political Parody on Tubal Cain)
The snow was fast descending (The Soldier's Boy)
So quietly one evening reclining (They say 'tis a Crime to be Poor)
A solicitor vile, in a high-flying way (Retaliation; or, Upstart Pride)
Some folks may boast of sense, egad (The Literary Dustman)
Some like to spend their leisure time (Up the Monument)
Some married men boast of their true happy state (Matrimonial Miseries)
Some people are always contending (The Overseer / The New / The Union Overseer)
Some people 'gainst women are railing (The Blessings / Charms of a Good Little Wife)
Some pity afford to a poor soldier's daughter (The Poor Soldier's Daughter)
Some thousands in England are starving (An Appeal by Unemployed Ex-Service Men / A Copy of Verses on the Unemployed and the Great Distress in England)
Some very good sayings I've heard in my time (A Pound or a Penny)
A song I am going to sing you and presently I shall bring you (The Pawn Shop / Pawnbroker's Shop / A Pawnbroker's Shop on a Saturday Night)

A song I will recite to you, I hope it will delight you (The Pawnbroker's Shop)
Soon after Polly Cox got wed, to Mr. Wick, lamplighter (Polly Cox's Party)
Stay lady—stay, for mercy's sake (The Orphan Boy / The Orphan Boy's Tale)
A story I'm going to tell ye (Belly and Back / The Back and the Belly / Flashy Back and Hungry Belly)
Strange times are come when stones must bleed (The Double Dealer)
Such a thing as true bliss in this life is a bubble (The Miseries of Living up Five Pairs of Stairs)
The sun had just risen / was just rising one fine summer's morning (Fortunate Factory Girl)
The sun had set behind the hill (The Farmer's / Lucky Farmer's Boy)
The sun was just rising one fine May-Day morning (The Factory Girl)
Supposing the rich to the poor man will give (Verses Composed on the Distress of the Times)
Sweet mother dear, I go (The Sailor Boy's Good Bye)
Sweet nosegays come buy my sweet nosegays (The Nosegay Girl)
Taking my walks on a cold winter's day (The Drunkard's Child / The Poor Drunkard's Child)
Tax-gatherers now how thick they swarm (Naked Truth / The Times)
Tell me little wanderer, why (The Orphan Boy)
Ten years ago I married a man who's such a drunken sot (The Wives Lamentation)
That boy? No, he's not mine exactly (The Policeman's Pet)
That mankind were always grumblers (The Iron Times)
That monster oppression behold how he stalks (W——'s Thirteen)
There came to the beach a poor exile of Erin (The Exile of Erin)
There is a man, you all must know (The Fasting Man Turned Hungry)
There is a sighing o'er the land, a voice upon the wind (The New Poor Law Bill)
There once was a time but it's happily past (The Reason Why)
There was a beauty bright (Marriage of the Blooming Lady and the Groom)
There was a lord lived in this town (Young Mat Hyland)
There was a naughty man (The St. Pancras Prigging Overseers)
There was a noble overseer, as crafty as a mouse sir (The Middleton Overseer / The Overseer / The Overseer and the Madman / The Overseer Outwitted)
There was a wedding held of late (Most Humorous Description of Irish Paddy's Wedding)
There was an old woman of Rumford (Old Woman of Rumford / Artichokes & Cauliflowers)
There's a class that bears the stamp of the great (The Working Man)
There's a difference to be seen 'twixt a beggar and a queen (Beggars and Ballad Singers)
There's a good time coming, boys (Comic Version of a Good Time Coming)
There's a good time coming, boys (A Good Time . . . / There's a Good Time Coming, Boys! / Wait a Little Longer)
There's a grim one-horse hearse in a jolly round trot (The Pauper's Drive)
There's a little man dressed all in grey (Merry Little Grey Fat Man)
There's a spot in Birmingham town (A New Comic Song of Dudley Street)
There's grinders enough, Sir, in every degree (The Knife Grinder)

There's lots of fun, the Corn Bill's done (Death of the Corn Bill)
There's ne'er a thriving trader who daily cheats the town (Satire on All Trades)
There's something new starts every day (The Tax on Gin!)
These, these, are the rigs of the times (The North Briton, or, Economy)
They call me little Joe, sir (Chimney Sweep / Little Joe, the Chimney Sweeper)
They call me poor old Farmer Bull, it's true I'm getting old (The State of Old England or, John Bull in Uniform)
They call me smirking Bobby (The Chandler's Shop)
They knew that I was poor (The Poor Voter's Song)
This farmer had ten thousand pounds in store (The Life and Awful Death of a Rich Miser)
This here's what I does, I, d'ye see, forms a notion (Honesty in Tatters)
This is a free and happy land (Justice in England)
This is my never failing bank (Lines Written on the Cover of an Old Bible)
This old hat was new once, but I cannot tell you when (When This Old Hat Was New)
This well may be called a wonderful age (Patent Bread)
This world may be a paradise quite (Rich and Poor)
Tho' I'm but a chimney-sweep I took a ticket (Shovel & Broom)
Tho' late and early I do pad (The Chimney Sweep)
Tho' to work your will is strong, glad to labour all the day ('Tis Hard to Leave This Land)
Thou great creator of this earth (The Farmer's Prayer)
Though a sweeper by trade, and though queer my estate (The Crossing Sweeper)
Though I'm a simple country lad (The Tread Mill)
Though some complain that trade is bad (Trust in the Lord)
Thousands in England are starving (Lines on the Unemployed and the Terrible Distress)
Thro' the town or village gay (The Nosegay Girl)
Thrown on the wide world, doomed to wander and roam (The Poor Peasant Boy)
The thunder roars loudly, the wind howls around me (The Orphan in Distress)
Tight lads I have failed with but none e'er so slightly (Bill Bobstay)
Times are getting worse and worse (Eat, Ye Paupers, Eat)
The times are much worse, our grandmothers declare (To Young Women)
Times never were so bad before (Hard Times Among the Farmers)
A tinker I am (Natty Sam)
'Tis a wonderful thing amongst all human creatures (The Biter & the Bitten)
'Tis all my cry by night and day (The Distressed Farmer)
'Tis down in yon valley my mother does dwell (The Cottager's Widow)
'Tis known old England long has been (Hercules Decapitating the Hydra of Corruption or, a Broom for the Boroughmongers)
'Tis myself dat/that was born now in Dublin (The Picture / The Irishman's Picture of England / London)
'Tis now some forty years ago (Forty Years Ago)
'Tis the way of the world I'm a going to review (Way of the World; or an Alteration to the Short Sketch of the Times)
To a fashionable theatre one evening I went (It is only the Way it was Played on the Stage)

To Hereford Old Town a new hero is come down (To Hereford Old Town)
To high and low of all degrees (Will You Go to California)
To high and low of each degree (California Gold)
To list a while you can't refuse (Open the Ports)
To the bum crushers truck you must tumble (A New Song on the Emancipation Bill for Debtors)
To the standard rally quick (The Corn Bill / They Must Repeal the Corn Bill)
To the tourist of London, who's curious in fact (St. James's and St. Giles's)
Tom Tackle was noble, was true to his word (Tom Tackle)
Tom Topsail he died and the folks piped their eyes (Tom Topsail)
The Tories are a sliding (They Are All Sliding)
T'other night as I slumbering lay on my bed (The Poor Man's Dream)
The trade of old England's decaying (England's Decline / If There's a Will There's a Way)
The trumpet of liberty sounds through the world (Fall, Tyrants, Fall!)
'Twas a keen frosty morn, and the snow heavy falling (The Little Chimney-Sweep / Poor Little Sweep)
'Twas at the hour, when sober cits (The Scullion Sprite)
'Twas in the autumn of the year, the evening it was fine (The Mechanic's / Poor Mechanic's Boy)
'Twas in the month of last December (Minstrel Girl)
'Twas in Yorkshire I were born and bred (The Poor Tradesman)
'Twas morn when the lark's cheerful note (The Village Maid)
'Twas night, and the farmer his fireside near (The Gipsey Wanderer)
'Twas night, the loving mother sat (The Soldier's Wife)
'Twas on a quarter's day, my money was nearly spent (The Quarter Day)
'Twas on a winter's morning (The Factory Girl's Last Day / The White Slave; or . . .)
'Twas on Good Friday eve, the neighbours all state (Mrs. Jenkins, of Billingsgate)
'Twas on one winter's evening when fast fell the snow (The Winter's Evening / Night)
'Twas on Saint Monday morning cross Mother Bung was snarling (The Pawnbroker)
'Twas on the 6th of September, that glorious day (A New Song on the Disagreeable Confusion Which Took Place on the Otmoor Inclosure)
'Twas one summer's eve all labours o'er (Poor Old / Poor Old Worn Out Sailor
'Twas Saturday night—the busy streets (The Market Basket)
Two orphan girls the tother day (Two Orphan Girls)
Underneath the gas light's glitter (Won't You Buy My Pretty Flowers)
Victoria she's got a daughter, and what shall we do now (State of the Times)
The villager born humbly, and bred hard (The Villager)
Was you at ———, or did you see (The Hiring Day)
The way/ways of the world I am going to review/show (The Way of the World / The Ways of the World)
We are all beggars, beg, beg, beggars (We Are All Beggars)
We are cotton spinners by our trade (Cotton Spinners from Manchester, for the Master or Mistress / Redditch in Worcestershire)

We are going to sing a song (A New Song on the Preston Tyranny)
We are in a mess. Oh, Dear! Oh, Dear! (Pity the Poor Costermongers)
We cotton spinners of Manchester (The Manchester Cotton Spinner's Petition)
We have all our shares of ups and downs (Kind Relations)
We have come to ask for assistance (Song of the Cotton Factory Operatives)
We have come to ask your assistance (Humanity is Calling)
We have heard it asserted a dozen times o'er (Shabby Genteel)
We may be happy yet, I think (Close the Ale-House Door)
We nail makers are in great distress (The Staffordshire Nail-Makers' Humble Petition)
We needle-makers are in great distress (Redditch in Worcestershire, for the Master or Mistress)
We plough and sow—we're so very, very low (The Song of the Lower Classes)
We say the times are grievous hard (Hard Times)
We talk of England's greatness (Old England is Going Down the Hill)
A wealthy citizen, who long (The Distressed Citizen)
Weary and worn with a face full of woe (Poor Joe)
Welcome now Victoria! (Queen Victoria / A New Song in Favour—Praise—of Her Majesty)
Welcome, pretty little stranger (Poor Robin)
Well done Robert Peel! You may say what you will (The Landowners Thrown Overboard)
Well met neighbour gossip, what news do you hear (The Balls in Mourning; or, the Downfall of Mr. Gripe, the Pawnbroker)
Well Mr. Skinflint, how do you do, sir (Curious Dialogue Between Four Selfish Landlords . . .)
The Welsh boy overhearing (The Welsh Boy's Answer)
We're brokenhearted gardeners, scarce got a bit of shoe (Poor Frozen-Out Gardeners)
We're werkin lads frae Lankisheer (Th' Surat Weyver)
We've sung of heroes brave and good (The Honest Working Man)
What a cry in this country about the free trade (A Laughable and Interesting Picture of Drunkenness)
What a dust the poor devils of farmers are making (Howls of the Farmers)
What a poor fellow I am sir (Two Bob a Week and My Board)
What a pother in this land about our French neighbours (A New Song)
What a row and a rumpus (The Chartists are Coming)
What confusion this act has made (The Golden Act / A New Song, Called the Golden Act)
What follies, what falsehoods were uttered in vain (An Address to the Meeting at Spa-Fields)
What funny times we see (Ladies Don't Go Thieving! / Rich & Poor Law!)
What ills my infant days await (The Beggar Boy)
What is the matter with the farmers, they all look so dull (What is the Matter with the Farmers)
What need of all this fuss and strife (There's Room Enough for All)
What news today? Why, one maintains (A New Song Called the "Turncoat")

What racket, disturbance, what strife and delusion (The Counterfeit Halfpence)
What will a drunkard do for ale (The Drunkard's Looking Glass)
What wonderous changes every day (Glorious Reformation)
When au had wark an brass to spend (Friends are Few When Foak / Folk are Poor)
When fell corruption's bands conspire (The Crisis, 1846)
When first a babe upon the knee (Little Bess the Ballad Singer)
When first I came to town (The Fancy Lad)
When first this humble roof I knew (The Humble Roof)
When hoary frost hung on each thorn (Spring Water Cresses)
When I married Miss Wiggins says she my dear Spriggins (The Chandler's Shop)
When I was gay and keen, and aged seventeen (My Husband was a Good for Nothing Man)
When I was young and healthy I rambled up and down (Bread, Cheese and Ale)
When I was young and in my prime (Dicky Numbscull's Ramble in Town)
When I was young and in my prime (The Hungry Army)
When I'd finished off my work last Saturday at neet (Oldham Workshops)
When morning streaks the east with gold (The Cottage Boy)
When Nature in the voice of pain (The Appeal of a Body of Unemployed Operatives to a Humane and Sympathizing Public / A Copy of Verses by a Poor Tradesman / To the Friends of Industry / The Tradesman's New Hymn)
When on these lands, which now are let so high (Lines on the Corn Bill)
When quite a babe my parents said (Chanting Benny or the Batch of Ballads)
When some people die (Gregory, the Wealthy Old Squire)
When the leaves had deserted the trees (The Robin's Petition)
When the winter wind whistles along the wild moor (The Wandering Boy)
When th' wars were o'er and peace proclaimed / When wild war's deadly blast was blown, and gentle peace returning (Poor But Honest Soldier)
When will America's cruel war cease? (The Weaver's Cry)
While strolling one night thro' London's gay throng (Poor Little Joe)
While strolling out one evening by a running stream (The Water-Cress Girl)
While thinking of some past events at home the other night (The Grand Dissolving Views)
Who is the prop and support of the land (Here's a Health to the Hard Working Man)
Who said that King William was not the Main Mast (Reform, and King William For Ever!)
Whoever may travel o'er Manchester gravel (Victoria Bridge on a Saturday Night)
Why did she leave him, they grew up together (Why Did She Leave Him Because He Was Poor)
Why good people all, at what do you pry (The Beggar)
Why is the world so busy is what I want to know ('S for Money)
Why, neighbours, what ails you? what makes you look sad? (General Distress of the Nation; or, the Downfall of Banks)
Why, Noddy, didst thou really say (A Word from Wm Rider to Edward Baines)
Why should the soldier or sailor—back stripped (Lay of the Lash)
Why should we at our lot repine (Never Dull Care)

The wife of a soldier was starving with hunger (He'll Be Back Bye-&-Bye)
Will you list the true but simple lay (Unfortunate Factory Girl)
William and Jonathan came to town together (The Cobbler and Poet)
With blue cold hands and stockingless feet (Out in the Cold)
With fingers jewell'd and gemm'd (The Song of the Truck)
With fingers weary and worn (The Song of the Shirt)
With lowly suit and plaintive ditty (With Lowly Suit)
With purest love Joe Bolland's heart (A New Hymn Composed on a Factory Boy & Girl Who were Found Drowned in the River Aire)
With sloe-black eyes and jet-black hair (Woodland Mary)
Work! work! work! (The Song of Work)
Working hard is my delight. Industry I crave (A Terror to the Rent Day)
The world was not made for one man alone (The World Was Not Made for One Man Alone)
Would you think that I who's now so grand (The Match Boy)
Ye ancient sons of ancient days (A Plaintive Pastoral)
Ye bakers of London beware (Pull Devil, Pull Baker!!!)
Ye British maids pray lend an ear (Lament of Charlotte Mills)
Ye British sons of freedom (Lamentation of Poor Mechanics)
Ye children, whom no absent joy (The Affectionate Mother; or, the Orphan Boy)
Ye children, whom no care or peril (The Affectionate Mother; or, the Orphan Girl)
Ye Englishmen of each degree (The Labouring Man and His Wife)
Ye friends of compassion, and friends of the brave (The Disabled Tar)
Ye gentlemen of England I pray you lend an ear (A New Song on the Times)
Ye grumblers and growlers attend and give ear (Joyful News for the Poor)
Ye kind-hearted souls pray attend to our song (Miseries of the Framework-Knitters)
Ye liberal I pray (The Trade Man's Lamentation)
Ye men of high and low degree, come listen to my song (The Rigs of the Times)
Ye merry men trotting along (The Big Bomb. In the Park)
Ye millions that so keenly feel (The Corn Laws)
Ye political critics who pore o'er the news (Peel's Income Tax, or a Miss at Popularity)
Ye poor men of Leicester come listen to me (The Baker Roasted)
Ye slaves who are treated like beasts (A New National Song, for the Wise, the Bold, and the Brave, Dedicated to the Oppressed and Starving People of this Country)
Ye sons of Briton lend an ear (A New Song Called Pills of Parliament)
Ye tradesmen of the nation, I am sorry it is true (A New Song, Called Times as They Are)
Ye true sons of freedom I pray you attend (The Transport's Return)
Ye wealthy and proud, while in splendour you roll (The Match Boy)
Ye working men both far and near (The Famine Fast Day)
Ye working-men where e'er ye dwell (The New Times)
Ye young and blooming females all (A Copy of Verses, on the Life and Death of Miss Sophia Wright)
You are not what you were, England (Won't You Tell Us Why, England?)

You ax me to sing, of course I shall (The Vorkus Gal / The Workhouse Girl)
You blooming lads and lasses gay, come listen to my song (Rigs and Flares-Up of Greenwich Fair)
You boatmen and colliers all (The Tommy Note)
You brave lads of Wardhill I pray lend an ear (Bonny Moor Hen)
You British subjects high and low (The State of Poor Old England)
You British subjects now attend (A New Song on the Times / The Times / A True Statement of the Present Times)
You Britons all attention give, and listen to my rhymes (The New Times)
You Britons all draw near (Britons Rights)
You Britons all where e'er you be (Forced / We are Forced to be Contented)
You Britons bold of each degree (Farmers Don't You Cry!)
You broken down farmers, give ear to my song (The Farmer's Downfall)
You constant lovers give attention (Mary and the Handsome Factory Boy / Rosetta / Rosetta, the Farmer's Daughter, and the / her gay Plough-Boy)
You country lads and lasses all (Rigs of Carlisle Hiring / Rigs of the Mops!)
You Englishmen, and Irishmen, Scotchmen and Welshmen too (Hard Times and No Beer)
You Englishmen of each degree (The Labouring Man)
You Englishmen wherever you be, come listen to what I say (The Tradesman's Complaint)
You fair sex we pray give attention (Protect the Soldiers Wives and Children)
You farmers all, both great and small (The Sporting Farmer)
You farmers' servants far and near (Jig, Jig, to the Hirings)
You feeling Christians lend an ear (Copy of Verses on the Lamentable Death of Mr. and Mrs. Jessup)
You friends of the poor, both high and low (The Poor Spinners)
You friends of the Union I pray give attention (The Union of Freedom)
You frolicksome sparks of game, ye being both wretched and old (Careless Billy)
You gentle and simple come listen awhile (Something or Other Starts New Every Day)
You gentlemen all give ear to my song (A Dialogue Between the Farmers and Landlords)
You gentleman all I understand (A New Song on the Times)
You gentlemen and ladies, I pray lend an ear (New Touch on the Times)
You gentlemen of England, wherever you be (The Request of the Poor)
You gentlemen who keep horses (The Times)
You gentles of England (The Distressed Sempstress)
You good folks of Nottingham I would have you draw near (A New Song, Call'd the Red Whig)
You hard working people attend to my rhymes (The Truth, the Whole Truth, and Nothing But the Truth)
You have heard a deal of talk about (Three Acres and a Cow)
You have heard of my grandfather— wonderful man! (My Uncle is a Most Kind-Hearted Man)
You heroes of England (King William IV and His Ministers Forever)
You jovial sons of Britain come listen unto me (A Touch on the Times)
You know I'm always singing songs (The Ballad Singer's List)

You ladies of old England (The Starving Times of England)
You lads and lasses blythe and gay (The Rigs and Sprees of Leeds Town)
You lads and you lasses give ear to my song (The New Times)
You lovers all, both great and small, attend unto my theme (The Servant Boy)
You married people high and low (One Pound One / The Contented-Pleasing Wife and Satisfied Husband
You married people high and low (The Way the Money Goes)
You married women draw near awhile (The Drunken Husband)
You may talk about taxes and say what you will (A Rare Row about the Income Tax; or, the Cat Let out of the Bag)
You miners all attend, these lines that I have penn'd (The Miners' Complaint)
You neighbours all listen, a story I'll tell (Pensioner's Complaint / The Pensioner's Complaint Against His Wife)
You noble patriots of reform (The Great Reform Bill)
You oft have told me, mother dear (The Child's Inquiry)
You Pimlico ladies of every degree (Who Prigged the Mutton)
You poor of old England (A Large Loaf for Sixpence)
You poor of old England give ear and attend (A New Song Called Little England)
You power-loom weavers far and near, come listen to my song (The Preston Steam-Loom Weavers)
You servant lads and lasses all come listen to my ditty (A Word of Advice / A New Song or a Word of Advice to Servants)
You servant lads and lasses, come listen for a while (A New Song on the Hirings)
You shall hear a funny ditty (The Subjects of the Times; or, Scenes of 1848)
You sons of Labour pay attention (Oastler is Welcome)
You sons of old England, now list to my rhymes (The Poor Labourers)
You surely have heard of great General Distress (General Distress)
You tell me you love me, I fain would believe (There's None Like a Mother, If Ever So Poor)
You tender Christians pay attention (Copy of Verses on the Dreadful Murder at Finsbury)
You tender mothers, parents dear (The Tooting Tragedy)
You tradesmen all, both high and low, come listen unto me (They're All Boxing)
You tradesmen all I pray attend (A Bundle of Truths)
You tradesmen all pray attend (The True State of Trade)
You tradesmen of England give attention to my song (The Poor Man's Companion)
You true sons of freedom, who join hand in hand (The True Sons of Freedom)
You weavers of England I pray now attend (The Weaver's Garland or the Downfall of Trade)
You working men are discontented (An Imaginary Conversation Between Gladstone and a Working Man)
You working men of England (The Great Battle for Freedom and Reform)
You working men of England one moment now attend (New Dialogue and Song on the Times)
You working men where e'er you be (The Poor Tradesman's Lamentation)

You workingmen where'er you be (How to Repeal the Corn Law, or the Six Points Explained)
You young men and maidens draw near for a while (A New Song on the Hiring of the Servants)
You'll own this is true, if you just pay attention (How the Poor Live)
You've heard about Macaulay, and the great New Zealander too (A Hundred Years to Come)
You've none of you heard, I suppose (The Suicide Club)
Young ladies and young gentlemen come listen to my song (The Fast Day)
Young ladies have pity on me (The Woman That Wished She'd Never Got Married)
Young men of each degree in life (The Drunken Wife)
Young William to his wife did say, my dear, I must away (Sailor's Return)
Your friendship I court (The Poet's Petition)

General Index

See the title list for source and page locations for broadsides on poverty, 1790–1870.

All broadsides of any date or subject not in the title list are listed together here under the entry "titles of other broadsides." Those concerned with poverty are marked P. Page locations are provided in the form noted below. Source locations are given in the notes to the two volumes.

Broadside authors named in the text appear here in appropriate alphabetical position. Page locations are given here for all their broadsides whether concerned with poverty or not. Locations are in boldface if the work is quoted in full, in italic if quoted in part, in regular type if discussed or mentioned. All those named authors whose works are significant to this book are also brought together under a single entry, "names of broadside authors." The entry identifies all those authors who are known or supposed to have written one or more ballads or prose works expressly for broadside publication—their names followed by B, all those whose works are used in full in the anthology or otherwise quoted in full or in significant part—their names followed by A, and all those authors whose works were apparently numerous or popular in broadside form whether those works were written for street, concert hall, theater, book, or other place—their names followed by R if their work is represented to any degree here, by N if it is not.

Aberdeen, Lord, 69, 71
Adelaide, Queen, 23, 49, 54
Ainsworth, Harrison, 43
Albert, Prince, 127, 134, 136, 303, 430, 453–54, 458
Aldridge: "The Workhouse Boy," first version, *168*, with attribution, 289, 430, 512; "Vorkus Gal," **169–71**, with corrected attribution, 289, 512
Althorp, Lord, 266
Arch, Joseph, 228
Argyll, duke of, 133, 134
Armstrong, Isobel, 18–19
Ashton, Eva, 418
Ashton, John, 38, 61, 65, 413, 506
Aspinall, A., 436

Bailey, William: ballads, *379*, 41, 274n. 20
bailiffs, 115, 202–4, 384–85
bakers, 84–85, 91, 202
balladmongers. *See* broadsides, sellers
Ballantine, Mr., 146–49
Bamford, Samuel, 336, 386–87
Barbauld, Anna, 22, 383–84
Barham, Richard, 324–25
Barrère, Albert, and Charles Leland, 537
bawdy ballads, **436–37**, 437–38, **438–39**, *440, 453–54,* 40, 45, 51, 66, 68–69, 77, 232, 414–15, 430
Bayly, Thomas Haynes, "I'll Be No Submissive Wife," *455*, 455; "The Mistletoe Bough," *167*, with notes on author and ballad, 42, 43, 45, 61, 63, 76, 167–68, 169, 512

GENERAL INDEX

Bedford, duke of, 87
Beggars Opera, 35, 36, 310–11, 500, 507–9, 521
beggary, 299–318, 500–501, 510, 548–49 n. 2
Bell, Robert, 403
Benyon's, 360
Bethnal Green, 86, 87, 181–89, 223, 260, 411
Billington, William: "Friends are Few When Foak are Poor," **251–53**, with notes on author and ballad, 24, 60, 236, 237, 253–55
Bishop, Sir Henry, 77, 164, 167
Blackburn, Judge, 155, 158
Blake, William, 20, 42
Blanchard, E. L., "Vilikins and His Dinah," *412–13*, 38, 43, 61, 270, 412–13
Bland, Mrs., 323
Boardman, Henry, 276 n. 49
Bonaparte, Napoleon, 105
boroughmongers, 41, 49, 110–11, 113, 514
Boulland, Frederick, 132
Bradley, Rev. Edward, 38, 273 n. 14, 274 n. 16
Brewer, E. C., 537
Bright, John, 127, 128, 129
broadsides, authors, 36–62; bards of Seven Dials and other poor authors, 34, 43–54, 59–60, 163–65, 251–55, 484; bards of all other sorts, 40–43, 55–60, 289; earnings from broadside printers, 17, 34, 39, 48, 431, 536; fictional bards and poetic personae, 480–99; learned authors, 39, 180, 274 n. 16, 281 n. 16,; named authors of ballads printed here in full, 27, 60–61, 289; naming of authors by printers, 20, 23, 27, 39, 51; popular and prolific authors (*see also* names of broadside authors), 46, 61–62; social classes represented, 34, 36–37, 40, 43–44, 60–62, 193–94, 289, 316, 351–52, 492–93; view of backgrounds, conventional, 34, 36–37, 78, 273 n. 8; view of backgrounds offered here, 37–39; women, 27, 152, 455–56. *See also* names of broadside authors
broadsides, audiences, 62–77; conventional description, 34, 36–37, 63, 65, 273 n. 8; diverse captive, 21, 62–63; diverse evident, 75, 501; opinion from Mayhew and others, 66–68, 180; opinion in contradiction of Mayhew, 68–76, 180; sales, cocks, 538, 539, 541; —gallows, 72–75, 498, 539; —other, 255 (*see also* Catnach, James, sales and editions); social classes addressed, 64, 69, 70, 78, 239–40; —inferred, 319, 493; summary estimate of broadside buying by the poor, 75; women and children, 66, 68, 180, 325, 533
broadsides, connections to concert, theater, book, etc., 36–39, 41–43, 60–61, 63, 75–77, 200–201, 319, 322–23, 429–30, 451, 512
broadsides, definition, 24, 37–39
broadsides, distinctive character, ballads, 21, 23, 27, 38, 49, 61, 70, 77–78, 88, 452, 480–82, 514
broadsides, government propaganda, 137–38
broadsides, kinds, 66–68
broadsides, piracy, 37, 39, 43, 52, 61, 62, 431
broadsides, plagiarism. *See* plagiarism
broadsides, prices, 34, 63, 72, 309, 508, 535
broadsides, print runs, editions, 100, 276 n. 52, 309, 429, 508. *See also* broadsides, audiences, sales
broadsides, reliable reportage, 73, 74, 247–48, 339–40, 372–73, 539–41; unreliable (*see* cocks)
broadsides, review of earlier literary and other judgments, 17–19, 271 nn. 1, 2, 3, 4
broadsides, sellers, 34, 66–68, 69, 73–75, 179–80, 529–41
Brome, Richard, 300–301
Brougham, Lord, 50, 113, 434, 435, 436, 514
Brown, George, notes on the author, 39, 44, 46, 61, 62, 274 n. 29. Works: "The Cruel Sea-Captain," *46–47*, 420; "The Ophan Child," *47*, 47, 48, 49; "Past, Present, and Future," *47*, 47, 48, 49; "The Poisoned Family," *48*, 48, 49; "The World's in a Terrible State," *47*, 47–48, 49

Bruton, James: "Bill Bounce," **389–91**, with notes on author and ballad, 132, 316, 391; "The Quarter Day, **204–6**, 206, with attribution, 289, 391
Bunn, Alfred, 144–45
Burke, Edmund, 109–12, 279 n. 19
Burke, William, 50, 392–93
Burnett, John, 234, 251
Burns, Robert, 19, 512
Bursnell, Sarah, 40, 481
butchers, 91, 202, 233–34
Byron, Lord, admired by William Billington, 254; appearance on broadsides, 37, 39, 42; John Morgan compared with, 49; mentioned in ballads, 244, 480, 487; misc., 512; social concern, 20, 95

Cambridge, duke of, 431
Cambridge, Prince George of, 360
Cane, Mr., 182–84
canon debate, 21–23, 24. *See also* broadsides, authors, audiences, distinctive character; poverty and poetry
canting ballads (flash ballads), **349–51**, 351–52; **352–53**, 353–54; **361**, 362; **389–91**, 391; *493;* other refs., 69, 72, 337, 481, 536
Captain Swing rebellion, 335, 336, 550 n. 12
Carlyle, Thomas, 375
Caroline, Queen: ballads and prose, *49–50, 55–56,* 342; other refs., 49–50, 53, 102
Carpenter, Joseph Edward, ballads, *232,* 391, 512
Catnach, James: associated printers, 200, 201, 433; author, *55, 56, 57,* 23, 39, 55–58, 557 n. 7, 559; background and family, 55, 539 (*see also* printers, broadside: Ryle, Anne); on Billy Waters, 33, 56, 308–11, 507–9; broadsides doubtfully his, 50, 275 n. 32, 558–59 n. 32; cocks, 535, 539; Hindley plagiarizing, 509; large sheets, 56–57, 309, 429, 559; misc. refs., 105, 432, 461, 465, 471, 475, 530; piracy by, on, 429, 431, 508, 509; preeminence, 33, 34, 55, 73, 74, 272 n. 2; printer, 33–36; in prison, 539; refs. to 1832 catalogue, 34, 203, 206, 239, 272–73 n. 2, 277 n. 75, 322, 328, 349, 391, 398, 412, 442–43, 465, 471, 500; relations with John Morgan, 39, 49, 50, 52; sales and editions, 63, 72–74, 276 n. 52, 309, 429, 498, 508; shop, 34, 35, 44–45, 76 (illus.); successors, 34, 51; on Tom and Jerry, 56–57, 63, 72, 308–11, 425, 429, 500, 506–9; variety of subjects, 75, 420
Cato Street conspirators, 339, 340, 343
caton wheel, 343, 344, 551 n. 24
Chadwick, Edwin, 195
Chandler, J. W.: "The Beggar Girl," **305–6**, 41, 42, 60, 61, 62, 63, 68, 69, 75, 277 n. 73, 306
charity schools, **243–45**, 100, 245
charlies, 56, 308, 309, 425, 429
Charlotte, Princess, 55
Chartism, 42, 58, 59, 335, 359, 550–51 n. 12
Chaucer, Geoffrey, 254
Cheap Repository Tracts, 58, 272 n. 2, 465
Child, Francis, 17
children on the street, 319–31
Cider Cellars, 37, 49, 269, 430
Civil War, American, 410
Clare, John, 20
clergy, heads of the church, 109, 110, 122, 141, 142, 206–9; incomes of the rich, 207–8, 277–78 n. 3; Parson Brown, 354–56, 357; others, 399
Clifton, Harry: "Polly Perkins," **449–50**; with notes on author and ballad, 60, 451
Coal Hole, 37, 38, 49, 430
coal owners, 375, 393–96
coal viewers, 394
Cobden, Richard, 127, 128, 225, 226
cockney ballads, **165–66**, 166–69; **484–88**, 488–94; **494–98**, 498–99, *493;* 431
cocks, 529–41; Charles Elliott, **338**, 340–43, 539–41; King / Mitchel, 531–32, 539; other refs., 66, 73, 247, 328, 373, 378, 499
Coleridge, Samuel Taylor, 42, 91, 337
Conway, Hugh, 120
Cook, Chris, 83
Cook, Eliza: "God Speed the Good Ship," **408–9**, with notes on author and ballad, 39, 42, 43, 60, 61, 68, 237, 384, 409–10

Corder, William, 57–58, 73–74, 499, 534, 558n. 17
Corinthian, 431
corn bill and law: ballads, **97–99**, 99–101; **126–28**, 128–31; **224–26**, 226–28; *266;* other refs. 22, 39, 41, 123, 125, 196, 374. *See also* free trade
Cornwall, Barry: "The Sea," **346–47**, with notes on author and ballad, 42, 43, 60, 61, 66, 77, 209, 345–47
cost of living, ballads, **93–94**, 94–95; **120–22**, 122–23; **126–28**, 128–30; **232–34**, 234; **248–51**, 251; other refs., 34, 83, 94–95, 122, 125, 128, 234, 236, 251, 277n. 2, 299, 500, 515
Cottenham, Lord, 129
Cowell, Sam, 270, 273n. 14
Cowper, William, 131, 132
Crabbe, George, 159
crime. *See* poverty and crime
Crimean War, 69–71, 172, 175, 387
Culley, Robert, 542–47
Cullum, Bob, 71
cultural poetics, 22–23, 24, 69–71. *See also* broadsides, authors; broadsides, audiences; broadsides, distinctive character; Morgan, John; poverty and poetry
Cunningham, Peter, 145

Davis, George, 276n. 49
Davison, Elizabeth, 65–66
Davy, John, 203
Dekker, Thomas, 351
Derby, earls of, 127, 129
Deserted Village, The, 20
Dibdin, Charles: "The Beggar," **303–5**, with notes on author and ballad, 41–42, 60, 61, 62, 63, 102, 305, 408, 430, 453, 501, 512
Dibdin, Charles, Jr.: "Hot Codlings," **505–6**, with notes on author and ballad, 38, 41, 42, 60, 506, 509
Dibdin, Thomas John, 102, 506, 509
Dickens, Charles, 169, 266, 289 (for revised dating information)
Disher, Maurice, 193, 506
Disraeli, Benjamin, 39, 41, 77, 129, 144, 145, 225–26, 266
D'Israeli, Isaac, 43–44, 480
drunkenness, 49, 463–66, 471–73, 510–11

Duggan family, 362–73
Duncan, James Elmslie/Elmzlie, 58–59, 276n. 48
Duncombe, John, 556n. 7
Dyos, Henry, and Michael Wolff. *See* Neuburg in bibliography

economic depression, 83–87, 96–97, 99, 104, 108–9, 122, 128
Egan, Pierce, 63–64, 308–10, 316, 422, 430, 500, 501, 506–9. *See also* Tom and Jerry
election broadsides, 6, 23, 49, 196–98
Elizabeth I, 257
Elliott, Charles, 338–43, 539–41
Elliott, Ebenezer, 19–20, 78
Embleton, John, ballads *162*, *370*, 40, 274n. 19
emigration, ballad, **408–9**, 409–10; other refs., 22, 98, 130, 132, 172, 258, 259, 378–81
Employment and unemployment, 374–410; children's, 360, 375, 393–99, 402–4 (*see also* Oastler, Richard); damage to health, 375, 393–99; other refs. to unemployment, 98, 99, 101, 103–5, 108–9, 240
enclosure, 47, 86, 105, 129, 226, 259, 374, 551n. 12
enemies of the poor. *See* bakers; Benyon's; Blackburn, Judge; butchers; Cane, Mr.; clergy; coal owners; coal viewers; Culley, Robert; Disraeli, Benjamin; factory masters; farmers, rich; Farnall, Harry Burrard; George III; George IV; Grey, Sir George; Gregory; guardians, workhouse; landowners; Lords, House of; Meyrick, Theobald; middle and upper classes; mill owners; Mr. W.; overseers of the poor; Pakington, J.; poor law, makers and the law; poor law, boards and commissioners; rich, the; rogues of several sorts; Ryan, Richard; Tories; Tyrrell, Sir, James; vestrymen; Wellington, duke of; William IV; workhouses, masters
Engels, Friedrich, 180
ESTC (*Eighteenth Century Short Title Catalogue*), 90, 91, 272n. 2, 557 appendix 1 n. 4, 558n. 23, 559n. 32
Evans, Colonel George de Lacey, 113, 116

GENERAL INDEX 661

factory masters, 196, 231–32, 255, 384–85, 397, 399. *See also* mill owners
famine, ballads, **92–93**, 93, **101–2**, **260–62**; other refs., 83–87, 260
farm laborers, 161, 209–12, 226–27, 337, 374, 408–9, 433–35, 440–42, 501–2
Farmer, J. S., 352, 537
farmers, small, ballad, **399–401**, 401–2; other refs., 97, 199–201, 226, 374
farmers, generous, 226, 237, 257
farmers, rich, ballads, **209–12**, 212; **224–25**, 226–28; other refs., 22, 23, 85, 99, 196, 201, 257, 259
Farnall, Harry Burrard, 184, 186, 192
Fauntleroy, Henry, 72–73
fever dens. *See* housing, discreditable
Fitz (author), 44–45
Fitzwilliam, Mr., 168
flash ballads. *See* canting ballads
Flint, R.: "The Workhouse Boy," **165–66**, 38, 60, 61, 68, 76, 163, 166–69, 171 (mistaken attribution; *see* Aldridge), 289, 430, 512
flogging, 149–52, 173–80, 408. *See also* whipping
forestallers, 85, 86, 94, 95, 209–10
Foster, Stephen Collins, 187
Fox, William Johnson, 19
Franco-Prussian War, 62
free and easies, 37, 43, 77, 466–67
free trade, ballads, **123–25**, 125; **126–28**, 128–30; **224–25**, 226; **262–63**, 263; **264–66**, 266, *122*. *See also* corn bill and law
Freeman, W. H.: "Happy Land!!" **130–31**, with notes on author and ballad, 60, 132, 512
French wars, 89–99, 303, 386
Friedman, Albert, 18
friends of the poor. *See* Bedford, duke of; Bright, John; Cobden, Richard; farmers, generous; Fox, William Johnson; Gavin, Hector; Gilpin, Charles; Greenwood, James; Grey, Charles; Harvey, Jane; Hone, William; Oastler, Richard; Onion, Robert; Otway, A. J.; Paine, Tom; Romilly, Sir Samuel

Gatrell, V. A. C., 19
Gavin, Hector, 195–96

George I, 90
George II, 257
George III, and famine, 84, 85–86, 93; other refs., 55, 87, 94, 95, 97, 112, 385, 386
George IV, 49, 55, 87, 137, 277–78 n. 3, 422
Gilpin, Charles, 157–58
Goldsmith, Oliver, 45
Gould, Rev. Sabine Baring, 17, 34, 90, 218, 403
Great Exhibition, 131, 132, 230
Green, Charles, 496, 498
Green, E.: "After Serving Seven Years," **361**, with notes on author and ballad, 289, 362
Green, F. W., 319
Greenacre, James, 73, 497, 498
Greenblatt, Stephen, 22
Green in France, 57, 63, 425, 429
Greenwood, James, 190–92, 194
Gregory, 199–201
Grey, Charles, second Earl Grey, 94, 95, 113, 114
Grey, Sir George, 155–58
guardians, workhouse, 163–65, 171–72, 176–78, 179, 183, 184–86, 187–88, 223–24. *See also* vestrymen

Halliday, Andrew, 378
Hanchant, W. L., 168
Handel, Georg Friedrich, 487
hard times, 83–136
Hardwick, J. A.: "Poor Married Man," **477–78**, with notes on author and ballad, 41 (with misspelling), 42, 43, 60, 193, 269–70, 478–79, 490; "St. James's and St. Giles's," **142–44**, 138, 144–45, attribution 479; workhouse ballad, *193*, 193
Hardy, Gathorne, 186
Hardy, Thomas, 23
Hare, William, 392–93
Harland, John, and T. T. Wilkinson, 386
Harvey, Jane: "Lines on the Corn Bill," **97–99**, with notes on the author and her work, 22, 39, 40, 60, 64, 88, 99–101, 140, 481
Hayden, James, ballad, *414*, 40, 41, 274 n. 20
Haynau, General Julius Jacob von, 39, 173, 175, 179–80, 274 n. 16

Heman, Felicia, 504
Henderson, William, 149
Hennessy, James Pope, 318
Henry V, 22
Hindley, Charles, on Billy Waters, Tom and Jerry, 311, 509; on broadside authors and audiences, 44, 75; carelessness of, 18, 50, 275n. 32, 509, 529, 533, 536; on Catnach as poet, 57; depiction of, information from, John Morgan, 37, 49–50, 51–53, 55, 73, 311, 429, 481; examples and mention of reputed and actual cocks, 529–31, 533–35, 539, 558–59n. 32; on gallows sales, 72, 73, 539; misc. refs., 57, 65; plagiarism by, 37, 273n. 11, 499, 509; printing verses by Morgan, 23; on Thomas Hudson, 429–30
history of the book, 21–23. *See also* Catnach, James; poverty and poetry; printers, broadside; several entries under broadsides
Hobhouse, Sir John Cam, 113, 116
Hogarth, George, 305
Holder, Reuben, ballads, 276n. 49
Hollingworth, Brian, 276n. 49
Holloway, John, and Joan Black, 18, 438
Hone, William, 87, 277–78n. 3
Hood, Thomas, 20, 24, 37, 39, 42, 43, 78, 167, 406, 429, 447
Hook, Theodore, 37
Hopkins, Mary, 58
Hotten, John Camden, 65, 347, 529, 530, 532. 533, 534, 535, 537
Houghton, Lord. *See* Milnes, Richard Monckton
housing, discreditable, 135, 136, 137, 195–96, 223, 517
Howe, General, 180
Hudson, Thomas: notes on the author, 42, 43, 60, 61, 168, 316, 429–32, 512; "The Bailiffs are Coming," **202–3**, with notes, 43, 69, 77, 168, 203–4, 431; "The Dogs-Meat Man," **425–29**, with notes, 43, 63, 168, 424 (illus.), 429–32, 519; "Flashy Back and Hungry Belly," *236*, 236, 431; "Follow the Drum," 430; "Her Majesty's Monkey," *430*, 430; "Mr. Walker, the Twopenny Postman," *451*, 451; "Pawnbroker's Shop on a Saturday Night," *216*, 216, 431; "Polly Cox's Party," 431, 514
Huges (Hughes?), R., 168–69
Hunt, C. J., 140, 359
Hunt, Henry, 248, 343
Hunt, Leigh, 487

income tax. *See* taxes
incomes of the poor, 87, 116, 277n. 3. *See also* taxes; wages
incomes of the rich, 87, 113, 136, 199–200, 207–8, 210, 277–78n. 3, 281 n. 10
industrial production, 1700–1900, 83
industrial revolution, 374–75
industrial struggle, 196, 550–51n. 12
Ingall, Thomas George, ballad, 42, 323

J. H., notes on author and ballads, *45–46*, 34, 37–38, 39, 54, 61, 62, 77, 78, 274n. 15
James V of Scotland, 301
Jerrold, Douglas, 69, 108, 145, 256, 266, 300, 311, 509
Jim Crow, 187, 411
Job, 22, 501, 503
Johns, B. G., 65, 279n. 27, 536
Johnson, T.: "Naked Truth," **399, 401**, with notes on author and ballad, 40, 60, 64, 226, 401–2
Jones, Jem, 536
Jones, Trevor, 276n. 49

Kean, Edmund, 315, 429–30
Keats, John, 24, 42, 254
King/Mitchel cocks, 539, 541
King Lear, 6, 20

Labern, John: notes on author and ballads, 41, 42, 60, 61, 269–70, 282–83 chap 6 nn. 6, 7, 512, 513; "The Cadger's Ball," 269, 514, 523; "Comic Version of a Good Time Coming," **267–69**, 269–70; "Life of a Cadger," *302*, 301–2
Lamb, Charles, 485
Lamborn, Edward: notes on author and ballad, 22–23, 24, 28, 40, 60, 77, 88, 139, 164–65, 370, 485, 505; "The New Poor Law and the Farmer's Glory," **163–64**

landlords, 124, 195–96, 204–6, 262, 263, 399–401
landowners, 129, 199–201, 228, 374
Lane, Samuel, notes on author and ballads, *59–60*, 39, 59–60, 71–72, 276n. 49
law. *See* poor law; poverty and law
Lees, Joseph, of Glodwick, 386, 552n. 12
Leybourne, George, 236
Life in London. *See* Egan, Pierce; Tom and Jerry
Lind, Jenny, 23, 53, 145
London Melodist, 349, 391
London Singer's Magazine, 41, 132, 245, 269, 282 chap. 6 n. 6, 322, 362, 430, 431, 488–90, 492, 493, 513 (correcting inaccuracy in vol. 1), 555n. 6
London Singer's Magazine and Reciter's Album, 512–13, 516
Lords, House of, 113, 141, 142, 207–8, 266, 436
Lloyd, A. L., 276n. 49
Luddism, 142, 335, 336, 383, 550n. 12
Lyon, Richard, notes on author and ballads, 44, 46, 274n. 28

Mackay, Charles: notes on the author, 42, 60, 260, 266; "Cheer, Boys, Cheer!" *410*, 43, 62, 172, 258, 266, 408, 409–10; "Wait a Little Longer" ("There's a Good Time Coming, Boys!"), **264–66**, 43, 61, 62, 68, 251, 256, 258, 266, 267–69, 270, 513
Macready, Charles, 315
Madden, Frederick, 272n. 2
Maidment, Brian, 18, 276n. 49
Mander, Raymond, and Joe Mitchenson, 451
Marchant, John William, 23, 50, 275n. 32
Martin, John: notes on the author, 41, 43–44, 60, 316, 480, 492–93, 555–56n. 6; "The Bard of Seven Dials," *488–90*, 488–90, 492; "Billy Nutts, the Poet," **484–88**, 42, 43–44, 269–70, 480, 481, 488–93; "Little Jessey, the Poor Flower Maid," **322**, 319, 322–23, 493; "When I Became an Author," *555–56n. 6*, 493, 555n. 6
Mat (Max) the Rhymer, ballads, 40, 274 n. 19
Mathews, Charles, 145
Mayhew, Henry, on broadside authors, 38, 44, 45–46, 53, 57, 62; on buyers and sellers of broadsides, 66–68, 69, 70; on Catnach as author, 57; on cocks, 378, 530, 533–38; his farce, *The Wandering Minstrel*, 412; on gallows sales, 72–74, 75, 530, 539; misc. refs., 18, 38, 44, 53; naïveté of, and of collaborator Halliday, 37, 378, 413, 274n. 24, 541
Melbourne, Lord, 144, 242, 430, 542, 544
Mendicity, Society for the Suppression of, 300, 303, 378, 495, 507, 508, 548n. 2
Meyrick, Theobald, 181–87
middle and upper classes, 195–96
mill owners, 228, 359–360, 374–75, 377–78, 384–85, 396–99. *See also* factory masters
Miller, John, 556n. 2
millers, 84–85, 91
Milnes, Richard Monckton, 42, 43, 76, 318
mines, 375, 393–96
Mitchel ballads, 342, 531–32, 539, 541
Model Song Book, 315, 362
Moeran, F. J., 418
Moncrieff, W. T.: "Beggars Opera," **506–8**, with notes on author and ballad, 57, 60, 63, 309, 316, 500, 508–9, 522
money and charity, 235–54
Monmouth Street, 34–36, 203, 236, 318, 484, 514–17, 519–23
Moore, Sir John, 393
Moore, Thomas, 37, 351, 512
More, Hannah: "Turn the Carpet," **381–83**, with notes on author and ballads, 39, 58–59, 60, 275–76n. 47, 383, 465, 501
More, Sally: ballad, 413–14
Morgan, John: life and character, 34, 49, 50, 51–53, 54, 60, 70–71, 481–82, 536; misc. refs. 27, 37, 55, 59, 60, 66, 289, 432; most popular ballads, 52, 61, 62, 63, 279n. 27, 473, 519; number of broadsides known, attributable, surmised, 21, 23, 34, 49, 51, 53, 54, 62, 116–17, 125, 263, 440; range of subjects 23, 49, 53–54, 440, 473; significance, 21, 23, 49, 481–82; social-political verse, 21, 23, 49, 66, 69–71, 78, 113, 481–82; workaday versifying, 38, 51, 54, 72, 116–17, 263, 279n. 24; writing for all classes, 71; "Advice to Country Maidens

Morgan, John *(continued)*
on the Poor Law Bill," **433–36**, 436, 481; "Agitation of Great Britain" (uncertain authorship), **262–63**, 117, 263, 482; "Assessed Taxes," **113–16**, 116–17, 481, 542–47; "Bachelor's Complaint," 453; "The Beautiful Muff" (uncertain authorship), *440*, 440; "Blow the Candle In," 52, 68, 77, 275, 440; "Britons Glory," 122; "Britons Rights," *54*, 116–17; "Camberwell & Reform," **114** (illus.), 113, 289, 482; "The Convict Lady's Maid," 39, 50; "The Drunken Husband," **471–72**, 473, 481; "England's Maiden Queen," *122*, 122, 263; "The Farmer's Daughter and the Gay Ploughboy," *412*, 412; "The Good Looking Man," 473; "Hertford Approaching Election," *6*, *53*, 53, 116, 197; "House and Window Taxes," *117*, 117, 279 n. 24; "The Humours of the Coronation," *122;* "Jim Crow's Description of the London Lasses," 187; "Jim Crow's Trip to the Royal Wedding," 187; "John Bull & the Taxes," *125*, 52, 63, 125, 275 n. 27; "Lamentation of Billy Barlow for the Loss of his Rib," *54*, 54; "The Life and Death of John William Marchant" (uncertain authorship), 23, 50, 275 n. 32; "The Life of an Honest Ploughman," 52; "Little Lord John out of Service," **70–71**, 23, 69–70, 78, 481–82; "The London Burkers," 50; "The Married Man's Complaint," 473, 555 n. 24; "My Grandfather's Days," *257*, 52, 257; "New Rigs of the Races," 440; "Our New Queen, the Flower of England," *123*, 122; "Petticoat Government," *457*, 122, 279 n. 24, 457; "The Pleasing Wife and Satisfied Husband," 52; "The Queen & the Taxes," **123–25**, 117, 125, 482; Queen Caroline ballad without title, *49–50*, 23, 49–50, 53; "Rigs and Flares-Up of Greenwich Fair," 440; "Rigs and Flares-Up of the Fair," **438–39**, 440, 481; Robert Stephenson ballad, 51; "There's Nothing Can Equal a Woman," 473, 555 n. 24; "The Trades Unions of England, Huzza!" 54, 275 n. 39; "A True Picture of the London Gin Palaces," *465;* "The Way to Live," **517–19**, 481, 519; "A Woman, Dear Woman for Me," 473, 555 n. 24

Morris, George Pope, 77
Moses & Son, 144, 145
Moulds, John, 322
Mr. W., 209–12, 213
Mudlarks, 328–31
Murray, William Henry: "The Fine Old English Gentleman," **216–18**; with notes on author and ballad, 41, 42, 60, 61, 63, 66, 76–77, 218–22, 237, 257, 258, 345
music hall, 37, 270, 452

names of broadside authors *(see the headnote for symbols B, A, R, N):*
Aldridge: A, R; Bailey, William: B; Bayly, Thomas Haynes: A, R; Billington, William: B, A, R; Blanchard, E. L: A, R; Brown, George: B, A, R; Bruton, James: A, R; Bursnell, Sarah: B; Catnach, James: B, A, R; Chandler, J. W.: A, R; Clifton, Harry: A, R; Cook, Eliza: A, R; Cornwall, Barry: A, R; Cullum, Bob: B, N; Davis, George: B; Dibdin, Charles: A, R; Dibdin, Charles Jr.: A, R; Dibdin, Thomas John, N; Duncan, James Elmslie (Elmzlie): B; Embleton, John: B, A; Fitz: B; Flint, R.: A, R; Freeman, W. H.: A; Green, E.: A; Hardwick, J. A.: A, R; Harvey, Jane: B, A; Hayden, James: B; Holder, Reuben: B; Hood, Thomas: N; Hudson, Thomas: A, R; Ingall, Thomas George: N; J. H.: B, A, R; Johnson, T.: B, A; Labern, John: A, R; Lamborn, Edward: B, A; Lane, Samuel: B, A, R; Lyon, Richard: B; Mackay, Charles: A, R; Martin, John: A, R; Mat (Max) the Rhymer: B; Moncrieff, W. T.: A, R; More, Hannah: B, A; Morgan, John: B, A, R; Murray, W. H.: A, R; Noel, Thomas: A; Praed, W. M.: N; Prest, Thomas Peckett: B, A, R; Purday, Charles: A, R; Smith, W.: B; Strickland, Miss: B, A; Taylor, John: B, A; Taylor, Samuel: B, N;

GENERAL INDEX

Thomas, J. / John: B; Valentine, Henry: B, A; White, Henry Kirk: N; Withy, Nathan: B; Wrigley, E.: B; Youd, John: B
National Melodist, 391
Neate, Alan, 178
Neuburg, Victor, 18, 442, 488
Neukom, Sigismund, 346
Newby, Howard, 201, 227
Nicholson, Renton, 273 n. 14, 275 n. 32
Noel, Thomas: "The Pauper's Drive," **311–12**, with notes on author and ballad, 42, 43, 60, 312–13
Northumberland, duke of, 300

O'Connor, Feargus, 129 , 533
Oastler, Richard, 255, 399, 553 n. 17
Old Bailey, 339–40, 341, 541
one nation or two, 39, 63, 75–77, 454
Onion, Robert, 186–87
Otway, A. J., 151–52
overseers of the poor, 64, 106, 162, 209–14, 399
Owen, Robert, 208
Owen, Wilfred, 20, 24
Oxford English Dictionary, 537

Paine, Tom, 58, 97
Pakington, J., 151–52
Pall Mall Gazette, 190–93, 194
Palmer, Roy, 18, 132, 168, 276 n. 49, 386
Palmerston, Lord, 69–70, 179
Parnell, John, 406
parody, imitation, and allusion, 76–77, 277 n. 75, 302, 362, 403, 412–13, 452–53, 516–17
Partridge, Eric, 245, 263, 351, 508, 537
pawnbrokers, **214–16**, 115, 144, 202, 216–18, 389, 458, 478, 489
Payne, J. H., 77, 164
Peel, Sir Robert, 111, 127–29, 226, 242, 303, 317, 331, 354
pensioners, placemen, 112, 241–42, 277–78 n. 3, 303
Percy, Thomas, 218
Peterloo, 87, 277–78 n. 3, 334, 335, 336, 550 n. 11
Pinto, Vivian de Sola, and A. E. Rodway, 17–18
piracy, 37, 39, 43, 218–22, 273 n. 12, 431, 508–9, 514

Pitt, William, the younger, 93, 95, 303
placemen. *See* pensioners, placemen
plagiarism, 46–47, 91, 218–22, 230, 276 n. 49, 342, 377–78, 420, 538, 541, 557 appendix 1 n. 4. *See also* Catnach, James; Hindley, Charles
Planché, J. R., 37
poaching and poaching ballads, *337*, 225, 228, 230, 337–38, 374
poet laureates, 112
political ballads, 66, 68, 69–72, 92–101, 109–17, 123–30. *See also* Morgan, John, social-political verse
poor law, ballads, **163–64**, 164–65; **433–35**, 436; boards and commissioners, 176–79, 182–87, 192, 241, 242, 303 (*see also* overseers of the poor; guardians, workhouse; vestrymen; workhouse masters); inspectors, 182–84, 186–87, 192; makers and the law, 22–23, 53, 119–20, 122, 131, 159–62, 164, 362–72, 436
poor relief, 47, 86–87, 104, 159–62, 260, 375
Pope, Alexander, 485
Pope, W. Macqueen, 269, 430
poverty and contentment, 138, 300–301, 318, 432–33, 501–28
poverty and crime, 332–73; beggarly criminals, 301–2, 313–14, 347–49; crimes of desperation, 332–33, 357–60, 362–73; criminal children, 324–25, 334, 338–42, 541; criminal lives, 347–54; poachers, 225, 228, 230, 337–38, 374; poor criminal versus rich, 146–49, 149–52, 152–58; prisons, prisoners, 336–37, 343–45, 361–62; statistics, kinds of crime, severity of sentence, 135–36, 333–34, 335, 340, 541; suggestive links between, 134–36, 162, 333, 336, 357–60. *See also* poverty and law; riot and rebellion; transportation; treadmills
poverty and friendship, 119, 236–38, 251–53
poverty and former times, 97–98, 107, 120, 126–28, 226–28, 256–60
poverty and law, favoritism, fraud, and wealth, 110, 139, 146–49, 152–58; law that is unjust, criminal, 98, 141, 149–52, 161–62, 207, 333, 334, 336, 339–40, 343, 370, 374. *See also* poor law

poverty and love, 236, 320, 411–51
poverty and marriage, 452–79
poverty and poetry, 17–24, 70, 77–79, 237, 302, 492. *See also* broadsides, distinctive character, ballads
poverty and religion, bible quoted, 160, 404; comfort, 237–38, 245–47, 303, 381–83, 410, 503–4, 556n. 2; despair, 362–66; God's avenging justice, 97–99, 140–42, 162, 163–64, 238, 504–5; indifference of clergy (*see* clergy); questioning, 323–25, 332, 387–89
poverty and sex, 68–69, 414–15, 433–40, 453–54
poverty and sin, 252, 253, 332, 421–22
poverty and war, government and other propaganda, 137–38; hungry army, 304, 407–8; war as cause of poverty, 89–93, 95–99, 301, 303, 386
Praed, W. M., 37, 43
Prest, Thomas Peckett: notes on the author, 40–41, 289, 316, 468, 511–14, 516; "The Coalheaver's Feast," **509–11**, 500, 511–14; "Monmouth Street," **514–16**, 36, 236, 503, 512, 516–17; "Mrs. Johnson," **466–67**, 467–68, 512
Preston 10 percent strike, 28, 196, 336
printers, broadside (London if not otherwise noted): Bailey, S., 393; Barnett, 533; Barr, John, of Leeds, 142; Barr, Richard, of Leeds and Holbeck, 142; Batchelar, T., 459; Beaumont, J., of Manchester, 488; Bebbington, J. O., of Manchester, 232, 318, 328, 488, 490; Birt, Mary, 33, 34, 520 (illus.); Birt, Thomas, 34, 272n. 2, 328, 351; Bloomer, Theophilus, of Birmingham, 416, 417, 419–20, 424; Bonner, Harry, of Bristol, 247, 343, 373, 532, 539, 540, 541, 551n. 23; Burbage & Stretton, of Nottingham, 91; Carpue & Son, 532; Catnach, James *(see separate entry for him)*; Croshaw, C., of York, 104; Dever, W., 526, 528; Disley, Henry, 51, 229, 230, 247, 248, 362, 372, 373, 416–17, 418, 419; Dodd, T., of Newcastle, 359; Evans (Long Lane), 239, 263; Ford, Thomas, of Chesterfield, 213, 398; Ford, William, of Sheffield, 247;

Fortey, W. S., 51, 74, 328, 372, 446 (illus.); Gilbert, John, of Newcastle, 325; Harkness, John, of Preston, 196, 403, 404, 442; Hill, J., 46; Hillatt & Martin, 46, 473; Hodges, Elizabeth Mary Ann, 34, 263, 318, 490, 499; Hook, Richard, of Brighton, 200–201, 433; Horsen, 532; Jackson & Son, of Birmingham, 92; Kyng, of Oxford, 111; Lucksway, 78, 528; Marshall, of Bristol, 201; Marshall, John, of Newcastle, 140; Marshall, John, 272 n. 2; Mate, Charles, Sr. and Charles Mate Jr., of Dover, 201; Mullins, 78, 149; Paul, C., 315, 373, 477; Paul, H., 362; Paul, J., 475; Phair, 50, 114; Pitts, John, 33, 34, 37, 104–5, 169, 239, 272n. 2, 305, 311, 321, 416, 422; Plumb, F. (unknown location), 93, 262; Randall, Mary, of Stirling, 90; Robson, W., of Durham, 109; Ryle, Anne, 34, 44, 51, 74, 76 (illus.). 275 n. 32, 328, 475; Sharp, J., 112; Shepherd, Henry, of Bristol, 342, 343, 532, 535; Shepherd, Mary, of Bristol, 104–5, 247, 340–43, 535, 539, 540, 541; Skinner, 78, 174; Smeeton, G., 541; Such, H. P., 51, 71, 260; Taylor (Brick Lane), 51; Taylor, W. (Waterloo Road), 39, 46, 50, 78, 354, 440, 471, 473, 513; Wardman, H., of Bradford, 404; Williams, J., of Portsea, 41, 417; Williamson, H., of Newcastle, 491, 492; Wilson, William, of Whitehaven, 208, 209; Wise, T., 90, 272n. 2
printers, broadside, character of, 21
printers, corrupt texts, 416–20, 483–84, 488–92
Proctor, Bryan Waller. *See* Cornwall, Barry
prostitution. *See* poverty and sex
Punch, 70, 145, 314, 316, 406, 496, 498
Purday, Charles (*see also* Murray, William Henry), 41, 42, 60, 61, 219–22
Pye, Henry James, 112

Queen Mother, 300

Radnor, Lord, 225, 226
Radzinowicz, Leon, 468
Rag Fair, 483

GENERAL INDEX 667

Ramsbotham, Mrs., 146–49
Raven, John, 18
Redgrave, Richard, 406
Reeve, William, 102
reform bill and act, ballads touching on, 23, 41, 109–11, 112–13, 114, 266, 514; other refs., 95, 119, 207
Rice, Thomas, 411
rich, the, 94, 98, 110, 111, 130, 133, 134–35, 137–58, 206–9, 209–12, 228–30, 238, 251, 258–59, 279n. 3, 381
Richmond, duke of, 127–29
Rimbault, E. F., 132
riot and rebellion, brief survey, 334–36, 550–51n. 12; detailed accounts, 1800 and 1833, 84–87, 542–47; other refs. 99, 117, 132, 142, 162, 230, 343, 359–60, 383, 384. *See also* Captain Swing rebellion; Chartism; Luddism; Peterloo
Robin Hood, 301
Rogers, Samuel, 167
rogues of several sorts, 195–99
Romilly, Sir Samuel, 207, 343
Ross, G., 270
Ross, J. W., 274n. 17
Rossetti, D. G., 447
Roud, Steve, 275n. 32, 316, 566
Roxburghe ballads, 452, 549nn. 4, 6; 550n. 1, 558–59n. 32
royal palaces, 106–7
Rush, James Bloomfield, 73, 75, 530–31
Russell, Henry, 172, 219, 266, 410
Russell, Lord John, 23, 59, 69–71, 113, 114, 123–25, 127, 128, 129
Ryan, Richard, 173–79

Sabine, Charles, 556n. 2
Scott, Harold, 269, 429, 430
Scott, J. W. R., 194
seamstresses, ballad, **405–6**, 119, 120, 135, 145, 228, 406, 414
Second Shepherd's Play, 20
Seven Dials, 33–36, 43–58, 315, 425, 484–94, 521, 522. *See also* Monmouth Street; St. Giles's
Shadwell, Thomas, 218
Shakespeare, William, *6*, 22, 485, 496, 254
Sharp, John W., 270, 484, 488
Sharp, Cecil, 417
Shelley, Percy Bysshe, *6*, 20, 42, 59

Shepard, Leslie, 37, 74, 90, 311, 272n. 2, 275–76n. 47
Sheppard, H. Fleetwood, 90
Sidney, Sir Philip, 20
Sims, Robert, 151
Singer's Penny Magazine and Reciter's Album, 289, 351, 468, 511–12
slavery, black and white, 228, 360, 375, 393–99, 405–6, 553n. 7
Smith, Charles Manby, 37, 39, 41, 44, 57, 61, 62, 536–37, 539
Smith, W., ballads, 41
Somerset, Charles, 167
Speaight, George, 430
Spence, Thomas, 112
Spinney, G. H., 58
St. Giles's, 33–36, 44–45, 142–45, 160–61, 299, 308–11, 315–16, 422, 425, 483, 500,
Stamfield, Rainer, 360
starvation, ballads, **117–19**, 119–20; **228–30**, 230; **245–47**, 247–48; **362–64**, 364–73; quoted passages and comment, *94, 96, 99, 106, 108, 123–25, 208, 209, 223–24,* 237, *238, 266, 332,* 333, 335, *376, 410, 495, 550 n. 12;* other ref., 303; starvation cocks, 247, 373; starving in the street, 247–48, 260
Strickland, Miss: "The Factory Child," **403–4**, with notes on author and ballad, 289, 404
Strickland, Sir George, 404
Stuart, Charles Douglas, and A. J. Park, 270
Sunday trading bill, 130, 132
supper clubs. *See* free and easies
Swell's Night Guide, The, 492–93
swinish multitude, 109–12
Sykes, George, 303

T. H. (author), 102
taxes, assessed, on goods, **113**, **115–16**, 93, 97, 116, 542; **123–25**, 125; burden on the poor, 97, 116; income tax, 93, 95, 97, 144, 267, 303; taxes in general, 23, 96, 106, 121, 131, 198, 228, 258; tax gatherers, **399–401**, 117, 96, 401
Taylor, John: "John Taylor, Cotton Spinner..., Being Out of Employ," **387–89**, with notes on author and ballad, 40, 60, 389, 503

Taylor, Samuel, 71
Tennyson, Alfred, Lord, 37, 39, 49, 78, 480
Thackeray, William Makepeace, 49, 61, 65, 66, 69, 78, 430
Thomas, J./John (author), 41
Thompson, E. P., 18
Thomson, Robert, 272 n. 2
three acres and a cow, 129
Tinsley, William, 194
titles of other ballads: An Account of the Sufferings of J. Castle, 152; Act on the Square, 451; Address to the Swinish Multitude, 112 P; Adieu My Native Land, Adieu, 306; After Many Roving Years, *362*, 362; All Round My Hat, 301, 549 n. 7; Always Put Your Shoulder to the Wheel, 451; Answer to Burns' Lovely Jean, 77; Answer to Home Sweet Home, 77; Answer to Sweet Lemminy, 275 n. 44; Answer to the Blue Ey'd Stranger, 77; Answer to the Wife's Dream, 77; Apparition of a Ghost to a Miller, 533–34; An Attempt to Exhibit...the Queen's Life, 56; An Authentic Account of the Riotous Meeting, 117, 541 P; The Bachelor of Sixty-Two, 453; The Bachelor's Complaint, 453; The Bachelor's Lesson, 454; The Beating of My Own Heart, 318; The Beautiful Muff, *440*, 440; The Beggar Wench of Hull, 301 P; The Beggar (Of all the trades), *301*, 301 P; The Beggar's Daughter of Bednall Green, 411 P; The Beggars Chorus, *300*, 300–301 P; Bellevue Gaol, 336–37; Betty Brill, 506; The Big Show Coming, 270; Bill Bobstay, 305; Black Bess, 38, 274 n. 15; Blow the Candle In, 52, 68, 77, 275, 440; Blow the Candle Out, 77; Bold Robin Hood, 301, 549 n. 5 P; Bonny Highland Laddie, 56; The Bonny Milk-Maid, 420; Bow thy Head, 56; A Brave Old Country Gentleman, 42 P; The Brixton Parson, 528; The Broken-Hearted Gardener, 451; The Brook-Side, *318*, 43, 76, 318; The Bunter's Wedding, *514*, 301, 514 P; Burning Them Out, 413; The Butcher Turned Devil, 91; The Cambridgeshire Tragedy, 238 P; Caroline, Queen, ballad without title, *49–50,* 23, 49–50, 53; Caroline, Queen, broadside, 342; Charlotte, Princess, ballad without title, 55; The Cholera is Coming, 204; A Christmas Carol Warbled in Newgate, 59; The Chummies' May-Day, 169; City Carting, 204; Confession and Execution of Samuel Wright, *157*, 73, 280 chap 2 n. 11; Confession and Execution of William Corder, *57*; 57–58; Confessions of a Bachelor, 362; The Constant Lady, 559; The Convict Lady's Maid, 39, 50; Coronation of Her Majesty Queen Victoria, 102, 278 n. 14; County Gaol, 336; Cruel and Inhuman Murder of Captain Lawson, *531*, 531; The Cumberland Tragedy, 247 P; The Dandy Cats-Meat Lass, 429; Death and the Gentleman, *213*; 212–13, 281 n. 11 P; Death and the Lady, *213*; 212–13. 281 n. 11 P; The Death of Nelson, 66; The Demon of the Sea, *45–46*, 38, 45; The Devil, *337*, 91, 337; The Devil and Baker, 91; The Devil and the Farmer's Wife, 90–91; Dirge, 56; Dives and Lazarus (As it fell out), 140 P; The Dorsetshire Garland, 301 P; Elegy on the Death of the Queen, 56; An Elegy on the Queen, *55*; The Exciseman Outwitted, 102; The Execution of James Bloomfield Rush, *530*, 530; Extraordinary & Funny Doings, *534–35*, 534–35; Farewell, Gay London (fragment), 57; The Fight, 346; The Fire Shovel, *456*, 456; The Flogging Colonel, 152; The Flogging Excitement at Hounslow, 152; Fly Away Pretty Moth, 455; Follow the Drum, 430; The Forsaken Shepherdess, *56*, 56; Full Particulars of the Dreadful Murder, *532*, 532–33; A Full...Account of...the Death of Three Atheists, *343*, 343, 535–36; A Funeral Dirge for the Queen, *55*; Gallant Poachers, *337*, 337–38; The Gay Cavalier, 66; General Haynau, 179; General Haynau's Quick March, 179; Generous Gift, 550 n. 1 P; Gentlemen Farmers, *227*, 227; George III ballad

without title, *55*, 201; Giles Scroggin's Ghost, 506; The Gin, 346; The Good Looking Man, 473; The Great and Important Battle, 533; Green in France, 57, 63, 425, 429; Grey and Victory!!!, 113; The Grunter's Ode, *112*, 112 P; The Happy Couple, 550 n. 1 P; Happy Land (Happy land! Happy land!), *132*, 132, 391; Haynau and Barclay and Perkins' Draymen, 179;; Haynau ballad without title, *180*, 179; Haynau's Adventure, 179; The Henpeck'd Husband, 456; Her Majesty's Monkey, *430*, 430; Home, 56; Honesty in Tatters, 305; Hot Codlins, *506*, 506 P; Humours of Rag Fair, 483 P; The Humours of the Coronation, 122; Hungry Army (Irish), 408 P; The Husband's Dream, 38, 77; I Am Going to be Married, *453*, 453; I Am Married at Last, 453; I Remember, 43; I Traced Her Little Footprints, **229**, 230; I Was Married on Monday, *453–54*, 454; I Will Never Deceive Him, 362; I Would That the Wars Were Well Over, 90; I'd Be a Butterfly, 455, 456; I'll Be No Submissive Wife, *455*, 455; I'm Afloat, 68, 409; I'm Ninety-Five, 454; I've Been to Australia, 552 n. 7; It May Be Some Day, 152; Jim Crow's Description of the London Lasses, 187; Jim Crow's Trip to the Royal Wedding, 187; Johnny Jiggletoes, 315; Johnstone's Escort into a Better Clime, 552 n. 38; The Jolly Beggar, 301 P; The Jolly London Beggars, 316; The Kentish Miracle, 238 P; King Cophetua and the Beggar Maid, 411 P; King, T./Thomas, broadsides on, 342, 531–32, 539, 541; Kitty of the Clyde, 506; Kitty the Cats-Meat Woman, 429; A Lament for Caroline, *55*; Lament of Charlotte Mills, 552 n. 38; Lamentation of Billy Barlow for the Loss of His Rib, *54*; Lamentation of the Smugglers, 552 n. 38; The Land, 346; The Lass of Teviot-Side, 56; The Last Words…of John and Joseph Bird, 342; Lemminy, 56; Lemminy's Grave, *56*, 56; The Life and Death of John William Marchant, 23, 50, 275 n. 32;

Life of Billy Waters, 56; The Life, Trial, Execution…[of] James Ward, *530–31*, 530–31; The Little Chimney Sweep, 323, 537–38; Little Lord John out of Service, **70–71**, 23, 69–70, 78, 481–82; The Liverpool Tragedy, *529–30*, 66, 276, 529–30, 535, 537, 538, 557 appendix 1 n. 4, 558 n. 32. 559 n. 32; The Liverpool Tragedy (ballad), 530, 533; The London Burkers, 50; Lord Lovel, 167; The Lost Child Found, 328; Lost Child Restored, 328; The Love Letter, *535*, 535; Lullaby, 56; The Mad-Brained Earl of K…, 528; The Maiden's Bantam Cock, 437; The Map of Mock-Beggar Hall, *301*, 301 P; The Married Man's Complaint, 473, 555 n. 24; The Maunding Soldier, 301 P; Men of Kent, 550 n. 12; The Merry Bells of England, 232; The Milk Maid, 420; The Milk-Maid and Squire, 420; Milk-Maid Coming from the Wakes, 420; The Milk-Maid, 420; The Mistletoe Bough, *167*, 42, 45, 76, 167–68, 169; Mitchel, Thomas, broadsides on, 342, 531–32, 539, 541; Moderation and Alteration, 218; Moll in the Wood, 454; Mother Be Proud of Your Boy in Blue, 409; Mr. Walker, the Twopenny Postman, *451*, 451; The Murder of Maria Marten, *57*, 57–58, 499, 534; My Eye and Betty Martin, 263; My Father Did So Before Me, 77; My Husband Has No Courage in Him, 68; My Lowland Queen, 56; My Mama Did So Before Me, *457–58*, 77, 457; National Convention and Murder, 117, 343, 541; The Naughty Poplar Man, 528; Never Flog Our Soldiers, 152; A New Ballad Shewing the Great Misery…, 373 P; The New Bury Loom, 437; A New Comic Song of Dudley Street, *517*, 517; The New Deserter, 152; The New Marriage Act, 57; A New Song on the Flogging Question, 152; A New Song on the Great Demonstration on Kersal Moor, 550 n. 12 P; A New Song on the Great Demonstration…on Kersal Moor, 550–51 n. 12 P; The Newcastle Treadmill, 347; Nine Times a Night, titles of other ballads *(continued)* 68, 437; The Nobleman's Generous Kindness to the Poor Man in Distress, *332*, 332, 333, 334, 550n. 1 P; The Nobleman's Generous Kindness; or, the Countryman's Unexpected Happiness, 282 chap 5 n. 1, 550n. 1 P; Nobody Coming to Woo, 452; Not a Drum Was Heard, 393; Number One, 43; O That the Wars Were All Over, 90; The Old Arm Chair, 409; Old Courtier, *219*, 218–21; The Old English Constable, 218; The Old English Publican, 218; The Old Lady & the Page, 414–15; The Omnibus, 346; The Oxfordshire Tragedy (The Scarborough Tragedy), 559n. 32; The Oxfordshire Tragedy; or, the Death of Four Lovers, 559n. 32; Paddle Your Own Canoe, 451; Particulars of a Riot, 550n. 12 P; Patient Grissel, 411 P; Petticoat Government, *457*, 122, 279 n. 24, 457; Petticoats Forever, 457; Petticoats is Master, 457; Pirate of the Isles, 38; The Poisoned Family, *48*, 49; Polly Brindle, 451; Poor Black Bess, 38, 274n. 15; Poor Little Blind Beggar Boy, 69 P; Pop Him into Limbo, *457*, 457; Preston Gaol, 337; Pretty Girls of London, *41*, 41, 511; Pretty Maid Milking Her Cow, 420; The Pretty Milk-Maid, 420; Prince Albert in England, 458; Princess Charlotte ballad without title, 55; Railway to Heaven, 465; The Remarkable Dream, 533; Return My Joey, 56; The Road, 346; Robin Hood and the Beggar, 301 P; Robin Hood Rescuing the Widow's Three Sons, 549n. 5 P; The Sailor's Dream, 77; Samuel Wright, 280 chap 2 n. 11; Sandman's Wedding, 301; Sarah Collins ballad without title, 40, 552n. 38; The Scarborough Tragedy, *558–59n. 32*, 66, 276n. 57, 537, 558–59n. 32; The Sea, **346–47**, 43, 61, 66, 77, 209, 345–47; Select Hymns for Christian Emigrants, *380*, 379–80; Sentences of the Prisoners...December 1830, 550n. 12; She Wore a Wreath of Roses, 455; A Single Life for Me, 454; Slavery in Yorkshire, 553n. 17 P; The Soldier's Dream, 77; Some Day, **118**, 120; Song of the Slaughter, 550n. 11 P; The Spree, 346; Squire and Thrasher, 550n. 1 P; Statement of...Persons...Committed to Newgate, 333, 550n. 2; Stephenson ballad without title, 51; The Story of Sinful Sally, 413–14; The Stout Cripple of Cornwall, 301 P; Strange Warning to a Reprobate Publican, 533–34; Strange...Account of the Rev. John Mills, 533–34; Subscription for Billy Waters, 56; Such a Getting out of Bed, 391; Sweet Lemminy, 275n. 44; Sweet Rosalind, 56; The Sweet Silver Moon, 56; The Tea, 346; Termagant Wife, 456; That's the Way She Sarves Me Now, *456*, 456; There's a Good Time Coming, Girls, 270; There's Nothing Can Equal a Woman, 473, 555n. 24; Tippetywitchet, 506; Tom, Jerry, and Logic at the Tread Mill, 347; Tragic Verses, 559n. 32; The Transport's Return, 552n. 38; Trial and Sentence of Dr. Barnard, *532*, 532–33; A True Picture of the London Gin Palaces, *465*, 465; The Ugly, Sea, 346; The Very Pretty Maid of this Town, 535; The Virtuous Milk-Maid, *418–19*, 411, 418–19, 420; Vulgar Little Boy, 324–25; Wakefield Gaol, 337; Wars Are All Over, 90; We Are Seven, 42; Weeping Parson in a Mess, 528; Welcome Frost to England, 550n. 12; What do People Marry For?, 454; When I Became an Author, *555–56n. 6*, 555n. 6 P; The White Cockade, *432*, 431–32; The Wife's Dream, 77; A Wife's Resolution, *457*, 456–57; Winter is Come, *55*; The Woes of Caroline, 55; The Woman that Conquered a Man, 457; A Woman, Dear Woman for Me, 473, 555n. 24; Wonderful, Just & Terrible Judgment, 534; Woodman, Spare That Tree, 77; The Wooing Maid, 452; Work, Boys, Work, and be Contented, 451; The Workhouse Cruelty, *160*, 160 P; The Workhouse Cruelty, Workhouses Turn'd Gaols, 160 P; Workhouse Wooing, 163; The Young Recruit, 152

Todd, William, 362, 459
Tolpuddle, 54, 111, 335
Tom and Jerry, **506–8,** 56, 57, 63, 72, 308–11, 422, 425, 429, 500, 508–9. *See also* Egan, Pierce
Tories, 53, 114, 122, 126, 128, 129, 218
Townley, George Victor, 152–58
trade unions, **109–11,** *218, 256,* 23, 46, 54, 99, 196, 256–57, 334–36
Traherne, Thomas, 20
transportation, 171, 228–30, 334, 335, 336, 340, 357–59
treadmills, **343–44,** 130, 133, 258, 311, 337, 344–45, 347, 361
Treuherz, Julian, 406
Tyrrell, Sir James, 196

upper and middle classes, 195–96
Upton, Mr., 323

Valentine, Henry: "The Beggar's Lament," **313–14,** with notes on author and ballad, 204, 289, 314–16, 324
Vauxhall Comic Song-Book, 132, 270, 431
Vestris, Madame, 315
vestrymen, 162, 163, 193, 196, 218, 222–24, 238
Vicinus, Martha, 18, 276 n. 49
Victoria, Queen, **123–25,** 46, 70–71, 122–23, 126, 127, 129, 430, 453–54, 455, 457, 458; misc. refs., 83, 102, 131, 179, 300, 513, 533
Vincent, David, 18

wages, 89, 94–95, 236, 248, 251, 259, 260, 386, 390, 406
Waters, Billy, and friends, 33, 56, 300, 307–11, 316, 509–11

Weber, Carl Maria von, 37
Wellings, Milton, 120
Wellington, duke of, 23, 49, 54, 110–11, 113, 127–29, 142, 180, 230, 242, 301, 533
Wheatley, Henry, 218, 420
Whigs, 53, 122, 125, 128, 129, 161–62, 381
whipping, 173–79, 180, 361, 362, 435, 436. *See also* flogging
White, Henry Kirk, *319,* 43, 319
White, James, 556 n. 2
Wilberforce, William, 22, 99
William IV, 23, 54, 110–11, 113, 114, 116, 141, 142, 248, 401, 438
Withy, Nathan, 484, 555 n. 3
Wolfe, Charles, 393
Wolff, Michael, 18
Wordsworth, William, 42
workhouses, diet, 172–73; historical background, ballads, and commentaries, 159–94; masters, 160, 165–66, 169, 173–79, 181–87; numbers, 375; other quoted broadside material concerning, *94, 98, 103, 105–7, 119, 122, 131, 133, 225, 241, 253, 370, 407;* other references, 22–23, 39, 95, 119–20. 132, 134, 226, 242, 270, 300, 364, 365–66, 370, 408
Wright, Harry, 229–30
Wright, Samuel, 152–58
Wright, Samuel (the other), 280 chap 2 n. 11
Wrigley, E., 41

York, duke of, 300
Youd, H., 269, 282–83, chap. 6 n. 6
Youd, John, 41

Poorly lived,

Poorly died,

Poorly buried,

Nobody cried.

Old epitaph, given in the *Bethnal Green Times*
21 April 1866

OHIO UNIVERSITY LIBRARY

Please return this book as soon as you have finished with it. In order to avoid a fine it must be returned by the latest date stamped below. All books are subject to recall after two weeks or immediately if needed for reserve.

CF